Childbirth, Vulnerability and Law

This book is inspired by a statement released by the World Health Organization directed at preventing and eliminating disrespectful and abusive treatment during facility-based childbirth.

Exploring the nature of vulnerability during childbirth, and the factors that make childbirth a site for violence and control, the book looks at the role of law in the regulation of professional intervention in childbirth. The WHO statement and other published work on 'mistreatment', 'obstetric violence', 'birth trauma', 'birth rape', and 'dehumanised care' all point to the presence of vulnerability, violence, and control in childbirth. This collected edition explores these issues in the experience of those giving birth, and for those providing obstetric services. It further offers insights regarding legal avenues of redress in the context of this emerging area of concern. Using violence, vulnerability, and control as a lens through which to consider multiple facets of the law, the book brings together innovative research from an interdisciplinary selection of authors.

The book will appeal to scholars of law and legal academics, specifically in relation to tort, criminal law, medical law, and human rights. It will also be of interest to postgraduate scholars of medical ethics and those concerned with gender studies more broadly.

Dr Camilla Pickles is a British Academy Postdoctoral Fellow at the Faculty of Law, University of Oxford. She explores issues related to pregnancy and childbirth, and has explored themes including abortion, obstetric violence, foetal personhood, involuntary sterilisations, and human rights within the contexts of pregnancy continuation and during labour and childbirth. She is currently leading a project titled 'Obstetric Violence and the Law' and is the author of several contributions, the most recent being *Pregnancy Law in South Africa: Between Reproductive Autonomy and Foetal Interests*.

Professor Jonathan Herring is a DM Wolfe-Clarendon Fellow in Law and the Vice Dean of the Faculty of Law at the University of Oxford. He works on themes related to criminal, family, and medical law and focuses on exploring how the law interacts with the important things in life such as love, family, friendship, and intimacy. Aside from authoring leading texts on criminal, medical, and family law, Jonathan regularly contributes to larger, challenging debates; some of his most recent contributions can be found in *Vulnerability, Childhood and the Law*; *Aging, Gender and Family Law*; and *Identity, Personhood and the Law*.

Childbirth, Vulnerability and Law

Exploring Issues of Violence and Control

Edited by
Camilla Pickles and
Jonathan Herring

Routledge
Taylor & Francis Group

LONDON AND NEW YORK

First published 2020
by Routledge
2 Park Square, Milton Park, Abingdon, Oxon OX14 4RN

and by Routledge
52 Vanderbilt Avenue, New York, NY 10017

Routledge is an imprint of the Taylor & Francis Group, an informa business

British Library Cataloguing-in-Publication Data
A catalogue record for this book is available from the British Library

Library of Congress Cataloging-in-Publication Data
Names: Pickles, Camilla, editor. | Herring, Jonathan, editor.
Title: Childbirth, vulnerability and law : exploring issues of violence and control / Edited by Camilla Pickles, Jonathan Herring.
Description: New York : Routledge, 2019. | Includes bibliographical references and index.
Identifiers: LCCN 2019027828 (print) | LCCN 2019027829 (ebook) | ISBN 9781138335493 (hardback) | ISBN 9780429443718 (ebook)
Subjects: LCSH: Medical personnel—Malpractice. | Childbirth. | Women—Crimes against. | Women—Violence against. | Health facilities—Risk management. | Pregnancy—Complications—Risk factors.
Classification: LCC K4365 .C55 2019 (print) | LCC K4365 (ebook) | DDC 344.04/19—dc23
LC record available at https://lccn.loc.gov/2019027828
LC ebook record available at https://lccn.loc.gov/2019027829

ISBN: 978-1-138-33549-3 (hbk)
ISBN: 978-0-429-44371-8 (ebk)

Typeset in Galliard
by codeMantra

Contents

Acknowledgements   vii
Contributors   ix

Introduction   1
CAMILLA PICKLES AND JONATHAN HERRING

1 *'Amigas, sisters: we're being gaslighted'*: obstetric
   violence and epistemic injustice   14
   SARA COHEN SHABOT

2 **Practices of silencing: birth, marginality and epistemic
   violence**   30
   RACHELLE CHADWICK

3 **Posttraumatic stress disorder following childbirth**   49
   ANTJE HORSCH AND SUSAN GARTHUS-NIEGEL

4 **Identifying the wrong in obstetric violence: lessons
   from domestic abuse**   67
   JONATHAN HERRING

5 **Midwives and midwifery: the need for courage to
   reclaim vocation for respectful care**   88
   SOO DOWNE AND NANCY STONE

6 **Health system accountability in South Africa: a driver
   of violence against women?**   111
   JESSICA RUCELL

7 Human rights law and challenging dehumanisation in
childbirth: a practitioner's perspective 132
ELIZABETH PROCHASKA

8 Leaving women behind: the application of evidence-
based guidelines, law, and obstetric violence by omission 140
CAMILLA PICKLES

9 Childbirth, consent, and information about options
and risks 161
LISA FORSBERG

10 Court-authorised obstetric intervention: insight and
capacity, a tale of loss 178
SAMANTHA HALLIDAY

11 Obstetric violence through a fiduciary lens 204
ELIZABETH KUKURA

12 Reflections on criminalising obstetric violence:
a feminist perspective 226
KAREN BRENNAN

Afterword 251
EMILY JACKSON

Index 257

Acknowledgements

Many people have made this collection possible and the editors would like to express their sincerest gratitude. We would like to thank all the contributors for sharing their time and knowledgeable insights, and for their commitment to this very important project. We thank Federica Giordano for her research assistance and reliable support throughout the project and Marthe Goudsmit for her assistance with indexing. Special thanks are due to the British Academy and the Oxford University Faculty of Law's Research Support Fund for funding our seminar. The generous funding enabled fruitful and exciting exchange of ideas at a seminar and this undoubtedly makes this book a better collection. Thanks to Exeter College for hosting our seminar and to all the administrative staff in the Faculty of Law who provided invaluable assistance throughout the project. Finally, we are so grateful to all at Routledge who were instrumental in bringing this collection to print.

Contributors

Karen Brennan is a Senior Lecturer in Law at the University of Essex.

Rachelle Chadwick is a Senior Lecturer in Sociology at the University of Pretoria.

Sara Cohen Shabot is an Senior Lecture at the Women's and Gender Studies Graduate Program at the University of Haifa.

Soo Downe is a Professor at the School of Community Health and Midwifery, University of Central Lancashire.

Lisa Forsberg is a British Academy Postdoctoral Fellow in Law and Philosophy at the University of Oxford.

Susan Garthus-Niegel is a Psychologist and a Research Professor at the Norwegian Institute of Public Health, and Head of the 'Epidemiology and Women's Health' research unit at the Dresden University of Technology.

Samantha Halliday is an Associate Professor of Law at Durham University.

Jonathan Herring is a Professor of Law at the University of Oxford and the DM Wolfe-Clarendon Fellow at Exeter College.

Antje Horsch is a clinical psychologist and an Assistant Professor at the Institute of Higher Education and Research in Healthcare, University of Lausanne, and at the Woman-Mother-Child Department, Lausanne University Hospital.

Emily Jackson is a Professor of Law at the London School of Economics and Political Science.

Elizabeth Kukura is a Visiting Assistant Professor of Law at Drexel University.

Camilla Pickles is a British Academy Postdoctoral Research Fellow in Law at the University of Oxford and a Fellow at the South African Institute for Advanced Constitutional, Public, Human Rights and International Law at the University of Johannesburg.

Elizabeth Prochaska is a Barrister, Legal Director at the Equality and Human Rights Commission, and founder of Birthrights.

Jessica Rucell is a Postdoctoral Research Fellow in Sociology at the University of Cape Town.

Nancy Stone is a Postdoctoral Researcher in maternal healthcare in Germany.

Introduction

Camilla Pickles and Jonathan Herring

This book explores the themes of vulnerability, violence, and control around childbirth. This might seem incongruous to some readers. Even if one does not accept the glorified accounts of childbirth as involving joy and wonder, but rather agony and distress, the terms 'violence' and 'control' might seem an exaggeration. Yet, in 2014 the World Health Organization (WHO) released a statement recognising that there is a growing body of research that 'paints a disturbing picture' of women's childbirth experiences:[1]

> Many women across the globe experience disrespectful, abusive or neglectful treatment during childbirth in facilities. ... While disrespectful and abusive treatment of women may occur throughout pregnancy, childbirth and the postpartum period, women are particularly vulnerable during childbirth. Such practices may have direct adverse consequences for both the mother and infant.[2]

Research reveals that women face discrimination within facilities, and they are sometimes sexually, physically, verbally, and/or emotionally abused by healthcare professionals.[3] Communication between women and healthcare professionals is sometimes inadequate and medical professionals give insufficient attention to women's concerns. This can lead to professionals failing to provide supportive care in general, objectifying women, and treating them as passive participants in their births.[4] There is evidence that health professionals fail to meet professional standards by neglecting to obtain women's informed consent and by performing procedures without due regard for women's right to privacy.[5] At times

---

1 World Health Organization, 'The Prevention and Elimination of Disrespect and Abuse During Facility-based Childbirth' (2014) <https://apps.who.int/iris/bitstream/handle/10665/134588/WHO_RHR_14.23_eng.pdf?sequence=1> accessed 11 February 2019.
2 Ibid.
3 Meghan A Bohren and others, 'The Mistreatment of Women during Childbirth in Health Facilities Globally: A Mixed-Methods Systematic Review' (2015) 12(6) PLOS Med e1001847.
4 Ibid.
5 Ibid.

healthcare professionals perform painful procedures without appropriate care and compassion, and women are denied access to pain relief medication. Some women have reported being neglected or completely abandoned during childbirth.[6] Further, facility and system deficiencies create birthing environments that compromise respectful and dignified care. Toxic facility cultures, caused by staff shortage, constraints on necessary supplies, problematic facility policies, are not women-centred and objectify women.[7] Women and their babies may survive childbirth but reports reveal that women's experience of facility-based care has left them traumatised and these circumstances may have dire consequences for mental well-being and the ability to bond with their babies.

In many ways these findings are surprising. Around the world there is greater awareness of and acceptance of women's rights.[8] There is a growing awareness of the problem of violence against women and a determination to address it. The quality of training for medical professionals is improving, including more importance being given to ethics. It is not hard to find fine-sounding professional and government documents setting out support for respecting women's choices in relation to childbirth.[9] Yet, despite all of this, it is clear that on the ground all too often women are abused during their labour.

Of course, these issues are not new. Abuse during facility-based childbirth has been occurring for decades, arguably for as long as childbirth became a medical event.[10] However, Hodges explains:

> [W]e are in about the same position we were in the 1950s and 1960s regarding domestic abuse and violence against women. Abuse and violence were happening, but we did not have a name for it. If your husband or boyfriend was verbally or physically abusive, well, that was just the way he was. It probably was your fault, and in any case, there was not much you could do about it.[11]

The WHO's statement (quoted above) makes it very clear that relevant stakeholders must do more to establish mechanisms to prevent and eliminate abuse during childbirth.

---

6 Ibid.
7 Ibid.
8 United Nations High Commissioner for Human Rights, 'Women's Human Rights and Gender Equality' (United Nations, 2019) <www.ohchr.org/en/issues/women/wrgs/pages/wrgsindex.aspx> accessed 11 February 2019.
9 Department of Health, 'Maternity Matters: Choice, Access and Continuity of Care in a Safe Service' (Department of Health 2007); The Royal College of Obstetricians and Gynaecologists, 'Providing Quality Care for Women: Obstetrics and Gynaecology Workforce' (The Royal College of Obstetricians and Gynaecologists 2016).
10 For instance, see Henci Goer, 'Cruelty in Maternity Wards: Fifty Years Later' (2010) 19 J Perinat Educ 33; Marsden Wagner, 'Confessions of a Dissident' in Robbie E Davis-Floyd and Carolyn F Sargent (eds), *Childbirth and Authoritative Knowledge* (University of California Press 1997) 366.
11 Susan Hodges, 'Abuse in Hospital-Based Birth Settings?' (2009) 18 J Perinat Educ 8.

The theme of abuse and violence during childbirth has connected researchers, activists, organisations, and other stakeholders across the globe from diverse disciplines. However, most of the literature available on the subject of abuse and violence during childbirth originates from disciplines other than law. In fact, debates in law are glaringly absent,[12] short of a small selection of contributions considering international human rights law and the different positions in South Africa, the United States, and Kenya.[13] We hope that this book can provide a starting point for legal debates over responses to this issue. This collection arose out of the need to initiate further legal debates on abuse during childbirth through the lens of violence, vulnerability, and control. Since this edited collection is one of the first contributions to take on this role, we considered it important to adopt an interdisciplinary approach by including contributions from other disciplines that are intended to provide much-needed context. These contextualising chapters unpack and explore the different dimensions and complexities of vulnerability, violence, and control during childbirth.

We certainly have come a long way in developing and understanding facility-based abuse and violence. We have a better grasp of how it manifests and why. We highlight here three aspects in particular. First, it is now recognised that abuse and violence during childbirth occur at an individual *and* a structural level.[14] That is, we are not dealing with only a few bad apples but a system that is structured in a way that oppresses women because it enables abuse and violence. The individual and structural systems are interrelated. Because the structures permit and authorise abusive practices against women, these are practised by medical professionals; and this practice is seen to normalise and justify

12 This is the case for English speaking countries. Several Latin American countries have enacted laws that recognise obstetric violence as a form of violence against women. Some recognise it a crime while others create a form of statutory right of action. See Grupo de Información en Reproducción Elegida, 'Obstetric Violence: A Human Rights Approach' (2015) <https://gire.org.mx/en/wp-content/uploads/sites/2/2015/11/ObstetricViolenceReport.pdf> accessed 11 February 2018.

13 Beatrice Odallo, Evelyne Opondo and Martin Onyango, 'Litigating to Ensure Access to Quality Maternal Health Care for Women and Girls in Kenya' (2018) 26(53) Reprod Health Matters 123; Elizabeth Kukura, 'Obstetric Violence' (2018) 106 Georget Law J 721; Maria T R Borger, 'A Violent Birth: Reframing Coerced Procedures during Childbirth as Obstetric Violence' (2018) 67 Duke Law J 827; Farah Diaz-Tello, 'Invisible Wounds: Obstetric Violence in the United States' (2016) 24(47) Reprod Health Matters 56; Rajat Khosla and others, 'International Human Rights and the Mistreatment of Women during Childbirth' (2016) 18 Health Hum Rights 131; Camilla Pickles, 'Eliminating Abusive "Care": A Criminal Law Response to Obstetric Violence in South Africa' (2015) 54(1) SACQ 5. Carlos Vacaflor provides a detailed account of the Argentinian position in Carlos Herrera Vacaflor, 'Obstetric Violence: A New Framework for Identifying Challenges to Maternal Healthcare in Argentina' (2016) 24(47) Reprod Health Matters 65.

14 For instance, see Miltenburg Solnes and others, 'Disrespect and Abuse in Maternity Care: Individual Consequences of Structural Violence' (2018) 26(53) Reprod Health Matters 88; Michelle Sadler and others, 'Moving beyond Disrespect and Abuse: Addressing the Structural Dimensions of Obstetric Violence' (2016) 24(47) Reprod Health Matters 47.

the structures in place. For example, the structures may perpetuate a view that women are not competent to make decisions during labour and so professionals do not seek to involve women in making decisions, a practice which silences women or against which women rebel, which reinforces the view that women are not competent.

Second, violence and abuse during childbirth is a gendered phenomenon shaped by hierarchical relationships of power and broader social inequalities.[15] Women's treatment during childbirth reflects their position in society because a health system 'wears the inequalities of the society in which it functions'.[16]

Third, abuse during childbirth reflects a particular model of doctor-female patients' relations. It is not just in childbirth, but in a range of medical and quasi-medical interventions that we see medical power exercised over women's bodies.

So, the issue of abuse during childbirth should be recognised as reflecting and being reinforced by wider social and institutional forces. It means also that we need to adopt a multipronged approach to tackling this issue. Adequate resources are essential but so too is the need to reshape embedded norms through improved training of professionals and effective accountability.[17] However, the broader issue requires responses at a wider social level. We must be committed to developing and providing women-centred, evidence-based care.[18]

As the chapters in this book demonstrate, the conceptualisations of violence, vulnerability, and control are contested. Indeed, not all contributors are equally comfortable with the use of these three words in this context. However, we deliberately did not confine contributors to a particular conception of the concepts of violence, vulnerability, or control, for two reasons. First, this is an interdisciplinary collection and conceptualisations of these terms will naturally vary according to discipline. Second, we consider 'conceptual freedom' necessary in this context because we are venturing into unchartered terrain. Most of the themes considered in this collection have not been aired before a court and this freedom brings with it innovative arguments and contributions, and we leave it to each contributor to define for themselves these terms according to the

---

15 Lydia Zacher Dixon, 'Obstetrics in a Time of Violence: Mexican Midwives Critique Routine Hospital Practices' (2015) 29 Med Anthropol Q 437, 440–41.

16 Joanna N Erdmann, 'Bioethics, Human Rights, and Childbirth' (2015) 17 Health Hum Rights 43, 48. Also see Stephanie Rose Montesanti and Wilfred E Thurston, 'Mapping the Role of Structural and Interpersonal Violence in the Lives of Women: Implications for Public Health Interventions and Policy' (2015) 15 BMC Womens Health 100, 103.

17 Diana Bowser and Kathleen Hill, 'Exploring Evidence for Disrespect and Abuse in Facility-Based Birth: Report of a Landscape Analysis' (USAID-TRAction Project and Harvard School of Public Health, 20 September 2010) <www.ghdonline.org/uploads/Respectful_Care_at_Birth_9-20-101_Final1.pdf> accessed 18 October 2018.

18 Suellen Miller and others, 'Beyond too Little, too Late and too Much, too Soon: A Pathway towards Evidence-Based, Respectful Maternity Care Worldwide' (2016) 388.10056 The Lancet 2176.

direction of their contribution. What we will do here is very briefly explore the three words used and highlight some of the tensions around them, particularly as applied to childbirth.

Violence

Violence is typically understood to involve an intentional act of excessive physical force used to cause suffering or injury.[19] However, this conceptualisation is increasingly recognised as being far too narrow for three main reasons.[20] First, there is widespread appreciation of the importance of mental and emotional well-being. In some cases, the emotional or psychological impact of being hit will be far more significant than the physical pain. Traditionally, the criminal law supports a conception of violence that focuses on attacks to the body (in the English context an assault occasioning actual bodily harm, inflicting grievous bodily harm, etc.). However, we are more recently seeing offences of stalking, coercive control, online abuse and harassment, recognising the importance of relational or psychological harms.[21] Second, and linked to the first point, there is a challenge to the division between mind and body. The argument that the body and mind can be separated (known as Cartesian Dualism in the philosophical literature) now has few supporters. Biology is clear that such a separation cannot be maintained. This indicates that restricting violence to attacks on the body and not including attacks on the emotional well-being can no longer be supported. Third, there is growing acknowledgement that violence need not be intentional, as traditionally understood. Harassment, for example, may be understood by the perpetrator as an expression of love. Indeed, it is common for men to fail to appreciate (or claim to fail to appreciate) that their wrongful and harmful conduct against women is such.

In the case of 'obstetric violence' we see the above listed themes reflected in the volume. Obstetric violence is usually defined as the appropriation of women's bodies and reproductive processes by health personnel which brings with it a loss of autonomy and the ability to decide freely about their bodies and sexuality, and which has a negative impact on the quality of women's lives.[22] This term is used to describe the wide range of abuses during childbirth, including unintentional and neglectful care and structural inadequacies. Clearly these kinds of harms do

---

19 Vittorio Bufacchi, 'Two Concepts of Violence' (2005) 3 Polit Stud Rev 197.

20 For instance, see Vittorio Bufacchi, *Violence and Social Justice* (Palgrave Macmillan 2007); Willem de Haan, 'Violence as an Essentially Contested Concept' in Sophie Body-Gendrot and Pieter Spierenburg (eds), *Violence in Europe: Historical and Contemporary Perspectives* (Springer 2007). Johan Galtung, 'Violence, Peace, and Peace Research' (1969) 6 J Peace Res 167.

21 For a more detailed discussion of this see Jonathan Herring, *Law and the Relational Self* (CUP 2019) ch 6.

22 Rogelio Pérez D'Gregorio, 'Obstetric Violence: A New Legal Term Introduced in Venezuela' (2010) 111 Int J Gynaecol Obstet 201.

not fit within the traditional image of a typical act of violence being one person hitting another. Yet they can be understood as violence in the sense outlined above as an attack on the psychological and emotional integrity of the person.

In this volume several chapters explore how different harms inflicted in childbirth can be understood as violence. In fact, the contributions in this collection go beyond the *usual* definition of obstetric violence and venture into more challenging areas of 'violence'. For instance, Chadwick offers an intersectional analysis of marginalised South African girls' experiences of 'silencing' during childbirth and she explores how modes of silencing amount to obstetric violence. Similarly, Cohen Shabot extends the scope of obstetric violence to instances of 'gaslighting', women during labour, and thereafter by loving family and friends. She draws from her personal experience of care during her miscarriage to theorise the experience of gaslighting as a form of obstetric violence. Pickles considers whether obstetric violence can occur in the case of an omission, and Herring innovatively teases out the unique harms associated with obstetric violence through an analogy with domestic violence.

Rucell's and Downe and Stone's contributions remind us to broaden our focus to include considerations of care providers and the oppressive contexts in which some healthcare professionals are expected to work. Rucell, for example, shifts our focus to the structural dimensions of obstetric violence and pinpoints important institutional failings, particularly in the context of accountability mechanisms that foster violence more generally and that maintain an environment that allows violence to persist.

These chapters are all a 'first' within the obstetric violence literature landscape; they directly challenge conventional conceptualisations of violence and work to problematise the conventional conception of violence. Nevertheless, it must be admitted that the traditional understanding of violence still holds sway, particularly, among the public. The WHO's researchers are expressly set on avoiding the use of 'violence'[23] in the context of childbirth and that is why it is possible to identify concerns about the terminology of violence in some chapters. For instance, Downe and Stone raise important issues with the current use of 'obstetric violence'. They explain that some midwives consider themselves excluded from the 'obstetric' scope and they are concerned by the fact that it is shaped by essentialist claims that this type of violence against women is rooted in male power, rendering birthing women and midwives subservient and subject to abuse by male obstetricians.

Despite there being a measure of pushback or resistance to expanding how we are to understand violence during childbirth, Horsch and Garthus-Niegel's exploration of post-traumatic stress disorder following childbirth highlights the severity of the consequences of inappropriate 'care' during childbirth. This contribution makes it clear that the traditional understanding of violence needs

---

23 Bohren and others (n 3) 210; J P Vogel and others, 'Promoting Respect and Preventing Mistreatment during Childbirth' (2016) 123 BJOG 671.

to be under constant consideration and it may also support understanding of violence in the broad ways presented in this collection.

Vulnerability

At one level it is an obvious point that a woman in childbirth is in a vulnerable state. Her movements may be limited; she may be attached to medical technology; she may be in considerable pain; and she may face some medical risks that are associated with childbirth. All of these put her in a position that she is at risk of harm and with limited authority to protect herself. However, a vulnerability analysis of the issue is more complex than this.

There is a powerful strand of feminist critiques of the use of vulnerability in political and popular discourse.[24] This strand claims that groups of people are labelled as vulnerable and this is used to subject them to paternalistic interventions designed to protect them from hurting themselves, being taken advantage of, or to restore them to a non-vulnerable state. This is clearly a concern in this context. Halliday tackles this very issue in her contribution on court-ordered obstetric interventions on women living with serious mental illness. She reveals how the clinical construct of 'insight' is used to assess capacity of women living with serious mental illnesses, particularly when they refuse medical advice during obstetric care. Their capacity to make decisions about their births is undermined if women are perceived to 'lack insight' and choice in maternity care becomes illusionary for them. The more the powerlessness of the woman is emphasised, the greater the risk that she is in 'need of protection' and interferences in her autonomy can be justified. This in part may explain the 'silencing of women' and 'epistemic violence' which is discussed in Chapter 2 by Chadwick. It is also reflected in the infantilisation explored by Cohen Shabot in Chapter 1.

The concept of vulnerability is drawn on by another strand of feminist critique, which is universal vulnerability. This approach is most prominently favoured by Fineman.[25] She claims that everyone is in their nature vulnerable:

> The vulnerability approach recognizes that individuals are anchored at each end of their lives by dependency and the absence of capacity. Of course, between these ends, loss of capacity and dependence may also occur, temporarily for many and permanently for some as a result of disability or illness. Constant and variable throughout life, individual vulnerability encompasses not only damage that has been done in the past and speculative harms of the distant future, but also the possibility of immediate harm. We are beings who live with the ever-present possibility that our needs and circumstances will change. On an individual level, the concept of vulnerability (unlike

24 Vanessa Munro and Jane Scoular, 'Abusing Vulnerability? Contemporary Law and Policy Responses to Sex Work in the UK' (2012) 20 Fem Leg Stud 189.
25 Martha Albertson Fineman, 'The Vulnerable Subject: Anchoring Equality in the Human Condition' (2008) 20 Yale J Law Fem 177.

that of liberal autonomy) captures this present potential for each of us to become dependent based upon our persistent susceptibility to misfortune and catastrophe.[26]

This approach recognises the universal nature of everyone's vulnerability. It is therefore sceptical of attempts to identify those who are particularly vulnerable and in need of protection and elevation from vulnerability.

This universal vulnerability approach might seem to be rather unhelpful to the issue of childbirth as it appears to argue against giving special protections to women in labour. Even though we are in our nature all vulnerable, society distributes resources to give different degrees of resilience to different groups.

It is true that at different times and in different circumstances we may be more overtly in use of societal resources but that should not disguise the fact that we are in need of communal and relational support for all our lives. We may be differently positioned within a web of economic and social relationships, and this will impact on our experience of vulnerability and the resources at our disposal.[27]

The significance of this observation is that there is nothing about being in labour which in and of itself renders a woman more vulnerable than everyone else; rather it is the social power structures that render a woman in labour open to abuse. The chapters in this contribution certainly support this understanding.

There are two reasons why this way of explaining the vulnerability is helpful. First, it makes it clear that the source of the particular vulnerability is not the woman, but the structure of medical and societal force acting on her during childbirth. Part of this theme is explored in Downe and Stone's chapter. They reveal that institutional management of maternity care prevents midwives from 'being with women' and instead results in the 'othering' of women and rendering them enemies of the system, thus creating fertile ground for abuse during childbirth. Second, it means that the legal protections should not be designed to remove the vulnerability by rendering the woman fully autonomous and putting her in sole charge of the situation as that would be impossible and undesirable. The message of universal vulnerability is that we need to cooperate together in respectful ways to find solutions to the challenges we face as we lack the resources alone to respond to them.[28]

Control

The concept of control is a complex one in relation to the birth process. For one thing it is in the nature of birth that the body cannot be controlled and contained. The process is about moving through bodies. It is a process that challenges the image of the body as a contained, static entity. The simple call for a woman to be in control of her childbirth is unrealistic in that sense.

---

26 Ibid.
27 Jonathan Herring, *Vulnerability, Childhood and the Law* (Springer 2018) 34.
28 Jonathan Herring, *Vulnerable Adults and the Law* (OUP 2016).

However, the experience of birth, as outlined above, is all too often an experience of other people taking control of a woman's body. That she becomes a baby producing machine for medical professionals to manipulate, tear, cut, and force at their bidding. Of course, this is typically done 'in order to produce a healthy baby' and is justified on the basis that this is what the woman would want. Halliday notes in this collection that 'women are supposed to remain in control, but what is actually meant is compliant'. Herring considers the concept of coercive control and uses it to explore the nature of obstetric violence as misuse of a trustful relationship to abuse the woman. Forsberg's chapter highlights how denying women access to information because it is too complex, too distressing, or cannot be processed undermines women's autonomy.

As these points indicate, the issue of power and who controls the process is complex. Too often the medical professionals take control of the woman's body during childbirth. However, women, through birthing, are in a position of power whether 'others' accept this or not. They bring life into the world and that is an incredibly powerful physiological and psychological process. Yet this is not power as it is commonly understood in patriarchy. First, because this power challenges patriarchal depictions of femininity.[29] Second, because it is not power in the sense of exercising control or domination over someone, as the concept is commonly understood in patriarchy. It is a generative power creating new life and new relationships. Similarly, in relation to control, birth is at one level a brute uncontrollable process. Yet it is one that only the woman concerned should be making decisions over. Again, not in the patriarchal sense of control as exercising domination over or subduing something, but in the sense of having the moral and legal authority to make decisions about the physiological process.

Legal responses to obstetric violence

One of the aims of this collection is to explore legal tools that could be used to provide an effective response to obstetric violence. One option is the use of human rights. Khosla and others argue that childbirth has not been adequately addressed or analysed under international human rights law.[30] This, they argue, is an essential first step because '[h]uman rights standards are an important accountability tool for recognizing and protecting the human rights of women during childbirth in facilities, and for supporting health system reform to prevent mistreatment in the future'.[31] Prochaska offers a practitioner's perceptive on this issue in the collection. She traces important international case law relevant to childbirth and reflects on their significance in the context of violence, vulnerability, and control during childbirth. She explains that human rights law offers women in the United Kingdom an opportunity to challenge hospital decisions

---

29 Sara Cohen Shabot explores this issue in 'Making Loud Bodies "Feminine": A Feminist-Phenomenological Analysis of Obstetric Violence' (2016) 39 Human Studies 231.

30 Khosla and others (n 13).

31 Ibid 138.

through litigation but she urges that the full might of human rights law lies in its potential to shape hospital culture. This is best achieved through the injection of human rights values within the maternity care context.

A second option is tort law. Borger and Diaz Tello consider this in the US context.[32] They emphasise that individual tort litigation is ineffective in the context of abuse, violence, or coercion. Dias Tello reveals that this avenue remains out of reach for many women and tort law tends to frame the issue as an individual problem rather than a structural one and it therefore hides the gendered dimensions of this phenomenon.[33] Kukura has earlier argued that

> obstetric violence will continue as long as doctors perceive that they risk liability by not intervening and thus force treatment on unwilling women out of fear of malpractice exposure. Courts must recognize and enforce informed treatment refusals as a necessary part of robust and meaningful informed consent.[34]

She emphasises that professional standard setting is an important avenue that needs further attention.[35] In this collection, Forsberg moves beyond these debates. She explores violations of women's autonomy during childbirth in relation to being deprived of information about treatment options and their risks. She demonstrates that depriving women of information or of the opportunity to decide amounts to a harm in and of itself, and negligence laws are ill-equipped to offer redress in this context.

A third option is the use of fiduciary law. In her contribution to this collection, Kukura explores the use of this doctrine in the context of US jurisprudence. Its attraction lies in the highlighting of the importance of trust in the medical professional-patient relationship and the strict liability approach. However, the chapter shows that the American courts have been reluctant to develop the concept of fiduciary obligations within a medical context. Despite this, her chapter offers a glimmer of hope to those seeking to employ the law in innovative ways.

A fourth option is the use of targeted legal interventions. Borger makes the case that obstetric violence laws are the most effective way to address current shortcomings; she recommends importing to the United States the obstetric violence law framework adopted in Latin America and thereby develop a criminal and civil law regime.[36] Pickles emphasises this point in her chapter on evidence-based guidelines and obstetric violence by omission. She argues that, in fact, governments are obligated by international human rights laws to enact legislation to tackle this very particular manifestation of gender-based violence.

---

32 Borger (n 13); Diaz-Tello (n 13).
33 Diaz-Tello (n 13).
34 Kukura (n 13) 800.
35 Ibid.
36 Borger (n 13).

A fifth option is the use of criminal law.[37] Brennan's chapter explores this in detail. She advocates for a specific offence of obstetric violence to ensure the wrong done to the victim is fully captured. She highlights how traditional criminal offences do not capture the severity of the issue. Nevertheless, as she acknowledges, there are limits to the role of the criminal law. It will be rare where sufficient *mens rea* can be proved and a jury may well be reluctant to convict medical professionals if they were seen as 'doing their best in a difficult situation'.

Concluding reflections

Abuse, violence, and control during childbirth and women's vulnerability during childbirth remain ill-defined and under-theorised from a legal perspective but this collection offers a promising start. It is necessary to see ourselves at the start because there are many themes not covered in this collection.

In the main, the more legally focused chapters in this collection have focused on the visible forms of violence and abuse during childbirth, rendering structural violence free from legal analysis. This is a particularly pressing issue because individual manifestations of violence are a consequence of structural inequalities.[38] It is not entirely clear what role the courts can play in the broader context of structural violence. The Kenyan experience in relation to strategic litigation brings home this point. The Centre for Reproductive Rights represented Majani; she was abused and neglected during childbirth in a Kenyan facility and the High Court of Bungoma ruled in her favour.[39] Nevertheless, Odallo, Opondo, and Onyango highlight several failures. They argue that the court failed to make an order that would facilitate much needed *structural changes* such as mandating human rights training for nurses, mandating the government to actively share information about complaints procedures for aggrieved patients, and failing to mandate the government to develop and implement policy guidelines on healthcare.[40] While this judgment reflects a promising development it also lays bare the reality that courts can play only a limited role in the fight against abuse and violence during childbirth. This limitation deserves deeper analysis and interrogation.

Further, we left open the question of whether medical negligence itself can constitute a manifestation of obstetric violence. Research reveals that obstetric violence is used to describe instances of medical negligence[41] and medical negligence is recognised as a manifestation of obstetric violence in some Mexican

---

37 Pickles (n 13).
38 Johan Galtung, 'Cultural Violence' (1990) 27 J Peace Res 291.
39 Odallo, Opondo, and Onyango (n 13).
40 Ibid 127.
41 For instance, see Simone Grilo Diniz and others, 'Abuse and Disrespect in Childbirth Care as a Public Health Issue in Brazil: Origins, Definitions, Impacts on Maternal Health, and Proposals for its Prevention' (2015) 25 J Hum Growth Dev 377.

states' laws.[42] However, it is not clear whether contemporary theories of violence are broad enough to include negligent conduct and what the law should do if negligence comes to be accepted as a form of violence.

This book seeks to start a discussion on where the violence in obstetric violence starts and where it ends. It has opened up debates about the nature and definition of obstetric violence. Until we are able to capture its multifaceted nature we will not be able to identify its core wrong(s) or produce an effective legal response to the issues raised. Our hope is that this volume and work flowing from it will generate a more effective legal response to violence in childbirth and more respectful treatment of women in labour.

Bibliography

Bohren M A and others, 'The Mistreatment of Women during Childbirth in Health Facilities Globally: A Mixed-Methods Systematic Review' (2015) 12(6) PLOS Med e1001847

Borger M T R, 'A Violent Birth: Reframing Coerced Procedures during Childbirth as Obstetric Violence' (2018) 67 Duke Law J 827

Bufacchi V, 'Two Concepts of Violence' (2005) 3 Polit Stud Rev 197

Bufacchi V, *Violence and Social Justice* (Palgrave Macmillan 2007)

Cohen Shabot S, 'Making Loud Bodies "Feminine": A Feminist-Phenomenological Analysis of Obstetric Violence' (2016) 39 Human Studies 231

D'Gregorio R P, 'Obstetric Violence: A New Legal Term Introduced in Venezuela' (2010) 111 Int J Gynaecol Obstet 201

De Haan W, 'Violence as an Essentially Contested Concept' in Body-Gendrot S and Spierenburg P (eds), *Violence in Europe: Historical and Contemporary Perspectives* (Springer 2007)

Department of Health, 'Maternity Matters: Choice, Access and Continuity of Care in a Safe Service' (Department of Health 2007)

Diaz-Tello F, 'Invisible Wounds: Obstetric Violence in the United States' (2016) 24(47) Reprod Health Matters 56

Diniz S G and others, 'Abuse and Disrespect in Childbirth Care as a Public Health Issue in Brazil: Origins, Definitions, Impacts on Maternal Health, and Proposals for its Prevention' (2015) 25 J Hum Growth Dev 377

Dixon L Z, 'Obstetrics in a Time of Violence: Mexican Midwives Critique Routine Hospital Practices' (2015) 29 Med Anthropol Q 437

Erdmann J N, 'Bioethics, Human Rights, and Childbirth' (2015) 17 Health Hum Rights 43

Fineman M A, 'The Vulnerable Subject: Anchoring Equality in the Human Condition' (2008) 20 Yale J Law Fem 177

Galtung J, 'Cultural Violence' (1990) 27 J Peace Res 291

Galtung J, 'Violence, Peace, and Peace Research' (1969) 6 J Peace Res 167

Goer H, 'Cruelty in Maternity Wards: Fifty Years Later' (2010) 19 J Perinat Educ 33

Herring J, *Law and the Relational Self* (CUP 2019)

Herring J, *Vulnerability, Childhood and the Law* (Springer 2018)

42 See Grupo de Información en Reproducción Elegida (n 12).

Herring J, *Vulnerable Adults and the Law* (OUP 2016)

Hodges S, 'Abuse in Hospital-Based Birth Settings?' (2009) 18 J Perinat Educ 8

Khosla R and others, 'International Human Rights and the Mistreatment of Women during Childbirth' (2016) 18 Health Hum Rights 131

Kukura E, 'Obstetric Violence' (2018) 106 Georget Law J 721

Miller S and others, 'Beyond too Little, too Late and too Much, too Soon: A Pathway Towards Evidence-Based, Respectful Maternity Care Worldwide' (2016) 388.10056 The Lancet 2176

Montesanti S R and Thurston W E, 'Mapping the Role of Structural and Interpersonal Violence in the Lives of Women: Implications for Public Health Interventions and Policy' (2015) 15 BMC Women's Health 100

Munro V and Scoular J, 'Abusing Vulnerability? Contemporary Law and Policy Responses to Sex Work in the UK' (2012) 20 Fem Leg Stud 189

Odallo B, Opondo E, and Onyango M, 'Litigating to Ensure Access to Quality Maternal Health Care for Women and Girls in Kenya' (2018) 26(53) Reprod Health Matters 123

Pickles C, 'Eliminating Abusive "Care": A Criminal Law Response to Obstetric Violence in South Africa' (2015) 54(1) SACQ 5

Sadler M and others, 'Moving beyond Disrespect and Abuse: Addressing the Structural Dimensions of Obstetric Violence' (2016) 24(47) Reprod Health Matters 47

Solnes M and others, 'Disrespect and Abuse in Maternity Care: Individual Consequences of Structural Violence' (2018) 26(53) Reprod Health Matters 88

The Royal College of Obstetricians and Gynaecologists, 'Providing Quality Care for Women: Obstetrics and Gynaecology Workforce' (The Royal College of Obstetricians and Gynaecologists 2016)

Vacaflor C H, 'Obstetric Violence: A New Framework for Identifying Challenges to Maternal Healthcare in Argentina' (2016) 24(47) Reprod Health Matters 65

Vogel J P and others, 'Promoting Respect and Preventing Mistreatment during Childbirth' (2016) 123 BJOG 671

Wagner M, 'Confessions of a Dissident' in Davis-Floyd R E and Sargent C F (eds), *Childbirth and Authoritative Knowledge* (University of California Press 1997) 366

1 'Amigas, sisters: we're being gaslighted'

Obstetric violence and epistemic injustice

Sara Cohen Shabot

Introduction

In 'Making Loud Bodies "Feminine"', I focused on how women live with and experience obstetric violence and why it is frequently described not only in terms of violence in general but specifically in terms of gender violence: as violence directed at women *because* they are women.[1] For this purpose, I used feminist phenomenology to explain and account for the feelings that many victims of this violence experience and report, including those of embodied oppression, of the diminishment of self, and of physical and emotional infantilisation.

In this chapter, I examine such feelings of diminishment of self and infantilisation through the epistemic aspects of the phenomenon of obstetric violence, mainly by observing it from the perspective of recent theories on epistemic injustice and specifically through the concept of 'gaslighting'. I argue that a central part of obstetric violence involves labouring women being disbelieved, distrusted, and (unjustifiably) questioned about their violent labouring experiences and, more pressingly, even being made to doubt their own experiences of violence and to feel deprived of epistemic authority altogether. I show that the distrust shown towards labouring women operates both during the experience of labour and afterwards, when they attempt to tell others about their (violent) labouring experiences and to obtain epistemic recognition from them. I emphasise that this experience of deep distrust needs to be understood not simply as a response to the phenomenon of obstetric violence but must be recognised as a core part of the phenomenon itself.

The idea of 'gaslighting' has recently been used to account for specific cases of epistemic injustice, where the victim is intentionally or unintentionally made to doubt and distrust her own experience and testimony, since her interlocutor (often her supposedly ally) heavily questions their truth. Thus, in this chapter, I argue that to be a victim of obstetric violence means (also) to be continuously gaslighted: first by the medical staff involved and then by those who listen to the victim's story.

---

1 Sara Cohen Shabot, 'Making Loud Bodies "Feminine": A Feminist-Phenomenological Analysis of Obstetric Violence' (2016) 39 Human Studies 231, emphasis added.

'But you cannot know for sure, can you?'

Last year, I went through several miscarriages. During one of them, I started bleeding at six weeks and five days into the pregnancy. I went to the hospital and was welcomed by a gynaecologist, a young woman. She seemed to be truly empathetic and kind. One of the first things she proceeded to do, after briefly conversing with me and my partner, was to examine me via ultrasound. She saw a tiny sac, with an approximately four-week-old embryo, a discovery she communicated to me optimistically. 'You are four weeks pregnant', she said, 'and you are bleeding, like so many women at this stage. Everything seems to be all right, do not worry too much'. 'But there is no heartbeat', I countered. 'Of course there is not', she replied, immutable: 'At four weeks we still cannot see any heartbeat'. Then I started impatiently explaining to her, for a second time now, that I was, in fact, not four, but rather almost seven weeks pregnant, and that this was surely an embryo that had stopped developing at four weeks (a situation similar to what had happened to me during several past pregnancies). It was then that a patronising dialogue of distrust began.

'But you do not really know *exactly* when you got pregnant, do you?' 'The truth is that I know the precise date', I responded. 'But you cannot know *for sure*', she continued. 'I do believe I can, though: I feel ovulation very clearly and I also used an ovulation predictor kit'. 'Well, this is what I see in the ultrasound', she said, attempting to bring this hierarchical conversation to a happy ending by using the ultimate silencing weapon: Technology.

'You just do not believe me; you do not believe me at all, right?' I desperately tried, one last time.

She wielded her final weapon, condescendingly: 'Well, we cannot base a diagnosis on your intuition, can we?'. And then I just shut up. I knew that this was pointless. I would not be able to convince her. In her view, I was still pregnant. To me, it was clear that I was miscarrying. I had experience, and I had knowledge, but this knowledge was being silenced mercilessly and turned by the 'epistemic authority' into 'pure intuition', just another suspicious female hunch not to be trusted. This is how I, an adult woman in her 40s, a responsible professional, a professor of philosophy, was sent home and told not to worry, since in eight more months I would most probably become a mother for the third time.

I went home, and I miscarried. Everything was all right and I needed no further intervention. However, that meeting with the kind doctor demanded reflection. After I went home that night, before I miscarried, I had noted that there was something else awakening in me alongside my anger and desperation at being disbelieved. I felt self-distrust, an uneasy feeling of not being sure whether I might be four weeks pregnant after all and not seven. That is, I had a feeling of not being sure whether I knew anything at all. In the end, I thought, it would be nice if she was right, and maybe she was, and how could I *really* know, after all?[2]

---

2 The similarities between my case and the one described by McLeod in her chapter on miscarriages and self-distrust as part of her analysis of reproductive autonomy and self-trust are

Reflecting on this experience in retrospect, I could not help but notice the similarities it had with some of the forms of obstetric violence I had undergone in my second childbirth, which I documented and analysed as examples of the broad experience of obstetric violence in my first paper on the subject. I suddenly understood that this experience of profound distrust and disbelief was a recurrent, aching theme in stories denouncing obstetric violence: women being infantilised and having our reports of pain or power – of knowing what our bodies were either suffering or enduring with strength during childbirth –dismissed by medical authorities (whether doctors or nurses) in the labour room[3] and, even more stressfully, by well-meaning allies listening to our labour experiences after the fact. But there was something else: this experience too often developed into one of self-distrust; it was eventually tainted by a disempowering feeling of deep self-doubt and, in consequence, loss of autonomy.[4] In other words, in addition

---

striking. She quotes a report by telling the story of Janet, who precisely and accurately charted her first pregnancy, and miscarried at seven and a half weeks of gestation:

> Every morning the bleeding stopped and every afternoon it started and on the Wednesday we went back to our doctor. He felt, palpated, and prodded and questioned that I had ever been pregnant at all: 'You told me you were pregnant and I believed you.' *And I, knowing that I had been pregnant, started to doubt myself and my knowledge of my body.* I felt concerned for the doctor, that he felt he had made a mistake, and it was my fault. You are very willing to believe everything is your fault. … I was afraid that the whole episode had just been hysteria, and he (the GP) was thinking 'neurotic woman.' … [She then explained that she had an ultrasound which confirmed her pregnancy.] … *I had known that I was pregnant, and I had doubted it, doubted me, doubted this little baby existence because some forms of knowledge are seen as more valid than others.*
>
> Valerie Hey and others, *Hidden Loss: Miscarriage and Ectopic Pregnancy* (2nd edn, Women's Press 1996) 44–45 quoted in Carolyn McLeod, *Self-Trust and Reproductive Autonomy* (MIT Press 2002) 38, emphasis added

3 The Internet is full of such reports these days. For instance, Birth Monopoly's Facebook page offers dozens of reports of women being mocked and patronised for bringing birth plans to their births. One such account reports:

> My first birth I handed over my birth plan and the nurse literally LOL'd and said to the other nurse 'Look. First time mom with a birth plan *laughs*' I was openly disrespected. I should have walked right out of that hospital and checked in somewhere else. The nurse mocked me for going pain med free, didn't believe me when I told her I was about to vomit, didn't believe me when I told her my water had broken. She was awful. My OB was so respectful, though. I didn't get anything in my birth plan (ended with a c-section after my cervix swelled), but I knew that was likely. That nurse made my birth experience traumatic. Not the c-section, the nurse did.
>
> Birth Monopoly (Facebook, 14 November 2017)

4 On self-distrust as eventually leading to loss of autonomy, see McLeod (n 2) 6. McLeod considers self-trust in patients to be the result of an intersubjective, relational process in which the patient trusts her healthcare provider and in consequence trusts herself and is able to make autonomous decisions about her own health. Referring to one particular case, she writes:

> Lee was not able to trust her health care providers to interpret the expression of her needs as legitimate, and as a result, she was not always able to trust herself to act in her own interests. Patients cannot trust themselves to be autonomous if they cannot trust physicians to give them room to express their autonomous desires, and also to inform them accurately about

to being condescendingly questioned regarding our most intimate embodied experiences, we were ultimately being convinced that 'they knew better'; we were truly made to feel and to believe that we had been exaggerating. Furthermore, it even seemed somewhat reasonable to assume that – precisely because of the pain of childbirth, because of our vulnerable state during it, because we were probably a little 'hysterical' – we had been magnifying 'what everybody goes through' and making a fuss over a 'normal' experience.[5] This is of course the ultimate silencing tool. It is one thing to know that our experiences are not trusted, but to be convinced that we are indeed wrong, exaggerating, crazy, or

---

their health and health care options. Patient self-trust does not replace the need for trust between patients and practitioners.

5 For more on the phenomenon of distrusting women in medical settings, mainly with respect to the reproductive process, because of sexist assumptions that women are oversensitive, overly emotional, and epistemologically and morally incompetent in consequence, see, for instance, McLeod (n 2) 8–9. Added to these sexist assumptions about women are assumptions about parenthood being a stressful and vulnerable condition, all of which are put onto women as they are going through the processes involved in becoming or trying to become mothers. Goering writes, for instance, about the experience of new parents in France when their babies are being taken care of in the newborn intensive care unit: '[P]arents whose infants are in the NICU are often treated paternalistically, with the presumption that they are "too emotional to be able to decide" or without "their whole decision-making capabilities because they are too stressed, for instance"'. Sara Goering, 'Postnatal Reproductive Autonomy: Promoting Relational Autonomy and Self-Trust in New Parents' (2009) 23 Bioethics 9. Racism adds another set of pernicious assumptions and frequently plays a part when women are disbelieved in the labour room as well as being involved in epistemic accountability in general: see Miranda Fricker, *Epistemic Injustice. Power and the Ethics of Knowing* (OUP 2007); Luvell Anderson, 'Epistemic Injustice and the Philosophy of Race' in Ian James Kidd, José Medina, and Gaile Pohlhaus (eds), *The Routledge Handbook of Epistemic Injustice* (Routledge 2017). The story of Serena Williams, the famous African-American tennis player, is a recent powerful example. After Williams gave birth to her first baby by emergency caesarean section, she started to experience a shortness of breath. Williams assumed that she was having a pulmonary embolism because of her history of blood clots, and because she was off her daily anticoagulant regimen due to the recent surgery. Williams informed her nurse of her concerns and requested an immediate CT scan and blood thinners. The nurse did not believe Williams and dismissed Williams' concerns, she thought that Williams' 'pain medicine might be making her confused.' Williams did finally manage to get what she needed and saved her own life in consequence. Rob Haskel, 'Serena Williams on Motherhood, Marriage, and Making Her Comeback' (*Vogue*, 10 January 2018) <www.vogue.com/article/serena-williams-vogue-cover-interview-february-2018> accessed 3 August 2018. But alas, this kind of happy ending is not at all what many African-American women experience in the labour room, as Gay reports:

> When discussing Williams's maternal-health emergency, it's vital to address the role played by racism and racial discrimination – a requirement to sustainably address the United States' growing maternal-health problem. Black women are nearly four times more likely to die from pregnancy and childbirth than white women, and are also more likely to experience a severe maternal morbidity such as a heart attack, hemorrhage, sepsis, or blood clots like Williams did, regardless of their level of education or income. In fact, data from the New York City Department of Health show that black college-educated women were more likely than white women who hadn't completed high school to experience adverse maternal-health outcomes. Knowledge and money aren't enough to save black women, because racism trumps all.
>
> Elizabeth Dawes Gay, 'Serena Williams Could Insist that Doctors Listen to Her. Most Black Women Can't' (*The Nation*, 18 January 2018) <www.thenation.com/article/serena-williams-could-insist-that-doctors-listen-to-her-most-black-women-cant/> accessed 3 August 2018

ultimately just not even capable of proper judgment: this is the most effective form of oppression. Such deep internalisation of self-distrust and of the idea of our selves not being worthy epistemic agents is certainly the ultimate tool through which hegemonic powers can continue unquestioned and untouched.

It was only recently that I learned that there was a name for this phenomenon. I have thus come to understand that other women and I have been continuously gaslighted as a part of our experience of obstetric violence and of our ensuing encounters with those to whom we tell our stories. In the following section, I will use the concept of gaslighting in order to give an account of this particular experience of self-distrust as a part of the scenarios of obstetric violence.

On gaslighting

The 1944 film *Gaslight* tells the story of Gregory, who attempts to drive his wife, Paula, crazy, in order to obtain the jewels she inherited. What is especially interesting in Gregory's manipulation of Paula is that he gradually succeeds in making her doubt her own perceptions, convincing her to distrust her own knowledge and judgment. Lately, the concept of 'gaslighting' has been analysed as a specific form of epistemic injustice, one according to which a (usually) more powerful person or group intentionally or unintentionally[6] causes a weaker one to distrust her/their own perceptions, thus contributing to a further diminution or oppression of the person or group that was weaker to begin with.[7] Abramson eloquently defines it as:

> [A] form of emotional manipulation in which the gaslighter tries (consciously or not) to induce in someone the sense that her reactions, perceptions, memories and/or beliefs are not just mistaken, but utterly without grounds – paradigmatically, so unfounded as to qualify as crazy. Gaslighting is, even at this level, quite unlike merely dismissing someone, for dismissal simply fails to take another seriously as an interlocutor, whereas gaslighting is aimed at *getting another not to take herself seriously as an interlocutor*. It almost always involves multiple incidents that take place over long stretches of time; it frequently involves multiple parties playing the role of gaslighter, or cooperating with a gaslighter; it frequently involves isolating the target in various ways.[8]

---

6 Researchers on gaslighting agree that an important feature of the phenomenon is that it can be done unintentionally. This raises substantive ethical and epistemological questions regarding the responsibility and accountability of gaslighters.

7 Kate Abramson, 'Turning Up the Lights on Gaslighting' (2014) 28 Philos Perspect 1; Elena Flores Ruíz, 'Musing: Spectral Phenomenologies: Dwelling Poetically in Professional Philosophy' (2014) 29 Hypatia 196; Rachel McKinnon, 'Allies Behaving Badly: Gaslighting as Epistemic Injustice' in Ian James Kidd, José Medina, and Gaile Pohlhaus (eds), *The Routledge Handbook of Epistemic Injustice* (Routledge 2017).

8 Abramson (n 7) 2, emphasis added.

Thus, when gaslighted, the victim is radically questioned, in the sense that she is not only questioned for a particular belief but also made to altogether doubt her own epistemic competence. Gaslighting usually involves others persistently distrusting her epistemic skills, and it is more effective when those doing the gaslighting are indeed many, rather than one, as Abramson rightly explains.

In the literature on gaslighting, the phenomenon has been quite loosely defined: in one place it is described as unintentional manipulation by impersonal institutions, invisible powers, or even normalised cultural practices; and in another place as something done by individuals, frequently even by supposed allies, people who are commonly regarded as those who should be the most supportive of and reliable for the victim of gaslighting.[9]

In her study of women in professional philosophy, Flores Ruíz uses gaslighting in order to explain how a minority might be manipulated into believing in and affirming its own inferiority. In dealing with the question of how philosophy has marginalised women and their experiences and methodologies (mainly those of non-white women), Flores Ruíz appeals to the concept of gaslighting and reminds us that in order to leave the philosophical canon unchallenged, and to uphold the supposed exceptionalism of the presence of women in professional philosophy, the most effective weapon is turning women against themselves: that is, convincing them to deeply distrust their power and their ability to create new methods and new philosophical knowledge. This gaslighting is, alas, particularly hard to tackle, in that it is not undertaken by a concrete manipulator but is part of a transparent power à la Foucault, one that is particularly pernicious and corrosive in its form, since it causes women to profoundly doubt their value as philosophers doing 'proper' philosophy. She writes:

> After hearing the increasingly lengthening scrolling narratives of women of colour in the profession of philosophy who dwell, whether briefly or constantly, in this sense of puncturing self-doubt, it finally hit me: Amigas, sisters, *we're being gaslighted*, predominantly by the somnambulatory policing in the form of normative practices and tacit methodological assumptions in mainstream philosophy. This is a kind of *professionalised, ambient abuse*; it has no 'mastermind' per se and it is done as a means of constructing the professional landscape of philosophy. Although in this case there is no grand architect, there is, however, the moving of justifications and the changing of standards all the while asking, 'how is this project philosophy, again?' This is why somnambulatory policing is a particularly hard form of gaslighting to counter, because there is no one admitting to being a mastermind, no culprit to hunt down, only sensibilities that emerge but are never (or are barely) acknowledged.[10]

---

9 Flores Ruíz (n 7); McKinnon (n 7).
10 Flores Ruíz (n 7) 201, emphasis in original.

McKinnon, on the other hand, deals with gaslighting as a frequent phenomenon within relationships among individuals of disempowered groups and their allies, ie their more powerful peers who 'work to end prejudice in their personal and professional lives, and relinquish social privileges conferred by their group status through their support of nondominant groups'.[11] Thus, in her paper 'Allies Behaving Badly: Gaslighting as Epistemic Injustice', she approaches gaslighting from the perspective of trans people who have experienced being disbelieved precisely by those whom they consider to be the most trustworthy and close: their 'allies'. McKinnon considers gaslighting in this context to be a kind of testimonial injustice, in which, for instance, a trans woman's testimony that she was continuously misreferred to as *he*[12] by a supposed ally during a party is put into question by another ally. Such gaslighting, McKinnon argues, happens largely due to the credibility deficit from which trans people (especially trans women) suffer, which is caused by an 'identity prejudice' (having to do both with being trans *and* with being a woman, that is, 'too hormonal', 'too emotional', and, in consequence, 'not rational enough').[13] This distrust affects the trans victim of gaslighting, sometimes to the point where they themselves begin to doubt their own experiences. Mainly, McKinnon argues, it leads to a severe dismissal of the victim as epistemic agent *qua* epistemic agent, in other words to an 'epistemic injustice circle (of hell)', happening:

> [W]hen something such as … emotion is treated as a reason to discount a speaker's testimony, whereby a normal response to this testimonial injustice is to become *more* emotional (eg, angry, frustrated, etc.). But this further emotionality is treated as a *further* reason to discount the speaker's testimony.[14]

On obstetric violence as gaslighting

The idea that certain instances of obstetric violence might be accurately explored through the concept of gaslighting definitively hit me when I read Abramson's phenomenological description of what it is like to be gaslighted:

> Think about one of your worst experiences, an experience which either itself, or in its effects, went on months. Now imagine that while you were going through that, all or most of the voices around you either flatly denied that anything worth being upset about was going on, or radically minimized it, or reconceptualized the experience so that it was not so

---

11 Kendrick T Brown and Joan M Ostrove, 'What Does It Mean to Be an Ally?: The Perception of Allies from the Perspective of People of Color' (2013) 43 J Appl Soc Psychol 2211, cited in McKinnon (n 7) 167–168.
12 This has been considered to be a serious form of gender harassment. McKinnon (n 7) 168.
13 McKinnon (n 7) 169.
14 Ibid, emphasis in original.

uncomfortable (for them) to live with. You protested. The protestations were greeted with 'that's crazy', 'it's not a big deal', 'you're overreacting'. Somehow you endured. But the very fact of your survival then became woven in to the rewriting of history, to confirm the minimizing and denials and later repression (eg 'Well, you survived, didn't you?', 'It all worked out in the end' or 'That was just a minor blip'). So, at no point during it did someone (or perhaps someone, but not enough, or perhaps just not the people most dear to you) look at you and confirm the reality of horror with which you were dealing. To the contrary, they said you're crazy for being upset, oversensitive, and any difficulty you might have is 'all in you'. That's what gaslighting is like.[15]

The phenomenon of gaslighting has been defined frequently as at least sexist, although not inherently so.[16] It is particularly done to women, as a weaker group whose epistemic capacity have always been put into question. Expressing disbelief, to the point of silencing the victim because she herself has been convinced that she probably is crazy, and what happened was not that terrible, is a constant in sexual violence. Rape victims are persistently disbelieved, and their silences over months and even years after the violent encounter are often due partly to shame, and the certainty that their testimony will be put into question.[17] But silence is often also due to the fact that they were gaslighted (probably by an 'ally', someone they loved and trusted, someone stronger than they were, at least in that moment, and whom they decided to tell in spite of the pain and shame) when they did tell someone, and in consequence they feel that they no longer know whether what happened really was violent or important. Abramson brings up the following (true) examples of gaslighting:

A female graduate student deals with sexual harassment. Confronts her harasser. He responds by first denying any problem, then, 'see, there wouldn't be this problem if there weren't any women in the department', and finally,

15 Abramson (n 7) 5–6.

16 Ibid 3.

17 On rape victims being disbelieved and the harmful consequences of this for their future lives, Whisnant writes:

Many rapes lead to additional harms beyond those intrinsic to the rape itself. … Victims who do not reveal their rapes to others, whether due to shame or to the expectation that they will not be believed, experience profound isolation and lack of support; and indeed, many who do report their rapes are disbelieved or blamed by friends, family, and/or police. Due to both low reporting levels and low conviction rates, relatively few victims see their rapists punished; many of those raped by relatives, co-workers, friends, or other ongoing acquaintances must then face continuing interaction with the rapist, while those raped by strangers often fear that the rapist will find and re-victimize them.

Rebecca Whisnant, 'Feminist Perspectives on Rape' in Edward N Zalta (ed), *The Stanford Encyclopedia of Philosophy* (Fall 2017 Edition) <https://plato. stanford.edu/archives/fall2017/entries/feminism-rape/> accessed 3 August 2018 'you're just a prude.' She talks to another student. The second graduate student retorts, 'he was just joking.'

And another account:

> A junior academic woman is standing at the department's front desk. A senior male colleague passes by and slaps her on the butt. She reports the incident to another senior colleague. The second colleague responds, 'Oh, he's just an old guy. Have some sympathy! It's not that big a deal.' A third colleague responds, 'Don't be so sensitive.'[18]

Thus, in order to understand gaslighting as part of obstetric violence, it is important to understand obstetric violence as a kind of gender violence. This understanding certainly has been available since the proclamation of the Venezuelan law against obstetric violence in 2007 (as a part of a general law, protecting women from violence and promoting women's rights)[19] and, later on, in several recent investigations into the subject.[20] Thus, 'Obstetric violence is violence done to women *because* they are women',[21] that is, women in the labour room are not simply undergoing medical violence but they are, in fact, undergoing gender violence: being dehumanised, humiliated, subjected to unnecessary interventions, shouted at, and turned into passive objects,[22] not only because this

---

18 Ibid 4–5.

19 Michelle Sadler and others, 'Moving Beyond Disrespect and Abuse: Addressing the Structural Dimensions of Obstetric Violence' (2016) 24(47) Reprod Health Matters 47.

20 S Bellón Sánchez, 'Obstetric Violence: Medicalization, Authority Abuse and Sexism within Spanish Obstetric Assistance: A New Name for Old Issues?' (Master's thesis, Utrecht University 2014); Meghan A Bohren and others, 'The Mistreatment of Women during Childbirth in Health Facilities Globally: A Mixed-Methods Systematic Review' (2015) 12(6) PLOS Med e1001847; Arachu Castro, Virginia Savage, and Hannah Kaufman, 'Assessing Equitable Care for Indigenous and Afrodescendant Women in Latin America' (2015) 38 Rev Panam Salud Pública 96; Camilla Pickles, 'Eliminating Abusive "Care": A Criminal Law Response to Obstetric Violence' (2015) 54 SACQ 5; Meghan A Bohren and others, '"By Slapping Their Laps, the Patient Will Know that You Truly Care for Her": A Qualitative Study on Social Norms and Acceptability of the Mistreatment of Women during Childbirth in Abuja, Nigeria' (2016) 2 SSM Popul Health 640; Cohen Shabot (n 1); Sadler and others (n 19); Carlos Herrera Vacaflor, 'Obstetric Violence: A New Framework for Identifying Challenges to Maternal Healthcare in Argentina' (2016) 24(47) Reprod Health Matters 65; Rachelle Chadwick, 'Ambiguous Subjects: Obstetric Violence, Assemblage and South African Birth Narratives' (2017) 27 Fem Psychol 489; Sreeparna Chattopadhyay, Arima Mishra, and Suraj Jacob, '"Safe", Yet Violent? Women's Experiences with Obstetric Violence during Hospital Births in Rural Northeast India' (2017) 20 Cult Health Sex 815.

21 Cohen Shabot (n 1) 233, emphasis added.

22 Bohren and others, 'The Mistreatment of Women' (n 20); Suellen Miller and Andre Lalonde, 'The Global Epidemic of Abuse and Disrespect during Childbirth: History, Evidence, Interventions, and FIGO's Mother–Baby Friendly Birthing Facilities Initiative' (2015) 131 Int J Gynecol Obstet S49; Michelle Gonçalves da Silva and others, 'Obstetric Violence According to Obstetric Nurses' (2014) 15 Rev RENE 720; Saraswathi Vedam and others, 'The Mothers on Respect (MOR) Index: Measuring Quality, Safety, and Human Rights in Childbirth' (2017) 3 SSM Popul Health 201.

is convenient and easy for the medical staff, but mainly as part of a general tendency to silence and trivialise women's embodied subjectivities.[23] It is in this sexist context that they are also being gaslighted, I will argue.

Gaslighting as part of the phenomenon of obstetric violence might correspond both to Flores Ruíz's idea of gaslighting as 'somnambulatory policing in the form of normative practices and tacit methodological assumptions'[24] – in this case on the part of medical authorities, rather than mainstream philosophers – and to McKinnon's, which specifically deals with gaslighting by allies and which illuminate mainly the kind of gaslighting that victims of obstetric violence undergo after their often-traumatic labours, when telling their stories to those close to them.

In the labour room, women are gaslighted by staff who frequently casts doubt on their pain, their capacities for labouring, and/or their knowledge of their own body processes. In her description of power relations in American maternity wards, for instance, Jordan offers a concrete example of this typical underestimation of labouring women's knowledge, describing a particular case in which the woman is infantilised and 'not allowed' to push until the doctor comes into the room and confirms that she is ready:

> She knows she has to push and says so clearly. She also expresses it in the visible, almost superhuman effort she marshals to suppress the urge to push. But every time she tries to get her desire – her expressed knowledge about the state of her body – acknowledged and made the basis for proceeding with the birth, her version of reality is overridden, is ignored, is denied, or, most frequently, is sidetracked, deflected, and replaced with some other definition of reality. Something else is offered up as being more relevant, as might happen to an obstinate child whose parent opts for distraction rather than confrontation.[25]

Martin offers another example of how the embodied knowledge of the labouring woman is contradicted by the instructions of the medical staff, creating confusion within her and deepening her feelings of ignorance, profound alienation, and detachment from the whole birthing process:

> And then there was that awful stage when they are telling me not to push and I couldn't [stop pushing]. You can't prevent yourself. One minute they are telling you that your uterus is an involuntary muscle and the next minute they are telling you not to push. I don't know whether you push with your uterus; I don't suppose you do.[26]

---

23 Cohen Shabot (n 1).
24 Flores Ruíz (n 7) 201.
25 Brigitte Jordan, 'Authoritative Knowledge and Its Construction' in Robbie E Davis Floyd and Carolyn F Sargent (eds), *Childbirth and Authoritative Knowledge. Cross-Cultural Perspectives* (University of California Press 1997) 67.
26 Ann Oakley, *Becoming a Mother* (Schocken 1979) quoted in Emily Martin, *The Woman in the Body: A Cultural Analysis of Reproduction* (Beacon Press 1987) 63.

After the labour is behind them, female victims of obstetric violence usually encounter harsh interlocutors for whom 'at least you have a healthy baby' is the ultimate response used to erase and shut up any further complaints regarding a violent labour, or a physical and emotional trauma deriving from labour. Thus, countless women undergo gaslighting at the hands of their natural allies: their most loved ones, their partners, women friends who have also given birth recently, their mothers, their healthcare providers. This is most often an unconscious attempt to gaslight, caused at least in part by the normalisation of violent practices in childbirth and the internalisation of the idea that birthing women are, after all, only vessels for their babies and must be willing to sacrifice themselves for them, as 'good' mothers do, and that they should be thankful just to have survived childbirth along with their babies.

Thus, because pain and suffering are perceived as integral to childbirth, and childbirth is perceived as a routine, even compulsory, process for women, the experiences, particularly the violent ones, of labouring women go unrecognised by both the women's immediate community and the medical staff. Birthing women who share traumatic, or even simply difficult birth stories are often silenced with comments like 'everybody goes through that', 'you should be grateful', or the quintessential 'all that matters is that the baby is healthy'. Shaming is a central part of this process, and it is also the perfect aid for a successful gaslighting. In her discussion of the shaming of mothers, Cokerill writes:

> It is the secret shame among mothers – birth trauma and the devastating effect it can have, not only physically but mentally, too. You are made to feel as though you cannot really be honest about a traumatic birth, you glaze over details only to relive them on your own later. You should be grateful your baby is here, shouldn't you?[27]

This is how birthing mothers are disciplined and silenced through shame and gaslighting. Phrases such as 'You should be grateful' express that whatever happens during childbirth is insignificant, given the labouring woman's sublime role in the creation of life and selfless engagement in mothering. Humphries recounts the responses she received when attempting to share with others the trauma she experienced after undergoing the violence of an emergency caesarean section:

> Wasn't I grateful? So many people said it to me, I started to wonder. People I trusted, people I respected, people I loved. Maybe I wasn't grateful for my babies? Maybe I didn't love my babies as much as I should or as much as other mothers did? ... I didn't *feel* a lot about them. I was depressed. Then I

---

27 Vicki Cokerill, 'The Secret Shame of Mothers' (*Huffington Post*, 17 August 2017) <www.huffingtonpost.co.uk/vicki-moore/the-secret-shame-of-mothe_1_b_17758548.html> accessed 1 May 2018.

began to realize how evil it is to tell a woman who's experienced a physically or emotionally traumatic birth that she should be grateful. ... It is evil to say, 'All that matters is a healthy baby' because you are saying that her pain, her damage, doesn't matter. You are telling her that not only is her body broken, but so is her mind. That if she is physically healthy, that's all that matters, and to be concerned with anything else is somehow wrong. ... Good mothers just don't have those feelings, and she's already afraid she isn't a good enough mother. And so she loses something precious, and so do we all. I discovered that there are a lot of women out there who hated the birth of their child; women who had bad surgeries, women who had good surgeries, rarely women who had necessary surgeries, women who didn't have surgery at all but did have horrible things done to them in the name of birth. I'm not the only one.[28]

The gaslighting of birthing women is made possible when it is inserted into a general context in which women are in principle already flawed epistemic agents, or not considered epistemic agents at all. Jordan describes power relations in the American hospital labour room, where the knowledge of doctors is clearly privileged over that of nurses, and the knowledge of nurses over that of the labouring woman, thus putting her at the bottom of the epistemic hierarchy. In this context, she states that:

[In] American hospital births ... medical knowledge supersedes and delegitimizes other potentially relevant sources of knowledge such as the woman's prior experience and the knowledge she has of the state of her body. Nonmedical knowledge is devalued by all participants, usually including the woman herself, who comes to believe that the course charted on the basis of professional medical knowledge is the best for her. ... In the labor room, authoritative knowledge is privileged, the prerogative of the physician, without whose official certification of the woman's state the birth cannot proceed.[29]

---

28 Gretchen Humphries, 'You Should Be Grateful' (Birth Matters, 2001) <www.plus-size-pregnancy. org/CSANDVBAC/shouldbegrateful.htm> accessed 15 December 2018, emphasis in original. In stories of early miscarriages, it becomes clear that there, too, women are made to feel ashamed in similar ways: Mothers are not really allowed to grieve for their early miscarriages, since the embryo is not considered developed enough to be called a baby, and many women are told that they should be grateful that this embryo did not develop into a baby that might have been 'defective':

   I found it really difficult to express just how difficult I was finding it emotionally after the miscarriage, and ... I guess partly because I didn't know anyone else who'd miscarried and I felt sort of like, well, it was only six weeks. It wasn't like I'd lost, ... lost a baby or that I'd had a stillbirth or something like that, ... and you know that maybe I shouldn't be as upset as I was.

   Cindy Leaney and Michelle Silver (producers, directors), *Unsung Lullabies* (film) (No Time to Cry Productions 1995) quoted in McLeod (n 2) 53

29 Jordan (n 25) 61, 64.

Conclusions

The dismissal of women's knowledge and the understanding of women as flawed epistemic agents do not occur exclusively in the realm of medicine or medicalised childbirth. Feminist epistemological theories show us that the underestimation of women's knowledge has been a pervasive motif within patriarchy and is not to be considered merely circumstantial. Women's knowledge has generally been considered unreliable and inferior, mainly because its origins are supposedly more emotional and less rational.[30] Alcoff compellingly articulates the conditions that make every discussion of knowledge and the validity of knowledge political, and maintains that 'Social hierarchies of power and privilege ... determine who can participate in epistemological discussions and whose views on epistemology have the potential to gain wide influence'; that is to say that some individuals, belonging to privileged groups, are more authorised than others to produce knowledge.[31] Men are undeniably more epistemically accountable than women.[32] Moreover, Alcoff shows how experience is frequently dismissed as a source of knowledge when privilege is missing: 'Midwives with extensive experience attending to women in labour as well as their own personal experience in childbirth are less likely to be believed than male obstetricians fresh out of medical school'.[33] Knowledge is also political with respect to its formal limitations. Alcoff argues that propositional knowledge and 'subject-less' knowledge are clearly privileged over other forms of knowledge: for example, knowledge that is known through a concrete subject's body or emotions (a form of knowledge that is usually strongly devalued):

> The tyranny of this subject-less, value-less conception of objectivity has had the effect of authorizing those scientific voices that have universalist pretensions and disauthorizing personalized voices that argue with emotion, passion and open political commitment.[34]

The way in which the quality of knowledge is measured is therefore in itself a product of power relations: certain kinds of knowledge have been privileged for the wrong reasons, not because of their true correspondence with reality but rather because of sexist, racist, and classist prejudices.[35]

30 Alison M Jaggar, 'Love and Knowledge: Emotion in Feminist Epistemology' (1989) 32 Inquiry 151; Genevieve Lloyd, *The Man of Reason: 'Male' and 'Female' in Western Philosophy* (University of Minnesota Press 1984).
31 Linda Martin Alcoff, 'How Is Epistemology Political?' in Alison Bailey and Chris Cuomo (eds), *The Feminist Philosophy Reader* (McGraw-Hill 2008) 706.
32 Ibid.
33 Ibid 708.
34 Ibid 711.
35 This view does not necessarily lead to an infinite plurality of equally valid discourses. The difficult paths that will need to be followed in order to provide us with a plurality through the erosion of power structures without automatically consigning us to an obscure absolute relativism have

Thus, we are being gaslighted in the ob-gyn office, in the labour room, and when telling our violent childbirth experiences to others, as part of a general devaluation of women's epistemological capacities and as part of the hegemonic patriarchal culture, which is sexist and misogynist to the core. But, if obstetric violence is the dehumanisation and objectification of women within obstetric practices, if it means infantilising us and depriving us of agency and autonomy over our birthing bodies, then this form of gaslighting must be recognised as obstetric violence too.

My story has a happy ending: I contacted the young doctor after I miscarried. I confronted her in writing, including in detail what finally happened and explaining to her why her distrust had been painful to me, and how it made me doubt my own knowledge. I told her that I believed this to be a form of obstetric violence, and I sent her my paper on the subject. She read, and reflected, and her views changed. She has since become one of the researchers and activists against obstetric violence within the medical system, and we are currently working together on common projects. But this only happened because I was a relatively privileged victim of gaslighting; because gaslighting did not, in fact, really work in my case. It also happened because the owner of the truly privileged epistemic status in this event was ready to listen and to think critically about her own position of power. I wish that this could happen more and more frequently. Gaslighting is a moral evil. My once-gaslighting doctor, and many other women and I are now working together to erode the practice: to make biased distrust a thing of the past, within obstetric care and, hopefully, beyond.

Bibliography

Abramson K, 'Turning Up the Lights on Gaslighting' (2014) 28 Philos Perspect 1

Alcoff L M, 'How Is Epistemology Political?' in Bailey A and Cuomo C (ed), *The Feminist Philosophy Reader* (McGraw-Hill 2008) 706

Anderson L, 'Epistemic Injustice and the Philosophy of Race' in Kidd I J, Medina J, and Pohlhaus G (eds), *The Routledge Handbook of Epistemic Injustice* (Routledge 2017)

Bellón Sánchez S, 'Obstetric Violence: Medicalization, Authority Abuse and Sexism within Spanish Obstetric Assistance: A New Name for Old Issues?' (Master's thesis, Utrecht University 2014)

---

been widely discussed by various feminist epistemologists, and are not for me to repeat here. See, for instance, Alcoff (n 31); Lorraine Code, *What Can She Know? Feminist Theory and the Construction of Knowledge* (Cornell University Press 1991); Lorraine Code, 'Taking Subjectivity into Account' in Alison Bailey and Chris Cuomo (eds), *The Feminist Philosophy Reader* (McGraw-Hill 2008); Sandra Harding, '"Strong Objectivity" and Socially Situated Knowledge' in Alison Bailey and Chris Cuomo (eds), *The Feminist Philosophy Reader* (McGraw-Hill 2008); Nancy C M Hartsock, 'The Feminist Standpoint: Developing the Ground for a Specifically Feminist Historical Materialism' in Sandra Harding and Merrill B P Hintikka (eds), *Discovering Reality: Feminist Perspectives on Epistemology, Metaphysics, Methodology, and the Philosophy of Science* (Reidel 1983).

Bohren M A and others, 'The Mistreatment of Women during Childbirth in Health Facilities Globally: A Mixed-Methods Systematic Review' (2015) 12(6) PLOS Med e1001847

Bohren M A and others, '"By Slapping Their Laps, the Patient Will Know that You Truly Care for Her": A Qualitative Study on Social Norms and Acceptability of the Mistreatment of Women during Childbirth in Abuja, Nigeria' (2016) 2 SSM Popul Health 640

Brown K T and Ostrove J, 'What Does It Mean to Be an Ally? The Perception of Allies from the Perspective of People of Color' (2013) 43 J Appl Soc Psychol 2211

Castro A, Savage V, and Kaufman H, 'Assessing Equitable Care for Indigenous and Afro-descendant Women in Latin America' (2015) 38 Rev Panam Salud Pública 96

Chadwick R, 'Ambiguous Subjects: Obstetric Violence, Assemblage and South African Birth Narratives' (2017) 27 Fem Psychol 489

Chattopadhyay S, Mishra A, and Jacob S, '"Safe", Yet Violent? Women's Experiences with Obstetric Violence during Hospital Births in Rural Northeast India' (2017) 20 Cult Health Sex 815

Code L, *What Can She Know? Feminist Theory and the Construction of Knowledge* (Cornell University Press 1991)

Code L, 'Taking Subjectivity into Account' in Bailey A and Cuomo C (eds), *The Feminist Philosophy Reader* (McGraw-Hill 2008)

Cohen Shabot S, 'Making Loud Bodies "Feminine": A Feminist-Phenomenological Analysis of Obstetric Violence' (2016) 39 Human Studies 231

Cokerill V, 'The Secret Shame of Mothers' (*Huffington Post*, 17 August 2017) <www.huffingtonpost.co.uk/vicki-moore/the-secret-shame-of-mothe_1_b_17758548.html>

Flores Ruíz E, 'Musing: Spectral Phenomenologies: Dwelling Poetically in Professional Philosophy' (2014) 29 Hypatia 196

Fricker M, *Epistemic Injustice. Power and the Ethics of Knowing* (OUP 2007)

Goering S, 'Postnatal Reproductive Autonomy: Promoting Relational Autonomy and Self-Trust in New Parents' (2009) 23 Bioethics 9

Gonçalves da Silva M and others, 'Obstetric Violence According to Obstetric Nurses' (2014) 15 Rev RENE 720

Harding S, '"Strong Objectivity" and Socially Situated Knowledge' in Bailey A and Cuomo C (eds), *The Feminist Philosophy Reader* (McGraw-Hill 2008)

Haskel R, 'Serena Williams on Motherhood, Marriage, and Making Her Comeback' (*Vogue*, 10 January 2018) <www.vogue.com/article/serena-williams-vogue-cover-interview-february-2018>

Hartsock N C M, 'The Feminist Standpoint: Developing the Ground for a Specifically Feminist Historical Materialism' in Harding S and Hintikka M B P (eds), *Discovering Reality: Feminist Perspectives on Epistemology, Metaphysics, Methodology, and the Philosophy of Science* (Reidel 1983)

Hey V and others, *Hidden Loss: Miscarriage and Ectopic Pregnancy* (2nd edn, Women's Press 1996)

Humphries G, 'You Should Be Grateful' (*Birth Matters*, 2001) <www.plus-size-pregnancy.org/CSANDVBAC/shouldbegrateful.htm>

Jaggar M A, 'Love and Knowledge: Emotion in Feminist Epistemology' (1989) 32 Inquiry 151

Jordan B, 'Authoritative Knowledge and Its Construction' in Davis Floyd R E and Sargent C F (eds), *Childbirth and Authoritative Knowledge. Cross-Cultural Perspectives* (University of California Press 1997) 67

Lloyd G, *The Man of Reason: 'Male' and 'Female' in Western Philosophy* (University of Minnesota Press 1984)

Martin E, *The Woman in the Body: A Cultural Analysis of Reproduction* (Beacon Press 1987)

McKinnon R, 'Allies Behaving Badly: Gaslighting as Epistemic Injustice' in Kidd I J, Medina J, and Pohlhaus G (eds), *The Routledge Handbook of Epistemic Injustice* (Routledge 2017)

McLeod C, *Self-Trust and Reproductive Autonomy* (MIT Press 2002)

Miller S and Lalonde A, 'The Global Epidemic of Abuse and Disrespect during Childbirth: History, Evidence, Interventions, and FIGO's Mother–Baby Friendly Birthing Facilities Initiative' (2015) 131 Int J Gynecol Obstet S49

Oakley A, *Becoming a Mother* (Schocken 1979)

Pickles C, 'Eliminating Abusive "Care": A Criminal Law Response to Obstetric Violence' (2015) 54 SACQ 5

Sadler M and others, 'Moving Beyond Disrespect and Abuse: Addressing the Structural Dimensions of Obstetric Violence' (2016) 24(47) Reprod Health Matters 47

Vacaflor C H, 'Obstetric Violence: A New Framework for Identifying Challenges to Maternal Healthcare in Argentina' (2016) 24(47) Reprod Health Matters 65

Vedam S and others, 'The Mothers on Respect (MOR) Index: Measuring Quality, Safety, and Human Rights in Childbirth' (2017) 3 SSM Popul Health 201

Whisnant R, 'Feminist Perspectives on Rape' in Zalta E N (ed), *The Stanford Encyclopedia of Philosophy* (Fall 2017 Edition) <https://plato.stanford.edu/archives/fall2017/entries/feminism-rape/> accessed 3 August 2018

2 Practices of silencing
Birth, marginality and epistemic violence

Rachelle Chadwick

Introduction

The mistreatment of women, girls and pregnant persons during pregnancy, labour and birth (usually in healthcare facilities) was formally recognised in 2014 by the World Health Organization as a global health problem. While instances of abuse and violence during hospitalised modes of childbirth have been reported since the 1950s in America,[1] mistreatment, or what is also known as maternity abuse, inhumane care or 'obstetric violence',[2] has become defined over the last decade or so as an urgent social and public health problem linked to adverse maternal health outcomes and recognised as an infringement of the human rights of pregnant women/persons. While broadly recognised as an unacceptable problem, there is little scholarly consensus about what to call this kind of violence, how best to conceptualise it or how to eradicate it. Since the early 2000s, childbirth abuse has broadly been defined as including instances of physical, emotional, sexual and verbal abuse, as well as neglect.[3] Early work on mistreatment and inhumane care in maternity settings was often framed by medical and public health professionals as a failure of evidence-based practices, health system shortcomings and quality of care issues.[4] Over the last decade, the structural aspects of birth violence and its links to intersectional and social forms of discrimination have been more widely recognised.[5] Furthermore, since 2010, abusive interactions during birth have been reframed as 'obstetric violence' in some contexts and identified as a form of gender violence. Emerging in Latin and Central American countries such as Venezuela, Argentina and Mexico with

1 Henci Goer, 'Cruelty in Maternity Wards: Fifty Years Later' (2010) 19 J Perinat Educ 33.
2 Rogelio Pérez D'Gregorio, 'Obstetric Violence: A New Legal Term Introduced in Venezuela' (2010) 111 Int J Gynaecol Obstet 201.
3 A F D'Oliveira, S G Diniz, and L B Schraibe, 'Violence against Women in Health-Care Institutions: An Emerging Problem' (2002) 359 The Lancet 1681.
4 J P Vogel and others, 'Promoting Respect and Preventing Mistreatment during Childbirth' (2016) 123 BJOG 671.
5 M Sadler and others, 'Moving beyond Disrespect and Abuse: Addressing the Structural Dimensions of Obstetric Violence' (2016) 24(47) Reprod Health Matters 47.

highly interventionist and medicalised obstetric systems, the emotive and highly charged term 'obstetric violence' has been defined as including:

> The appropriation of the body and reproductive processes of women by health personnel, which is expressed as dehumanized treatment, an abuse of medication, and to convert the natural processes into pathological ones, bringing with it a loss of autonomy and the ability to decide freely about their bodies and sexuality, negatively impacting the quality of life of women.[6]

Both unnecessary medical interventions and the absence or untimely administration of medical interventions when necessary have thus been defined as birth violence. Furthermore, the above definition also names the *appropriation*, or what I would term the medical *colonisation* of labouring/birthing bodies, as itself a form of obstetric violence. This is a productive move echoing earlier feminist arguments regarding the oppressive and dehumanising aspects of medicalised birth.[7] It also potentially allows for a more complex conceptualisation of obstetric violence that exceeds the bounds of neatly defined incidents of physical, verbal or medical abuse with clear perpetrators, which often works to minimise this violence as the work of a few 'bad apples' in the medical system.[8] This chapter is interested in thinking through the more insidious forms of violence that are linked to 'the appropriation of the body and reproductive processes'[9] of labouring/birthing persons (in this case girls). Using the concept of 'epistemic violence' and drawing on the work of Dotson on 'practices of silencing',[10] I explore the muting of (marginalised) girls' voices, haptic knowledge and embodied selves during labour and birth as a form of violence. I argue that the systematic silencing, smothering and dismissal of girls' embodied knowledge during birth functions as a form of epistemic or hermeneutical violence that shrinks agency and reiterates social and gendered relations of power. It is also intimately intertwined with other forms of obstetric violence, including loss of autonomy, dehumanised treatment and coercive medical practices.

Practices of silencing, birth and epistemic violence

Most research on childbirth abuse, mistreatment and obstetric violence has focused on describing abusive interactions in which women/girls and pregnant

6 D'Gregorio (n 2).
7 Barbara Katz Rothman, *In Labour: Women and Power in the Birthplace* (WW Norton & Company 1982); Emily Martin, *The Woman in the Body: A Cultural Analysis of Reproduction* (OUP 1987); Ann Oakley, *Women Confined: Towards a Sociology of Childbirth* (Martin Robertson 1980).
8 R Jewkes, N Abrahams, and Z Mvo, 'Why Do Nurses Abuse Patients? Reflections from South African Obstetric Services' (1998) 47 Soc Sci Med 1781.
9 D'Gregorio (n 2).
10 Kristie Dotson, 'Tracking Epistemic Violence, Tracking Practices of Silencing' (2011) 26 Hypatia 236.

persons have reported being physically assaulted, shouted at, neglected or otherwise treated in an inhumane and degrading manner during labour/birth. Several scholars have framed this research within an intersectional analysis of social relations of power, stigma and discrimination linked to class, race, gender and other inequalities.[11] In this chapter, I argue that obstetric violence is not just the product of gendered and classed/racialised oppression that acts in a top-down fashion to coerce, diminish and oppress selves. Obstetric violence also functions as a form of epistemic violence in which the privileged embodied knowledge of labouring/birthing persons is systematically silenced and suppressed. While the 'authoritative knowledge'[12] of obstetric medicine has been theorised by feminist scholars as part of the disempowering apparatus of biomedical birth, the processes whereby women/girls' haptic and bodily knowledge is silenced, constrained and denied during labour/birth have not received a great deal of attention. Furthermore, these modes of silencing have not been conceptualised as aspects of obstetric violence. In this chapter, I use Dotson's[13] work on the interrelations between 'practices of silencing' and epistemic violence in order to think through the muting of girls' voices and embodied selves during labour/birth as forms of hermeneutical violence.

According to Dotson, epistemic violence is 'a type of violence that attempts to eliminate knowledge possessed by marginal subjects'.[14] Marginalised subjects are thus, by virtue of race, ethnicity, age, ability, sexuality or class membership/s, systematically not granted status as credible knowers. As a result, such forms of silencing or epistemic violence damage the 'ability to speak and be heard'.[15] Much has been written about epistemic violence in relation to racial oppression/s and coloniality. In particular, black feminist writers such as Hill Collins, Lorde and Mohanty have explored epistemic silencing as a particularly insidious form of oppression facing black women.[16] There have, however, been few attempts to think about 'epistemic violence' in relation to medicalised practices[17] and reproductive health issues. An exception is the work of Bell[18] who

---

11 Lydia Dixon, 'Obstetrics in a Time of Violence: Mexican Midwives Critique Routine Hospital Practices' (2015) 29 Med Anthropol Q 437; Vania Smith-Oka, 'Managing Labour and Delivery among Impoverished Populations in Mexico: Cervical Examinations as Bureaucratic Practice' (2013) 115 Am Anthrop 595; Vania Smith-Oka, 'Micro Aggressions and the Reproduction of Social Inequalities in Medical Encounters in Mexico' (2015) 143 Soc Sci Med 9.
12 Brigitte Jordan, 'Authoritative Knowledge and Its Construction' in Robbie Davis-Floyd and Carol Sargent (eds), *Childbirth and Authoritative Knowledge* (University of California Press 1997).
13 Dotson (n 10).
14 Ibid 236.
15 Ibid.
16 Ibid.
17 See these exceptions: Alistair Wardrope, 'Medicalization and Epistemic Injustice' (2015) 18 Med Health Care Philos 341; Havi Carel and Ian Kidd, 'Epistemic Injustice in Healthcare: A Philosophical Analysis' (2014) 17 Med Health Care Philos 529.
18 Karen Bell, 'Exploring Epistemic Injustice Through Feminist Social Work Research' (2014) 29 Affilia 165.

uses the concept of 'epistemic injustice'[19] to explore women's experiences of assisted reproduction (AR). She argues that the dominant medicalised discourse of AR works to silence women's emotional and experiential knowledge and functions as a form of epistemic injustice. Epistemic injustice is defined by Bell as occurring when 'the value of a marginalised group or individual's knowledge is diminished by a more powerful group or individual'.[20] While the invalidation of women/girls' bodily and affective knowledge of pregnancy, labour and birth has been identified as a central current of biomedical approaches,[21] it has not been conceptualised as a form of epistemic violence. This chapter argues that epistemic violence, or the dismissal, silencing and repudiation of women/girls' status as embodied knowers during labour/birth, is a systematic form of harm occurring in obstetric contexts.

While the silencing of embodied selves is often a constitutive part of medicalised birth for women *in general*, intersecting social inequalities mean that poor black women and girls are more likely to be the recipients of coercive and persistent forms of silencing during labour/birth. According to Dotson,[22] epistemic violence occurs in communicative exchanges when the required reciprocity between the speaker and listener breaks down due to prejudices and harmful assumptions (held by the listener). In such exchanges, the audience fails to reciprocate, interact with or hear what the speaker is saying. Epistemic violence occurs when such communicative failures become reliable and systematic, damaging an entire group's ability to enact epistemic agency and claim authorial voices. Such linguistic violence also results in partial and oppressive forms of knowledge in which alternative epistemic perspectives are denied and muted.[23] Dotson describes two key forms of silencing associated with epistemic violence, namely testimonial quieting and testimonial smothering. Quieting occurs when an audience 'fails to identify a speaker as a knower'[24] because of race, class, gender and/or other marginalised group memberships. This is an 'active practice of unknowing'[25] in which marginalised persons are denied epistemic authority resulting in 'epistemically disadvantaged identities'.[26] In quieting, marginalised subjects do speak and attempt to articulate epistemic authority; however, their voices and knowledge/s are actively dismissed or remain unheard. In testimonial smothering, speakers effectively censor their own voices/testimony because they believe that their audience is unable or unwilling to hear them. This amounts

---

19 Miranda Fricker, *Epistemic Injustice: Power and the Ethics of Knowing* (OUP 2007).
20 Bell (n 18) 165.
21 R Root and C Browner, 'Practices of the Pregnant Self: Compliance with and Resistance to Prenatal Norms' (2001) 25 Cult Med Psychiatry 195. Rachelle Chadwick, *Bodies that Birth: Vitalizing Birth Politics* (Routledge 2018).
22 Dotson (n 10).
23 Bell (n 18) 165.
24 Dotson (n 10).
25 Ibid 243.
26 Ibid.

to the 'truncating of one's own testimony'[27] in which marginalised subjects 'smother' their own voices. According to Dotson, this amounts to a type of 'coerced self-silencing'[28] in which speakers mute themselves because they perceive the content of their stories/experiences to be unsafe, dangerous and risky in the context of particular audiences and socio-epistemic conditions.

Using Dotson's work on practices of silencing, including epistemic quieting and smothering, this chapter explores an often unacknowledged form of linguistic and affective violence that occurs in obstetric contexts. While most work on childbirth abuse has focused on explicit or obvious instances of physical violence and dehumanisation, my argument is that *other*, less visible and often subterranean forms of violence (such as epistemic violence) produce and enable outbursts of direct violence. As I have argued elsewhere, drawing on the work of Žižek,[29] it is hidden, normalised and often invisible forms of violence that 'create the conditions of possibility for outbreaks of physical violence'.[30] While writers such as Žižek argue that objective or 'hidden' violence is embedded in everyday discursive and linguistic modes of life, Dotson's work offers a practical framework with which to begin to think through and trace practices of coercive silencing as forms of violence. Other theorists have underlined the harmful effects of the systemic self-silencing of marginalised subjects in the face of socio-epistemic inequalities. According to Medina,[31] profound 'hermeneutical harms' occur when individuals' efforts to make meaning are unfairly blocked and muted and they are 'preventing from developing and exercising a voice'.[32] These harms can be so severe, according to Medina, that selves are effectively 'annihilated', producing what he refers to as 'hermeneutical death'.[33] Elsewhere Medina, however, underlines the importance of acknowledging that 'communicative contexts are always polyphonic', involving shifting performative positionalities and relationalities.[34] This opens the possibility to explore practices of silencing alongside moments of resistance or epistemic agency. Thus, similarly to Bell,[35] I seek to explore both coerced silencing and articulations of testimonial resistance in girls' birth stories.

The analysis that follows explores forms of coerced silencing and resistance in/through the pregnancy and birth narratives of black, poor and young mothers. These stories were collected as part of a larger longitudinal study of the transition to first-time mothering for 30 poor, marginalised women/girls living in

---

27 Ibid 244.
28 Ibid 251.
29 Slavoj Žižek, *Violence: Six Sideways Reflections* (Picador 2008).
30 Rachelle Chadwick, 'Ambiguous Subjects: Obstetric Violence, Assemblage and South African Birth Narratives' (2017) 27 Fem Psychol 489.
31 José Medina, 'Varieties of Hermeneutical Injustice' in Ian Kidd, José Medina and Gaile Polhaus (eds), *The Routledge Handbook of Epistemic Injustice* (Routledge 2017).
32 Ibid 41.
33 Ibid.
34 José Medina, 'Hermeneutical Injustice and Polyphonic Contextualism: Social Silences and Shared Hermeneutical Responsibilities' (2012) 26 Soc Epistemol 201.
35 Bell (n 18) 165.

informal settlements in the Western Cape region of South Africa. Participants were interviewed three times over a period of approximately nine months as they transitioned from pregnancy to early mothering. In the analysis that follows, I focus on five stories, exploring the multiple modes of marginalisation/silencing facing young mothers as they traverse pregnancy, labour/birth and early motherhood.

Histories of violence and silencing

This chapter explores practices of coercive silencing and epistemic violence in/through the birth stories of the following five young mothers: Esther, Selma, Juno, Roxanne and Christina.[36] Before tracing and analysing specific instances of epistemic silencing, it is important to provide some general introduction to the lives of these young mothers in order to contextualise, frame and make sense of their pregnancy/birth stories. Significantly, most of these participants did not just narrate 'obstetric violence'; they told of lives that were intimately shaped with/in the resonances and lived realities of domestic and partner violence, familial homicides and incarcerations, mental illness, substance abuse, parental separation and dispersed (often disconnected) family networks. All of these young mothers were adolescents at the time of the research interviews and ranged in age from 16 to 19 years. All were of mixed racial descent (locally known as 'Coloured'), lived in informal settlements and were poor, with many living 'hand-to-mouth' in households with no fixed income. Others lived in households (consisting of multiple extended family members) with a joint income of no more than 180 USD per month. As these young mothers talked about their lives and pregnancies, they told stories involving multiple histories of violence. Most of the participants had experienced family violence and abuse. For example, Esther, 19 years old at the time of the interview, spoke of her father who was murdered when she was just six years old and who subjected her mother to severe physical abuse. Christina, 18 years old, was in an abusive relationship in which her boyfriend regularly assaulted her, although he stopped doing so during her pregnancy. Violence was thus a tangible and persistent thread in many of these young mothers' stories and lives. As a result, for many of the participants, mistreatment and abuse were not unfamiliar experiences. It is therefore not surprising that some of the girls struggled to recognise forms of maternity abuse, silencing and dehumanisation during labour/birth as unjust, wrong or problematic. For these girls, positioned precariously within multiple, intersecting and marginalised identities involving age, race, poverty and gender, violence, abuse and silencing were all too familiar as experiences and attunements in their personal, material, affective and emotional landscapes.

In addition to narrating histories of violence, participants also spoke about the painful forms of silencing they experienced as pregnant teenagers and young

36 All of these names are pseudonyms.

mothers. Instead of the news of pregnancy being received by family and friends as a joyful and celebratory moment, many of the girls experienced pregnancy as a time of muting and isolation in which their embodied selves and experiences were rejected and shamed. For example, 16-year-old Selma was faced with a wall of silence and rejection after her pregnancy became public. Her mother would not speak to her after she refused to agree to an abortion and during the first few months of her pregnancy, Selma avoided her mother and father, darting from place to place to escape them. When she did eventually run into her mother, there was no communication – 'I wouldn't greet her and she wouldn't greet me, and wouldn't speak to me'. For the first few months of her pregnancy Selma thus experienced a wall of silence in which nobody (including herself) would speak about her pregnancy: 'We never spoke about the pregnancy'. Being black, teen-age and pregnant in the context of poverty was a source of shameful silencing for Selma and several other girls. Juno, 18 years old, beautiful, sociable and success-ful at school, was rejected by her friends and her mother when she became preg-nant. Similar to Selma, Juno's mother refused to speak to her when she found out that she was pregnant. However, this silence was maintained throughout the pregnancy as her mother continued to refuse to visit her (Juno lived with her grandmother). When Juno realised she was pregnant, her first instinct was want-ing to disappear: 'I wanted to run away, I don't know where I would run to, but I just wanted to run away'. The desire to disappear or become invisible persisted throughout her pregnancy as she largely hid herself away (inside her home) from the outside eyes of her community and neighbours. A pregnant Juno told me 'I only come out at night' because 'people look at me otherwise'. Other girls told stories with similar themes of rejection, isolation and silencing. Being a pregnant teenager was experienced by several girls as a difficult, tense and lonely time in which they were shunned by family, school and friends.

As a result, many girls came to the birth event from positions, contexts and histories marked by struggle, abuse, rejection and shaming. Multiple modes of marginality (being young, unmarried, poor and black) also coalesced to make them likely targets of further forms of mistreatment during labour/birth.[37] While all women and pregnant persons are quintessentially *vulnerable* at the time of labour/birth and dependent on the support, care, help and affirma-tion of others, it can be argued that these girls, who occupied complex po-sitions of marginality, were especially vulnerable given histories of violence and shaming. Birth could either be experienced as an event that reiterated their marginalisation and embodied shame or one that affirmed their value and worth as persons, mothers and young women. Work on women's experiences of childbirth often tends to de-contextualise birth as if it were a stand-alone event apart from broader socio-epistemic currents and separate from the real-ities and histories of embodied lives. As argued by Lyerly,[38] it is important to

---

37 Smith-Oka (n 11).
38 Ann Drapkin Lyerly, 'Shame, Gender, Birth' (2006) 21 Hypatia 101.

underline that birth does not stand apart from (psycho)social life; instead it is an event 'to which women bring a lifetime of experiences relating to the shame of female embodiment: Of demeaning treatment and subordination'.[39] For the young mothers represented in this chapter, a 'lifetime of experiences' typically included violence, abuse, the embodied shame of teenage pregnancy and the hardships and stress of poverty. Experiences of obstetric violence and 'practices of silencing' during labour/birth cannot be understood in isolation from wider lives and histories. As argued by others, obstetric violence is not just the outcome of a faulty health system or a few 'rotten apples' among a population of healthcare workers;[40] it reflects, reproduces and is intertwined with localised sociocultural inequalities.

Practices of silencing and the appropriation of girls' birth experiences

As outlined earlier, Dotson describes 'quieting' as a form of epistemic violence in which an audience 'fails to identify a speaker as a knower'.[41] While this kind of silencing has not been recognised or conceptualised as obstetric violence, it is, in my view, a key epistemic mechanism that enables biomedical machineries to effectively 'colonise' women's bodily and emotional experiences of birth. As noted earlier, the legal definition of obstetric violence (as outlined in Venezuelan law) describes 'the appropriation of the body and reproductive processes of women by health personnel'[42] as a key feature of this kind of violence. My argument in this chapter is that forms of epistemic silencing, including quieting, smothering and erasure, function as powerful mechanisms whereby the birth process is 'appropriated' or 'colonised' by medical personnel. In processes of quieting, dismissal, smothering and erasure, the power to define, name and make meaning of the embodied experience of labour/birth is taken away from women/girls themselves. As such, it is a form of hermeneutical injustice in which birthing women/girls find their meaning-making efforts 'constrained or undermined'[43] and in which they are preventing from articulating or developing an authorial voice about their own bodily experience/s.

Systematic erasure and epistemic colonisation

Many of the girls spoke of their experiences within public sector healthcare services, both in relation to antenatal care and during labour/birth, as encounters in which they were unacknowledged as speakers, persons and knowers. Across the board, they spoke of systematic patterns of communicative erasure in which

39 Ibid 111.
40 Jewkes (n 8).
41 Dotson (n 10) 242.
42 D'Gregorio (n 2).
43 Medina (n 31).

any kind of reciprocity between the speaker and listener was denied. This was often 'quieting' taken to the extreme in the sense that not only were girls un-recognised as knowers, but also often unrecognised as human beings. Esther, 19 years old and employed as a cleaner of public toilets at the time of her first post-birth interview, told a story in which she was systematically erased – both as speaker and as human person during labour/birth. Esther describes lying in the hospital for three days in pain. In this time, she recalls shouting and asking for help from nurses but repeatedly receiving no response.

ESTHER: By X [public hospital] they didn't even help me, they walked past me, walked up and down. I lay there screaming for them to help me, but they didn't help me.

In these failed communicative encounters, Esther desperately tries to reach out to those around her but is repeatedly dismissed and ignored. This is, in fact, not just 'quieting' but systematic erasure and the refusal to enter into any kind of reciprocal communicative exchange. According to Dotson, speakers are inher-ently vulnerable and require listeners/audiences to be 'willing and capable of hearing us'.[44] Epistemic violence occurs when communicative encounters fail due to 'pernicious ignorance'. This kind of ignorance does not require intention-ality but is marked by its repetitive, reliable and harmful qualities. Throughout Esther's birth story, she makes repeated reference to similar communicative fail-ures in which she tries to reach out to healthcare providers but is met by silence and lack of recognition (of her pain, her embodied experience and her human-ity). Esther also describes the use of more overt physical violence during her labour in which she was tied up and put into stirrups against her will.

ESTHER: In the labour ward they didn't help me, I just lay there. They left me there till that evening. I was pushing and shouting by myself. And then they tied me up as well! They tied me up because I was walking up and down. Then I said, 'I can't lie here the whole time'. They didn't help me so must I just lie there the whole time in pain? Then they tied me up till they cut me [caesarean section].
INTERVIEWER: And how did you feel when they tied you up?
ESTHER: I cried! I cried my heart out.

Left by herself to deal with labour, Esther shouts, pushes and walks up and down in order to try to find some way of actively coping with her body pains. Unfor-tunately, this is not well received by nurses and she is tied up in order to force her to stop walking around. In addition to receiving no help, support, commu-nicative encouragement or assistance from her 'caregivers', and being subjected to the systematic erasure of her paining, embodied self, Esther is also forced into

44 Dotson (n 10) 242.

stirrups and thereby also denied the possibility of finding a means of coping, via active movement, with her paining body.

As shown by Akrich and Pasveer,[45] in their analysis of over 70 birth stories, a positive and empowering birth experience is characterised by the birth-giver's ability to forge a productive and agentic relationship between the embodied self and the paining, labouring body. This kind of relational dynamic is facilitated by modes of labour allowing active and free movement, expression and inform-ative relational exchanges. In the violent encounter narrated by Esther, her pain and embodied experience of labour is 'appropriated', dismissed and colonised by those around her. She is forcibly restrained, interfering with her ability to agentically inhabit and take ownership of her bodily experience of labour and visceral pain. Nurses act within the epistemic authority of biomedicine in order to control/discipline her labouring body so that it complies with a medicalised interpretive view of how birthing bodies should behave/act – ie as passive and silent entities devoid of knowledge, power or active agency. This amounts to the forceful muting of the 'loud'[46] labouring body so that its epistemic status as the logical centre of the labour/birth process is denied, obstructed and silenced.

Childbirth is a unique event in which bodily pain is *normal and productive* and which is also a powerful subjective experience for women/girls in which they creatively bring new life into the world with/through their embodied selves. This normal and potentially personally transformative and emotionally significant bodily experience has been redefined by biomedical modes of knowl-edge as pathological, risky and in need of intervention, control and regulation. As a result, the 'appropriation' of women's bodily experiences of labour/birth, as evidenced in Esther's birth narrative, is typically normalised within obstet-rics but is, in fact, tantamount to modes of epistemic colonisation. Further-more, legal definitions of 'obstetric violence' allude to this in their reference to the 'appropriation' of reproductive processes as a form of violence.[47] In such in-stances of colonisation or appropriation, women/girls are often estranged from their own bodily experiences of labour. Later in her story, Esther described becoming an incidental and insignificant character in her own birth drama. As her labour became increasingly 'medicalised' and she was forcibly restrained via stirrups to the labouring bed and connected to a series of machines, the epis-temic centre of her own birth experience became located elsewhere, outside of her own bodily sensations, to the point where it resided more in the machine and medicalised interpretation/s thereof than in her own embodied sensations. As a marginalised – young, black and poor mother – she was denied access to this alternative epistemic world and thus left effectively estranged from her own labouring body.

---

45 Madeleine Akrich and Bernike Pasveer, 'Embodiment and Disembodiment in Childbirth Narra-tives' (2004) 10 Body Soc 63.
46 Sara Cohen Shabot, 'Making Loud Bodies 'Feminine': A Feminist-Phenomenological Analysis of Obstetric Violence' (2016) 39 Human Studies 231.
47 D'Gregorio (n 2).

ESTHER: They just came in and out to look at the screen and the heart monitor. And then they walked away again, they just looked at that thing and then they walked off. I asked the one sister, I asked her: 'Now what do you see on that thing because I don't know what is going on' and then she said to me 'shut your mouth, you talk too much!'.

In this failed communicative exchange, complex processes of silencing are evident. First, Esther's labouring body is disciplined and made orderly and passive (or 'muted') via confinement through stirrups to the maternity bed. Second, she is connected to obstetric machinery which effectively become vitalised, pulsing, beeping and agentic forces and the epistemic centre of the birth drama. It is these machines that are looked at, touched and deciphered rather than Esther's paining, labouring body. Given that she cannot read the machines, Esther becomes an unknowing bystander to her (now medicalised) labour/birth and her own embodied sensations/knowledge become insignificant. Third, when she tries to communicate with a nurse and ask for information she is sharply and rudely told to shut up. Her silencing is underlined in this narrative moment. Instead of meeting her halfway in a reciprocal communicative exchange, Esther is dismissed as unknowing, incidental and reprimanded for trying to exercise any 'voice' at all. Her efforts to incorporate the surrounding obstetric machinery and biomedicalised epistemic knowledge into her attempts to make meaning of labour are, as a result, *disabled* by this healthcare provider. The moment at which Esther's communicative efforts are silenced in the narrated exchange represents the final appropriation of her birthing experience. At this point, a reciprocal exchange was still possible in which she could have drawn on technical obstetric knowledge to *make sense* of her own bodily experience/ sensations and thus to enhance her own position as epistemic participant. Instead, her 'meaning-making capacities encounter unfair obstacles'[48] amounting to what Medina refers to as hermeneutical injustice and she is prevented from 'developing and exercising a voice'[49] in relation to her own birth experience. At this point, it is important to note that obstetric technology and machinery do not always alienate and mute birth-givers as evidenced in Esther's story. Instead, technology can be administered and used in a way which potentially enhances women/girls' embodied experiences of labour/birth.[50] As argued by Lyerly,[51] it is the affective and communicative contexts within which obstetric technologies/interventions are applied that either enhance or disable women's attempts to make meaning and construct epistemic and embodied modes of agency in relation to birth.

Erasure was a repeated mode of silencing narrated by most of the girls as they told birth stories. For example, 16-year-old Selma spoke about being

48 Medina (n 31).
49 Ibid 41.
50 Akrich and Pasveer (n 45); Drapkin Lyerly (n 38); Chadwick (n 21).
51 Drapkin Lyerly (n 38).

systematically ignored by healthcare workers. Given that she was not allowed to have her mother or friend with her during labour, she was left alone and unsupported throughout most of the birth process.

SELMA: I couldn't lay for long and then the pain came, and then I got up and I read the stuff on the wall and the doctors weren't taking note of me, they were all doing their own thing. And no one was allowed to be in the room with you, so my mom and my friend left ... and then I walked around a bit, crying and rubbing my own back and ... because no one is worried about you ... I was like in pain and nobody would help me.

INTERVIEWER: And then the nurses weren't responding when you were crying?

SELMA: No, like they didn't even come and check like – 'am I okay?' They only came when like, when they had to do an observation ... they were all just doing their own thing ... nobody came to me and asked 'hey are you fine?' and 'how are you coping?', it was just like everybody was doing their own thing.

Being left alone and ignored by caregivers was distressing for Selma. As she put it, 'I felt upset because I was alone and nobody was caring'. An important part of her dissatisfaction was the fact that none of the nurses or medical staff bothered to communicate with her or respond to her distress and crying. She was left feeling erased, unheard and invisibilised, not only in her status as a knower but also as a communicative human being. She is treated simply as a passive body, there to be 'observed' and monitored, and not as a speaker or linguistic being.

Smothering of voices and embodied agency

While no comforting or supportive communicative exchanges were forthcoming from healthcare providers (see above), in her birth narrative, 16-year-old Selma nonetheless also recognised that she could be the target of abuse from her 'caregivers' if she stepped out of line. As a result, she describes censoring and disciplining her expressions and actions in efforts to avoid abuse from healthcare workers.[52]

INTERVIEWER: Did you feel free to do what you wanted to do when you were walking around? Could you shout? Could you scream?

SELMA: No, they didn't want people to go on ... I didn't, I was only crying because I knew they would come and maybe they would shout at me if I shout, or be nasty if I start screaming, or be rude and stuff like that. So I held it in, and I was just crying because I was in pain.

INTERVIEWER: So you couldn't shout or express yourself? How did that make you feel?

SELMA: Like I was upset, because I couldn't do what I wanted to do. All I could do was cry and nobody even took note of that.

52 Chadwick (n 30).

In this extract, Selma describes a process of self-silencing, akin to what Dotson[53] refers to as 'testimonial smothering'. Smothering is a form of coercive silencing in which speakers censor their own testimonies or expressions because they perceive their audience to be unable or unwilling to hear them. According to Dotson, 'smothering' or self-silencing occurs when speakers regard their own articulations, expressions or testimonies to be 'unsafe and risky'.[54] In Selma's birth story, she describes herself as not free to express herself, shout or scream for fear of being targeted and abused by nurses. She says 'I held it in', thus effectively smothering her own pain and screams in order to avert the possibility of violence.

Juno spoke of being left alone, unsupported and erased as speaker, knower and person during labour/birth in her birth narrative.

JUNO: They left me there, just in pain. They didn't even help me. ... I started getting restless and impatient and I think that's when my blood started getting higher, and then they put me on the drip. I started getting restless and wanted to pull my hair out and they were like 'mommy, we're not going to help you if you're going to be like that'.

Communicative refusals in which healthcare workers (for whatever reason) would not respond, listen to or talk to Juno characterised a lack of reciprocity whereby her meaning-making efforts were obstructed or frustrated. When she tries to performatively resist – 'I started getting restless', she is threatened with the withdrawal of care and help – 'we're not going to help you'. Later she describes giving her hand to one of the nurses, hoping and expecting that the nurse would take it and help her to get up. The nurse refuses her hand and she is told 'no, I have to help myself'. This upsets Juno to the point that she starts 'banging on the table' in frustration. This unruly act is once again met with hostility and threats as nurses warn her that they will 'put me out' [drug and/or anaesthetise her] if she insists on being difficult. Via threats of violence and literal muting (ie anaesthetic), Juno's unruly body is forcibly and coercively 'smothered' and disciplined into compliance and silence.

Acts of quieting and the denial of girls' embodied knowledge of labour/birth

Eighteen-year-old Christina told a birth story in which her embodied knowledge of her labour/birth process was systematically dismissed by healthcare workers, akin to what Dotson[55] refers to as 'testimonial quieting' or the refusal to acknowledge that a speaker is the source of credible knowledge.

53 Dotson (n 10) 242.
54 Ibid 244.
55 Ibid 242.

CHRISTINA: The Sunday night I told them, I lay the whole night in pain, crying, the pain comes, goes, comes, goes, I told them the child is going to come now but they wouldn't believe me, I told them I can feel the head is lying just here. They argued, they argued … I lay there, then I pushed, I probably didn't push right, then they said they are going to cut me because I am not pushing right. The more I said, 'I am pushing right, the child is coming now', then they walked out of the room. Oh my gosh! It's a good thing I didn't go to the toilet, then the child came! Then, then, her father saw her head, then he ran, then he went to call them.

In this extract, Christina describes a clear case of 'quieting' as healthcare providers refuse to acknowledge and believe her interpretations of her own corporeal pain/labour sensations. Her bodily intuitive knowledge that her baby is about to be born is dismissed and silenced – as she says: 'They wouldn't believe me' and later on they left the room, abandoning her despite her pleas and insistence that delivery was imminent. In this exchange, which is not unusual in public sector healthcare services in South Africa,[56] labouring women/girls' epistemic status as knowers in relation to their own embodied experiences of birth is not recognised. As a result, many are disbelieved when they say they are in active labour (and are sent home)[57] and are ignored and dismissed when they say that delivery is about to occur.

Such acts of silencing and muting are underpinned by the biomedical belief that birthing women have no epistemic authority, knowledge or status to define or interpret their own bodily experiences of labour/birth. Knowledge, in relation to birth, is regarded as the exclusive remit of biomedical actors trained in technologies of measurement and intervention. Such 'quieting' and silencing is not only a mode of hermeneutical violence in which women/girls are stripped of epistemic agency and dismissed as knowers, it is also potentially dangerous and risky for mothers and babies. Women birthing in public sector services in South Africa regularly report experiences in which their babies' heads were out and crowning without any medical assistance or personnel present.[58] This amounts to unassisted delivery and giving birth with no caregiver and is highly risky. For example, Christina spoke about friends of hers who had given birth to their babies in toilet pots in local healthcare facilities; this is why she said (see above) that 'it's a good thing I didn't go to the toilet' otherwise she too might have delivered her baby into a toilet. Hermeneutical violence in the form of epistemic modes of silencing in which women/girls' embodied knowledge is dismissed is thus intimately tied to poor quality of care and potentially adverse maternal health outcomes.

---

56 R J Chadwick, D Cooper, and J Harries, 'Narratives of Distress about Birth in South African Public Maternity Settings: A Qualitative Study' (2014) 30 Midwifery 862.
57 Chadwick (n 21).
58 Chadwick, Cooper, and Harries (n 56).

Perhaps understandably, given their histories of violence and silencing, some of the girls represented in this chapter did not recognise the treatment they received in healthcare services as wrong or problematic. Thus, when she was later asked by the interviewer how the nurses had treated her, Christina (who had been ignored, disbelieved and left alone to deliver her baby) replied, 'no, they were alright with me, how can I say, they weren't rude to me'. Other girls, however, clearly articulated 'testimonies of resistance'[59] against poor treatment, acts of quieting and silencing. For example, 18-year-old Roxanne, highly articulate and very mature for her age, spoke about how her status as a pregnant teenager impacted on the treatment she received while in labour at the local maternity centre. Asked directly by the interviewer whether she thought she was treated differently because of her age, she replied, 'yes, they did, they think, "oh she's immature, she doesn't know what's happening"'. Roxanne thus recognised that she was not identified as a knower by nurses and healthcare providers. Like Christina, she talked about being disbelieved when she tried to report and interpret her own bodily experiences to nurses.

ROXANNE: There were quite a few females [nurses] who came into the labour ward and they were like, 'no, you're not in labour yet so you need to lay down', and they were much older than I was ... I told my boyfriend I'm gonna report her [nurse] because the way she was handling me wasn't up to standard. When I told her I couldn't urinate, she just told me 'just go pee' and when my water broke I was sitting on the toilet and I told her, 'I think my water just broke' cause I just felt like this popping feeling. And she was like, 'how do you know your water broke?' ... she was unhelpful. Telling me to calm down and breathe – she didn't tell me it, I had to tell myself that, and I expected more.

Roxanne's efforts to interpret, speak about and name her bodily feelings and sensations are thus thwarted at every turn, thus effectively damaging and obstructing her 'ability to speak and be heard'[60] during labour/birth. Her haptic and intuitive knowledge is systematically dismissed and refused. Interestingly, Roxanne also noted similar experiences or acts of quieting in relation to interactions with ordinary community members. The assumption that she was a teenage mother with no status as a knower/epistemic agent was thus not only held by healthcare workers but also functioned as a wider form of socio-epistemic injustice. However, attempts to silence and deny Roxanne's voice and epistemic agency as a young mother were not always fully successful and she described ways in which she managed to 'speak back' against instances of (attempted) silencing.

59 Chadwick (n 21).
60 Dotson (n 10) 242.

ROXANNE: Even now [after birth] people still judge you, like when I go to clinics for his [baby's] check-ups, like there's a certain period where you have to wait until they call your name and people just stare at you and think 'look at this stupid child, she doesn't even know what she's doing', like they are so judgemental. It makes me very angry. There was this one incident where this lady was like, 'oh no, my first baby, I wasn't even on the calendar' – I don't even know what that means, it's got something to do with my age. And then I told her, 'you know what – I know you are not talking *to me* but you are talking about me, don't you have better things to do? You are older than I am, you are supposed to be mature, these things happen.' ... I feel like people just push me aside like, 'oh she's young, she has a baby, she's stupid so let's talk about her'.

Roxanne was thus not always successfully silenced or 'quieted' by instances of socio-epistemic oppression in which she was judged to be stupid, ignorant and unknowing on the basis of her embodied identity as a 'teenage mother'. Similarly to Bell, I thus found that marginalised subjects can and do offer resistance to epistemic modes of violence and silencing and that 'epistemic agency can survive, even if it is not validated within the dominant frame of reference'.[61]

Conclusion

This chapter has explored practices of coerced silencing in/through the pregnancy and birth narratives of five, multiply marginalised, young South African mothers. Drawing on the work of Dotson,[62] I argued that practices of coerced silencing function as forms of epistemic violence during birth and are intimately entangled with other forms of obstetric violence, including the loss of autonomy, physical and verbal abuse, dehumanised treatment and the coercive use of medical interventions. While substantial literature exists on the mistreatment and abuse of women and pregnant persons during childbirth, most of this research has focused on direct and overt forms of physical and verbal abuse. There have, so far, been few explorations of other, more subterranean forms of violence (such as epistemic violence) in relation to birth. At the same time, the legal definition of 'obstetric violence' in Venezuela defines 'the appropriation of the body and reproductive processes of women'[63] as a defining feature of obstetric violence. I have argued in this chapter that references to 'appropriation' as a core feature of obstetric violence allude to the subtle, normalised and widespread biomedical and socio-epistemic processes whereby women/girls' embodied experiences of labour/birth are 'colonised'. Practices of silencing and erasing authorial voices and epistemic agency are key mechanisms that enable the appropriation and

61 Bell (n 18) 173.
62 Dotson (n 10) 242.
63 D'Gregorio (n 2).

colonisation of women/girls' birth experiences. In this chapter, I have shown that epistemic violence, defined as 'a type of violence that attempts to eliminate knowledge possessed by marginal subjects'[64] is a central aspect of obstetric violence and, in my view, underpins and enables more overt forms of physical, verbal and emotional abuse during labour/birth. Epistemic modes of silencing which position birth-giving women and girls as unknowing, incompetent and unreliable speakers, and which erase their unique haptic and embodied forms of knowledge, are intimately intertwined with acts of dehumanisation and disrespect during birth.

While all women/girls and pregnant persons are vulnerable to silencing during birth, intersecting social inequalities mean that poor, black and young teenage girls are even more likely to be on the receiving end of harmful modes of coercive silencing. As reiterated by black feminist writers, black women/girls are often systematically devalued as knowers on the basis of intra-acting race, class and gender inequalities and prejudices.[65] This chapter drew on the pregnancy and birth narratives of five, multiply marginalised young mothers to explore the ways in which coercive modes of silencing function as forms of epistemic violence. The analysis outlined three key forms of silencing identified in girls' narratives, namely, systematic erasure, smothering and acts of quieting. These forms of silencing were argued to be central mechanisms that enable the broader 'appropriation' and colonisation of girls' experiences of labour/birth. Via systematic acts of erasure, threats of violence, the coercive smothering of voices and embodied agency, and acts of quieting in which girls' embodied sensations/knowledge are unrecognised, the power to define, name and make meaning of their own bodily experiences is curtailed and obstructed. As a result, such forms of silencing functioned as forms of hermeneutical injustice as girls found their meaning-making efforts 'constrained or undermined'[66] and were prevented from developing an authorial voice in relation to their own labour/birth experiences. However, at the same time, girls' narratives also showed that practices of coercive silencing were not always entirely successful and some girls continued to find ways of exerting epistemic agency and articulating 'testimonies of resistance' in the face of attempts to silence their voices.

In summary, this chapter argued that epistemic violence, enacted through different forms of silencing, is a key mode of obstetric violence. Furthermore, the systematic silencing and erasure of women/girls' status as epistemic knowers and speakers in relation to labour/birth also enables and underpins other, often more overt, forms of violence (ie physical and verbal violence, the abuse of medical technologies and disrespectful treatment). As such, the dehumanising and colonising nature of obstetric epistemologies and medical practices that valorise technocratic knowledge while dismissing and silencing the lived, haptic

---

64 Dotson (n 10) 242.
65 Ibid.
66 Medina (n 31).

and embodied knowledge of birth-givers needs to be challenged and recognised as a mode of oppression. Furthermore, the complex intertwining between oppressive biomedical practices and authoritative modes of knowledge, and broader socio-epistemic prejudices (of race, class, gender, ableism, sexuality and ageism) which result in the broader epistemic agency of marginalised subjects being unrecognised, also needs recognition. Birth does not occur in a socio-epistemic vacuum and patterns of abuse, mistreatment, violence and silencing during birth reflect, reproduce and are entangled with localised sociocultural inequalities, epistemic injustices and modes of marginalisation.

Bibliography

Akrich M and Pasveer B, 'Embodiment and Disembodiment in Childbirth Narratives' (2004) 10 Body Soc 63

Bell K, 'Exploring Epistemic Injustice through Feminist Social Work Research' (2014) 29 Affilia 165

Carel H and Kidd I, 'Epistemic Injustice in Healthcare: A Philosophical Analysis' (2014) 17 Med Health Care Philos 529

Chadwick R, 'Ambiguous Subjects: Obstetric Violence, Assemblage and South African Birth Narratives' (2017) 27 Fem Psychol 489

Chadwick R, *Bodies that Birth: Vitalizing Birth Politics* (Routledge 2018)

Chadwick R, Cooper D and Harries J, 'Narratives of Distress about Birth in South African Public Maternity Settings: A Qualitative Study' (2014) 30 Midwifery 862

Cohen Shabot S, 'Making Loud Bodies 'Feminine': A Feminist-Phenomenological Analysis of Obstetric Violence' (2016) 39 Human Studies 231

D'Gregorio R P, 'Obstetric Violence: A New Legal Term Introduced in Venezuela' (2010) 111 Int J Gynaecol Obstet 201

D'Oliveira A, Diniz S, and Schraibe L, 'Violence against Women in Health-Care Institutions: An Emerging Problem' (2002) 359 The Lancet 1681

Dixon L, 'Obstetrics in a Time of Violence: Mexican Midwives Critique Routine Hospital Practices' (2015) 29 Med Anthropol Q 437

Dotson K, 'Tracking Epistemic Violence, Tracking Practices of Silencing' (2011) 26 Hypatia 236

Drapkin Lyerly A, 'Shame, Gender, Birth' (2006) 21 Hypatia 101

Fricker M, *Epistemic Injustice: Power and the Ethics of Knowing* (OUP 2007)

Goer H, 'Cruelty in Maternity Wards: Fifty Years Later' (2010) 19 J Perinat Educ 33

Jewkes R, Abrahams N and Mvo Z, 'Why Do Nurses Abuse Patients? Reflections from South African Obstetric Services' (1998) 47 Soc Sci Med 1781

Jordan B, 'Authoritative Knowledge and Its Construction' in Davis-Floyd R and Sargent C (eds), *Childbirth and Authoritative Knowledge* (University of California Press 1997)

Martin E, *The Woman in the Body: A Cultural Analysis of Reproduction* (OUP 1987)

Medina J, 'Hermeneutical Injustice and Polyphonic Contextualism: Social Silences and Shared Hermeneutical Responsibilities' (2012) 26 Soc Epistemol 201

Medina J, 'Varieties of Hermeneutical Injustice' in Kidd I, Medina J and Polhaus G (eds), *The Routledge Handbook of Epistemic Injustice* (Routledge 2017) 41

Oakley A, *Women Confined: Towards a Sociology of Childbirth* (Martin Robertson 1980)

Root R and Browner C, 'Practices of the Pregnant Self: Compliance with and Resistance to Prenatal Norms' (2001) 25 Cult Med Psychiatry 195

Rothman B K, *In Labour: Women and Power in the Birthplace* (WW Norton & Company 1982)

Sadler M and others, 'Moving beyond Disrespect and Abuse: Addressing the Structural Dimensions of Obstetric Violence' (2016) 24(47) Reprod Health Matters 47

Smith-Oka V, 'Managing Labour and Delivery among Impoverished Populations in Mexico: Cervical Examinations as Bureaucratic Practice' (2013) 115 Am Anthropol 595

Smith-Oka V, 'Microaggressions and the Reproduction of Social Inequalities in Medical Encounters in Mexico' (2015) 143 Soc Sci Med 9

Vogel J and others, 'Promoting Respect and Preventing Mistreatment during Childbirth' (2016) 123 BJOG 671

Wardrope A, 'Medicalization and Epistemic Injustice' (2015) 18 Med Health Care Philos 341

Žižek S, *Violence: Six Sideways Reflections* (Picador 2008)

3 Posttraumatic stress disorder following childbirth

Antje Horsch and Susan Garthus-Niegel

Introduction

Childbirth is an intense event that is of emotional, social, and cultural significance as well as involving great physical stress.[1] Physically, women have to cope with acute changes and a high degree of pain as the uterus contracts, the cervix dilates, and the baby and placenta are born.[2] Emotionally, labour and the birth of the baby may involve both intense positive and negative emotions. Interpersonal dynamics between the woman, her (birth) partner, and maternity staff may be supportive or may increase stress if birth attendants are perceived as unhelpful, dismissive, or even abusive.[3] Culturally, birth and motherhood are associated with many cultural expectations and norms, as commonly childbirth is considered a merely positive life event.[4]

However, as this book sheds light on diverse aspects of childbirth, it becomes clear that it is more complex than that. Indeed, research evidence from the last two decades shows that labour and delivery may have the potential to fulfil the traumatic stressor criteria, as defined in the Diagnostic and Statistical Manual of Mental Disorders.[5] Approximately three to four per cent of women develop the full constellation of symptoms of posttraumatic stress disorder (PTSD) and thus qualify for a clinical diagnosis.[6] Hence, with approximately 136 million births

1 Antje Horsch and others, 'Improving Maternal Mental Health Following Preterm Birth Using an Expressive Writing Intervention: A Randomized Controlled Trial' (2016) 5 Child Psychiatry Hum Dev 780.

2 Susan Garthus-Niegel and others, 'The Role of Labor Pain and Overall Birth Experience in the Development of Posttraumatic Stress Symptoms: A Longitudinal Cohort Study' (2014) 41 Birth 108; Antje Horsch and Susan Ayers, 'Childbirth and Stress' in George Fink (ed), *Stress: Concepts, Cognition, Emotion, and Behavior* (Academic Press 2016) 325.

3 Horsch and others (n 1).

4 Ibid.

5 American Psychiatric Association, *Diagnostic and Statistical Manual of Mental Disorders* (4th edn, American Psychiatric Association 1994).

6 Rebecca Grekin and Michael W O'Hara, 'Prevalence and Risk Factors of Postpartum Posttraumatic Stress Disorder: A Meta-Analysis' (2014) 34 Clin Psychol Rev 389; Lydia King, Kirstie McKenzie-McHarg, and Antje Horsch, 'Testing a Cognitive Model to Predict Posttraumatic Stress Disorder following Childbirth' (2017) 17 BMC Pregnancy Childbirth 32; Pelin Dikmen

worldwide,[7] more than 4.7 million women and their families are affected, every single year. As recent research on the intergenerational transmission of stress and trauma underlines the relevance and far-reaching consequences not only for the mother but also for her offspring, PTSD following childbirth thus represents a major public health issue.[8]

This chapter provides an overview of the current evidence and understanding of PTSD following childbirth by focusing on (i) childbirth as a traumatic stressor; (ii) definition and prevalence rates; (iii) protective and risk factors; (iv) the impact on maternal, child, and couple outcomes; (v) the economic costs; and (vi) evidence-based interventions.

Childbirth as a traumatic stressor

Symptoms of posttraumatic stress were first identified in relation to war experiences. However, in contrast to previous diagnostic criteria, triggers are not considered anymore to be restricted to events that are outside of the range of 'usual human experience' such as war, rape, or road traffic accidents.[9] Indeed, for many years clinicians have been aware that also health-related events such as heart attacks, stroke, miscarriage, stillbirth, or childbirth may act as precipitants for posttraumatic stress responses.[10] This comprises a peculiarity of PTSD following childbirth, because – as mentioned above – childbirth is typically associated with positive connotations (opposed to other potential traumatic events such as war or sexual/physical abuse).[11] Also, in the Western world, births normally take place within the context of regular medical care, which actually represents

---

Yildiz, Susan Ayers, and Louise Phillips, 'The Prevalence of Posttraumatic Stress Disorder in Pregnancy and After Birth: A Systematic Review and Meta-Analysis' (2017) 208 J Affect Disord 634.

7　Central Intelligence Agency, 'The World Factbook' (2018) <www.cia.gov/library/publications/download/download-2018/index.html> accessed 24 September 2018.

8　Malloy E Bowers and Rachel Yehuda, 'Intergenerational Transmission of Stress in Humans' (2016) 41 Neuropsychopharmacology 232; S Garthus-Niegel and others, 'The Impact of Subjective Birth Experiences on Post-Traumatic Stress Symptoms: A Longitudinal Study' (2013) 16 Arch Womens Ment Health 1; King, McKenzie-McHarg, and Horsch (n 6).

9　Pauline Slade, 'Towards a Conceptual Framework for Understanding Post-Traumatic Stress Symptoms Following Childbirth and Implications for Further Research' (2006) 27 J Psychosom Obstet Gynaecol 99.

10　Helen Allott, 'Picking up the Pieces: The Post-Delivery Stress Clinic' (1996) 4 BJM 534; Antje Horsch, Ingo Jacobs, and Kirstie McKenzie-McHarg, 'Cognitive Predictors and Risk Factors of PTSD Following Stillbirth: A Short-Term Longitudinal Study' (2015) 28 J Traum Stress 110; C Lee, P Slade, and V Lygo, 'The Influence of Psychological Debriefing on Emotional Adaptation in Women Following Early Miscarriage: A Preliminary Study' (1996) 69 Br J Med Psychol 47; Josephine E Tedstone and Nicholas Tarrier, 'Posttraumatic Stress Disorder Following Medical Illness and Treatment' (2003) 23 Clin Psychol Rev 409; Slade (n 9).

11　Kirstie McKenzie-McHarg and others, 'Post-Traumatic Stress Disorder Following Childbirth: An Update of Current Issues and Recommendations for Future Research' (2015) 33 J Reprod Infant Psychol 219.

the helper system (as opposed to crimes rated as criminal acts).[12] Further, pertaining to PTSD following childbirth, at least two individuals must always be considered: The mother and the child (see also in the 'Impact on maternal, child, and couple outcomes' section).[13] This can be challenging for the mother, as her role is to care for her baby who may be a strong reminder of the traumatic event.

Regarding posttraumatic stress responses in the context of childbirth, it is important to distinguish whether a woman suffering from PTSD following childbirth already suffered from PTSD during pregnancy, or whether the disorder has occurred only as a result of birth.[14] Traumatic memories such as previous sexual abuse may be triggered by child movements as well as vaginal delivery and can lead to an actualisation of trauma symptoms.[15] Clinical experience shows that in case of prior traumatisation, flashbacks may occur during childbirth triggered by a feeling of loss of control. They may also be the result of other trigger stimuli such as physical sensations (eg pain, birth injuries, bleeding) or sentences such as 'it's over soon', reminding the woman of the perpetrator's language that refers to earlier trauma.[16] Women who have suffered from childhood abuse appear to have an increased risk of dissociation during delivery (especially in the context of additional risk factors).[17] In addition to previous biographical traumatisation, women may also live under present adverse conditions such as domestic violence which may increase their risk of suffering from PTSD already during pregnancy.[18]

Definition and prevalence rates

Studies have shown that up to one third of women perceive their delivery as traumatic, fulfilling the Diagnostic and Statistical Manual of Mental Disorders, fourth edition (DSM-IV) Criterion A1 (ie witness or experience death, threat of death, or serious injury to themselves or a significant other – in the case of postpartum PTSD usually the baby).[19] However, a much smaller part of women

12 Ibid.

13 Ibid.

14 Grekin and O'Hara (n 6).

15 Kristina Hofberg and Ian Brockington, 'Tokophobia: An Unreasoning Dread of Childbirth. A Series of 26 Cases' (2000) 176 Br J Psychiatry 83.

16 Kerstin Weidner, Susan Garthus-Niegel, and Juliane Junge-Hoffmeister, 'Traumatische Geburtsverläufe: Erkennen und Vermeiden' (Traumatic Birth: Recognition and Prevention) (2018) Z Geburtshilfe Neonatol 189.

17 Kristen R Choi and Julia S Seng, 'Predisposing and Precipitating Factors for Dissociation during Labor in a Cohort Study of Posttraumatic Stress Disorder and Childbearing Outcomes' (2016) 61 J Midwifery Womens Health 68.

18 Jacquelyn C Campbell, 'Health Consequences of Intimate Partner Violence' (2002) 359 The Lancet 1331; Weidner, Garthus-Niegel, and Junge-Hoffmeister (n 16).

19 American Psychiatric Association (n 5); Susan Ayers, 'Delivery as a Traumatic Event: Prevalence, Risk Factors, and Treatment for Postnatal Posttraumatic Stress Disorder' (2004) 47 Clin Obstet Gynecol 552; Eelco Olde and others, 'Posttraumatic Stress Following Childbirth: A Review' (2006) 26 Clin Psychol Rev 1; Slade (n 9); Johanna E Soet, Gregory A Brack, and

eventually develops a PTSD profile, indicating that a traumatic childbirth experience does not automatically lead to a pathological response.[20] Recent meta-analyses suggest, in community samples, PTSD following childbirth affects between three and four per cent of women after birth at diagnostic levels and 16–19 per cent of women in high-risk groups, eg after preterm birth or neonatal death.[21] Still, a substantial number of women suffer from clinically significant PTSD symptoms, even though their symptoms remain below the diagnostic threshold level.[22] This is because sub-threshold symptomatology may also considerably impact on women's functioning, particularly if they are having symptoms of re-experiencing.[23]

Whether or not women develop PTSD symptoms depends to a large degree on the subjective perception of the birth. In fact, regarding childbirth, both clinical observations and scientific evidence indicate that what may be considered as a medically normal labour and delivery in terms of duration and mode of delivery may still be associated with subsequent posttraumatic stress responses.[24] Being aware of the essential role of subjective birth experiences offers a unique opportunity to prevent traumatisation. If women feel safe and well taken care of, it may be easier for them to abstain from catastrophic interpretations during birth and to focus instead on the joyful outcome of their labour – the baby. Training programs to improve communication between labouring women and staff may help healthcare workers to be more sensitive and responsive to women's needs, thus potentially increasing their subjective birth experience.

Regarding the long-term course of PTSD following childbirth, there are hardly any studies available. While relatively high remission rates of up to 44 per cent have been found for general PTSD,[25] future prospective studies need to show whether the clinical course of PTSD following childbirth (eg in terms of severity, duration, and remission with and without treatment) is comparable to that of general PTSD.[26] Case reports at least suggest that women with PTSD following childbirth often suffer from their symptoms for months, without being diagnosed and treated.[27]

Colleen DiIorio, 'Prevalence and Predictors of Women's Experience of Psychological Trauma during Childbirth' (2003) 30 Birth 36.

20 Olde and others (n 19).

21 Grekin and O'Hara (n 6); Yildiz, Ayers, and Phillips (n 6).

22 Horsch and Ayers (n 2).

23 McKenzie-McHarg and others (n 11).

24 Louise B Andersen and others, 'Risk Factors for Developing Post-Traumatic Stress Disorder Following Childbirth: A Systematic Review' (2012) 91 Acta Obstet Gynecol Scand 1261; Garthus-Niegel and others (n 2); Garthus-Niegel and others (n 8); Slade (n 9).

25 Nexhmedin Morina and others, 'Remission from Post-Traumatic Stress Disorder in Adults: A Systematic Review and Meta-Analysis of Long Term Outcome Studies' (2014) 34 Clin Psychol Rev 249.

26 McKenzie-McHarg and others (n 11).

27 Hofberg and Brockington (n 15).

Several studies have found substantial comorbidity between PTSD and depression in the postpartum period,[28] with comorbidity rates ranging between 20 and 75 per cent.[29] Anxiety or other mental health problems have also been suggested to be comorbid with PTSD following childbirth, although concrete numbers are largely unknown.[30]

One possible explanation for the high correlation with depression is the potential symptom overlap in some of the PTSD clusters,[31] because measures of hyperarousal and numbing symptom clusters within the PTSD criteria tend to correlate highly with measures of depression.[32] It is important to keep in mind that most studies investigating comorbidity have relied on DSM-IV criteria. The addition of the fourth symptom cluster 'negative alterations in cognitions and mood' in DSM-5 (eg 'persistent negative beliefs and expectations about oneself or the world' or 'loss of interest or participation in significant activities') might imply an increase in symptom overlap (as these symptoms could also be attributed to depression),[33] and thus further increase comorbidity rates in future studies.

The course and onset of comorbid PTSD and depression are still unknown. On the one hand, depression in pregnancy has been shown to be an important predictor of PTSD following childbirth.[34] On the other hand, regarding the postpartum period only, clinicians have suggested that postpartum depression is usually secondary to PTSD following childbirth.[35] In any case, epidemiological research has shown that postpartum depression is more prevalent (10–15 per cent) than PTSD following childbirth.[36] Still, from a clinical perspective, it is important that PTSD is considered as an independent diagnosis in postpartum women, because many women, who (also) suffer from PTSD following childbirth, are diagnosed with depression (only) and therefore do not receive appropriate treatment.[37]

28 Jo Czarnocka and Pauline Slade, 'Prevalence and Predictors of Post Traumatic Stress Symptoms Following Childbirth' (2000) 39 Br J Clin Psychol 35; Grekin and O'Hara (n 6); Johan Söderquist, Barbro Wijma, and Klaas Wijma, 'The Longitudinal Course of Post-Traumatic Stress after Childbirth' (2006) 27 J Psychosom Obstet Gynaecol 113; Claire A I Stramrood and others, 'Posttraumatic Stress Following Childbirth in Homelike and Hospital Settings' (2011) 32 Psychosom Obstet Gynaecol 88; Tracey White and others, 'Postnatal Depression and Post-Traumatic Stress after Childbirth: Prevalence, Course and Co-Occurrence' (2006) 24 J Reprod Infant Psychol 107.
29 McKenzie-McHarg and others (n 11); Stramrood (n 28); White and other (n 28).
30 McKenzie-McHarg and others (n 11); Stramrood (n 28).
31 McKenzie-McHarg and others (n 11).
32 Grekin and O'Hara (n 6).
33 McKenzie-McHarg and others (n 11).
34 S Ayers and others, 'The Aetiology of Post-Traumatic Stress Following Childbirth: A Meta-Analysis and Theoretical Framework' (2016) 46 Psychol Med 1121; Grekin and O'Hara (n 6).
35 McKenzie-McHarg and others (n 11).
36 Susan Ayers and others, 'Post-Traumatic Stress Disorder Following Childbirth: Current Issues and Recommendations for Future Research' (2008) 29 J Psychosom Obstet Gynaecol 240; Ian Brockington, 'Postpartum Psychiatric Disorders' (2004) 363 The Lancet 303.
37 McKenzie-McHarg and others (n 11).

Protective and risk factors

In 2006, Slade suggested a framework for the development of postpartum PTSD, comprising predisposing, precipitating, and maintaining factors. Predisposing and precipitating factors may again be subdivided into internal, external, or interactional factors.[38] According to Slade's framework, predisposing factors are often pregnancy-related or may have been present already before conception, increasing the risk of PTSD symptoms.[39] Examples of predisposing factors are fear of childbirth or mental health problems (either in the woman's history or during pregnancy), an unplanned pregnancy, or low social support. Precipitating factors are birth related; they act together with predisposing factors to determine if a woman develops PTSD symptoms after giving birth.[40] Examples of precipitating factors are perceived low control during birth or a negative gap between expectation and experience of the birth, a lack of support of partner or staff, an emergency caesarean section (ECS), or an instrumental vaginal delivery.[41] Maintaining factors are those that may either increase or reduce PTSD symptoms over time such as insomnia during the postpartum period.[42]

Another theoretical approach represents the diathesis-stress model of the aetiology of postpartum PTSD by Ayers that was first introduced in 2004 and recently updated in 2016.[43] The diathesis-stress model has similarities to Slade's theoretical framework, and it is based on the results of a meta-analysis. The model incorporates vulnerability factors in pregnancy, risk factors during birth, and postnatal factors. Important vulnerability factors are depression in pregnancy, fear of childbirth, complications in pregnancy, or a history of mental health problems.[44] Vulnerability factors may predict trauma responses directly, but they are also proposed to interact with or to be mediated by risk factors during birth. Risk factors during birth represent a negative subjective birth experience, operative birth, lack of support from staff during birth, and dissociation.[45] Crucial for whether or not subsequent traumatic stress responses occur is the appraisal of the birth as traumatic or not. Postnatal factors might also predict initial traumatic stress responses. In addition, they may determine whether those responses get resolved or maintained over time. Postnatal factors comprise depression as well as poor coping and stress.

---

38 Slade (n 9).
39 Ibid.
40 Ayers (n 19); Slade (n 9).
41 Slade (n 9).
42 Susan Garthus-Niegel and others, 'Maintaining Factors of Posttraumatic Stress Symptoms Following Childbirth: A Population-Based, Two-Year Follow-up Study' (2015) 172 J Affect Disord 146; Slade (n 9).
43 In this regard see figure 1 in Ayers (n 19) 562 and figure 3 in Ayers and others (n 34) 1130.
44 Ibid.
45 Ibid.

Cognition also plays an important role in the development of PTSD following childbirth.[46] The cognitive model proposed by Ehlers and Clark is a third theoretical approach and suggests that a sense of current threat is produced by negative cognitive appraisals both during and after the traumatic event, ie in our case the birth.[47] This threat, together with a fragmented and poorly integrated traumatic memory, can be unintentionally triggered by situations resembling some aspect of the birth. PTSD may then be maintained through unfavourable cognitive (eg thought suppression) and behavioural (eg reminder avoidance) strategies.[48] Even though these strategies are meant to control the sense of threat, they may directly produce symptoms and/or prevent change in negative appraisals of the trauma or the nature of the trauma memory.[49]

Impact on maternal, child, and couple outcomes

Women with PTSD following childbirth report high levels of distress; some talk about feelings of panic, anxiety, grief, anger, and tearfulness.[50] Sometimes the distress experienced can become unbearable and some women report having suicidal thoughts and ideations following traumatic childbirth. One qualitative study quoted a mother who had thoughts about harming her baby: 'I just thought oh, I wanta strangle, you know I didn't want to, it just came into my head, strangle'.[51] Women describe being haunted by traumatic memories for many years, as one woman explained: 'It was sort of a long black hole, just endless, endless pain'.[52] Women may experience a loss of identity and self-esteem, particularly with regard to their competencies as a mother.[53]

Following traumatic childbirth, women may decide not to have further children.[54] Traumatised women who do embark on a new pregnancy are more likely

46 Elizabeth Ford, Susan Ayers, and Robert Bradley, 'Exploration of a Cognitive Model to Predict Post-Traumatic Stress Symptoms following Childbirth' (2010) 24 J Anxiety Disord 353; King, McKenzie-McHarg, and Horsch (n 6); McKenzie-McHarg and others (n 11); Anna N Vossbeck-Elsebusch, Claudia Freisfeld, and Thomas Ehring, 'Predictors of Posttraumatic Stress Symptoms Following Childbirth' (2014) 14 BMC Psychiatry 200.

47 Anke Ehlers and David M Clark, 'A Cognitive Model of Posttraumatic Stress Disorder' (2000) 38 Behav Res Ther 319; King, McKenzie-McHarg, and Horsch (n 6).

48 King, McKenzie-McHarg, and Horsch (n 6).

49 Ibid.

50 Giliane Fenech and Gill Thomson, '"Tormented by Ghosts from Their Past": A Meta-Synthesis to Explore the Psychosocial Implications of a Traumatic Birth on Maternal Well-Being' (2014) 30 Midwifery 185.

51 Susan Ayers, Andrew Eagle, and Helen Waring, 'The Effects of Childbirth-Related Post-Traumatic Stress Disorder on Women and Their Relationships: A Qualitative Study' (2006) 11 Psychol Health Med 389, 395.

52 C Nilsson, T Bondas, and I Lundgren, 'Previous Birth Experience in Women with Intense Fear of Childbirth' (2010) 39 J Obstet Gynecol Neonatal Nurs 298, 304.

53 Ayers, Eagle, and Waring (n 51).

54 Karin Gottvall and Ulla Waldenström, 'Does a Traumatic Birth Experience Have an Impact on Future Reproduction?' (2002) 109 BJOG 254.

to have a negative experience of subsequent pregnancies, with some women experiencing distress when they found out they were pregnant again: 'I took the test and crumpled over the edge of our bed, sobbing and retching hysterically for hours'.[55] This may be accompanied by an increased risk of maternal stress and its associated risks of negative pregnancy outcomes such as intrauterine growth retardation, low birth weight, and premature birth.[56] PTSD following childbirth is also related to an extreme fear of subsequent pregnancy and childbirth (tokophobia), sexual problems, and avoidance of medical care.[57]

Apart from the distress experienced by the mother, PTSD following childbirth can have negative consequences for the whole family. Following traumatic childbirth, women may blame their partners for the events that took place.[58] A recent prospective study showed that maternal PTSD symptoms following childbirth were prospectively related to low couple relationship satisfaction at two years postpartum, mediated by postpartum depression symptoms.[59]

Some studies found that PTSD following childbirth can also negatively interfere with the mother-infant relationship.[60] For some women, caring for their baby continues to be a reminder of traumatic experiences, which may, in turn, make it harder for them to develop strong bonds and secure attachments with their baby. One of the symptoms of PTSD is emotional detachment, and mothers may therefore be unable to feel and show affection towards their baby, as was described by one mother: 'Mechanically I'd go through the motions of being a good mother. Inside I felt nothing'.[61] Traumatised mothers have been shown to be more controlling and less sensitive towards their child. They also report being overprotective towards their children. This may be a consequence of hypervigilance, one of the symptoms of PTSD.[62] Mothers have an important role in supporting the infant's development of self-regulation skills and prosocial behaviour. Some evidence shows that traumatised mothers

55 Cheryl Tatano Beck and Sue Watson, 'Subsequent Childbirth after a Previous Traumatic Birth' (2010) 59 Nurs Res 241, 245.

56 Shari S Rogal and others, 'Effects of Posttraumatic Stress Disorder on Pregnancy Outcomes' (2007) 102 J Affect Disord 137; Julia S Seng and others, 'Posttraumatic Stress Disorder and Pregnancy Complications' (2001) 97 Obstet Gynecol 17.

57 Hofberg and Brockington (n 15); Leslie Morland and others, 'Posttraumatic Stress Disorder and Pregnancy Health: Preliminary Update and Implications' (2007) 48 Psychosomatics 304.

58 Karen Nicholls and Susan Ayers, 'Childbirth-Related Post-Traumatic Stress Disorder in Couples: A Qualitative Study' (2007) 12 Br J Health Psychol 491.

59 Susan Garthus-Niegel and others, 'The Impact of Postpartum Posttraumatic Stress and Depression Symptoms on Couples' Relationship Satisfaction: A Population-Based Prospective Study' (2018) 9 Front Psychol 1.

60 Ayers, Eagle, and Waring (n 51); Ylva M Parfitt and Susan Ayers, 'The Effect of Post-Natal Symptoms of Post-Traumatic Stress and Depression on the Couple's Relationship and Parent-Baby Bond' (2009) 27 J Reprod Infant Psychol 127.

61 Cheryl Tatano Beck, 'Post-Traumatic Stress Disorder due to Childbirth: The Aftermath' (2004) 53 Nursing 216, 220.

62 Horsch and Ayers (n 2).

struggle to be available for the regulation of their infants' emotions, arousal, and aggression during and immediately following a stressful interaction.[63] This, in turn, may interfere with the development of emotion regulation in these children.

PTSD following childbirth is also related to other negative infant outcomes such as behavioural and cognitive development.[64] Further, a prospective study found that maternal PTSD symptoms eight weeks after birth were associated with poor social-emotional development at two years, especially among boys and children with difficult temperament.[65] Although a recent systematic review stated that evidence for an association between maternal PTSD and mother-infant interaction, the mother-infant relationship, or child development was inconclusive, it concluded there was enough evidence for associations between maternal PTSD following childbirth with low birth weight and lower rates of breastfeeding.[66] A prospective relationship between PTSD following childbirth and breastfeeding initiation as well as breastfeeding continuation was recently confirmed in a large cohort.[67] This is likely due to dysfunctional coping mechanisms in order to avoid traumatic intrusion often triggered by mothers' close contact with their baby.[68] At the same time, as the mother is usually the primary caregiver during the first postpartum weeks, the constant confrontation with the baby – and thus the trauma – might also constitute a mechanism of recovery and healing.[69]

The economic costs

Given the negative impact of PTSD following childbirth not only on the mother herself but also on her partner and her child, it is important to identify potential signs and symptoms of PTSD early on in order to offer appropriate treatment. It has clearly been shown that undetected perinatal mental health problems carry significant economic costs for society (only in the United Kingdom at least £8.1 billion for each one-year cohort of births) and that the majority of those

63 Daniel S Schechter and others, 'Subjective and Objective Measures of Parent-Child Relationship Dysfunction, Child Separation Distress, and Joint Attention' (2010) 73 Psychiatry 130.

64 Debra K Creedy, Ian M Shochet, and Jan Horsfall, 'Childbirth and the Development of Acute Trauma Symptoms: Incidence and Contributing Factors' (2000) 27 Birth 104; E S Paykel, 'Life Events and Affective Disorders' (2003) 108 Acta Psychiatr Scand 61; Richard J Shaw and others, 'The Relationship between Acute Stress Disorder and Posttraumatic Stress Disorder in the Neonatal Intensive Care Unit' (2009) 50 Psychosomatics 131; Söderquist, Wijma, and Wijma (n 28).

65 S Garthus-Niegel and others, 'The Impact of Postpartum Post-Traumatic Stress Disorder Symptoms on Child Development: A Population-Based, 2-Year Follow-up Study' (2017) 47 Psychol Med 161.

66 Natalie Cook, Susan Ayers, and Antje Horsch, 'Maternal Posttraumatic Stress Disorder during the Perinatal Period and Child Outcomes: A Systematic Review' (2018) 225 J Affect Disord 18.

67 Susan Garthus-Niegel and others, 'The Influence of Postpartum PTSD on Breastfeeding: A Longitudinal Population-Based Study' (2017) 54 Birth 193.

68 Fenech and Thomson (n 50).

69 Ayers, Eagle, and Waring (n 51).

costs are linked to the child, ie the future generation.[70] Indeed, given the increasingly complex medical needs of women who become pregnant, for example, when older and/or obese, an increase in the number of women experiencing traumatic births is likely to be expected.[71]

Prevention and intervention

Given the mounting evidence for the negative impact of PTSD following childbirth, questions regarding its prevention and intervention arise. Childbirth is a predictable event and valuable opportunities for primary prevention therefore exist.[72]

Primary prevention may include preparing pregnant women in a more realistic way for labour and birth.[73] Evidence shows that pre-existing beliefs and cognitive appraisals of the impending birth play an important role in the development of postpartum PTSD. Birth preparation should therefore also include discussing the fact that labour and childbirth may not be as planned and women and their partners should be provided with information on the incidence of obstetric interventions and the associated risks and benefits.[74] Given that a prediction prior to the birth of who will or will not require medical interventions is often impossible,[75] the development of a 'birth flow chart' with different pathways for 'what if labour starts with induction/starts preterm/ends with caesarean section' might be a way forward.[76] In that way, women are prepared for a range of possible processes and outcomes, thus preventing them from going into labour with an idealistic picture (eg of natural childbirth).[77]

Based on the evidence from previous risk factor studies regarding the aetiology of postpartum PTSD, another form of primary prevention may include the targeted detection of those pregnant women who may be particularly vulnerable such as those with a history of PTSD or severe fear of childbirth.[78]

Primary prevention in women with a history of PTSD could include psychoeducation on PTSD and potentially comorbid disorders (eg depression) as well as teaching skills as of how to deal with trauma-associated anxiety symptoms,

70 Annette Bauer and others, 'The Costs of Perinatal Mental Health Problems' (Centre for Mental Health and London School of Economics 2014).
71 Gwyneth Lewis (ed), 'Saving Mothers' Lives: Reviewing Maternal Deaths to Make Motherhood Safer 2003–2005' (The Seventh Report of Confidential Enquiries into Maternal and Child Health in the United Kingdom, CEMACH 2007).
72 Olde and others (n 19).
73 Ibid.
74 Creedy, Shochet, and Horsfall (n 64); Horsch and Ayers (n 2); Olde and others (n 19).
75 Olde and others (n 19).
76 McKenzie-McHarg and others (n 11); Gill Thomson and Soo Downe, 'A Hero's Tale of Childbirth' (2013) 29 Midwifery 765.
77 Julia Frost and others, 'Utopian Theory and the Discourse of Natural Birth' (2006) 4 Soc Theory Health 299; McKenzie-McHarg and others (n 11).
78 Ayers and others (n 34); Grekin and O'Hara (n 6); Olde and others (n 19).

tensions, and dissociative conditions.[79] However, whether and at what point women should be confronted with profound biographical experiences through trauma exposure ought to get decided individually. The potential benefit of such emotionally demanding treatment must be weighed against the risk of intrauterine stress exposure or even preterm contractions.[80] However, if a history of PTSD remains unaddressed, an upcoming birth may cause severe fear of childbirth and may hold the potential to reactivate prior trauma and related trauma symptoms.[81]

Fear of childbirth is another important risk factor for a traumatic birth experience and is therefore also relevant for the primary prevention of postpartum PTSD.[82] Childbirth information and advice on coping with specific birth-related problems, delivered in antenatal classes, may help reduce fear of childbirth.[83] The application of relaxation techniques in order to reduce physical tensions and the knowledge about the availability of effective painkillers during childbirth can also have a calming effect on pregnant women.[84] If women suffer from severe fear of childbirth, psychological counselling may help to increase both their motivation to deliver vaginally[85] and their trust in the healthcare staff,[86] thereby increasing the chances of a positive birth experience.[87] On the other hand, women who actively seek treatment for their fear of childbirth seem to belong to a particularly vulnerable group of women who, despite psychological support, often develop postpartum posttraumatic stress reactions.[88]

Perinatal care represents an area where there is clear potential to prevent or minimise posttraumatic stress reactions, as a considerable proportion of postpartum

79 Julia Martini and others, 'Posttraumatische Belastungsstörung (PTBS) in der Peripartalzeit: Bedingungsfaktoren, diagnostische Besonderheiten und Implikationen für Mutter und Kind' (Posttraumatic Stress Disorder (PTSD) in the Peripartal period: Conditional Factors, Diagnostic Features and Implications for Mother and Child) (2017) 11(4) Trauma und Gewalt 280; Weidner, Garthus-Niegel, and Junge-Hoffmeister (n 16).

80 Martini and others (n 79).

81 Ibid; Hilde Nerum and others, 'Maternal Request for Cesarean Section due to Fear of Birth: Can It Be Changed through Crisis-Oriented Counseling?' (2006) 33 Birth 221.

82 Susan Garthus-Niegel and others, 'The Influence of Women's Preferences and Actual Mode of Delivery on Post-Traumatic Stress Symptoms Following Childbirth: A Population-Based, Longitudinal Study' (2014) 14 BMC Pregnancy Childbirth 191; Martini and others (n 79).

83 Martini and others (n 79).

84 Ibid.

85 Nerum and others (n 81); H Rouhe and others, 'Obstetric Outcome after Intervention for Severe Fear of Childbirth in Nulliparous Women–Randomised Trial' (2013) 120 BJOG 75; Terhi Saisto and others, 'Therapeutic Group Psychoeducation and Relaxation in Treating Fear of Childbirth' (2006) 85 Acta Obstet Gynecol Scand 1315; Berit Sjögren, 'Fear of Childbirth and Psychosomatic Support. A Follow Up of 72 Women' (1998) 77 Acta Obstet Gynecol Scand 819.

86 Sjögren (n 85).

87 Rouhe and others (n 85).

88 Elsa Lena Ryding and others, 'An Evaluation of Midwives' Counseling of Pregnant Women in Fear of Childbirth' (2003) 82 Acta Obstet Gynecol Scand 10.

PTSD may be preventable if appropriate care and support is provided during labour and childbirth.[89] Given that perceived safety during childbirth appears to be a particularly important predictor of PTSD following childbirth,[90] sensitive and supportive management of events during the labour process may contribute to the woman's sense of control and positively influence their appraisals of these events. It is crucial that healthcare staff provide the labouring woman and her partner with as much information and choice as possible and that they are sensitive to the fact that even routine procedures during labour may be stressful and cause anxiety.[91] Even in emergency situations that are not life threatening or if medical procedures are unavoidable, maternity staff should provide reassurance.[92] Indeed, recent studies suggest that increasing psychological mindedness of the maternity service through specific perinatal mental health training may lead to a decrease in the onset of postpartum PTSD symptoms in the cared for women.[93]

To date, evidence-based interventions for women after traumatic childbirth are lacking,[94] particularly early interventions that could improve longer term outcomes for both the mother and the child.[95] A recent meta-analysis of trauma-focused psychological therapies (TFPTs) for PTSD following childbirth found evidence for the effectiveness of TFPTs for reducing PTSD symptoms in the short term (up to three months postpartum) and medium term (three to six months postpartum). However, the authors concluded a lack of robust evidence for the effectiveness of TFPT in improving women's recovery from clinically significant PTSD symptoms.[96]

An early intervention so far tested is expressive writing.[97] The evaluated intervention consisted of 20 minutes of expressive writing according to

---

89 Ayers and others (n 34); Horsch and Ayers (n 2).

90 King, McKenzie-McHarg, and Horsch (n 6).

91 Horsch and Ayers (n 2).

92 Ibid; King, McKenzie-McHarg, and Horsch (n 6).

93 King, McKenzie-McHarg, and Horsch (n 6); Kirstie McKenzie-McHarg and others, 'Think Pink! A Pink Sticker Alert System for Women with Psychological Distress or Vulnerability during Pregnancy' (2014) 22 BMJ 590; Richard J Shaw and others, 'Prevention of Postpartum Traumatic Stress in Mothers with Preterm Infants: Manual Development and Evaluation' (2013) 34 Issues Ment Health Nurs 578.

94 Maria Helena Bastos and others, 'Debriefing Interventions for the Prevention of Psychological Trauma in Women following Childbirth' (2015) 4 (CD007194) Cochrane Database Syst Rev, Cochrane Library; Lisanne F de Graaff and others, 'Preventing Post-Traumatic Stress Disorder Following Childbirth and Traumatic Birth Experiences: A Systematic Review' (2018) 97 Acta Obstet Gynecol Scand 648.

95 McKenzie-McHarg and others (n 11).

96 Marie Furuta and others, 'Effectiveness of Trauma-Focused Psychological Therapies for Treating Post-Traumatic Stress Disorder Symptoms in Women Following Childbirth: A Systematic Review and Meta-Analysis' (2018) 9 Front in Psychiatry 1.

97 P Di Blasio and others, 'The Effects of Expressive Writing on Postpartum Depression and Posttraumatic Stress Symptoms' (2015) 117(3) Psychol Rep 856; P Di Blasio and others, 'Emotional

Pennebaker's method,[98] noting down thoughts, expectations, and emotions related to the delivery (two or three days postpartum, respectively). This was compared to a control group of mothers who had to write about their daily activities in behavioural terms, not emotional ones. In both studies, mothers in the intervention group showed a significantly greater decrease in symptom load compared to the control group.[99] Similar encouraging results were found for mothers who had given birth to very premature babies who carried out expressive writing for 15 minutes during three consecutive days when their babies were three months old.[100]

Further, cognitive psychology research suggests that visual aspects of (traumatic) memory that underpin intrusions can be disrupted by actively engaging in visuospatial tasks, since these compete for resources with the brain's sensory-perceptual resources.[101] In a proof-of-principle randomised controlled study, intrusive traumatic memories after ECS were markedly reduced by a cognitive computerised intervention (ie playing the computer game Tetris for approximately 15 minutes during the first six hours following ECS), representing a first step in the development of an early intervention to prevent PTSD following childbirth.[102]

Even though research on prevention and intervention is preliminary, early treatment of PTSD following childbirth should be provided, given the negative impact also on the relationship with the partner and child, and the development of the child.

Several studies have looked at structured psychological interventions for women with postpartum PTSD but no standard intervention with proved effectiveness is available for women with postpartum PTSD.[103] In international

---

Distress Following Childbirth: An Intervention to Buffer Depressive and PTSD Symptoms' (2015) 11(2) EJOP 214.

98 J W Pennebaker, 'Expressive Writing in Psychological Science' (2018) 13(2) Perspect Psychol Sci 226.

99 Di Blasio and others, 'The Effects of Expressive Writing' (n 97); Di Blasio and others, 'Emotional Distress Following Childbirth' (n 97).

100 Horsch and others (n 1).

101 Jackie Andrade, David Kavanagh, and Alan Baddeley, 'Eye-Movements and Visual Imagery: A Working Memory Approach to the Treatment of Post-Traumatic Stress Disorder' (1997) 36 Br J Clin Psychol 209; A D Baddeley and J Andrade, 'Working Memory and the Vividness of Imagery' (2000) 129 J Exp Psychol Gen 126; Emily A Holmes and others, 'Can Playing the Computer Game "Tetris" Reduce the Build-Up of Flashbacks for Trauma? A Proposal from Cognitive Science' (2009) 4(1) PLOS ONE e4153; David J Kavanagh and others, 'Effects of Visuospatial Tasks on Desensitization to Emotive Memories' (2001) 40 Br J Clin Psychol 267.

102 Antje Horsch and others, 'Reducing Intrusive Traumatic Memories after Emergency Caesarean Section: A Proof-of-Principle Randomized Controlled Study' (2017) 94 Behav Res Ther 36.

103 Claire A I Stramrood and others, 'The Patient Observer: Eye-Movement Desensitization and Reprocessing for the Treatment of Posttraumatic Stress Following Childbirth' (2012) 39 Birth 70.

guidelines on the management of general PTSD, trauma-focused cognitive behavioural therapy and eye-movement desensitisation and reprocessing (EMDR) are recommended as the interventions of choice.[104] Initial results of studies investigating the effects in women who experienced the delivery as traumatic are promising,[105] but predominantly comprise case studies.[106] Hence, randomised controlled trials are needed in order to prove the effectiveness in this particular population as well.[107]

Bibliography

Allott H, 'Picking up the Pieces: The Post-Delivery Stress Clinic' (1996) 4 BJM 534

American Psychiatric Association, *Diagnostic and Statistical Manual of Mental Disorders* (4th edn, American Psychiatric Association 1994)

American Psychiatric Association, 'Practice Guidelines for the Treatment of Patients with Acute Stress Disorder and Posttraumatic Stress Disorder' (2004) <https://emdria.omeka.net/items/show/15786>

Andersen L B and others, 'Risk Factors for Developing Post-Traumatic Stress Disorder following Childbirth: A Systematic Review' (2012) 91 Acta Obstet Gynecol Scand 1261

Andrade J, Kavanagh D, and Baddeley A, 'Eye-Movements and Visual Imagery: A Working Memory Approach to the Treatment of Post-Traumatic Stress Disorder' (1997) 36 Br J Clin Psychol 209

Ayers S, 'Delivery as a Traumatic Event: Prevalence, Risk Factors, and Treatment for Postnatal Posttraumatic Stress Disorder' (2004) 47 Clin Obstet Gynecol 552

Ayers S and others, 'Post-Traumatic Stress Disorder following Childbirth: Current Issues and Recommendations for Future Research' (2008) 29 J Psychosom Obstet Gynaecol 240

Ayers S and others, 'The Aetiology of Post-Traumatic Stress following Childbirth: A Meta-Analysis and Theoretical Framework' (2016) 46 Psychol Med 1121

---

104 American Psychiatric Association, 'Practice Guidelines for the Treatment of Patients with Acute Stress Disorder and Posttraumatic Stress Disorder' (2004); National Collaborating Centre for Mental Health, *Post-Traumatic Stress Disorder: The Management of PTSD in Adults and Children in Primary and Secondary Care* (Gaskell 2005).

105 Susan Ayers, Kirstie McKenzie-McHarg, and Andrew Eagle, 'Cognitive Behaviour Therapy for Postnatal Post-Traumatic Stress Disorder: Case Studies' (2007) 28 J Psychosom Obstet Gynaecol 177; Leann K Lapp and others, 'Management of Post Traumatic Stress Disorder after Childbirth: A Review' (2010) 31 J Psychosom Obstet Gynaecol 113; Marianne Sandström and others, 'A Pilot Study of Eye Movement Desensitisation and Reprocessing Treatment (EMDR) for Post-Traumatic Stress after Childbirth' (2008) 24 Midwifery 62; Stramrood and others (n 103).

106 McKenzie-McHarg and others (n 11).

107 M A M Baas and others, 'The OptiMUM-Study: EMDR Therapy in Pregnant Women with Posttraumatic Stress Disorder after Previous Childbirth and Pregnant Women with Fear of Childbirth: Design of a Multicentre Randomized Controlled Trial' (2017) 8(1) Eur J Psychotraumatol; Astrid George and others, 'Effectiveness of Eye Movement Desensitization and Reprocessing Treatment in Post-Traumatic Stress Disorder after Childbirth: A Randomized Controlled Trial Protocol' (2013) 92 Acta Obstet Gynecol Scand 866; Martini and others (n 79).

Ayers S, Eagle A and Waring H, 'The Effects of Childbirth-Related Post-Traumatic Stress Disorder on Women and Their Relationships: A Qualitative Study' (2006) 11 Psychol Health Med 389

Ayers S, McKenzie-McHarg K, and Eagle A, 'Cognitive Behaviour Therapy for Postnatal Post-Traumatic Stress Disorder: Case Studies' (2007) 28 J Psychosom Obstet Gynaecol 177

Baas M A M and others, 'The OptiMUM-Study: EMDR Therapy in Pregnant Women with Posttraumatic Stress Disorder after Previous Childbirth and Pregnant Women with Fear of Childbirth: Design of a Multicentre Randomized Controlled Trial' (2017) 8(1) Eur J Psychotraumatol 1293315.

Baddeley A D and Andrade J, 'Working Memory and the Vividness of Imagery' (2000) 129 J Exp Psychol Gen 126

Bastos M H and others, 'Debriefing Interventions for the Prevention of Psychological Trauma in Women following Childbirth' (2015) 4(CD007194) Cochrane Database Syst Rev, Cochrane Library <https://www.cochranelibrary.com/cdsr/doi/10.1002/14651858.CD007194.pub2/abstract>

Bauer A and others, *The Costs of Perinatal Mental Health Problems* (Centre for Mental Health and London School of Economics 2014) <eprints.Lse.ac.uk/59885/> accessed 21 July 2019

Beck C T, 'Post-Traumatic Stress Disorder due to Childbirth: The Aftermath' (2004) 53(4) Nursing 216

Beck C T and Watson S, 'Subsequent Childbirth after a Previous Traumatic Birth' (2010) 59 Nurs Res 241

Bowers M E and Yehuda R, 'Intergenerational Transmission of Stress in Humans' (2016) 41 Neuropsychopharmacology 232

Brockington I, 'Postpartum Psychiatric Disorders' (2004) 363 The Lancet 303

Campbell J C, 'Health Consequences of Intimate Partner Violence' (2002) 359 The Lancet 1331

Choi K R and Seng J S, 'Predisposing and Precipitating Factors for Dissociation during Labor in a Cohort Study of Posttraumatic Stress Disorder and Childbearing Outcomes' (2016) 61 J Midwifery Womens Health 68

Cook N, Ayers S and Horsch A, 'Maternal Posttraumatic Stress Disorder during the Perinatal Period and Child Outcomes: A Systematic Review' (2018) 225 J Affect Disord 18

Creedy D K, Shochet I M and Horsfall J, 'Childbirth and the Development of Acute Trauma Symptoms: Incidence and Contributing Factors' (2000) 27 Birth 104

Czarnocka J and Slade P, 'Prevalence and Predictors of Post-Traumatic Stress Symptoms following Childbirth' (2000) 39 Br J Clin Psychol 35

De Graaff L F and others, 'Preventing Post-Traumatic Stress Disorder following Childbirth and Traumatic Birth Experiences: A Systematic Review' (2018) 97 Acta Obstet Gynecol Scand 648

Di Blasio P and others, 'Emotional Distress following Childbirth: An Intervention to Buffer Depressive and PTSD Symptoms' (2015) 11(2) EJOP 214

Di Blasio P and others, 'The Effects of Expressive Writing on Postpartum Depression and Posttraumatic Stress Symptoms' (2015) 117(3) Psychol Rep 856

Ehlers A and Clark D M, 'A Cognitive Model of Posttraumatic Stress Disorder' (2000) 38 Behav Res Ther 319

Fenech G and Thomson G, '"Tormented by Ghosts from Their Past": A Meta-Synthesis to Explore the Psychosocial Implications of a Traumatic Birth on Maternal Well-Being' (2014) 30 Midwifery 185

Ford E, Ayers S and Bradley R, 'Exploration of a Cognitive Model to Predict Post-Traumatic Stress Symptoms following Childbirth' (2010) 24 J Anxiety Disord 353

Frost J and others, 'Utopian Theory and the Discourse of Natural Birth' (2006) 4 Soc Theory Health 299

Furuta M and others, 'Effectiveness of Trauma-Focused Psychological Therapies for Treating Post-Traumatic Stress Disorder Symptoms in Women following Childbirth: A Systematic Review and Meta-Analysis' (2018) 9 Front in Psychiatry 1

Garthus-Niegel S and others, 'The Impact of Subjective Birth Experiences on Post-Traumatic Stress Symptoms: A Longitudinal Study' (2013) 16 Arch Womens Ment Health 1

Garthus-Niegel S and others, 'The Influence of Women's Preferences and Actual Mode of Delivery on Post-Traumatic Stress Symptoms following Childbirth: A Population-Based, Longitudinal Study' (2014) 14 BMC Pregnancy Childbirth 191

Garthus-Niegel S and others, 'The Role of Labor Pain and Overall Birth Experience in the Development of Posttraumatic Stress Symptoms: A Longitudinal Cohort Study' (2014) 41 Birth 108

Garthus-Niegel S and others, 'Maintaining Factors of Posttraumatic Stress Symptoms following Childbirth: A Population-Based, Two-Year Follow-up Study' (2015) 172 J Affect Disord 146

Garthus-Niegel S and others, 'The Impact of Postpartum Post-Traumatic Stress Disorder Symptoms on Child Development: A Population-Based, 2-Year Follow-up Study' (2017) 47 Psychol Med 161

Garthus-Niegel S and others, 'The Influence of Postpartum PTSD on Breastfeeding: A Longitudinal Population-Based Study' (2017) 54 Birth 193

Garthus-Niegel S and others, 'The Impact of Postpartum Posttraumatic Stress and Depression Symptoms on Couples' Relationship Satisfaction: A Population-Based Prospective Study' (2018) 9 Front Psychol 1

George A and others, 'Effectiveness of Eye Movement Desensitization and Reprocessing Treatment in Post-Traumatic Stress Disorder after Childbirth: A Randomized Controlled Trial Protocol' (2013) 92 Acta Obstet Gynecol Scand 866

Gottvall K and Waldenström U, 'Does a traumatic birth experience have an impact on future reproduction?' (2002) 109 BJOG 254

Grekin R and O'Hara M W, 'Prevalence and Risk Factors of Postpartum Posttraumatic Stress Disorder: A Meta-Analysis' (2014) 34 Clin Psychol Rev 389

Hofberg K and Brockington I, 'Tokophobia: An Unreasoning Dread of Childbirth. A Series of 26 Cases' (2000) 176 Br J Psychiatry 83

Holmes E A and others, 'Can Playing the Computer Game "Tetris" Reduce the Build-up of Flashbacks for Trauma? A Proposal from Cognitive Science' (2009) 4(1) PLOS ONE e4153

Horsch A and Ayers S, 'Childbirth and Stress' in Fink G (ed), *Stress: Concepts, Cognition, Emotion, and Behavior* (Academic Press 2016) 325

Horsch A and others, 'Improving Maternal Mental Health following Preterm Birth Using an Expressive Writing Intervention: A Randomized Controlled Trial' (2016) 5 Child Psychiatry Hum Dev 780

Horsch A and others, 'Reducing Intrusive Traumatic Memories after Emergency Caesarean Section: A Proof-of-Principle Randomized Controlled Study' (2017) 94 Behav Res Ther 36

Horsch A, Jacobs I, and McKenzie-McHarg K, 'Cognitive Predictors and Risk Factors of PTSD following Stillbirth: A Short-Term Longitudinal Study' (2015) 28 J Traum Stress 110

Kavanagh D J and others, 'Effects of Visuospatial Tasks on Desensitization to Emotive Memories' (2001) 40 Br J Clin Psychol 267

King L, McKenzie-McHarg K, and Horsch A, 'Testing a Cognitive Model to Predict Posttraumatic Stress Disorder following Childbirth' (2017) 17 BMC Pregnancy and Childbirth 32

Lapp L K and others, 'Management of Post Traumatic Stress Disorder after Childbirth: A Review' (2010) 31 J Psychosom Obstet Gynaecol 113

Lee C, Slade P, and Lygo V, 'The Influence of Psychological Debriefing on Emotional Adaptation in Women following Early Miscarriage: A Preliminary Study' (1996) 69 Br J Med Psychol 47

Lewis G (ed), *Saving Mothers' Lives: Reviewing Maternal Deaths to make Motherhood Safer 2003–2005* (The Seventh Report of Confidential Enquiries into Maternal and Child Health in the United Kingdom, CEMACH 2007)

Martini J and others, 'Posttraumatische Belastungsstörung (PTBS) in der Peripartalzeit: Bedingungsfaktoren, diagnostische Besonderheiten und Implikationen für Mutter und Kind' (Posttraumatic Stress Disorder (PTSD) in the Peripartal period: Conditional Factors, Diagnostic Features and Implications for Mother and Child) (2017) 11(4) Trauma und Gewalt 280

McKenzie-McHarg K and others, 'Think Pink! A Pink Sticker Alert System for Women with Psychological Distress or Vulnerability during Pregnancy' (2014) 22 BMJ 590

McKenzie-McHarg K and others, 'Post-Traumatic Stress Disorder following Childbirth: An Update of Current Issues and Recommendations for Future Research' (2015) 33 J Reprod Infant Psychol 219

Morina N and others, 'Remission from Post-Traumatic Stress Disorder in Adults: A Systematic Review and Meta-Analysis of Long Term Outcome Studies' (2014) 34 Clin Psychol Rev 249

Morland L and others, 'Posttraumatic Stress Disorder and Pregnancy Health: Preliminary Update and Implications' (2007) 48 Psychosomatics 304

National Collaborating Centre for Mental Health, *Post-Traumatic Stress Disorder: The Management of PTSD in Adults and Children in Primary and Secondary Care* (Gaskell 2005)

Nerum H and others, 'Maternal Request for Cesarean Section due to Fear of Birth: Can It Be Changed Through Crisis-Oriented Counseling?' (2006) 33 Birth 221

Nicholls K and Ayers S, 'Childbirth-Related Post-Traumatic Stress Disorder in Couples: A Qualitative Study' (2007) 12 Br J Health Psychol 491

Nilsson C, Bondas T and Lundgren I, 'Previous Birth Experience in Women with Intense Fear of Childbirth' (2010) 39 J Obstet Gynecol Neonatal Nurs 298

Olde E and others, 'Posttraumatic Stress following Childbirth: A Review' (2006) 26(1) Clin Psychol Rev 1

Parfitt Y M and Ayers S, 'The Effect of Post-Natal Symptoms of Post-Traumatic Stress and Depression on the Couple's Relationship and Parent-Baby Bond' (2009) 27 J Reprod Infant Psychol 127

Paykel E S, 'Life Events and Affective Disorders' (2003) 108 Acta Psychiatr Scand 61

Pennebaker J W, 'Expressive Writing in Psychological Science' (2018) 13(2) Perspect Psychol Sci 226

Rogal S and others, 'Effects of Posttraumatic Stress Disorder on Pregnancy Outcomes' (2007) 102 J Affect Disord 137

Rouhe H and others, 'Obstetric Outcome after Intervention for Severe Fear of Childbirth in Nulliparous Women–Randomised Trial' (2013) 120 BJOG 75

Ryding E L and others, 'An Evaluation of Midwives' Counseling of Pregnant Women in Fear of Childbirth' (2003) 82(1) Acta Obstet Gynecol Scand 10

Saisto T and others, 'Therapeutic Group Psychoeducation and Relaxation in Treating Fear of Childbirth' (2006) 85 Acta Obstet Gynecol Scand 1315

Sandström M and others, 'A Pilot Study of Eye Movement Desensitisation and Reprocessing Treatment (EMDR) for Post-Traumatic Stress after Childbirth' (2008) 24 Midwifery 62

Schechter D S and others, 'Subjective and Objective Measures of Parent-Child Relationship Dysfunction, Child Separation Distress, and Joint Attention' (2010) 73 Psychiatry 130

Seng J S and others, 'Posttraumatic Stress Disorder and Pregnancy Complications' (2001) 97 Obstet Gynecol 17

Shaw R J and others, 'The Relationship between Acute Stress Disorder and Posttraumatic Stress Disorder in the Neonatal Intensive Care Unit' (2009) 50 Psychosomatics 131

Shaw R J and others, 'Prevention of Postpartum Traumatic Stress in Mothers with Preterm Infants: Manual Development and Evaluation' (2013) 34 Issues Ment Health Nurs 578

Sjögren B, 'Fear of Childbirth and Psychosomatic Support. A Follow up of 72 Women' (1998) 77 Acta Obstet Gynecol Scand 819

Slade P, 'Towards a Conceptual Framework for Understanding Post-Traumatic Stress Symptoms following Childbirth and Implications for Further Research' (2006) 27 J Psychosom Obstet Gynaecol 99

Söderquist J, Wijma B, and Wijma K, 'The Longitudinal Course of Post-Traumatic Stress after Childbirth' (2006) 27 J Psychosom Obstet Gynaecol 113

Soet J E, Brack G A, and DiIorio C, 'Prevalence and Predictors of Women's Experience of Psychological Trauma during Childbirth' (2003) 30 Birth 36

Stramrood C A I and others, 'Posttraumatic Stress following Childbirth in Homelike- and Hospital Settings' (2011) 32 Psychosom Obstet Gynaecol 88

Stramrood C A I and others, 'The Patient Observer: Eye-Movement Desensitization and Reprocessing for the Treatment of Posttraumatic Stress following Childbirth' (2012) 39 Birth 70

Tedstone J E and Tarrier N, 'Posttraumatic Stress Disorder following Medical Illness and Treatment' (2003) 23 Clin Psychol Rev 409

Thomson G and Downe S, 'A Hero's Tale of Childbirth' (2013) 29 Midwifery 765

Vossbeck-Elsebusch A N, Freisfeld C and Ehring T, 'Predictors of Posttraumatic Stress Symptoms following Childbirth' (2014) 14 BMC Psychiatry 200

Weidner K, Garthus-Niegel S, and Junge-Hoffmeister J, 'Traumatische Geburtsverläufe: Erkennen und Vermeiden' (Traumatic Birth: Recognition and Prevention) (2018) Z Geburtshilfe Neonatol doi:10.1055/a-0641-6584

White T and others, 'Postnatal Depression and Post-Traumatic Stress after Childbirth: Prevalence, Course and Co-occurrence' (2006) 24 J Reprod Infant Psychol 107

Yildiz P L, Ayers S, and Phillips L, 'The Prevalence of Posttraumatic Stress Disorder in Pregnancy and After Birth: A Systematic Review and Meta-Analysis' (2017) 208 J Affect Disord 634

4 Identifying the wrong in obstetric violence

lessons from domestic abuse

Jonathan Herring

Introduction

In this chapter I seek to identify the wrongs of obstetric violence. I am not talking about the wrongs in obstetric violence which would be wrongs in any other context: such as the touching of a person without their consent or the use of force on someone without legal justifications. Rather, I want to explore the particular wrongs that arise in the context of obstetric violence which are over and above the kind of wrongs that would be recognised in any other context. What is it about an unwanted touching during birth that makes it different from an unwanted touching on another context? In other words, I seek an explanation for what is uniquely wrong with abuse in the context of obstetric violence.

In engaging in this discussion I use the literature on the wrongs of domestic violence as providing a framework. While these two topics may appear somewhat unconnected, I think the comparison is fruitful,[1] in part because domestic abuse has received considerable academic attention and there is already sophisticated analysis of it, thus providing a rich resource when seeking to build an analysis of obstetric violence. Another reason is that both domestic abuse and obstetric violence are powerful examples of how patriarchy uses violence to reinforce its expectations of how women ought to behave. They are also linked to conduct which may appear to be private under the traditional private/public distinction, but in fact have significant public ramifications. Exploring the particular wrongs in obstetric violence will help us understand the nature of the phenomenon and tailor appropriate legal and non-legal responses to it.

This chapter will explore three particular wrongs that are associated with domestic abuse, which I believe will provide insights into the wrongs of obstetric violence. First is the concept of coercive control. Second is the extent of breach of trust involved in obstetric violence. Third is the interaction with patriarchy. Before developing those I will start with a discussion of obstetric violence.

---

1 Sonya Charles, 'Obstetricians and Violence against Women' (2011) 11 Am J Bioeth 51 is the only other work where I have seen an extended comparison of these themes.

Obstetric violence

At a basic level obstetric violence can be described as behaviour during birth which involves abuse of women and/or a failure to show respect for women. In a much cited analysis in 2010 Bowser and Hill have divided obstetric violence into seven categories:

- physical abuse,
- non-consented care,
- non-confidential care,
- non-dignified care,
- discrimination based on patient attributes,
- abandonment of care, and
- detention in facilities.[2]

Notably, in 2015 Bohren and others suggested that it was better to replace the language of 'obstetric violence' with the terminology of 'obstetric mistreatment'.[3] They proposed an amendment to the following seven categories:

- physical abuse,
- sexual abuse,
- verbal abuse,
- stigma and discrimination,
- failure to meet professional standards of care,
- poor rapport between women and providers, and
- health system conditions and constraints.

This proposed shift in terminology (from violence to mistreatment) reflects a concern that engaging with professionals may be problematic if the terminology of violence is used. It also reflects a broader concern over the elasticity of the concept and concerns that it may be stretching violence beyond its natural meaning. However, most academic commentators have stuck with the language of obstetric violence. Chadwick argues powerfully in favour of this:

> There is ... consensus that obstetric violence includes both direct violence (physical, verbal, and sexual abuse), subtler forms of emotional violence (dehumanization, disrespect, non-dignified care), and structural violence (stigma, discrimination, and system deficiencies). Importantly, recent conceptualizations seek to name phenomena which are often not easily or normatively recognized as forms of violence (humiliation, shaming, dehumanized

---

2 Diana Bowser and Kathleen Hill, *Exploring Evidence for Disrespect and Abuse in Facility-Based Childbirth* (Harvard School of Public Health University Research Co 2010).
3 Meghan A Bohren and others, 'The Mistreatment of Women during Childbirth in Health Facilities Globally: A Mixed-Methods Systematic Review' (2015) 12(6) PLOS Med e1001847.

treatment) *as violence.* It is this very insistence that gives the concept of obstetric violence its disruptive and radical edge.[4]

The term is intended to be 'unexpected, jarring and provocative'[5] in part to catch attention, but also to counter the assumptions that childbirth must be a time of joy and medical intervention is in its nature beneficial. It seeks to capture the experiences of the women suffering it, rather than the language of the professionals.

Nevertheless, there is no denying that the concept is not concrete. Obstetric violence includes physical violence (hitting, slapping, kicking and pinching); use of gags and restraints; rough, frequent, and unnecessary vaginal examinations;[6] sexual assault;[7] verbal abuse (abusive language, judgmental comments); racial and ethnic minority discrimination; degrading and inhuman treatment; and denying treatment causing emotional harm. Few would deny that such practices are harmful[8] and an interference in human rights.[9] Sando and others in their review of studies on 'disrespect and abuse' during childbirth found prevalence rates ranging from 15 to 98 per cent.[10] This variance existed even though the very similar definitions were used in the surveys, which reflects the difficulty in producing a hard and fast definition. I argue, however, that this is appropriate. As will become clear in the chapter the nature of the wrongs of obstetric violence is such that it cannot be reduced to a list of set behaviours or the kind of 'tick box definition' that is beloved of surveys. It is in its nature personalised and involves heavily subjective elements. The difficulty in producing a survey-appropriate definition is a strength, not a weakness of the concept.

Obstetric violence has been recognised by national and international bodies. The World Health Organization has issued a statement on obstetric violence:

> Every woman has the right to the highest attainable standard of health, which includes the right to dignified, respectful health care throughout pregnancy and childbirth, as well as the right to be free from violence and discrimination. Abuse, neglect or disrespect during childbirth can amount

4 Rachelle Chadwick, 'Ambiguous Subjects: Obstetric Violence, Assemblage and South African Birth Narratives' (2017) 27 Fem Psychol 489, 492, emphasis in the original.

5 Lydia Zacher Dixon, 'Obstetrics in a Time of Violence: Mexican Midwives Critique Routine Hospital Practices' (2015) 29 Med Anthropol Q 437.

6 Umber Darilek, 'A Woman's Right to Dignified, Respectful Healthcare during Childbirth: A Review of the Literature on Obstetric Mistreatment, Issues in Mental Health' (2018) 39 Issues Ment Health Nurs 538.

7 Rajat Khosla and others, 'International Human Rights and the Mistreatment of Women during Childbirth' (2016) 18(2) Health Hum Rights 131.

8 Anand Grover, UN Special Rapporteur on the Right to the Highest Attainable Standard of Health (UN Doc No A/66/254 2011) para 17.

9 *C v Slovakia*, No 18968/07, 2012 European Court of Human Rights.

10 David Sando and others, 'Methods Used in Prevalence Studies of Disrespect and Abuse during Facility Based Childbirth: Lessons Learned' (2017) 14 Reprod Health 127.

to a violation of a woman's fundamental human rights … . In particular, pregnant women have a right to be equal in dignity, to be free to seek, receive and impart information, to be free from discrimination, to enjoy the highest attainable standard of physical and mental health, including sexual and reproductive health.[11]

The term was adopted by the Venezuelan legislature in 2007, Argentina in 2009 and Mexico in 2014. The Venezuelan law criminalises obstetric violence and under art 15 of the 'Organic Law on the Right of Women to a Life Free of Violence' it defines obstetric violence as:

The appropriation of the body and reproductive processes of women by health personnel, which is expressed as dehumanized treatment, an abuse of medication, and to convert the natural processes into pathological ones, bringing with it a loss of autonomy and the ability to decide freely about their bodies and sexuality, negatively impacting the quality of life of women.

Furthermore, art 51 specifies the acts that constitute obstetric violence including:

untimely and ineffective attention to obstetric emergencies; forcing the woman to give birth in a supine position; impeding early attachment of the child with his/her mother without a medical cause; altering the natural process of low-risk labour and birth using augmentation techniques; and performing caesarean sections when natural childbirth is possible, without obtaining the voluntary, expressed and informed consent of the woman.

In other jurisdictions the issue is not specifically addressed and receives little attention. There are several reasons for this. First, in many Western countries childbirth is said to be governed by 'individual choice' and so there is no scope for criticism about the way a woman has been treated as long as there is 'choice'. The emphasis on choice will be critiqued later in this chapter. Second, there is the common response: 'You have a healthy child, why are you complaining?'. The implication here is that a woman who has a healthy child is lucky. Given that many women have disabled children they should not be objecting to the birth procedures, especially if they are seen by healthcare professionals as necessary to ensure the safe delivery of the child. Indeed this may lead to women being reluctant to complain about how they were treated. Third, there is the simple point that many women are so overtaken with care of the new baby that their energy for mounting a formal complaint is limited.

I will now explore the three themes from the domestic abuse literature which I believe will be helpful in understanding obstetric violence: coercive control, breach of trust, and patriarchy.

---

11 World Health Organization, 'The Prevention and Elimination of Disrespect and Abuse during Facility-Based Childbirth' (2014) <http://apps.who.int/iris/bitstream/handle/10665/134588/WHO_RHR_14.23_eng.pdf?sequence=1> accessed 2 January 2019.

Obstetric violence as 'coercive control'

The concept of 'coercive control' has been developed to explain domestic abuse. Traditionally lawyers define crimes in terms of the injury done to the body. Does the defendant's act cause a cut or a bruise? Is it just an unwanted touching? This can lead to an assessment of whether the crime is one of a battery or an assault occasioning actual bodily harm. Yet, the assessment of the severity of the harm by focusing on the extent of bodily impact at the moment in time is a narrow construction of harm. This way of understanding legal wrongs does not capture the wider context of the relationship between the parties and of the broader social circumstances within which the act is done.[12] In this way the law can miss serious elements of the wrong. In the literature on domestic violence the concept of 'coercive control' has become significant. It seeks to understand violence, not simply as a series of violent or abusive acts, but rather as a program of 'coercive control'.[13]

Psychologist Dutton, writing in the context of domestic abuse, explains:

> Abusive behaviour does not occur as a series of discrete events. Although a set of discrete abusive incidents can typically be identified within an abusive relationship, an understanding of the dynamic of power and control within an intimate relationship goes beyond these discrete incidents. To negate the impact of the time period between discrete episodes of serious violence – a time period during which the woman may never know when the next incident will occur, and may continue to live with on-going psychological abuse – is to fail to recognize what some battered woman experience as a continuing 'state of siege'.[14]

The aim of this domestic abuse is to dominate the victim. By diminishing her sense of self-worth; restricting access to work, money and friends; and psychological manipulation the abuser seeks to render the victim utterly dependent on him. The programme of coercive control may involve violence, but that may be only one tool that is used.[15] Where it is used, or there is the threat of it, it is designed to ensure further compliance.

Another aspect of coercive control is that the victim can fail to recognise domestic abuse for what it is. Nicolson quotes from Connie, a victim of domestic abuse:

> At the time I didn't really know, I didn't recognise it for what it was because I mean it was things like not speaking to you, like nudging you and

---

12 Deborah Tuerkheimer, 'Recognizing and Remedying the Harm of Battering' (2004) 94 J Crim L & Criminology 959.
13 Evan Stark, *Coercive Control* (OUP 2007).
14 Mary Ann Dutton, 'Understanding Women's Response to Domestic Violence' (2003) 21 Hofstra L Rev 1191, 1204.
15 Orly Rachmilovitz, 'Bringing Down the Bedroom Walls: Emphasizing Substance Over Form in Personalized Abuse' (2007) 14 Wm & Mary J Women & L 495.

bumping into you and at one point he pulled my hair and pushed me over, things like that. I just thought that was sort of life a bit over zealous but I didn't really recognised it from the start off.[16]

Accounts explain that there tends to be a cycle of abuse whereby the victim may not be aware of the control that is being exercised. Where there is violence or verbal abuse the victim blames herself for what has happened. As Tadros argues: 'Domestic abuse is not just that the defendant denies the victim options, but also that he denies her the freedom to recognise and exploit the options that she has'.[17] A programme of coercive control is not just a single attack on the body of the victim. It is a challenge to her whole way of life, an attempt to rob her of her autonomy and her dignity.

I believe that this concept of coercive control is a helpful one to understand obstetric violence.[18] It makes it clear that the wrong is best understood not as a one off incident or set of incidents, but rather as an on-going relationship of control. It may be that an incident described with no context can appear relatively minor. However, when seen in the context of an on-going circumstance where control has been exercised over the woman this becomes all the more serious. Obstetric violence during birth should be seen in the context of an on-going relationship where the pregnant woman is controlled by authority figures. The strictures on behaviour during pregnancy, for example over diet, drinking alcohol, have already sought to severely limit her behaviour during the pregnancy. As Bristow claims:

> [T]here is something deeply unhealthy about a culture in which a pregnant woman is terrified of the effect of everything she does, and encouraged to conceive of herself as little more than a malfunctioning incubator ... . In recent years, the significant and necessary accommodations that pregnant women already make to the new life they are nurturing have been taken for granted, and now they are coerced into adhering to a set of rules that are about something else entirely.[19]

As Bristow argues, during pregnancy the woman is seen as uniquely responsible for the foetus and as its guardian. The message sent by a wide range of professional and social sources is clear: her own interests must take second place to those of the foetus. That message is reinforced in the extensive preparations, classes, tests and examinations prior to child's birth. Not only do these reinforce

---

16 Paula Nicolson, *Domestic Violence and Psychology: A Critical Perspective* (OUP 2010) 35.

17 Victor Tadros, 'The Distinctiveness of Domestic Abuse: A Freedom Based Account' (2005) 65 La L Rev 989, 999.

18 Charles (n 1).

19 Jennie Bristow, 'Policing Pregnancy Is Bad for Babies' (*Spiked*, 11 January 2016) <www.spiked-online.com/2016/01/11/policing-pregnancy-is-bad-for-babies/#.WkpcJzfLi70> accessed 14 December 2018.

the image of the sacrificial mother but also reinforce a message that others know better than the woman about birth and she needs advice and help to see her through the process. Hence women receive warnings from professionals, family members and passers-by about eating sushi, drinking coffee, exercising, drinking alcohol and lifting heavy packages.[20] These practices have received judicial recognition in the United States:

> [D]uring the period of gestation, almost all aspects of a woman's life may have an impact, for better or for worse, on her developing fetus. A fetus can be injured not only by physical force, but by the mother's exposure, unwitting or intentional, to chemicals and other substances, both dangerous and non dangerous, at home or in the workplace, or by the mother's voluntary ingestion of drugs, alcohol, or tobacco. A pregnant woman may place her fetus in danger by engaging in activities involving a risk of physical harm or by engaging in activities, such as most sports, that are generally not considered to be perilous. ... She also may endanger the well-being of her fetus by not following her physician's advice with respect to prenatal care or by exercising her constitutional right not to receive medical treatment.[21]

There is also the implied message that the woman may not be able to trust herself. She might give into the temptation to put her own interests above those of the foetus and must constantly be on her guard. This all undermines the woman's self-confidence. In light of this lack of respect, abuse, violence, high intervention rates during childbirth itself are simply a continuation of control exercised over the woman during the pregnancy.[22]

By the time it comes to birth, the woman has been taught to put her own interests behind those of the foetus; to obey the advice of the experts; and to trust her own feelings.[23] The irony is that women are particularly encouraged in Western countries to develop 'birth plans' that give them the expectation of being in control of the process. The continual pressure on what being a 'good mother' involves has become overwhelming. Verbal abuse received by women reflects and reinforces this pressure during childbirth. Jenkinson and others recorded women being called 'aggressive'; 'stupid'; 'crazy'; 'completely bonkers'; 'asking for trouble ... naught'; 'selfish'; 'ridiculous ... she's nuts'; 'control freak'.[24] These terms all draw on and reinforce the larger context of messages around pregnancy.

---

20 Dara E Purvis, 'The Rules of Maternity' (2017) 84 Tenn L Rev 367.

21 *Remy v MacDonald*, 801 N.E.2d 260, 263 (Mass 2004).

22 Michelle Sadler and others, 'Moving beyond Disrespect and Abuse: Addressing the Structural Dimensions of Obstetric Violence' (2016) 24(47) Reprod Health Matters 47.

23 Bec Jenkinson, Sue Kruske, and Sue Kildea, 'The Experiences of Women, Midwives and Obstetricians when Women Decline Recommended Maternity Care: A Feminist Thematic Analysis' (2017) 15 Midwifery 1.

24 Ibid.

There are of course some important differences between coercive control in the domestic abuse setting and obstetric violence setting. The control on obstetric violence comes from a range of sources and not a single abuser, as commonly occurs in domestic abuse. The motive of medical professionals is not obviously malevolent as it is in domestic abuse. Indeed Jenkinson and others found in their study that many doctors supported women's autonomy in birth, but had a 'line in the sand' which if crossed would justify intervention.[25] That would be where there was a threat to the well-being of the foetus by the woman's choice. The language of autonomy is a pretence. The concept of coercive control better captures the obstetric experience for all too many women.

Obstetric abuse as a breach of trust

The second particular wrong of domestic abuse which I wish to highlight is that it involves a grave breach of trust. This has been emphasised in the context of domestic abuse. Our intimate relationships are key to our identity.[26] Without those close to us to love us and to be loved by us our lives would have little meaning. It is through our caring and loving relationships that we flourish. Eekelaar has argued that trust is at the heart of the intimacy, which enables love and autonomy to develop.[27] It is in being able to be completely honest and vulnerable with a partner that relationships can deepen, an understanding of self can grow, and lives can flourish. But all of that requires a deep trust. In the case of domestic abuse, the access gained in the relationship to private information, bodies and spaces is misused against the victim. It is a profound breach of trust. It involves turning what should be a life-enhancing experience into a soul-destroying one.

I argue that this deep breach of trust is also part of obstetric violence. Birthing involves 'thick interpersonal trust'.[28] It involves giving access to physical, emotional and personal places one would not normally give access to. Birth is a highly intimate experience, which involves making public parts of the body most women choose not to make public, and in a context in which there is little control over who has access to those parts of the body or how they are viewed or dealt with.

Birth is also a highly emotional and significant time. For women who have given birth, for good or bad, it will be a highlight and a life-changing and dramatic event, which means that its understanding and form will be important for the identity and self-perception of woman concerned. She invests in the birth extraordinarily in personal, bodily, economic and emotional terms. Those around her at the time of birth have significant power to make it go well or make it go bad and share this enormous experience. The woman herself will have little

25 Ibid.
26 Jonathan Herring and Charles Foster, *Identity, Personhood and the Law* (Springer 2017).
27 John Eekelaar, *Family Law and Personal Life* (OUP 2006) 47.
28 Dmitry Khodyakov, 'Trust as a Process: A Three Dimensional Approach' (2007) 41 Sociology 116.

control over what happens. She trusts those around her to protect her interests and respect her wishes. Indeed, by informing them of any birth plan, a woman gives those around her the power to comply with the goals in birth or to choose to undermine them. In obstetric violence the access gained in birth is misused to render the birth, not an enriching uplifting one, but a self-destructive one.

The breach of trust in birth, where a woman's interests are ignored or she is mistreated or abused, causes a particular harm to the self. An intimate experience such as birth is central to our identity and sense of self. Where a birthing experience is used to send negative messages about us or degrade our sense of self, the harm is uniquely personal.[29] In the context of domestic abuse Stark writes:

> In the romantic vernacular, love and intimacy compensate women for their devaluation in the wider world. Personal life does something more. It provides the state where women practice their basic rights, garner the support needed to resist devaluation, experiment with sexual identities, and imagine themselves through various life projects. Coercive control subverts this process, brining discrimination home by reducing the discretion in everyday routines to near zero, freezing feeling and identity in time and space, the process victims experience as entrapment. Extended across the range of activities that define women as person, this foreshortening of subjective development compounds the particular liberty harms caused by coercive control.[30]

Oberman describes obstetric violence as a breach of fiduciary duty.[31] She explains that physicians breach this because they perceive the foetus as the second patient. Treating a patient in this way can mean, as Wolf puts it, that there is 'metaphysical violence'.[32] As she explains this can take various forms:

> Erasure of the being's self or identity-constituting aspects, denial that the being is a self or a legitimate entity with moral standing in the universe, preventing someone from doing what is needed to be a self or making it impossible for one to develop oneself, or an obfuscation of key aspects of oneself (or of things needed in order to connect to oneself or identify it).[33]

What is particularly painful is that these situations arise from the particular vulnerable position of the woman who has placed her trust in medical professionals, a trust that is often misused in obstetric violence.

---

29 Rachmilovitz (n 15).
30 Starks (n 13) 363.
31 Michelle Oberman, 'Mothers and Doctors' Orders: Unmasking the Doctor's Fiduciary Role in Maternal-Fetal Conflicts' (2000) 94 Nw UL Rev 451.
32 Allison B Wolf, 'Metaphysical Violence and Medicalized Childbirth' (2013) 27 Int J Appl Philos 101.
33 Ibid 102.

Obstetric violence and patriarchy

The third and final point is the relationship between obstetric violence and patriarchy. Much has been written on the definition of patriarchy and I will only sketch an outline of it.[34] Madden Dempsey defines patriarchy as 'A collection of social forms which constitute a structural inequality, whereby men hold systematic social power in society more generally'.[35]

Patriarchy is a range of forces that restrict the ability of women to access valuable resources and exercise their options. This can be through active misogyny (hatred of women) but can also be through a failure to value the work or characteristics of women. It can be expressed in a range of ways: from sex discrimination where barriers are put in place to social resources which favour men over women; to sex harassment in the street which discourages women from accessing public spaces; to a devaluing of care which is predominantly performed by women. It involves denying women access to resources they need to live valuable lives. Patriarchy works to restrict women to domestic spaces and deny them access to economic, material and public resources.

Returning to our analogy with domestic abuse there is much literature on the links between how domestic violence reinforces and relies upon power exercised by men over women in society more generally.[36] This is a two-way relationship: patriarchy enables and reinforces domestic abuse; and domestic abuse enables and reinforces patriarchy. As the Parliamentary Assembly, Council of Europe, Committee on Equal Opportunities for Women and Men puts it:

> Violence against women is a question of power, of the need to dominate and control. This in turn is rooted in the organization of society, itself based on inequality between the sexes. The meaning of this violence is clear: it is an attempt to maintain the unequal relationship between men and women and to perpetuate the subordination of women.[37]

Domestic violence reflects the negative attitudes and forces that women face in society. It also contributes to them. Madden Dempsey explains:

> [T]he patriarchal character of individual relationships cannot subsist without those relationships being situated within a broader patriarchal social structure. Patriarchy is, by its nature, a social structure – and thus any particular instance of patriarchy takes its substance and meaning from that social context. If patriarchy were entirely eliminated from society, then patriarchy

---

34 Sylvia Walby, *Theorizing Patriarchy* (OUP 1990).
35 Michelle Madden Dempsey, *Prosecuting Domestic Violence: A Philosophical Analysis* (OUP 2009) 136.
36 Stark (n 13) 363.
37 Parliamentary Assembly – Committee on Equal Opportunities for Women and Men, 'Domestic Violence' (Council of Europe 2002) para 12.

would not exist in domestic arrangements and thus domestic violence in its strong sense would not exist … . Moreover, if patriarchy were lessened in society generally then *ceteris paribus* patriarchy would be lessened in domestic relationship as well, thereby directly contributing to the project of ending domestic violence in its strong sense.[38]

The specific ways in which domestic abuse reinforces patriarchy include the following. Domestic abuse reinforces the messages sent more broadly by patriarchy that women should be subservient to men and are inferior to them. The Convention on the Elimination of All Forms of Discrimination against Women General Recommendation 19 states that domestic abuse is based on 'traditional attitudes by which women are regarded as subordinate to men'. Gender stereotypes typically underpin domestic abuse. The abuse often echoes the many societal messages that women's primary role is to care for their husbands and family. That women should try and meet the wishes of their spouses and children. Accounts of domestic abuse commonly involve behaviour which is designed not just to humiliate a partner, but to reinforce a particular role for women (eg as home maker) and a particular status (eg as lesser than men).[39] This echoes similar messages found in advertising, street harassment and the media.

Before exploring this further there is an obvious issue to address that many health professionals involved in obstetric services are women. Jewkes and others examining why in a South African context nurses abuse women write:

> Nurses are thus engaged in an unremitting struggle to claim a status and respect as a middle class profession within environments in which political, professional, historical and personal factors continuously undermine this claim. Nurses at a clinic level thus become embroiled in continuous struggles to assert a middle class identity through continuous striving to create social distance from patients. In this struggle, uniform and insignia (epaulettes), verbal assertions of distance, displays of lack of compassion and ultimately physical violence are all deployed.[40]

Patriarchy has worked to demean the role of women healthcare professionals and abuse can be understood as an attempt to regain control. These professionals retain patient inferiority to maintain their position of power in an environment that disempowers them (as Black women in South Africa).

I will argue that in the same way, obstetric violence should not be seen as simply inappropriate treatment by medical professionals but should be understood in the context of broader patriarchal forces. Obstetric violence is gender violence

---

38 Michelle Madden Dempsey, 'Towards a Feminist State: What Does "Effective" Prosecution of Domestic Violence Mean?' (2007) 70 MLR 908, 921.

39 Ibid.

40 Rachel Jewkes, Naeemah Abrahams, and Zodumo Mvo, 'Why Do Nurses Abuse Patients? Reflections from South African Obstetric Services' (1998) 47 Soc Sci Med 1781, 1793.

'directed at women because they are women'.[41] It reinforces and is reinforced by patriarchy. I will now identify some of the specific ways it does this.

Women subservient

First, obstetric violence reinforces messages sent more broadly by patriarchy that women should be subservient to men. We see this in the way that women are told to behave and be degraded if they fail to follow the medical professional's advice. A 'good mother' is compliant and obedient in the face of doctor's orders.

A good example of this is provided by a letter written by an American hospital to one mother recorded by Diaz-Tello:

> While we recognize that you have the right to consent to a Cesarean section, you have elected to refuse this procedure despite the advice of your treating physicians. This decision places both you and your unborn child at risk for death or serious injury. We will act in the best interests of you, your family, and your unborn child.[42]

The carefully worded letter notes the right to a caesarean section, but no right to refuse one. The woman is seen as posing a risk to the foetus, while the hospital is presented as the one who will ensure that child's interests are made paramount. The barely concealed threat is to use a caesarean section regardless of her wishes. We can see a similar point in cases where there is a threat to remove the child at birth as the mother has shown herself as an unsuitable mother due to her behaviour during childbirth.[43] Earlier I cited some of the terminology used against women who were not compliant to doctor's demands. Again this echoes the repeated messages of patriarchy that good women comply with male orders, or else ... .

Women as mothers

Second, obstetric violence reinforces the patriarchal idea that women have a particular role in life: as bearers of children and carers of children.[44] This is the message that is prayed and reinforced from the start of pregnancy in the birthing process. To ensure performance in this role women must put their own interests below those of children, or even foetuses. This image of the 'good mother' who is willing to sacrifice all to promote the interests of others echoes similar messages

41 Sara Cohen Shabot, 'Making Loud Bodies "Feminine": A Feminist-Phenomenological Analysis of Obstetric Violence' (2016) 39 Human Studies 231.
42 Farah Diaz-Tello, 'Invisible Wounds: Obstetric Violence in the United States' (2016) 24(47) Reprod Health Matters 56.
43 Ibid.
44 Ellen Reese, Ian Breckenridge-Jackson, and Julisa McCoy, 'Maternalist and Community Politics' in Holly J McCammon and others (eds), *The Oxford Handbook of US Women's Social Movement Activism* (OUP 2017).

found in advertising, street harassment and the media. Purvis explores this powerfully in her article 'The Rules of Maternity'.[45] She explains:

> Motherhood is all about judgment. Sometimes the judgment is external and positive, as motherhood is a respected status that is customarily rewarded with praise. Sometimes the judgment is internal and empowered, as mothers themselves exercise judgment as to when to become a mother, how to become a mother, where to give birth, what parenting philosophy to follow (if any), and what kind of parent to be.[46]

She goes on to explain not only how the regulation can be by open coercion and punishment for making unacceptable decisions but also the myriad of ways that make women doubt their own capacity. Thus 'Mothers cannot be trusted with autonomy'.[47]

So we have the dual messages promoted by patriarchy: that good women become mothers who will sacrifice all for their children, and that mothers cannot be trusted to fulfil their role properly. These messages are acted out, reinforced and reflected in obstetric violence.

Women's bodies

According to Cohen Shabot the process of birth is 'antithetical to the myth of femininity'.[48] It is noisy, sweaty, powerful, bloody, painful. Of course it is the myth of femininity that must be challenged here not birth, an entirely natural process, unlike much of what makes up so-called beauty and assumptions about the ideal feminine body. Cohen Shabot suggests that the abuse of women during labour can be a form of gender discipline, shock and outrage at the woman's body defying beauty norms, while engaging in what might be seen as a uniquely feminine act. The woman's body at its most powerful and creative, doing what a man's body cannot do, is challenging patriarchy. Cohen Shabot explains:

> I propose that the active, creative, powerful, open body in labor, which is not shy or weak but loud and almost irreverent at its core, is precisely the 'anti-feminine' body that has to be 'put in its place,' the threatening body that requires domestication by medical authorities. The violence performed against the birthing body is not only an expression of the general control and objectification characteristic of medical scenarios but specifically an action against a subversive, rebelling femininity, one that contests alienation, attempting to be one with its body, to feel at home within its embodied existence.[49]

---

45 Purvis (n 20).
46 Ibid 2.
47 Ibid 5.
48 Cohen Shabot (n 41) 245.
49 Ibid 243.

Birth challenges patriarchy's image of the feminine body as passive, commodified, designed for the male gaze, an image perpetuated through pornography. Here, in birthing, the female is active, powerful and creative, existing not for the male gaze. Obstetric violence can be seen then as an attempt by patriarchy to gain control over the female body and restore it to male control.[50] The same might be said of the phenomena of birth pornography, which is seen as an attempt to regain birth as sexual to the male gaze.[51] The link between sexuality and birth requires further consideration.

Sexuality

To take up the point just made, it is important to note how women through discussions about childbirth interact with sex. Malacrida and Boulton explain that:

> The idealized feminine body is expected to be blemish free, young, smooth, sexual, tight, and always available for heterosexual viewing and pleasure. Against this ideal form of feminine embodiment, it is not difficult to imagine how vaginal birthing can come to be seen as inappropriate because of the stretching and messiness of birth and because of an imagined problem of 'matter out of place', which can occur when a baby occupies a vaginal space normalized as solely appropriate to heteronormative sexual pleasure. In an ironic twist, given the current discursive and normative framing of the ideal feminine body as pure, clean, tight, and childlike, the process of vaginal birth can be seen as a violation of feminine purity.[52]

In their study of women's birth decisions it was surprising to Malacrida and Boulton how often heterosexual sex impacted women's birth decisions.[53] For example Melanie, a nursing student, said:

> I've seen C-sections and natural births and I don't want my husband seeing me in that situation; like, there's a lot of lost dignity [in] giving birth naturally. ... And if there's tearing it can be quite severe. ... I don't want my husband getting that sort of image, when I plan to still have a sexual life after I have children. ... And you're naked ... and lots of times stool is passed giving birth ... and I don't want my husband to be involved with that.[54]

---

50 Sadler (n 22).
51 Robyn Longhurst, 'A Pornography of Birth: Crossing Moral Boundaries' (2006) 5 ACME: An International Journal of Critical Geographies 209.
52 Claudia Malacrida and Tiffany Boulton, 'Women's Perceptions of Childbirth "Choices" Competing Discourses of Motherhood, Sexuality, and Selflessness' (2012) 26 Gend Soc 748, 751.
53 Ibid 761.
54 Ibid.

Concerns were expressed that after birth a vagina would be 'floppy' and that heterosexual intercourse after birth would be 'throwing a hot dog in a hallway'.[55] Another woman, Mackenzie, was considering a caesarean section rather than vaginal delivery because:

> If you've ever picked up any kind of men's magazine and read what they write ... well, you're not as attractive, you're not able to please your husband. ... I can imagine it would be very painful, and then afterwards you're not able to do the same things, and you're not as well appreciated.[56]

Malacrida and Boulton note that these concerns (on the impact of vaginal delivery on sex) relate to the pleasure men will receive from sex and women's own sexual appeal, rather than their own enjoyment of sexual relations. The sexual element is also reflected in the consideration of the links between rape and obstetric violence to which I now turn.

Rape

It is notable how obstetric violence is linked to rape in the literature. Sometimes the link is explicitly made. Cohen Shabot argues that 'The laboring experience also appears to be deeply sexual, one reason why obstetric violence is interpreted by some women as nothing less than rape'.[57] In other descriptions it is implicit such as where women complain the experience felt like being treated like a 'lump of meat', feelings of helplessness and alienation with echoes of some accounts of rape. For women who have been the victims of sexual assault the links are explicit. Richland quotes one woman:

> I had, without warning, been taken back to the scene of a crime – a rape. My daughter's birth contained all the elements of a rape. I was taken to a strange place and told what to do. My clothes and personal possessions were taken from me. I was forced into an uncomfortable position and bound. I was threatened (it's hospital policy, don't make trouble). I was drugged and knocked unconscious. I was sexually assaulted: My vagina was cut and a man's tool (forceps) was inserted into my body. I was robbed. That which was most precious to me, my baby, was taken from me. All this was done against my will. Like most rape victims, I dried my tears, stuffed my pain and proceeded to get on with my life. Like many rape victims, I didn't report the crime nor did I seek help. I also didn't have a clue how profoundly or for how long these acts of violence would affect my life.[58]

---

55 Ibid 764.
56 Ibid 764–65.
57 Cohen Shabot (n 41) 233.
58 Shea Richland, 'Birth Rape: Another Midwife's Story' (2008) 85 Midwifery Today 2.

Darilek reports the account of another woman:

> [M]y cervix was manually dilated forcefully after pleading for the doctor to stop. This caused me to re-experience a previous rape. Later in my birth my doctor performed a deep episiotomy after being told repeatedly that I did not want one … Images and fears from my past sexual abuse/ assaults became constant in my mind after birth.[59]

Choice under patriarchy

As mentioned earlier most official publications and many ethical declarations place weight on the principle of autonomy. In short the patient gets to decide what happens during the pregnancy. Many Western legal systems uphold this principle, providing the patient freedom that he or she has the capacity to consent.

There are straightforward cases where women's autonomy is limited and any consent must be of questionable validity. One woman recorded by Jenkinson, Kruske and Kildea described what must be a common experience:

> They [were] making all of these decisions for me … I should have asked to hop up and walk around for a while, take five minutes … re-check the baby. But instead I just agreed to be rushed off for an emergency caesarean which … probably wasn't necessary.[60]

Their study found other cases where women were misinformed and badgering with requests. Perhaps the most obvious interference is by not offering alternatives. The Supreme Court in the United Kingdom recently heard a case where a doctor determined that caesarean section should not be offered and did not propose it as an option.[61] Lady Hale was particularly critical of the doctor's approach because it involved the doctor using his or her values to make decisions when it was a decision for the patient:

> A patient is entitled to take into account her own values, her own assessment of the comparative merits of giving birth in the 'natural' and traditional way and of giving birth by caesarean section, whatever medical opinion may say, alongside the medical evaluation of the risks to herself and her baby. She may place great value on giving birth in the natural way and be prepared to take the risks to herself and her baby which this entails. The medical profession must respect her choice, unless she lacks the legal capacity to decide.[62]

---

59 Darilek (n 6) 539.
60 Jenkinson (n 23) 5.
61 *Montgomery v Lanarkshire Health Board* [2015] UKSC 11 [2015] AC 1430 [115].
62 Ibid.

More problematic is where there is no overt manipulation of these kinds, but the decision reached by the woman in the context of patriarchy is complex.[63] Indeed it can all too easily become a justification for abusive practices.[64] Patriarchy can claim to be reinforced because that is what women want. That is the ultimate success of patriarchy.

The problem is, as already identified in this chapter, that there are a wide range of pressures that impact on the 'choices' made: the assumptions about motherhood; the perception of birth as an event of risk; idealisations of femininity; self-confidence which mean that we cannot be users whether choices reflect an authentic choice or not.[65] The complex pressures and power relations mean that subtle and overt pressures compromise choice in the childbirth context.[66] As McAra-Couper and others put it:

> It became clear that women's choices were strongly influenced and determined by social change, by the gendering of women, and by values such as control, predictability, convenience, the 'quick fix' and the normalization of surgery. We argue that the prevailing notion of 'informed' choice obscures the structural and social influences on 'choice'.[67]

This issue is of broader significance and a major theme of debate among feminists. Of course, the danger is, the more impact of patriarchy on women's choices is emphasised, the greater the danger that woman's voices will be discounted and, ironically, paternalism increases.[68] Or there is the danger that other discriminations between women being made, with only the autonomy of educated, 'aware' women being protected. This is apparent in the following suggestion:

> Unless women are aware of the sexist underpinnings of medicine and the increasing normalization of 'surgical childbirth', it is impossible for them to make an informed choice.[69]

---

63 Diaz-Tello (n 42).
64 Donna Cherniaka and Jane Fisher, 'Explaining Obstetric Interventionism: Technical Skills, Common Conceptualisations, or Collective Countertrans-Ference?' (2008) 31 Women's Stud Int Forum 270.
65 Katherine Beckett, 'Choosing Cesarean: Feminism and the Politics of Childbirth in the United States' (2005) 6 Fem Theory 251.
66 Heather A Cahill, 'Male Appropriation and Medicalization of Childbirth: An Historical Analysis' (2008) 33 J Adv Nurs 334.
67 Judith McAra-Couper, Marion Jones, and Liz Smythe, 'Caesarean-Section, My Body, My Choice: The Construction of "Informed Choice" in Relation to Intervention in Childbirth' (2017) 22 Fem Psychol 81.
68 Claudia Malacrida, 'Always, Already-Medicalized: Women's Prenatal Knowledge and Choice in Two Canadian Contexts' (2015) 63 Curr Sociol 636.
69 McAra-Couper (n 67) 84.

This discussion addresses the question raised by Abrams, which is why there is so little disagreement between women and their doctors.[70] As she notes, despite the literature on obstetric violence, it is surprising how in few cases there seems disputes between physicians and doctors. She acknowledges that doctors commonly prioritise the interest of the foetus, but this is agreed with by women. As she notes the problem is not so much as one of breach of autonomy, but that women have come to accept this automatic and overwhelming prioritising. The consequence of this is that the women agree to wide range of interventions and acceptance that her role is, as foetal incubator to do all to ensure a healthy birth, whatever the personal costs. Worse is that if there is not the 'perfect birth' she has failed in her responsibility and it is she who carries the blame not the physicians.

The solution is not to abandon listening to women but to challenge the wider social forces that impact on women's assumptions and expectations during pregnancy. Another point is to ensure women are informed of alternative understandings and to provide them with friends and support to navigate these decisions. At their best midwives are well positioned to perform this role and there is no doubt that some take that on.

Intersectionality

Of course, although I have been focusing on patriarchy, obstetric violence can reflect the interaction between disadvantage and assumptions based not only on sex but also on race, class and age; and intersections between them. A study of obstetric violence in India, for example, found poor and indigenous women being particularly subject to violence and abuse.[71] It being assumed they lacked the intelligence to make decisions or to complain about their treatment. It would be wrong to assume that it is only patriarchy which is at work here. Obstetric violence can reflect racial-, class- and age-based assumptions. It involves multiple axes of social disadvantage. For instance, in Mexico, an ethnic Mazatec woman was denied medical attention and had to give birth on a lawn in front of the health centre in Oaxaca.[72] Intersectionality is explored further in the chapter by Rachelle Chadwick.

Conclusion

This chapter has sought to identify what are the particular wrongs at the heart of obstetric violence that make it different from violence in other settings. It has used some of the writing on domestic abuse to identify three

---

70 Jamie R Abrams, 'The Illusion of Autonomy in Women's Medical Decision-Making' (2014) 42 Fla St U L Rev 1.
71 Sreeparna Chattopadhyay, Arima Mishra, and Suraj Jacob, '"Safe", Yet Violent? Women's Experiences with Obstetric Violence during Hospital Births in Rural Northeast India' (2017) 15 Cult Health Sex 1.
72 Chadwick (n 4).

characteristics of obstetric violence that generate its particular wrongfulness. First, it should be understood as a programme of coercive control of women. This means that acts of violence in the obstetric context cannot be understood in isolation but must be examined in their broader context and part of a broader control of women through pregnancy and childbirth. Second, it has been argued that obstetric violence is a breach of trust, meaning that an experience that should lead to human flourishing for the woman is turned against her. Third, obstetric violence is a reflection of patriarchy. Obstetric violence reflects and reinforces a range of patriarchal attitudes and forces such as women should be subservient, women's primary role is as mothers, and women's bodies must live up to an ideal designed of the heterosexual male gaze and for heterosexual intercourse. An understanding of these aspects of the wrongs of obstetric violence assists in understanding its nature and power. Also, a very urgent response to this issue is called for. However, the depth of the endemic forces that underpin obstetric violence is also highlighted, meaning it is all the harder to combat.

Table of cases

Remy v MacDonald, 801 NE2d 260, 263 (Mass 2004)
C v Slovakia, No 18968/07, 2012 European Court of Human Rights
Montgomery v Lanarkshire Health Board [2015] UKSC 11 [2015] AC 1430

Bibliography

Abrams J R, 'The Illusion of Autonomy in Women's Medical Decision-Making' (2014) 42 Fla St U L Rev 1

Beckett K, 'Choosing Cesarean: Feminism and the Politics of Childbirth in the United States' (2005) 6 Fem Theory 251

Bohren M A and others, 'The Mistreatment of Women during Childbirth in Health Facilities Globally: A Mixed-Methods Systematic Review' (2015) 12(6) PLOS Med e1001847

Bowser D and Hill K, *Exploring Evidence for Disrespect and Abuse in Facility-Based Childbirth* (Harvard School of Public Health University Research Co 2010)

Cahill H A, 'Male Appropriation and Medicalization of Childbirth: An Historical Analysis' (2008) 33 J Adv Nurs 334

Chadwick R, 'Ambiguous Subjects: Obstetric Violence, Assemblage and South African Birth Narratives' (2017) 27 Fem Psychol 489

Charles S, 'Obstetricians and Violence against Women' (2011) 11 Am J Bioeth 51

Chattopadhyay S, Mishra A and Jacob S, '"Safe", Yet Violent? Women's Experiences with Obstetric Violence during Hospital Births in Rural Northeast India' (2017) 15 Cult Health Sex 1

Cherniaka D and Fisherb J, 'Explaining Obstetric Interventionism: Technical Skills, Common Conceptualisations, or Collective Countertrans-Ference?' (2008) 31 Women's Stud Int Forum 270

Cohen Shabot S, 'Making Loud Bodies "Feminine": A Feminist-Phenomenological Analysis of Obstetric Violence' (2016) 39 Human Studies 231

Darilek U, 'A Woman's Right to Dignified, Respectful Healthcare during Childbirth: A Review of the Literature on Obstetric Mistreatment, Issues in Mental Health' (2018) 39 Ment Health Nurs 538

Dempsey M M, 'Towards a Feminist State: What Does "Effective" Prosecution of Domestic Violence Mean?' (2007) 70 MLR 908

Dempsey M M, *Prosecuting Domestic Violence: A Philosophical Analysis* (OUP 2009)

Diaz-Tello F, 'Invisible Wounds: Obstetric Violence in the United States' (2016) 24(47) Reprod Health Matters 47

Dixon Z, 'Obstetrics in a Time of Violence: Mexican Midwives Critique Routine Hospital Practices' (2015) 29 Med Anthropol Q 437

Dutton M A, 'Understanding Women's Response to Domestic Violence' (2003) 21 Hofstra L Rev 1191

Eekelaar J, *Family Law and Personal Life* (OUP 2006)

Grover A, UN Special Rapporteur on the Right to the Highest Attainable Standard of Health, UN Doc No A/66/254 (2011)

Herring J and Foster C, *Identity, Personhood and the Law* (Springer 2017)

Jenkinson B, Kruske S and Kildea S, 'The Experiences of Women, Midwives and Obstetricians When Women Decline Recommended Maternity Care: A Feminist Thematic Analysis' (2017) 15 Midwifery 1

Jewkes R, Abrahams N and Mvo Z, 'Why Do Nurses Abuse Patients? Reflections from South African Obstetric Services' (1998) 47 Soc Sci Med 1781

Khodyakov D, 'Trust as a Process: A Three Dimensional Approach' (2007) 41 Sociology 116

Khosla R and others, 'International Human Rights and the Mistreatment of Women during Childbirth' (2016) 18(2) Health Hum Rights 131

Longhurst R, 'A Pornography of Birth: Crossing Moral Boundaries' (2006) 5 ACME: An International Journal of Critical Geographies 209

Malacrida C, 'Always, Already-Medicalized: Women's Prenatal Knowledge and Choice in Two Canadian Contexts' (2015) 63 Curr Sociol 636.

Malacrida C and Boulton T, 'Women's Perceptions of Childbirth "Choices" Competing Discourses of Motherhood, Sexuality, and Selflessness' (2012) 26 Gend Soc 748

McAra-Couper J, Jones M, and Smythe L, 'Caesarean-Section, My Body, My Choice: The Construction of "Informed Choice" in Relation to Intervention in Childbirth' (2017) 22 Fem Psychol 81

Nicolson P, *Domestic Violence and Psychology* (OUP 2010)

Oberman M, 'Mothers and Doctors' Orders: Unmasking the Doctor's Fiduciary Role in Maternal-Fetal Conflicts' (2000) 94 Nw UL Rev 451

Parliamentary Assembly – Committee on Equal Opportunities for Women and Men, *Domestic Violence* (Council of Europe 2002)

Purvis D E, 'The Rules of Maternity' (2017) 84 Tenn L Rev 367

Rachmilovitz O, 'Bringing Down the Bedroom Walls: Emphasizing Substance Over Form in Personalized Abuse' (2007) 14 Wm & Mary J Women & L 495

Reese E, Breckenridge-Jackson I, and McCoy J, 'Maternalist and Community Politics' in McCammon H J and others (eds), *The Oxford Handbook of US Women's Social Movement Activism* (OUP 2017)

Richland S, 'Birth Rape: Another Midwife's Story' (2008) 85 Midwifery Today 2

Sadler M and others, 'Moving Beyond Disrespect and Abuse: Addressing the Structural Dimensions of Obstetric Violence' (2016) 24(47) Reprod Health Matters 47

Sando D and others, 'Methods Used in Prevalence Studies of Disrespect and Abuse during Facility Based Childbirth: Lessons Learned' (2017) 14 Reprod Health 127

Stark E, *Coercive Control* (OUP 2007)

Tadros V, 'The Distinctiveness of Domestic Abuse: A Freedom Based Account' (2005) 65 La L Rev 989

Tuerkheimer D, 'Recognizing and Remedying the Harm of Battering' (2004) 94 J Crim L & Criminology 959

Walby S, *Theorizing Patriarchy* (OUP 1990)

Wolf A B, 'Metaphysical Violence and Medicalized Childbirth' (2013) 27 Int J Appl Philos 101

World Health Organization, 'The Prevention and Elimination of Disrespect and Abuse during Facility-Based Childbirth' (2014)

5 Midwives and midwifery

The need for courage to reclaim vocation for respectful care

Soo Downe and Nancy Stone

Introduction

> [We are] trading the ease of the machine for the grace of our souls ... nothing will change if we cherish our fear as a blessing. If we are afraid to tear down the old and lose what we may in that unmaking, we will never build the new.[1]

Childbirth is a time of intense experiences, with the potential for profound achievement, and positive transformation. It is a liminal space that, for most women, only requires guardianship and support rather than intensive clinical surveillance and treatment. The midwifery professional project aligns itself, rhetorically, with childbearing women. In this narrative, what midwives do is always led by what women want and need. However, this assumption is regularly disrupted in practice. Challenges can come from neoliberal employing organizations that are focused on profit and/or on the benefits of standardisation; from the constraints of shift working and of surveillance cultures that marginalise therapeutic touch and intuitive interaction; and from the modernist project that interprets the state of 'being with child' through the lens of machine imaging and computerised record keeping. In low-income countries, challenges come from extreme workloads, the need to prioritise the most acutely ill women and babies, leaving other women to labour and give birth alone, staff being underpaid (or not paid at all), long and unsafe travel distances for pregnant and labouring women, and structural and domestic power imbalances.

The social shift towards the super-valuation of technocracy is evident in the widespread use of personal devices to record and report back to us our physical and even psychological well-being. As our trust in the output of these machines increases, we perceive our own embodied sensations to be increasingly less reliable. This turn increases maternal acceptance of surveillance by machine and monitor in pregnancy and labour, creating both physical and emotional distance between labouring women and attending midwives. Ultimately, increasing dependence by both women and midwives on technology and medical

---

1 Jay Kristoff, *Kinslayer* (Pan Macmillan 2013) 131.

interventions in pregnancy, labour and birth is a social move that directly challenges midwifery expertise in physiological processes and outcomes, and that creates increasing distance between labouring women and midwives, raising questions about how far the midwifery philosophy can be sustained in some settings.

One consequence is the potential for some midwives to become divorced from their vocational roots through the pursuit of a professionalising agenda that is more aligned with neoliberal health policy and practice than with childbearing women. This has been expressed as midwives being 'with institution'[2] rather than being 'with woman', or 'compliance'.[3] The consequence is a disruption of the claim midwives make of being aligned with women, and the subsequent potential for traumatic relations and disrespectful behaviours between midwives and women. The Lancet Series on Midwifery[4] made a clear separation between midwives (the professional group) and midwifery (the philosophy of being with women), noting that not all midwives do midwifery. However, the Series did point out that where midwives do midwifery, especially where this is integrated in functioning maternity care systems with respectful, effective relationships with other care providers such as obstetricians, the quality and outcomes of care are likely to be optimal. Indeed, this very point was made more than two decades ago by Louden in his sociological analysis of maternal mortality in Europe between 1800 and 1950.[5]

Where care is not optimal, the use of shocking statistics can be a wake-up call. In many settings, the term obstetric violence, and the activities and behaviours that it surfaces, has had the effect of raising awareness about disrespectful and non-consented maternity care, especially at the political level. However, this specific terminology can have the paradoxical effect of making midwives feel that violence and abuse are not their problem, especially if they work in countries where 'obstetric' only means what doctors do. If midwives in search of professional power align themselves with institutional and modernist imperatives of standardisation, control and extreme risk aversion, especially where this is strongly focused on the baby alone, women become invisible to them. Once someone is invisible, they can be 'othered', ignored and mistreated.[6] On the other hand, where midwives actively engage with women as part of their vocation to optimise safety and positive well-being of both mother and baby, they can catalyse transformative experiences that resonate throughout women's lives,

2 Billie Hunter, 'Conflicting Ideologies as a Source of Emotion Work' (2004) 20 Midwifery 261.

3 Rhona O'Connell and Soo Downe, 'A Metasynthesis of Midwives' Experience of Hospital Practice in Publicly Funded Settings: Compliance, Resistance and Authenticity' (2009) 13 Health 589.

4 Mary J Renfrew and others, 'Midwifery and Quality Care: Findings from a New Evidence-Informed Maternity Care Framework' (2014) 384 The Lancet 1129.

5 Irvine Loudon, *Death in Childbirth: An International Study of Maternal Care and Maternal Mortality 1800–1950* (Clarendon Press 1994) 1.

6 Michal Krumer-Nevo, 'The Arena of Othering: A Narrative Study with Women Living in Poverty and Social Marginality' (2002) 1 Qual Soc Work 303.

and those of their families, for years to come.[7] Midwives can, therefore, be both the solution and the problem.

This chapter will address the earlier issues, in an exploration of how the increasing gap between the midwifery vocation and the midwife profession is played out in women's experiences of traumatic or transformative care throughout the childbearing episode. It will also explore the role of midwives doing or not doing midwifery in women's experiences of violence or harm, or joy and strength, in the context of horizontal or vertical power and control as it operates in institutional settings. The analysis includes consideration of what this means for midwives, other maternity care workers and, critically, for childbearing women themselves.

Siting the issues

The feminist critiques from Simone de Beauvoir in 1949 to Germaine Greer in the 1970s were catalytic in illustrating the fundamental power disparities between men and women in all levels of society.[8] Although feminism as a movement is multi-layered, and, in some cases, splintered, the fundamental mission of gender equality is critical for any analysis of the impact of gender in healthcare. There is a particular resonance for maternity care, since all those having babies are female (or, for transgender people, physiologically female at the time of pregnancy and childbirth). The majority of immediate maternity caregivers are also female. Doctors have been traditionally male. Based on this, binary claims are commonly made about the gendered nature of power and submissiveness in relation to the position of midwives, obstetricians and childbearing women. The first text to address this directly was probably that of Jane Sharp, written in 1671,[9] and it is from this that the notion of meddlesome midwifery by man midwives has been taken forward. Many authors have explored the way in which female midwifery power (allied with women as those bearing children) has been usurped by (antagonistic) male power, based on a Cartesian duality which opposes male and female, midwife and doctor, humanistic ways of doing birth with technocratic or, even more essentialist, medical ways of doing birth, where 'medical' is seen as a negative phenomenon. This is then interpreted as an example of the general power of the patriarchy, with midwives and women being aligned as victims, together against the system, and particularly in opposition to the male medical gaze. In this analysis, the growing concern with disrespect and abuse in

---

7 Rachel Reed, Rachael Sharman, and Christian Inglis, 'Women's Descriptions of Childbirth Trauma Relating to Care Provider Actions and Interactions' (2017) 17 BMC Pregnancy Childbirth 1; Annika Karlström, Astrid Nystedt, and Ingegerd Hildingsson, 'The Meaning of a Very Positive Birth Experience: Focus Groups Discussions with Women' (2015) 15 BMC Pregnancy Childbirth 251.

8 Simone de Beauvoir, *The Second Sex* (Knopf 1953); Germaine Greer, *The Female Eunuch* (McGraw-Hill 1970).

9 Jane Sharp, *The Midwives Book: Or the Whole Art of Midwifery Discovered* (Elaine Hobby ed, OUP 1999).

maternity care has coalesced around the term 'obstetric violence', as discussed in other volumes in this book. While this term is not used to mean that every (male) obstetrician is violent, or that violence in maternity care is only restricted to obstetrics, the direction of travel of much of the literature in this field is that obstetric violence is a male patriarchal outworking of misogyny against (female) midwives and women. Indeed, the current Wikipedia entry for violence against women cites the UN definition of such violence as 'violence against women is a manifestation of historically unequal power relations between men and women' and 'violence against women is one of the crucial social mechanisms by which women are forced into a subordinate position compared with men', and includes obstetric violence in the list of examples.[10] Some of these analyses are useful in identifying and challenging damaging taken-for-granted power divisions, but they can result in essentialist rhetoric that hides some much more nuanced realities on the ground.

The direct challenge to essentialist claims about the gendered roots of disrespectful maternity care comes from current studies in the area. Most of these have been undertaken in low- or middle-income countries, where an increasing percentage (and in some countries and settings a majority) of obstetricians are women, and a relatively high percentage of midwives and nurses working in maternity care are men. The data seem to suggest that, in contrast to some of the prior assumptions, women are more likely to report abuse at the hands of female professional caregivers (nurses or midwives) than from male professional care providers (nurses, midwives or doctors) or from other providers such as the (non-professional, vocational) traditional birth attendants (TBAs) or dayas. For example, 'On certain days she [the midwife] is so rude'; '[i]f I want to talk about something, I fear approaching her, although she could advise me'.[11] Further,

> The descriptions of the midwifery staff given by women included 'silly', 'rude', 'ridiculous', 'unhuman', 'not caring', and 'not kind'. They were said to speak to patients as if 'talking to a child', and patients reported that 'nobody showed any kindness'. This was particularly important to patients as they described labour and delivery as times of great 'anxiety' and 'worry' and time that were very 'difficult' (an expression of pain).[12]
>
> The hospital is not where you go always, so you have to keep going to know the place very well and even get to know the nurses very well. You know nurses are very wicked, you doctors are better and very caring.[13]

10 Wikipedia, 'Violence against Women' (16 February 2019) <https://en.wikipedia.org/wiki/Violence_against_women> accessed 22 February 2019.

11 Paul Conrad and others, 'Antenatal Care Services in Rural Uganda: Missed Opportunities for Good-Quality Care' (2012) 22 Qual Health Res 619, 624, 625.

12 Naeemah Abrahams, Rachel Jewkes, and Zodumo Mvo, 'Health Care-Seeking Practices of Pregnant Women and the Role of the Midwife in Cape Town, South Africa' (2001) 46 J Midwifery Womens Health 240.

13 O U Umeora and others, 'Implementing the New WHO Antenatal Care Model: Voices from End Users in a Rural Nigerian Community' (2008) 11 Niger J Clin Pract 260, 262.

We return to the earlier quote below.

One of the most prevalent explanations of this kind of finding is that male power has created technocratic systems in which childbearing women and midwives are subservient and subject to abuse, and that, in order to obtain positions of power within the system, or to be legitimised, female obstetricians (and nurses and midwives) must behave in the same way as their male counterparts, or even more aggressively. It could also be, simply, that childbearing women are more likely to encounter female midwives and nurses as their immediate care providers, and so are more likely to report disrespect and abuse from these caregivers.

There is some empirical evidence that structural patriarchy might explain the paradox (from the perspective of the midwifery professional project) of abuse from female maternity caregivers, as is evident in other chapters in this book. Indeed, the recent report by the International Confederation of Midwives (ICM), the World Health Organization (WHO) and the White Ribbon Alliance, 'Midwives' Voices, Midwives' Realities' showed how such factors are the everyday backdrop to the lives of midwives in many parts of the world.[14] But there are also indications that while action on these issues is necessary to move midwifery and maternity care into a space where practice is always genuinely aligned with women, it is not sufficient to do so in and of itself. Self-critique is also needed to ensure that midwives authentically work in collaboration with other stakeholders in the system, in genuine alignment with childbearing women. This is essential to ensure that women, babies, families and communities can expect and receive optimal maternity care to ensure that their experience is a positive, safe and life transforming one, and where all care providers actively enjoy their job, with the ultimate aim of long-term human flourishing.

Profession and vocation

There are a range of definitions of profession, both within disciplines such as sociology, philosophy and political science, and between them. At one extreme, only religious orders, law and medicine were traditionally accepted as 'true' professions, with other aspiring professional groups given a range of titles, including 'aspiring' or 'pseudo' professional.[15] As Johnson pointed out in the introduction to his seminal book *Professions and Power*, theorists from Marx to Durkheim have variously seen professionalism as a power for (moral and societal) good, or for ill.[16] More recently, there has been increasing evidence of populist rejection of the perceived elitism of professional claims of 'expertise'.[17]

---

14 International Confederation of Midwives, World Health Organization, and White Ribbon Alliance, 'Midwives' Voices, Midwives' Realities' (2016) <www.who.int/maternal_child_adolescent/documents/midwives-voices-realities/en/> accessed 22 February 2019.

15 Keith M MacDonald, *The Sociology of the Professions* (Sage 1995).

16 Terence J Johnson, *Professions and Power* (Routledge 1972).

17 Ben Stanley, 'The Thin Ideology of Populism' (2008) 13 J Political Ideol 95.

Claims to professional status are grounded in formal training and education in a specific and bounded discipline, formal standards of skilled practice, restricted discipline-specific organisations, legal barriers to entry and to claims of belonging, and exclusiveness.[18] These characteristics of standardised norms and particular legitimised practices are reinforced by the scientific bureaucratic norms that tend to typify managerial governance. This is expressed in rules and procedures that demand adherence to particular kinds of knowledge and processes. In this context, 'professional practice' is increasingly redefined as adherence to governance-driven norms, in a range of professional disciplines, including the classical professions of law and medicine. This turn prioritises the formal knowledge and norms of professions: the 'science' of profession, while marginalising the vocational wisdom of experience-based professional expertise: professional artistry. The vocational elements tend to be the moral and virtuous components that typify a 'calling', rather than those that typify a job or career. Enacting vocation can sometimes conflict with enacting profession.

When the midwifery professional vocational project meets structural and institutional imperatives

In the technocratic/managerial healthcare context that typifies most maternity care provision, minimisation of error through standardisation and industrial safety and care delivery processes is the driving force for service design and delivery.[19] When healthcare becomes industrialised, care provision is organised as systems work processes that are fragmented, and carried out by different caretakers. In this context, standardisation becomes essential to minimise communication and procedural errors. The prevailing belief in such systems is that standard tools and procedures ensure that everyone understands what is being talked about and what should be done at any specific time, and in response to any specific event, thus lowering the incidence of communication errors in teams that don't know each other well (or at all). Because standardisation is considered to be the product of rational thought-processes, it is assumed to be (inevitably) safer, due to the reproducibility of procedures that must, therefore, lead to good outcomes. It also becomes reified as 'what professionals do' and, ultimately, as (morally good) 'professional practice'.

Although standardisation has led to increased safety in industry (automotive, aviation), the complexity of individual healthcare needs prevents care delivery from being straightforwardly deconstructed and restructured according to production line methods. When standards are not used appropriately for the individual being cared for, and not updated as new knowledge emerges, they can

18 Stephen Timmons and Judith Tanner, 'A Disputed Occupational Boundary: Operating Theatre Nurses and Operating Department Practitioners' (2004) 26 Sociol Health Illn 645.

19 Darius A Rastegar, 'Health Care Becomes an Industry' (2004) 2(1) Ann Fam Med 79; F Moffatt, P Martin, and S Timmons, 'Constructing Notions of Healthcare Productivity: The Call for a New Professionalism?' (2014) 36 Sociol Health Illn 686.

even pose a risk. According to Wears, 'overly ambitious efforts to standardise are likely to create disorder, either in the target area or elsewhere in the system. These problems are euphemistically labelled "side effects," or "unintended consequences"'.[20] In this analysis, 'problems' could be read as staff (midwives) who are disconnected from service users, emotionally blunted by the need to adhere to systems processes and not to undertake their vocational work, and, thus, more prone to seeing childbearing women who do not (choose to) fit the standard systems processes as inconvenient, awkward or even morally deviant. In this context, there is an (unacknowledged) risk that staff align themselves with colleagues from their own and other disciplinary groups as a supportive and defensive mechanism against managerial critique. To do this successfully, they discipline service users (in this case childbearing women) as their 'professional duty' to ensure they come into line with what is seen as locally normative. This is fertile ground for disrespectful and abusive treatment of women who are seen to be transgressive, by wanting, for example, support, attention, or care and treatment that is 'outside of guidelines'.[21] Indeed, when used to imply that care should not take place outside of guideline recommendations, this phrase becomes almost oxymoronic, given that guidelines are not rules, and are not intended to set boundaries outside which all alternatives are deviant.

The creation and application of standards as a techno-rational process is also meant to fill gaps in knowledge and experience that care providers may have, and to create pathways of care based on the highest level of scientific evidence, thought to be randomised controlled trials and systematic reviews. The model of scientific bureaucratic healthcare rejects personal experience as an instrument to regulate and standardise care.[22] Scientific bureaucratic healthcare can be summarised as follows: decision-making based on rules about what ought to be done in particular circumstances (hence 'best practice' is defined increasingly in terms of following 'if … then' algorithms); a rise in managerialism over professionalism; and trust redefined in terms of reliability of systems and procedures instead of virtues of the doctor.[23]

Without the skilled, present-moment input of the practitioner, healthcare is reduced to routines enforced by institutional management. Institutionalised standards in hospital maternity wards, when not normatively and routinely subjected to reflexivity through processes such as reflective practice, can lead to alienation of staff from women.[24] The consequence can be midwives who

20 Robert L Wears, 'Standardisation and Its Discontents' (2015) 17 Cogn Technol Work 89.
21 Claire Feeley, Gill Thomson, and Soo Downe, 'Caring for Women Making Unconventional Birth Choices: A Meta-ethnography Exploring the Views, Attitudes, and Experiences of Midwives' (2019) 72 Midwifery 50.
22 Stephen Harrison, 'New Labour, Modernisation and the Medical Labour Process' (2002) 31 J Soc Policy 465.
23 Ellen Annandale, 'EC Dimensions of Patient Control in a Free-Standing Birth Center' (1987) 25 Soc Sci Med 1235.
24 Donald A Schön, *The Reflective Practitioner: How Professionals Think in Action* (Basic Books 1984).

pressure women to accept interventions and procedures they do not want, or to forgo procedures, treatments or interventions they would choose, because these interventions are not deemed to be in the best interest of childbearing women in general, based on accepted organizational standard.[25]

Risk orders theory: when person (woman)-centred care conflicts with institutional demands

Risk orders theory can be used to understand the conflict that midwives have when attempting to deliver person-centred care and endeavouring to adhere to practices that support countercultural practices such as physiological birth, appropriate use of technology and women's choice for or against certain interventions, treatments and procedures.[26] Risk orders theory describes three levels of risk. The first order describes dangers and injuries that are imagined as preventable through personal agency and behaviour, either through a specific action or through inaction. In risk discourse, these are the risks to the individual that should be minimised.

First-order risks are implicitly intertwined with societal values that make each individual responsible for the good or bad outcomes that occur through action and inaction. In addition to this, there is an added value gained by the individual who can, through discipline, avoid harmful outcomes, whether for herself or another individual. Trust in expert systems is inherent in this process, since risk categories are validated and reified by professional experts.[27] In maternity care, the consequence is, usually, a very high valuation of the need to reduce increasingly rare pathological outcomes (mortality and severe morbidity) that affect a few individuals very profoundly. Even more particularly, the outcomes that are valued in settings where both maternal and neonatal risks are low tend to be those associated with death or damage to the baby, over that of the mother. Positive outcomes, particularly for the mother, may have a place in systems rhetoric, but they are rarely listed as targets to be counted, or by which maternity care provision is measured, judged or funded. Systems are set up to control these rare adverse events, and any adverse event is judged to be a professional (and not a system) failure.

In the case of maternity care, Striley and Field-Springer found that maternity nurses in their study were expected to make choices when caring for labouring women that will lead to the best outcomes. Even more, it is expected that midwives will discipline women to make the 'right' choices. Paradoxically, even where maternity care systems ostentatiously value choice and control of the healthcare

25 Ibid.
26 Katie Striley and Kimberly Field-Springer, 'When It's Good to Be a Bad Nurse: Expanding Risk Orders Theory to Explore Nurses' Experiences of Moral, Social and Identity Risks in Obstetric Units' (2016) 18 Health Risk Soc 77.
27 Anthony Giddens, *Modernity and Self-Identity: Self and Society in the Late Modern Age* (Stanford University Press 1991).

user, based on a rhetorical prioritisation of the individual over the group, the actual choices that are available are directed at the protection of the group over the individual. That is, for example, women are told that their risk of stillbirth 'doubles' if their pregnancy is more than ten days overdue. On this basis, they are advised that they should take up the 'choice' of induction of labour. In fact, the risk goes from 1:1000 to 2:1000. This means that 998 healthy women and babies are exposed to the iatrogenic risks of labour induction for the sake of one baby that will be saved from stillbirth as a consequence. Further, those women who decline this 'choice' often come under strong pressure to acquiesce 'for the sake of their baby': and it is midwives who are expected to perform this disciplining activity.

Second-order risks arise when an individual tries to prevent a first-order risk, but, in the process, is threatened with the loss of social status and identity and is excluded from a group to which they belong. An example of this from Striley and others' study showed how, in three separate cases, US labour ward nurses made the decision to disobey physician's orders that the amount of pitocin (oxytocin) being administered to a labouring woman should be increased. In all three cases, the nurses were reprimanded. They believed that:

> [T]heir actions would decrease first-order risks to patients. However, in doing so, they experienced their own social risks. Nancy and Olivia faced public shame for their actions, and risked becoming valued less as co-workers due to their perceived disobedience to doctor's orders. Kaitlyn's official censure put her at risk for job loss, with the ultimate exile from her social group.[28]

These nurses made decisions based on their perceptions of the safety of the particular women they were working with. However, other labour ward nurses in the same study acted against their clinical judgment, to avoid being reprimanded, and to prevent the expected social marginalisation and shame that would follow, despite their beliefs that acting on physicians' orders risked the safety of the woman and foetus. The choice in these situations was between 'moral deviance' and 'social deviance'.[29]

As a result of this kind of response, a number of third-order risks emerge. Striley uses the term 'agency-constraining' risk for one of these. This can be explained as the loss of agency that the nurses experienced when having to decide between patient safety or obedience to the physician's/manager's orders, or the institutional guidelines. This loss of agency in a particular situation affects a more profound capacity to be creative and to imagine another solution to future practice dilemmas: 'Third-order risks threaten our ability to imagine the world otherwise. Our fear of first-order risks and desire to avoid second-order risks (re) produce habituated social practices and ideas'.[30]

---

28 Striley and Field-Springer (n 26) 85.
29 Ibid 89.
30 Katie Striley, Katie Margavio, and Kimberly Field-Springer, 'The Bad Mother Police: Theorizing Risk Orders in The Discourses of Infant Feeding Practices' (2014) 29 Health Commun 552, 560.

Risk orders theory is one way of explaining what prevents midwives from doing what women need and want, and what might help women feel safe.

Reading the individual through the technocracy

There is currently a moment of tension in the world of maternity care. On the one hand, as noted earlier, technical training approaches and personalised surveillance devices/medicine signal an increasing distancing of midwives from the bodies of women in labour, and from the subtle relationships that form when in close attendance on labouring women. On the other hand, there is a rapidly growing recognition that the current ways of doing birth are associated with very high levels of unnecessary intervention in some places and too little intervention in others,[31] with longer term consequences for children and societies[32] and growing rates of maternal mental ill-health.[33] It is also becoming clear that in contrast to the promise of scientific bureaucratic standardised maternity care, healthcare systems that spend high levels on surveillance and intervention in pregnancy and childbirth (such as the United States) have some of the highest rates of adverse outcomes for mother and baby.[34] The way in which professional knowledge is gained provides another insight into why reading women through technocracy and artefacts might lead to distancing of midwives from childbearing women.

From hands on empirical training to the skills lab

Traditionally, midwifery skills were passed on through empirical apprenticeship training. Through the institutionalisation and standardisation of midwifery studies, new approaches to learning have been incorporated into training. One of these is the skills lab where simulation training takes place, allowing midwives to practice care.[35] The purpose of simulation training is to create circumstances in the lab that are as close to a real event as possible, either through audio-visual

31 Suellen Miller and others, 'Beyond too Little, too Late and too Much, too Soon: A Pathway Towards Evidence-Based, Respectful Maternity Care Worldwide' (2016) 388 The Lancet 2176.

32 H G Dahlen and others, 'Childbirth and Consequent Atopic Disease: Emerging Evidence on Epigenetic Effects Based on the Hygiene and EPIIC Hypotheses' (2016) 16 BMC Pregnancy and Childbirth 1.

33 Tiffany Field, 'Postnatal Anxiety Prevalence, Predictors and Effects on Development: A Narrative Review (2018) 51 Infant Behav Dev 24.

34 Peter Conrad, Thomas Mackie, and Ateev Mehrotra, 'Estimating the Costs of Medicalization' (2010) 71 Soc Sci Med 1943; Nan H Troiano and Patricia M Witcher, 'Maternal Mortality and Morbidity in the United States: Classification, Causes, Preventability, and Critical Care Obstetric Implications' (2018) 32 J Perinat Neonatal Nurs 222.

35 Simon Cooper, Ruth Endacott, and Robyn Cant, 'Measuring Non-Technical Skills in Medical Emergency Care: A Review of Assessment Measures' (2010) 2 Open Access Emerg Med 7; Robin Lewis, Alasdair Strachan, and Michelle McKenzie Smith, 'Is High Fidelity Simulation the Most Effective Method for the Development of Non-Technical Skills in Nursing? A Review of the Current Evidence' (2012) 6 Open Nurs J 82.

training, games and role play, with and without manikins.[36] Simulation training is believed to address several issues in medical, nursing and midwifery training, including what has come to be seen as the unethical practice of 'learning at the bedside', which is seen as risky for patients. Simulation training is thought to prepare future practitioners to behave satisfactorily in clinical situations and to learn skills such as leadership, teamwork, situation awareness and decision-making, so-called 'soft' skills or non-technical skills.

One of the benefits reported with the use of simulation training is:

> [T]he opportunity [for students] to familiarize themselves with equipment and procedures within a safe, supervised environment. The students are encouraged to 'have a go', and acquaint themselves with the feel, use, safe handling and appropriate disposal of equipment.[37]

While there is a logic to this explanation, there are problems with the acquisition of procedural skills that are learned by rote, and on models that are always the same, without interaction with dynamic, variant, unique human bodies. In one study, students needed to learn to 'get past the plastic' and 'stop seeing them as a manikin and start seeing them as a patient'.[38] This imposes an additional need to unlearn, with the risk that such unlearning does not happen, and that expectations of bodily response become standardised. With the loss of practical training, clinical situations, whether emergencies or routine care, become disembodied, with the risk of rendering the women's experience invisible and irrelevant. McGaghie writes that simulation-based medical education '*complements* clinical education but cannot substitute for training grounded in patient care in real clinical settings'.[39]

Midwives and professional power: the loss of vocation

While the rhetoric of vocation is strongly present in midwifery policy documents, the emphasis on professionalism (particularly when it is aligned with scientific bureaucratic managerialism) has crowded out the practice of vocational midwifery in many settings. Increasingly, professional midwives are allocated management or supervisory roles, or the job of watching and recording the data produced by machines attached to pregnant or labouring women. The human interactive space that is left, including physical touch and supportive contact with women, is increasingly being occupied by other neo-professionalising groups such as maternity care workers (in the United Kingdom) and doulas and other birth

---

36 Angela Hope, Joanne Garside, and Stephen Prescott, 'Rethinking Theory and Practice: Pre-Registration Student Nurses Experiences of Simulation Teaching and Learning in the Acquisition of Clinical Skills in Preparation for Practice' (2011) 31 Nurse Educ Today 711.

37 Ibid 713.

38 Tamara Power and others, 'Plastic with Personality: Increasing Student Engagement with Manikins' (2015) 35 Nurse Educ Today 126, 128.

39 William C McGaghie and others, 'A Critical Review of Simulation-Based Medical Education Research': 2003–2009 (2010) 44 Med Educ 50, 57, emphasis in the original.

companions in many countries around the world.[40] The ideal of 'midwifery' as a philosophical and practical ethos, as expressed in The Lancet Series on Midwifery, is thus less and less attainable by midwives themselves in some settings. This, in turn, is associated with an increasing loss of identification with women in practice. As midwifery practice becomes focused more and more on managerial and bureaucratic concerns, and/or defensive measuring, recording and 'just in case' interventions, women are seen not just as 'other' but even as the enemy:

> The interviews with the midwives confirm the patient reports. The main reason for the abuse were when women broke the rules such as booking late, arguing with a midwife about whether in labor, requesting attention, pushing without the midwife telling them to, delivering without the midwives' presence, or not having the required items such as baby clothes or cleaning items such as soap. Although many of these abuses can be viewed as ways in which the midwife tried to ensure the safe birthing process, some were purely punitive.[41]

Increasing disengagement in the context of consumerist neoliberal healthcare, and/or in settings where staffing levels and shifts do not allow for personal relationships to be formed leads to fear that any woman could complain or sue, and that, therefore, no woman is to be trusted. This feeds back into the woman's experience, increasing a sense of being traumatised, both by physical interventions that are imposed 'just in case', and by lack of interpersonal engagement and care. In these circumstances, women are more likely to complain, sue, go onto social media, contact journalists and so on – and then the distrust and fear become further amplified both by employing organisations that put in place even more restrictive risk-averse policies, forcing staff to become even more 'professionally' distanced and divorced from childbearing women, and perpetuating the vicious cycle. In this toxic mix, disrespect and abuse are increasingly likely to occur.

'Expertise' and professional vocation, rather than knowledge and professional managerialism?

In a systematic review of expert midwifery practice, Downe and others concluded that expert midwifery is a synthesis of *wisdom, skilled practice* and *enacted vocation*.[42] In this analysis, 'wisdom' is characterised as:

> [A] state of the human mind characterized by profound understanding and deep insight. It is often, but not necessarily, accompanied by extensive formal knowledge. Unschooled people can acquire wisdom, and wise people

---

40 Jenny McLeish and Maggie Redshaw, 'A Qualitative Study of Volunteer Doulas Working Alongside Midwives at Births in England: Mothers' and Doulas' Experiences' (2018) 56 Midwifery 53.
41 Abrahams, Jewkes, and Mvo (n 12) 245.
42 Soo Downe, Louise Simpson, and Katriona Trafford, 'Expert Intrapartum Maternity Care: A Meta-Synthesis' (2007) 60 J Adv Nurs 127.

Table 5.1 Expertise by skill level from Dreyfus and Dreyfus (1980)

Skill level/ mental function	Novice	Advance beginner	Competent	Proficient	Master
Recollection	Non-situational	Situational	Situational	Situational	Situational
Recognition	Decomposed	Decomposed	Holistic	Holistic	Holistic
Decision	Analytical	Analytical	Analytical	Intuitive	Intuitive
Awareness	Monitoring	Monitoring	Monitoring	Monitoring	Absorbed

can be found among carpenters, fishermen, or housewives. Wherever it exists, wisdom shows itself as a perception of the relativity and relationships among things. It is an awareness of wholeness that does not lose sight of particularity or concreteness, or of the intricacies of interrelationships.[43]

Wisdom is not the same as knowledge. It is an applied art that integrates formal evidence and learning with experiential skills and reflexive practice, and with patterning-type intuitive understanding based on respectful attunement to individuals.[44] Aristotle claimed that there were three types of knowledge. *Episteme,* which can be translated as 'science' (*theōria*); *Téchnē*, technical and artistic skills; and *Poiēsis*, the art of production, or bringing into being.[45] The first two are more likely to be associated with professionalism. Vocation seems to include both of these, but to also incorporate *phronesis*, or practical wisdom, including both ethics and action (praxis). The combination of all of these is associated with expertise. Dreyfus and Dreyfus[46] captured the nature of expertise in an exploration of a range of professional groups, and proposed that competence in any profession, occupation or trade area could be described at five levels, and four types of capacity (Table 5.1).

The novice works on the basis of rules and procedures. They may be knowledgeable, but only in terms of general training and principles. They think about situations in components, and their decision-making is based on linear analysis, based on standardised predetermined rules, or on the application of instruction from more expert others. At the basic level, this becomes 'tell me what to do and I'll do it'.

In contrast, the expert recognises the 'unusual normal', based on patterns of understanding built up over years of reflexive engagement. They understand rules and they have extensive knowledge that they can call on, but their reasoning

---

43 Joseph W Meeker, 'The Wisdom and Wilderness' (*The Wisdom Page*, 1981) <www.wisdompage. com/meekart.html> accessed 22 February 2019.

44 Sietse Wieringa and others, 'How Knowledge Is Constructed and Exchanged in Virtual Communities of Physicians: Qualitative Study of Mindlines Online' (2018) 20(2) J Med Internet Res e34.

45 Aristotle, *The Nicomachean Ethics* (J A K Thomson tr, Penguin Classics 2004).

46 Stuart E Dreyfus and Hubert L Dreyfus, 'A Five-Stage Model of the Mental Activities Involved in Directed Skill Acquisition' (University of California – Berkeley, February 1980) <https:// apps.dtic.mil/dtic/tr/fulltext/u2/a084551.pdf> accessed 22 February 2019.

in any specific situation seems to be 'intuitive' because they don't need to go through the logical train of decision-making based on linear processes. This is embodied knowledge – a form of wisdom. Usually, people operating at this level rapidly move to assessing a situation as if it is 'like' another similar particular case they have encountered before. They then add in other pieces of knowledge and experience to move rapidly to understanding it as a unique, dynamic event that may or may not require the application of standard rules and procedures. Experts who work at this level are finely attuned to each situation, and can seem to be in what has been called a 'flow state'.[47]

Patricia Benner used this taxonomy to analyse the work of nurses and concluded that expert nurses 'have a deep understanding of the total situation'.[48] This deeply engaged wisdom is the kind of 'enacted vocation'. While some midwives express it in practice, others seem to align more closely to the characteristics of the novice. This is especially the case when evidence-based medicine is translated as ensuring that women follow guidelines based on quantitative systematic reviews, in contrast to the classic definition of evidence-based practice presented by Sackett and his colleagues in 2000:

> Evidence-based medicine (EBM) is the integration of best research evidence with clinical expertise and patient value ... when these three elements are integrated, clinicians and patients form [an] ... alliance which optimises clinical outcomes and quality of life.[49]

This definition is actually aligned to the concepts of expertise and enacted vocation, as outlined earlier, where evidence from a range of sources (qualitative and quantitative) is equally valued, and is practiced in combination with values and skills, taking account of what matters and what is appropriate for each individual, in a therapeutic alliance.

Even the assumption that the guidelines that underpin professional practice should be followed routinely by midwives, doctors and service users because they are based on classic (randomised trial or systematic review) evidence is undermined by what actually happens. In fact, some evidence is valued and applied by professionals, and other equally (or better) supported practices are not. Examples are rife in maternity care. The rapid uptake of the findings of the Term Breech Trial[50] versus the persistent use of electronic foetal monitoring despite decades of research that shows it does more harm than good;[51] the attention

47 Mihaly Csikszentmihályi, *Flow: The Psychology of Optimal Experience* (Harper & Row 1990).

48 Patricia Benner, *From Novice to Expert, Excellence and Power in Clinical Nursing Practice* (Prentice Hall 1984).

49 David L Sackett and others, *Evidence-Based Medicine: How to Practice and Teach EBM* (2nd edn, Churchill Livingston 2000).

50 K L Hogle and others, 'Impact of the International Term Breech Trial on Clinical Practice and Concerns: A Survey of Centre Collaborators' (2003) 25 J Obstet Gynaecol Can 14.

51 Zarko Alfirevic and others, 'Continuous cardiotocography (CTG) as a Form of Electronic Fetal Monitoring (EFM) for Fetal Assessment during Labour' (*Cochrane Library*, 3 February 2017)

paid to the 'A Randomized Trial of Induction Versus Expectant Management' (ARRIVE trial)[52] despite its lack of external generalisibility, and the evidence that companionship in labour has similar or better effects;[53] and the lack of uptake of midwifery-led continuity of care despite clear evidence of benefit, including a large decrease in the incidence of prematurity[54] are all examples. Even in a system where safety is super valued over women's experiences of respectful care, professionals (including professional midwives) continue to use routine technical interventions that they know to be harmful for the majority of women and/or babies, because these interventions are mandated in managerially driven protocols and rules. In some cases, professionals, including midwives, deny women choice for these interventions even if they have a deeply held reason for wanting to make this kind of choice. In the case of midwives, this breaks the promise of being 'with woman' that is embedded in the very name midwifery. It also directly contradicts the rhetoric of women-centred care. As illustrated earlier, practitioners who resist this standardisation in the name of service user well-being, based on their vocational alignment with childbearing women, are often marginalised or even dismissed from their jobs, sometimes for 'non-professional' behaviour. Given the emotional, intellectual and physical energy it takes each time a midwife tries to argue for each woman to be able to have 'out of guideline' care, over time it becomes easier for all except the most dedicated just to tell women this kind of care is not possible, or to neglect to offer choice at all, for fear of being seen by peers to oppose local normative professional behaviours if women make 'difficult' choices.

The combination of the above-mentioned factors risks an increasing rift between midwives and childbearing women and families. Studies have shown that midwives are seen by women as the most important factor in both positive and fulfilling births, and in traumatic ones.[55] In the latter case, these are often births following labour induction and then a cascade of associated intervention, accompanied by disengaged or uncaring midwives and other staff, or even a more or less complete absence of staff, either physically or emotionally, as midwives concentrate on reading machines and writing notes rather than

---

<www.cochranelibrary.com/cdsr/doi/10.1002/14651858.CD006066.pub3/full> accessed 22 February 2019.

52 Ben Spencer, 'Inducing Pregnant Women a Week before Their Due Date Could Reduce Risk of Birth Complications and Emergency C-sections, Trial Finds' (*Daily Mail*, 9 August 2018) <www.dailymail.co.uk/news/article-6041163/Inducing-pregnant-women-week-date-reduce-risk-birth-complications.html> accessed 27 February 2019.

53 Meghan A Bohren and others, 'Continuous Support for Women during Childbirth' (*Cochrane Library*, 6 July 2017) <www.cochranelibrary.com/cdsr/doi/10.1002/14651858.CD003766.pub6/full> accessed 22 February 2019.

54 Jane Sandall and others, 'Midwife-led Continuity Models Versus Other Models of Care for Childbearing Women' (Cochrane Database Syst Rev, Cochrane Library 2016) <www.cochranelibrary.com/cdsr/doi/10.1002/14651858.CD004667.pub5/full> accessed 22 February 2019.

55 Madeleine Simpson and Christine Catling, 'Understanding Psychological Traumatic Birth Experiences: A Literature Review' (2016) 29 Women Birth 203.

being with the woman.[56] The sense of betrayal that is evident in research, and in popular social media, is even more acute as women generally expect that even if no-one else is their ally in childbirth, midwives will be. Once this trust is broken, it is very difficult to repair. Negative stories begin to circulate that set up fear and uncertainty in pregnant women, who then begin to see 'normal' birth (ie any vaginal birth in this interpretation) as inherently traumatic and to be avoided. More and more women then begin to ask for interventions that they perceive to protect themselves from this kind of trauma, including elective caesareans, or early epidurals. Midwives see this as counter to the core of midwifery expertise, which is in physiological labour and birth, and, more profoundly, perceive that women are exposing themselves and their babies to harm in the short and longer term by making such choices, but, at the same time, they perceive themselves to be powerless to provide the kind of care women need in order to avoid traumatic births, and to optimise positive, fulfilling experiences. This situation results in a vicious downward cycle, and a rupture in the midwife-women relationship at a fundamental level, as the rhetoric of woman-centred care is directly challenged daily in practice, on social media and in the mainstream press. Both women and midwives become distanced, and the interpersonal relationship that is fundamental to respectful care is undermined.

Courage: when midwives do professional vocational expert midwifery based on what women want and need

In the review undertaken by Downe and others, 'enacted vocation' had three components: *values* (belief, courage, trust), *intuition*, and *connected companionship*. Some aspects of this have been addressed earlier, including the need to believe in the capacity of women to give birth, trust and the notion of intuition. Connected companionship captures both the relationship-based care with women discussed earlier, and positive relationships with co-workers and peers. The component of courage has not yet been unpacked.

Based on the foregoing text, it could be argued that midwives are subject to pressures from healthcare systems that are oppressive for both midwives and women (either in a gender sense or in a range of other senses) and, indeed, there is a great deal of evidence for this and discussion of it. However, systems are created by people. Only people can change them. In this context, one of the most cited theorists in the nursing and midwifery field is Foucault, most specifically in relation to technical surveillance, and the power of panoptical control.[57] However, Foucault did not only discuss 'power-over'. He made it

---

56 Christina Nilsson, 'The Delivery Room: Is It a Safe Place? A Hermeneutic Analysis of Women's Negative Birth Experiences' (2014) 5 Sex Reprod Health 199.

57 D Holmes, 'From Iron Gaze to Nursing Care: Mental Health Nursing in the Era of Panopticism' (2001) 8 J Psychiatr Ment Health Nurs 7; Elizabeth C Newnham, Lois V McKellar, and Jan I

clear that systems are always subject to resistance to power.[58] Such resistance requires courage.

In the context of maternity care, it takes courage to challenge systems that see good quality 'professional' practice as that based on following institutional rules and procedures, even when these are manifestly not ideal for some (or even many) women and babies who are subject to them. Resistance in this situation can operate both on an hour to hour, day to day basis in authentic alignment with labouring women and with peers, colleagues, managers and funders, and also across the longer term, in campaigns to change policy and funding mechanisms. In the United Kingdom, the recent Better Births initiative[59] is the latest example of such resistance that has been in place for at least the last 30 years, since before the seminal Changing Childbirth report[60] was published. Globally, The Lancet Series on Midwifery and on Caesarean Section,[61] and the WHO guidelines for antenatal[62] and intra-partum care[63] for positive maternal experiences are examples of the consequence of steady resistance for years. The recent upswing in research and legal rulings on disrespect and abuse and on obstetric violence, many of which are discussed elsewhere in this volume, are also examples of long-term, patient resistance by activists, healthcare professionals and others, to the status quo that has until recently disregarded such concerns in the name of standardised care provision designed to optimise safety in specific areas, without regard to unintended consequences.

Everyday courage enacted in the name of individuals who want and need something that is 'out of guidelines' for the specific unique case of them or their babies also happens everywhere, around the world. It is highly rewarding for expert vocational professionals, but it is done every time with an awareness that such practices, while safe, could expose the practitioner to appropriation from peers and superiors, to job loss, the risk of being struck off professional registers, or even to criminal charges, and, ultimately, jail. Sometimes, this is what it takes for midwives to be 'with woman'.

What women want is simple. A recent meta-synthesis review of global literature undertaken to examine what matters to women in pregnancy found that

Pincombe 'Paradox of the Institution: Findings from a Hospital Labour Ward Ethnography' (2017) 17 BMC Pregnancy Childbirth 1.

58 Michel Foucault, *The History of Sexuality: The Will to Knowledge* (Penguin 1998).

59 National Maternity Review, 'Better Births: Improving Outcomes of Maternity Services in England – A Five Year Forward View for Maternity Care' (NHS England 2016) <www.england.nhs.uk/wp-content/uploads/2016/02/national-maternity-review-report.pdf> accessed 11 January 2019.

60 Expert Maternity Group, *Changing Childbirth: The Report of the Expert Maternity Group* (Stationery Office Book 1993).

61 Ana Pilar Betrán and others, 'Interventions to Reduce Unnecessary Caesarean Sections in Healthy Women and Babies' (2018) 392 The Lancet 1358.

62 World Health Organization, 'WHO Recommendations on Antenatal Care for a Positive Pregnancy Experience' (2016) <www.who.int/reproductivehealth/publications/maternal_perinatal_health/anc-positive-pregnancy-experience/en/> accessed 11 January 2017.

63 World Health Organization, 'WHO Recommendation: Intrapartum Care for a Positive Childbirth Experience' (2018) <www.who.int/reproductivehealth/publications/intrapartum-care-guidelines/en/> accessed 11 January 2019.

they want both safety (expressed in a number of ways) and a positive experience.[64] The key components were:

- Maintaining physical and sociocultural normality;
- Maintaining a healthy pregnancy for mother and baby (including preventing and treating risks, illness and death);
- Effective transition to positive labour and birth;
- Achieving positive motherhood (including maternal self-esteem, competence, autonomy).

Similar components were found in a parallel review of what matters to women in labour and birth.[65] This is the very opposite of disrespectful and abusive care. It should not be problematic for any system of care, or for any individual caregiver to provide such care. It depends on the exercise of emotional intelligence, and on the confidence of professional midwives to enact the midwifery vocation with enduring skill, compassion and wisdom. Sometimes, this depends on midwives having the courage to consciously be seen as positive deviants, who are:

> [P]eople whose uncommon but successful behaviors or strategies enable them to find better solutions to a problem than their peers, despite facing similar challenges and having no extra resources or knowledge.[66]

Often this is worked out through individuals who act on the basis of their vocational values, beliefs, skills and knowledge rather than waiting for permission obtained through bureaucratic processes: 'It is easier to act your way into a new way of thinking than think your way into a new way of acting'.[67]

Crucially, this is not reckless behaviour. To return to Aristotle, there is a crucial difference between recklessness, courage and cowardice. The former involves taking risks that are not justifiable. The latter is to fear, and not to act. Courage, the 'golden mean', is seen in someone who:

> fears and endures the things he ought to, for the right purpose, as he ought to and at the time he ought to, as well as the one who dares accordingly, is a courageous man; for the courageous man feels and acts in as much as merit requires and reason prescribes.[68]

64 Soo Downe and others, 'What Matters to Women: A Systematic Scoping Review to Identify the Processes and Outcomes of Antenatal Care Provision that Are Important to Healthy Pregnant Women' (2016) 123 BJOG 529.
65 Soo Downe and others, 'What Matters to Women during Childbirth: A Systematic Qualitative Review' (2018) 13(4) PLoS ONE e0194906.
66 Lyle Berkowitz and Chris McCarthy (eds), *Innovation with Information Technologies in Healthcare* (Springer 2013) 288.
67 Richard Pascale, Jerry Sternin, and Monique Sternin, *The Power of Positive Deviance: How Unlikely Innovators Solve the World's Toughest Problems* (Harvard Business Review Press 2010) 37.
68 Aristotle, 'What Courage Is and How It Stands Between Cowardice and Rashness' (*Aristotelian Philosophy*, 14 August 2016) <www.aristotelianphilosophy.com/what-courage-is-and-how-it-stands-between-cowardice-and-rashness/> accessed 27 February 2019.

To illustrate the point that individuals can subvert disrespectful system norms, we return to one of the earlier quotes used, and include the final element:

> The descriptions of the midwifery staff given by the women included 'silly', 'rude', 'ridiculous', 'unhuman', 'not caring', and 'not kind'. They were said to speak to patients as if 'talking to a child', and patients reported that 'nobody showed any kindness'. This was particularly important to patients as they described labor and delivery as times of great 'anxiety' and 'worry' and time that were very 'difficult' (an expression of pain). The women perceived that the care that they received substantially 'depended on the midwife' and many of the narrative accounts of abuse and neglect also included mention of rescue by the intervention of a 'nice' midwife at some stage.[69]

Reclaiming vocation and respectful, fulfilling maternity care

> A society in which vocation and job are separated for most people gradually creates an economy that is often devoid of spirit, one that frequently fills our pocketbooks at the cost of emptying our souls.[70]

Resistance to the power of the systemic depersonalisation in neoliberal healthcare services is crucial if midwives are to rebuild trusting, respectful relationships with childbearing women. This means sustaining both safety and authentically individualised care for all women, babies and families everywhere, to optimise the possibility for a positive, or even joyous, outcome in both the short and the longer term. Reconnecting to enacted vocation seems to be a powerful route to achieve this.

Doing this at an individual level is hard. Linking with others to share difficulties and achievements, hints, tips and resources helps. Communities of Practice[71] have formed both locally, face to face and on social media, sometimes of women only or midwives only, locally, nationally or internationally, and sometimes of people from a wide range of professional, activist and social groups. Such groups have changed the law to ban obstetric violence in Venezuela,[72] raised the issue of what women want across India into political consciousness,[73] supported home birth practitioners, and influenced political awareness of the 'too much, too soon, too little, too late' agenda in terms of childbirth interventions. They have kept birth centres and local hospitals open, changed local clinical policies and practice, and increased the space in which women and midwives can rebuild

---

69 Abrahams, Jewkes, and Mvo (n 12) 245.
70 BrainyQuote, 'Sam Keen Quotes' <www.brainyquote.com/quotes/sam_keen_178455> accessed 27 February 2019.
71 Etienne Wenger, *Communities of Practice: Learning, Meaning, and Identity* (CUP 1998).
72 C R Williams and others, 'Obstetric Violence: A Latin American Legal Response to Mistreatment during Childbirth' (2018) 125 BJOG 1208.
73 The White Ribbon Alliance for Safe Motherhood, 'Hamara Swasthya, Hamari Awaaz' (*The White Ribbon Alliance India*, 2016) <www.whiteribbonallianceindia.org/whats-latest/hamara-swasthya-hamari-awaz> accessed 27 February 2019.

trust in each other and in the physiological processes of labour and birth. They have supported individual midwives who are burnt out from fighting for unusual normal care for women, and individual women who are desperate to make choices that are seen as countercultural or even immoral through the lens of current social norms around childbirth.

One of the ways in which practitioners can move along the continuum from novice to expert, and thus become more able to exercise courage rather than recklessness in non-standard situations is to consciously engage with reflexivity through regular reflective practice.[74] Schön recognises the difference between the 'pure', population level knowledge that is produced by scientific enquiry (and sometimes captured in guidelines, as discussed earlier) and the reality of everyday practice:

> In the varied topography of professional practice, there is a high, hard ground overlooking a swamp. On the high ground, manageable problems lend themselves to solution through the application of research-based theory and technique. In the swampy lowland, messy, confusing problems defy technical solution.[75]

For Schön, the reflective practitioner is able to move '*from technical rationality to reflection in action*'.[76] This process is reinforced by 'reflection on action' after the event, in which the practitioner consciously spends time after an unusual event, thinking about what kind of knowledge they tapped into, and how they used it, with a view to integrating what worked and what did not into future ('expert') practice.

These two techniques – seeking out and engaging with Communities of Practice, and conscious reflection on and in action – provide a strong basis for the courage to enact professional vocation.

Conclusion: beyond victimhood – building a positive future

This chapter has addressed and critiqued the assumption that midwives are inevitably subjected and victimised by a patriarchal social and healthcare system in which male medical doctors are the dominant and oppressive force, and that this relieves midwives from responsibility to ensure maternity care is authentically responsive to what women want and need. The argument is that this framing does explain many of the issues in maternity care today, but it also restricts the potential for Foucauldian 'resistance to power' that might act as a force for positive change. As a way forward, we argue that, on both an everyday and long-term basis, midwives need to actively resist the current normative professional-managerial ethos of maternity care, which results in standardisation

---

74 Schön (n 24) 202.
75 Ibid 14.
76 Ibid 33, emphasis added.

of the human response, and a consequent 'othering' of all who do not fit with these narrow, population-based, rule-enforced standards. Disrespect, abuse and even violence are a consequence of such 'othering'. A move back to courageous (but not reckless) expert professional reflective vocational practice (for doctors as well as for midwives, and for others working with childbearing women and families) is likely to increase the potential for positive relationships and, therefore, to re-valuation of the individual. This maximises the potential for human flourishing for the childbearing woman and her family, and for maternity care staff members, in both the short and the longer term.

Bibliography

Abrahams N, Jewkes R, and Mvo Z, 'Health Care-Seeking Practices of Pregnant Women and the Role of the Midwife in Cape Town, South Africa' (2001) 46 J Midwifery Womens Health 240

Annandale E, 'EC Dimensions of Patient Control in a Free-Standing Birth Center' (1987) 25 Soc Sci Med 1235

Aristotle, *The Nicomachean Ethics* (J A K Thomson tr, Penguin Classics 2004)

Beauvoir S, *The Second Sex* (Knopf 1953)

Benner P, *From Novice to Expert, Excellence and Power in Clinical Nursing Practice* (Prentice Hall 1984)

Berkowitz L and McCarthy C (eds), *Innovation with Information Technologies in Healthcare* (Springer 2013)

Conrad P and others, 'Antenatal Care Services in Rural Uganda: Missed Opportunities for Good-Quality Care' (2012) 22 Qual Health Res 619

Conrad P, Mackie T, and Mehrotra A, 'Estimating the Costs of Medicalization' (2010) 71 Soc Sci Med 1943

Cooper S, Endacott R, and Cant R, 'Measuring Non-Technical Skills in Medical Emergency Care: A Review of Assessment Measures' (2010) 2 Open Access Emerg Med 7

Csikszentmihályi M, *Flow: The Psychology of Optimal Experience* (Harper & Row 1990)

Dahlen H G and others, 'Childbirth and Consequent Atopic Disease: Emerging Evidence on Epigenetic Effects Based on the Hygiene and EPIIC Hypotheses' (2016) 16 BMC Pregnancy and Childbirth 1

Downe S and others, 'What Matters to Women: A Systematic Scoping Review to Identify the Processes and Outcomes of Antenatal Care Provision that Are Important to Healthy Pregnant Women' (2016) 123 BJOG 529

Downe S and others, 'What Matters to Women during Childbirth: A Systematic Qualitative Review' (2018) 13(4) PLoS ONE e0194906

Downe S, Simpson L, and Trafford K, 'Expert Intrapartum Maternity Care: A Meta-Synthesis' (2007) 60 J Adv Nurs 127

Expert Maternity Group, *Changing Childbirth: The Report of the Expert Maternity Group* (Stationery Office Book 1993)

Feeley C, Thomson G, and Downe S, 'Caring for Women Making Unconventional Birth Choices: A Meta-ethnography Exploring the Views, Attitudes, and Experiences of Midwives' (2019) 72 Midwifery 50

Field T, 'Postnatal Anxiety Prevalence, Predictors and Effects on Development: A Narrative Review (2018) 51 Infant Behav Dev 24

Foucault M, *The History of Sexuality: The Will to Knowledge* (Penguin 1998)

Giddens A, *Modernity and Self-Identity: Self and Society in the Late Modern Age* (Stanford University Press 1991)

Greer G, *The Female Eunuch* (McGraw-Hill 1970)

Harrison S, 'New Labour, Modernisation and the Medical Labour Process' (2002) 31 J Soc Policy 465

Hogle K L and others, 'Impact of the International Term Breech Trial on Clinical Practice and Concerns: A Survey of Centre Collaborators' (2003) 25 J Obstet Gynaecol Can 14

Holmes D, 'From Iron Gaze to Nursing Care: Mental Health Nursing in the Era of Panopticism' (2001) 8 J Psychiatr Ment Health Nurs 7

Hope A, Garside J, and Prescott S, 'Rethinking Theory and Practice: Pre-Registration Student Nurses Experiences of Simulation Teaching and Learning in the Acquisition of Clinical Skills in Preparation or Practice' (2011) 31 Nurse Educ Today 711

Hunter B, 'Conflicting Ideologies as a Source of Emotion Work' (2004) 20 Midwifery 261

Johnson T J, *Professions and Power* (Routledge 1972)

Karlström A, Nystedt A, and Hildingsson I, 'The Meaning of a Very Positive Birth Experience: Focus Groups Discussions with Women' (2015) 15 BMC Pregnancy Childbirth 251

Kristoff J, *Kinslayer* (Pan Macmillan 2013) 131

Krumer-Nevo M, 'The Arena of Othering: A Narrative Study with Women Living in Poverty and Social Marginality' (2002) 1 Qual Soc Work 303

Lewis R, Strachan A, and Smith M M, 'Is High Fidelity Simulation the most Effective Method for the Development of Non-Technical Skills in Nursing? A Review of the Current Evidence' (2012) 6 Open Nurs J 82

Loudon I, *Death in Childbirth: An International Study of Maternal Care and Maternal Mortality 1800–1950* (Clarendon Press 1994)

MacDonald K M, *The Sociology of the Professions* (Sage 1995)

McGaghie W C and others, 'A Critical Review of Simulation-Based Medical Education Research: 2003–2009' (2010) 44 Med Educ 50

McLeish J and Redshaw M, 'A Qualitative Study of Volunteer Doulas Working Alongside Midwives at Births in England: Mothers' and Doulas' Experiences' (2018) 56 Midwifery 53

Miller S and others, 'Beyond too Little, too Late and too Much, too Soon: A Pathway Towards Evidence-Based, Respectful Maternity Care Worldwide' (2016) 388 The Lancet 2176

Moffatt F, Martin P, and Timmons S, 'Constructing Notions of Healthcare Productivity: The Call for a New Professionalism?' (2014) 36 Sociol Health Illn 686

National Maternity Review, 'Better Births: Improving Outcomes of Maternity Services in England – A Five Year Forward View for Maternity Care' (NHS England 2016)

Newnham E C, McKellar L V, and Pincombe J I, 'Paradox of the Institution: Findings from a Hospital Labour Ward Ethnography' (2017) 17 BMC Pregnancy Childbirth 1

Nilsson C, 'The Delivery Room: Is It a Safe Place? A Hermeneutic Analysis of Women's Negative Birth Experiences' (2014) 5 Sex Reprod Health 199

O'Connell R and Downe S, 'A Metasynthesis of Midwives' Experience of Hospital Practice in Publicly Funded Settings: Compliance, Resistance and Authenticity' (2009) 13 Health 589

Pascale R, Sternin J, and Sternin M, *The Power of Positive Deviance: How Unlikely Innovators Solve the World's Toughest Problems* (Harvard Business Review Press 2010)

Pilar Betrán A and others, 'Interventions to Reduce Unnecessary Caesarean Sections in Healthy Women and Babies' (2018) 392 The Lancet 1358

Power T and others, 'Plastic with Personality: Increasing Student Engagement with Manikins' (2015) 35 Nurse Educ Today 126

Rastegar D A, 'Health Care Becomes an Industry' (2004) 2(1) Ann Fam Med 79

Reed R, Sharman R, and Inglis C, 'Women's Descriptions of Childbirth Trauma Relating to Care Provider Actions and Interactions' (2017) 17 BMC Pregnancy Childbirth 1

Renfrew M J and others, 'Midwifery and Quality Care: Findings from a New Evidence-Informed Maternity Care Framework' (2014) 384 The Lancet 1129.

Sackett D L and others, *Evidence-Based Medicine: How to Practice and Teach EBM* (2nd edn, Churchill Livingston 2000).

Sandall J and others, 'Midwife-led Continuity Models Versus Other Models of Care for Childbearing Women' (Cochrane Database Syst Rev, Cochrane Library 2016)

Schön D A, *The Reflective Practitioner: How Professionals Think in Action* (Basic Books 1984)

Sharp J, *The Midwives Book: Or the Whole Art of Midwifery Discovered* (Elaine Hobby ed, OUP 1999)

Simpson M and Catling C, 'Understanding Psychological Traumatic Birth Experiences: A Literature Review' (2016) 29 Women Birth 203

Stanley B, 'The Thin Ideology of Populism' (2008) 13 J Political Ideol 95

Striley K and Field-Springer K, 'When It's Good to Be a Bad Nurse: Expanding Risk Orders Theory to Explore Nurses' Experiences of Moral, Social and Identity Risks in Obstetric Units' (2016) 18 Health Risk Soc 77

Striley K, Margavio K, and Field-Springer K, 'The Bad Mother Police: Theorizing Risk Orders in the Discourses of Infant Feeding Practices' (2014) 29 Health Commun 552, 560

Stuart E Dreyfus and Hubert L Dreyfus, 'A Five-Stage Model of the Mental Activities Involved in Directed Skill Acquisition' (University of California – Berkeley, February 1980)

Timmons S and Tanner J, 'A Disputed Occupational Boundary: Operating Theatre Nurses and Operating Department Practitioners' (2004) 26 Sociol Health Illn 645

Troiano N H and Witcher P M, 'Maternal Mortality and Morbidity in the United States: Classification, Causes, Preventability, and Critical Care Obstetric Implications' (2018) 32 J Perinat Neonatal Nurs 222

Umeora O U and others, 'Implementing the New WHO Antenatal Care Model: Voices from End Users in a Rural Nigerian Community' (2008) 11 Niger J Clin Pract 260

Wears R L, 'Standardisation and Its Discontents' (2015) 17 Cogn Technol Work 89

Wenger E, *Communities of Practice: Learning, Meaning, and Identity* (CUP 1998)

Wieringa S and others, 'How Knowledge Is Constructed and Exchanged in Virtual Communities of Physicians: Qualitative Study of Mindlines Online' (2018) 20(2) J Med Internet Res e34

Williams C R and others, 'Obstetric Violence: A Latin American Legal Response to Mistreatment during Childbirth' (2018) 125 BJOG 1208

World Health Organization, 'Midwives' Voices, Midwives' Realities Report 2016' (2016)

World Health Organization, 'WHO Recommendation: Intrapartum Care for a Positive Childbirth Experience' (2018)

World Health Organization, 'WHO Recommendations on Antenatal Care for a Positive Pregnancy Experience' (2016)

6 Health system accountability in South Africa

A driver of violence against women?

Jessica Rucell

Introduction

Pillay J emphasised: 'As unreasonable as the conduct of the [state's] employees was, any cost order drains the health budget at the expense of health services for all. It does not punish the wrong doers'.[1]

The term 'violence against women' encompasses a broad range of violence women and girls systemically face.[2] One of these forms of violence is the control of women's reproductive capacity during childbirth. Sexual and reproductive health and rights (SRHR) have been especially developed to acknowledge this vulnerability and to protect women from violations of our unique reproductive capacity.[3]

In this chapter I focus on the issue of 'obstetric violence' which I define as 'direct physical, psychological violence and/or unnecessary or coerced medical interventions' carried out within reproductive healthcare services.[4] I argue that obstetric violence therefore is a *particular* form of violence against women.

Recently, the World Health Organization (WHO) reached consensus that 'disrespect and abuse' of women during childbirth is a widespread and normalised practice affecting women in high- and low-income countries.[5] (The phrase 'disrespect and abuse,' regularly used in writing on birth in public health literature, is almost synonymous with the term 'obstetric violence' used in feminist literature.) The WHO statement can be interpreted then to mean that the evidence shows that it is *likely* for women to experience physical and/or psychological violence during hospital facility-based childbirth. Thus, the prevalence of obstetric violence is similar to more commonly discussed violence against

---

1 *Madida v MEC for Health for the Province of KwaZulu-Natal* 2016 JDR 0477 (KZP) [71].
2 See for example, the Convention on the Elimination of All Forms of Discrimination against Women (1979).
3 For instance, see General Comment 14 of the Committee on Economic, Social and Cultural Rights, 'Transforming our World: The 2030 Agenda for Sustainable Development' (A/RES/70/1, United Nations 2015).
4 Jessica Rucell, 'Obstetric Violence and Colonial Conditioning in South Africa's Reproductive Health System' (DPhil thesis, University of Leeds 2017) 17.
5 World Health Organization, 'The Prevention and Elimination of Disrespect and Abuse during Facility-based Childbirth' (2014) <http://apps.who.int/iris/bitstream/handle/10665/134588/WHO_RHR_14.23_eng.pdf?sequence=1> accessed 6 June 2018.

women.[6] This disturbing information signals to us that violence against women is systemic in health systems globally. As the opening quotation from Pillay J suggests, this context of gross injustice has legal, financial and social implications.

Direct obstetric violence continues to be poorly addressed and understood despite the fact that there is international consensus that its incidence has reached global proportions. The subordination of women, based on gender discrimination, and resultant inequalities in power are at the centre of all forms of violence against women.[7] Considering this I have found it useful and necessary to theorise the systemic drivers of this global problem facing women and their kin.

Taking into account a breadth of feminist theorisation on the violation of SRHR[8] coupled with my empirical research has led me to advance the thesis that this global phenomenon occurring across race, class, cultural and geographical differences is 'obstetric structural violence'.[9] By which I mean 'the socio-political causes of the systematic violation of sexual and reproductive health rights carried out by health systems, and/or policy, resulting in: The constraint of individuals' and in some circumstances whole groups capability to have children safely and with dignity, and prevent maternal and neonatal disability, morbidity and mortality'.[10] Furthermore, I have argued that obstetric structural violence is the cause of *direct* obstetric violence.

I argue that there are three key factors that generate and sustain 'obstetric structural violence': *social norms, political-economic arrangements, and health systems and their policies.*[11] Health systems reflect and reinforce the legal and policy frameworks guiding service delivery and society's dominant social values. In this way, health systems are products of their sociopolitical environments.[12] Thus, the predominance of gender discrimination and inequality facilitates and sustains this global problem at the institutional level.

6 Ibid.
7 Rashida Manjoo, 'Report of the Special Rapporteur on Violence Against Women Its Causes and Consequences' (A/HRC/26/38, United Nations General Assembly 2014) ss 29, 62.
8 Angela Davis, 'Racism, Birth Control and Reproductive Rights' in Angela Y Davis, *Women, Race and Class* (Random House/Women's Press 1982) 202, 217; Dorothy Roberts, *Killing the Black Body: Race, Reproduction, and the Meaning of Liberty* (Pantheon Books 1997); Imrana Qadeer, 'Unpacking the Myths: Inequities and Maternal Mortality in South Asia' (2005) 48 Development 120, 126. Jael Silliman, Anannya Bhattacharjee, and Angela Davis, *Policing the National Body: Sex, Race, and Criminalization* (South End Press 2002); Mohan Rao, *From Population Control to Reproductive Health: Malthusian Arithmetic* (Sage Publications 2004); Loretta J Ross and Rickie Solinger, *Reproductive Justice: An Introduction* (University of California Press 2017); Diana Bowser and Kathleen Hill, *Exploring Evidence for Disrespect and Abuse in Facility-Based Childbirth* (Harvard School of Public Health University Research Co 2010). Michelle Sadler and others, 'Moving beyond Disrespect and Abuse: Addressing the Structural Dimensions of Obstetric Violence' (2016) 24(47) Reprod Health Matters 47.
9 Rucell (n 4).
10 Ibid.
11 Ibid.
12 Sjaak van der Geest and Kaja Finkler, 'Hospital Ethnography: Introduction' (2004) 59 Soc Sci Med 1995.

In this chapter, I use my earlier theorisation to inform this investigation into one of the three key factors driving obstetric structural violence: 'Health systems and their policies'. My specific focus here is: health system accountability. To help identify the role of gender discrimination and inequality this examination is considered in relation to transparency of and participation in monitoring mechanisms as well as investigating the structure, distribution and functioning of health system oversight authority. Meaning, I ask: who is empowered with authority to oversee reporting and determine remedial actions, and how accessible are these powers and mechanisms to healthcare managers.

I apply these questions to the South African context. South Africa is a middle-income country although with one of the most significant income inequalities in the world. Its governing legal frameworks are lauded for their progressive stances, including with regard to SRHR.[13] This enabling legal and policy environment, coupled with the resources to support a functioning public health system, provides an instructive case to examine the influence of systems of accountability on obstetric violence. Adding to this relevance there is a documented history of obstetric violence in South Africa.[14] However, only a few of these studies offer detailed examinations of the role of health system factors.[15]

The analysis in this chapter is based on data from primary and secondary sources of research. I used qualitative research methods to map the district health system and evaluate the functioning of the governance of service delivery of seven public hospitals (consisting of primary and tertiary levels of care) in the Cape Town metro area.[16] Further, to consider the extent to which obstetric-related medical negligence litigation raises issues of obstetric structural violence I reviewed the available data on case law nationally up until 2017. Based on my analysis of this data I advance the argument that – broadly – accountability

13 Diane Cooper and others, 'Ten Years of Democracy in South Africa: Documenting Transformation in Reproductive Health Policy and Status' (2004) 12(24) Reprod Health Matters 70.

14 Rachel Jewkes and others, 'Why Do Nurses Abuse Patients? Reflections from South African Obstetric Services' (1998) 47 Soc Sci Med 1781; Lou-Marié Kruger and Christiaan Schoombee, 'The Other Side of Caring: Abuse in a South African Maternity Ward' (2010) 28 J Reprod Infant Psychol 84; Human Rights Watch, 'Stop Making Excuses: Accountability for Maternal Health-Care in South Africa' (*Reliefweb*, 8 August 2011) <www.ngopulse.org/resource/stop-making-excuses-accountability-maternal-health-care-south-africa> accessed 19 December 2018; Zaynab Essack and Ann Strode, '"I Feel Like Half a Woman all the Time": The Impacts of Coerced and Forced Sterilisations on HIV-Positive Women in South Africa' (2012) 26 Agenda 24; Ann Strode, Sethembiso Mthembu, and Zaynab Essack, '"She Made up a Choice for Me": 22 HIV-Positive Women's Experiences of Involuntary Sterilisation in Two South African Provinces' (2012) 20(s39) Reprod Health Matters 61; Rachelle J Chadwick, Diane Cooper, and Jane Harries, 'Narratives of Distress about Birth in South Africa Public Maternal Settings: A Qualitative Study' (2014) 30 Midwifery 862.

15 For example, Jewkes and others (n 14); Kruger and Schoombee (n 14).

16 I gained ethical approvals for this research from the University of Leeds (No. AREA 12-013), the University of Cape Town (No. HREC 290/2013) and the Western Cape Department of Health (No. RP093/2013). All field-sites are anonymised, and ethnically congruent pseudonyms are used to refer to participants and informants.

mechanisms encourage the tolerance of direct, and structural obstetric violence in several overlapping and reinforcing ways. This argument is based on the findings that these accountability mechanisms tolerate and invisibilise these gross violations of SRHR.

The first part outlines the relationship between obstetric violence and poor birth outcomes illustrated by data on South Africa. I take this approach to foreground the harmful consequences of a system that fails to protect women's SRHR. Then I provide the legal and policy contexts that guide the delivery of SRHR protections. The second part maps and analyses the structure, distribution and functioning of health system oversight authority. Then I provide an examination of relevant negligence case law, settlements and legislative response thereto. I conclude with an overview of my analysis of how the structures and functioning of health system accountability drive obstetric structural violence and propose solutions.

The problem of obstetric violence in South Africa

Obstetricians, gynaecologists[17] and nurses working in South Africa,[18] and global health experts confirm that it is likely for birthing women to be subjected to physical and/or psychological violence during facility-based care.[19] Forms of physical assault include: slapping, pulling and applying pressure to the fundus during active labour.[20] Coercive and unnecessary medical procedures include caesarean sections,[21] episiotomies,[22] vaginal examinations,[23] sterilisations and the administration of the contraception Depoprovera.[24]

17 E Farrell and R C Pattison, 'Out of the Mouths of Babes – Innocent Reporting of Harmful Labour Ward Practices' (2004) 94 SAMJ 896; D J Mets, 'Out of the Mouths of Babes – Innocent Reporting of Harmful Labour Ward Practices' (2005) 95 SAMJ 284; Simone Honikman, Sue Fawcus, and Ingrid Meintjes, 'Abuse in South African Maternity Settings Is a Disgrace: Potential Solutions to the Problem' (2015) 105 SAMJ 284.

18 Marie Hastings-Tolsma, Anna G W Nolte, and Annie Temane, 'Birth Stories from South Africa: Voices Unheard' (2018) 31(1) Women Birth e42.

19 Mickey Chopra and others, 'Saving the Lives of South Africa's Mothers, Babies, and Children: Can the Health System Deliver?' (2009) 374 The Lancet 835.

20 The fundus is the base or upper part of the uterus, which protrudes during pregnancy. Applying pressure to this organ during pregnancy is not part of evidence-based practice. Farrell and Pattison (n 17).

21 Rachelle Chadwick, 'Obstetric Violence in South Africa' (2016) 106 SAMJ 5.

22 'Episiotomy' refers to a surgical incision into the opening of the vagina. Clinical guidance advises a restriction of this practice. See World Health Organization, 'Recommendations for Prevention and Treatment of Maternal Peripartum Infections' (2015) <www.who.int/reproductivehealth/publications/maternal_perinatal_health/peripartum-infections-guidelines/en/> accessed 19 December 2018.

23 Women who participated in on and offline mobilisations in 2018 organised by the national #TheTotalShutDown social movement have reported that this is experienced as a form of sexual assault and occurs during cervical checks (to determine dilation in childbirth), during gynaecological examinations performed in cases concerning suspected miscarriage and in the contexts of post-abortion services.

24 Data on coercive sterilisation continues to emerge in South Africa. For instance, see South African National AIDS Council, 'The People Living with HIV Stigma Index, South Africa:

Psychological violence ranges from neglect to verbal assaults. Neglect refers to girls and women being turned away from healthcare facilities when they are in active labour.[25] And additionally, when labour ward staff do not attend to girls and women who have been admitted under their care.[26] Verbal assaults often take the form of healthcare professionals judging girls and women's sexuality and fertility choices.[27] In practice this means that girls and women who turn to the health system for care are met with accusations of having little morals, and blamed for poor birth outcomes.[28] Moreover, my empirical research found that verbal assault is normalised to the point that it is routinely practiced.[29] Research has also found that lack of material resources (staff, hygienic consumables and emergency obstetric equipment amongst others) contribute to certain forms of obstetric violence, for instance neglect.[30]

Relatedly, evidence has consistently shown that poor patient-provider relations, poor quality of care and patient's not finding services acceptable create barriers to women accessing sexual reproductive healthcare.[31] Importantly, acceptable, quality maternal healthcare is required to reduce preventable deaths.[32] Furthermore, the international community has reached consensus that 'preventable' rates of maternal morbidity and mortality are violations of women's rights.[33] Some South African scholars and government oversight bodies[34] single out avoidable provider and administrative health system factors as contributing to poor obstetric outcomes (including South Africa's high rate of maternal mortality). For instance, scholars[35] have noted that provider neglect contributed to

---

Summary Report' (May 2015) <www.stigmaindex.org/sites/default/files/reports/Summary-Booklet-on-Stigma-Index-Survey%20South%20Africa.pdf> accessed 19 December 2018. Strode, Mthembu, and Essack (n 14).

25 Interview with Dr Naledi, Family Physician, Primary-care Hospital (Cape Town, South Africa, 23 September 2013); Interview with Eleanor Grant, Professor of Obstetrics and Gynaecology (Cape Town, South Africa, 3 May 2017).

26 Human Rights Watch (n 14).

27 Rucell (n 4) 197–8. Grant (n 25); Interview with Thomas Gordon, Family Physician, Tertiary Hospital (Cape Town, South Africa, 10 August 2013).

28 Ibid.

29 Rucell (n 4) 197–8.

30 Bowser and Hill (n 8).

31 Chopra and others (n 19).

32 Suellen Miller and others, 'Beyond Too Little, Too Late and Too Much, Too Soon: A Pathway Towards Evidence-Based, Respectful Maternity Care Worldwide' (2016) 388 The Lancet 2176.

33 United Nations High Commissioner for Human Rights, 'Technical Guidance on the application of a human rights-based approach to the implementation of policies and programmes to reduce preventable maternal morbidity and mortality' (A/HRC/21/22, UN Human Rights Council 2012); United Nations High Commissioner for Human Rights, 'Follow-up report on the application of the technical guidance on the application of a human rights-based approach to the implementation of policies and programmes to reduce preventable maternal mortality and morbidity' (A/HRC/33/24, UN Human Rights Council 2016).

34 National Committee for the Confidential Enquiries into Maternal Deaths, 'Saving Mothers 2014–2016: Seventh Triennial Report on Confidential Enquiries into Maternal Deaths in South Africa (Short Report)' (Health Department Republic of South Africa 2018) 72–74, 128.

35 Farrell and Pattison (n 17); Chopra and others (n 19).

maternal and neonatal deaths.[36] Additionally, they outline that transportation and medical consumables (non-provider health system factors) also contribute to maternal deaths.

Furthermore, an assessment of maternal mortality in South Africa during the Millennial Development Goals (MDG) challenge (1990–2015) found 'forty per cent of all (maternal deaths) were classified as avoidable, indicating health systems failures'.[37] South Africa has created three mortality committees to capture and interpret primary data on maternal, perinatal and child mortality.[38]

Preventable maternal and neonatal disability (for instance anaemia, hormonal imbalances, pelvic inflammatory disease for mothers and cerebral palsy for newborns) and mortality has been a long-term problem in South Africa. Furthermore, with regard to mortality, of the 40 per cent of all deaths classified as avoidable during the MDG, these related to mortalities due to obstetric haemorrhage and hypertension being thought to be preventable in 81 per cent and 61 per cent of cases, respectively.[39] A significant increase of early pregnancy deaths were reported (37 per cent) in 2008–2010 as compared to 2005–2007.[40] The majority of these deaths resulted from complications following miscarriage and ectopic pregnancies. Moreover, 53 per cent of ectopic pregnancy deaths and 32 per cent of miscarriage deaths were classed as avoidable.[41] The latest review on maternal deaths found 61 per cent to be preventable, and resulting from 'mostly poor quality of care'.[42]

These egregious violations of women's rights, which include preventable deaths and disabilities, additionally signal the failures of protective legal and policy frameworks. This has been highlighted by the Human Rights Council as the ineffectiveness of health system accountability.[43] Furthermore, the Council states key components of effective accountability are resourced and appropriate monitoring mechanisms guided by transparency, equality and iterative participation.[44] The remaining sections of this chapter discuss South Africa's SRHR laws and analyse health system accountability mechanisms to explain why such violations of women's rights continue to take place.

36 Ibid.
37 Diane Cooper, Jane Harries, and Marriette Momberg, 'Assessing the Cycle of Accountability for Maternal and Child Health and Human Rights South Africa Report' (UN High Commissioner on Human Rights 2015) 6.
38 The National Committee for the Confidential Enquiries into Maternal Deaths established in 1998; the National Perinatal Mortality and Morbidity Committee, and the Committee on Mortality and Morbidity in Children, which were both established in 2008.
39 National Committee for the Confidential Enquiries into Maternal Deaths, 'Saving Mothers 2008–2010: Fifth Report on Confidential Enquiries into Maternal Deaths in South Africa' (Health Department Republic of South Africa 2011).
40 Ibid.
41 Ibid.
42 (n 34) 174.
43 UN High Commissioner for Human Rights (n 33) 16–19.
44 Ibid.

Reproductive rights, accountability and legal redress

South Africa has a developed public health system and sophisticated medical fraternity and policy system. A progressive legal and policy framework was established over 20 years ago to address, amongst other problems, the staggering rates of maternal and neonatal disability and mortality inherited from centuries of colonialism and decades of apartheid.[45]

SRHR received particular attention which is explicitly protected in the South African Constitution[46] and other legislation. Section 4 of the National Health Act[47] mandates the provision of free healthcare services to all pregnant and breast-feeding women, and in 1996 legislation was passed to mandate free abortion services.[48] In addition, Sections 3–5 of the National Health Act mandate decentralisation of power over health governance and service delivery. This includes a framework requiring community oversight, which is a key lever for women's empowerment. Indeed, the majority participating in community health structures are older women.[49] However, unfortunately, in practice the empowered community oversight stipulated in the Act is largely non-existent. Where community oversight has been organised it takes the form of Community Health Committees (CHCs) and Regional Health Forums which are separate from the more powerful Hospital Boards. The existing CHCs and forums are fragmented, unclear of their mandate, and lack operational and skilled resources.[50] At times community oversight structures are entirely absent.[51] Despite this gross lack of policy implementation I raise this mechanism here because community oversight is one of the key levers able to support women's participation and SRHR.[52]

Still, the changes in law and policy in favour of rights to health are significant achievements. For instance, the legalisation of abortion decreased maternal mortality and morbidity significantly.[53] Despite this step forward evidence suggests that many women still use illegal and unsafe abortion providers.[54] One likely

45 Cooper, Harries, and Momberg (n 37).
46 See sections 12(2)(a) and 27(1)(a) of the Constitution of the Republic of South Africa, 1996.
47 National Health Act (No. 61 2003).
48 Cooper, Harries, and Momberg (n 37).
49 Hanne Jensen Haricharan, 'Extending Participation: Challenges of Health Committees as Meaningful Structures for Community Participation: A Study of Health Committees in the Cape Town Metropole' (University of Cape Town and the Learning Network on Health and Human Rights 2011) 8–9.
50 Ibid. Tracey Naledi, Peter Barron, and Helen Schneider, 'Primary Health Care in South Africa since 1994 and Implications of the New Vision for PHC Re-Engineering' in A Padarath and R English (eds), *South African Health Review 2011* (Health Systems Trust 2011) 20.
51 Ibid.
52 A/HRC/21/22 (n 33) 17.
53 Rachel K Jewkes and others, 'Why Are Women Still Aborting Outside Designated Facilities in Metropolitan South Africa?' (2005) 112 BJOG 1236.
54 Ibid.

reason for this is that the state has not adequately distributed its funds to ensure easy access to safe abortion services.[55]

As values and policies change over time, they reshape patient/provider relations with them.[56] The embrace of a rights-based approach to SRH is one aspect of changing patient/provider relations and removing practices of violence and control. Despite these extensive legislative and policy efforts the evidence provided earlier as well as that on abortion here establishes that systemic violations persist. Health systems reflect the changing societal values (and policies) they exist within. Thus, the partiality of these gains signals the continued constraint on women's power. The following analysis of the operations of health system accountability illustrates how women's power is constrained.

Locating power and inequality in health system governance

The progressive legislative environment described earlier and appropriate monitoring mechanisms are key elements to maintaining SRHR and health system accountability. To understand the spectrum of challenges posed to ensuring the protection of SRHR and the empowerment of women through them, the next section analyses the structures of health system accountability. It does so by first engaging with the empirical data drawn from my research in the Western Cape Metro district health system. Internal (national and provincial) health system accountability mechanisms, their accessibility to the public and the distribution of power and oversight are mapped in Figure 6.1. The left side maps the guidelines and functioning of the Department of Health's (DoH) internal complaints procedures, and the often-parallel disciplinary hearings carried out under the internal Office of Labour Relations. Importantly, the Director of Labour Relations oversees complaint management relating to the internal investigation of staff transgressions. As is evident from the figure, this is a hierarchical and non-community participatory structure.

The primary role of Directors of Districts is to translate strategic policy decisions into long, mid-term, short and immediate operational service delivery.[57] Their main responsibility is to manage district health services through hospitals and clinic facilities.[58] These authorities are also responsible for overseeing all complaints, including those reported to the national Minister of Health,

55 Gilda Sedgh and others, 'Induced Abortion Incidence and Trends Worldwide from 1995 to 2008' (2012) 379 The Lancet 625.

56 Lucy Gilson, 'Trust and the Development of Health Care as a Social Institution' (2003) 56 Soc Sci Med 1453.

57 For clarity, it is important to note that in the Western Cape Metro districts are designated as 'sub-structures'. I use the term districts as that designation is more commonly used in South Africa and globally.

58 Soraya Elloker and others, 'Crises, Routines and Innovations: The Complexities and Possibilities of Sub-District Management' in A Padarath and R English (eds), *South African Health Review 2012/13*' (Health Systems Trust 2013) 161, 164; Vera Scott and others, 'Exploring the

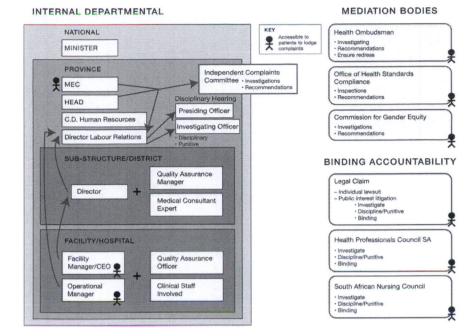

Figure 6.1 Internal and external accountability mechanisms (author's own).[59]

provincial Member of Executive Council (MEC), and those reported to the various institutions (labelled *Mediating Bodies* on the right side in Figure 6.1). If a complaint or negligence case is escalated through the Labour Relations office its Director oversees and appoints the presiding officers who hear and make the final determinations on internal investigations and disciplinary hearings.

Gilson and her colleagues argue that the health system is both complex and adaptive.[60] The governance structure examined earlier confirms the complexity of the administrative and political power overseeing the system. Transparency is key to determining the level of functioning of an accountability system. This is because information facilitates answerability and enforceability.[61] For instance, staff, managers and community members who are informed about procedures

Nature of Governance at the Level of Implementation for Health System Strengthening: The DIALHS Experience' (2014) 29(s2) Health Policy Plan ii59, ii61.

59 This figure builds on the Western Cape Department of Health's organogram, see Western Cape Department of Health, 'Organogram of Senior Management' (2010) <www.westerncape.gov.za/other/2010/10/health_organogram_2010.pdf> accessed 20 December 2018.

60 Lucy Gilson and others, 'Development of the Health System in the Western Cape: Experiences since 1994' in A Padarath and P Barron (eds), *South African Health Review 2017* (Health Systems Trust 2017) 59.

61 Rosie McGee and John Gaventa, 'Shifting Power? Assessing the Impact of Transparency and Accountability Initiatives' (2011) 383 IDS Working Papers 1.

and active cases are empowered to provide oversight, whereas the absence of information disempowers stakeholders from participation.

I was only able to engage with one of the four District Directors in the Metro District during my research. After more than five appointments with District Directors were made and rescheduled, it appeared clear that these authorities wanted little to do with a study focused on the quality of health system accountability relating to obstetric care. Therefore, I have limited direct information from this important level of authority. Cooper, Harries and Momberg's assessment of accountability for SRHR similarly found issues with transparency, '[al]though monitoring and evaluation mechanisms *appear* to be transparent and readily available, there appears to be a significant delay in the publication of data through the various governmental departments and committees'.[62] Furthermore, in my interviews, several nurses and managers at the primary level of care were reportedly confused about lines of governance and authority within the health system. Lack of transparency contributed to this. In addition, staff were unsure about how reporting functions in instances of negligence apart from initial reporting to heads of units and primary care hospitals.[63]

Staff confusion seems to be driven by at least three factors: (1) The lack of answerability staff and clinic managers experienced when patients, staff and managers themselves reported complaints and grievances (this lack of answerability from empowered authorities included cases of serious operational failures and medical negligence. Cases reported ranged from the physical assault and neglect of patients on the one hand, and stock-outs, chronic absenteeism and crony management on the other hand). (2) I found the staffs' sense of confusion is compounded by the seemingly unending structural reforms to the health system initiated since democracy. Scott and her colleagues similarly found managers and staff described the result of this continuous restructuring as 'change fatigue'.[64] Additionally, a long-term research team examining structures of district health governance argues that the change fatigue, habits of authoritarianism and growing patient demands lead to district and hospital level managers developing 'collective mind-sets of passivity and risk avoidance'.[65] (3) The lack of guidelines to manage complaints and grievances has also contributed to staff's disempowerment. For instance, at the provincial level, guidelines were first established

---

62 Cooper, Harries, and Momberg (n 37) 12, emphasis added.

63 Interview with Mthwakazi Qumza, Midwife, Primary Care Hospital (Cape Town, South Africa, 22 August 2013); Interview with Babalwa Mfiki, Midwife, Primary Care Hospital (Cape Town, South Africa, 29 October 2013); Interview with Dineo Ngoqo, Operations Manager, Primary Care Hospital (Cape Town, South Africa, 5 September 2013); Interview with Crystal Abrahams, Midwife, Primary Care Hospital (Cape Town, South Africa, 10 October 2016).

64 Vera Scott, Verona Mathews, and Lucy Gilson, 'Constraints to Implementing an Equity-Promoting Staff Allocation Policy: Understanding Mid-Level Managers' and Nurses' Perspectives Affecting Implementation in South Africa' (2011) 27 Health Policy Plan 138, 141.

65 Lucy Gilson and others, 'Advancing the Application of Systems Thinking in Health: South African Examples of a Leadership of Sense-Making for Primary Health Care' (2014) 12 Health Res Pol Syst 1, 10.

in 2014, and at the national level guidelines to manage complaints were only released in 2017.[66]

My argument here is that lack of transparency and the hierarchical structure of accountability mechanisms contribute to the disempowerment of low-level staff (the majority of whom are black women nurses), primary care hospital CEOs (who are also often nurses) and obstetric patients (the majority of whom are working class black women). I have identified the category of healthcare professional and gender and race markers of the staff and patients here to raise that their disempowerment within the health system corresponds their continued disempowerment in South African society. As the below data show, this lack of transparency and structural dis-empowerment often results in reported cases of obstetric violence being ignored and left unpunished. In this way the disenfranchisement of staff enables the health system to *encourage* direct and structural obstetric violence. By disciplining these civil servants into adopting passive approaches to governance, the health system *tolerates* and *normalises* this particular form of violence against women.

Another contributing issue is the oversight authority of health system accountability being ignored and broken at primary care Midwifery Obstetric Units (MOU). This was found in three of the four districts in the Cape Metro that I studied. This breakdown in oversight caused isolation of clinics and a lack of reporting to and accountability from responsible authorities. In all the cases the exclusion was entrenched and fed confusion about lines of authority. In two of the clinics this led not only to tolerance of obstetric violence but also to poor procurement of necessary consumable goods (which as mentioned earlier can relate to obstetric violence).[67]

An interview with Family Physician Naledi illustrates the level of isolation that one MOU faced for several years from the CEO of the hospital (facility manager) the unit is housed in and how a policy intervention impacted this neglect:

DR: 'Engagement with MOU started with this "Patient Centred Care" meeting'.
INTERVIEWER: 'You mean with the facility manager?'

66 Western Cape Department of Health, 'Adverse Incident Reporting and Management System: Guideline and Training Manual' (2014) emailed from Asher Swartz, Health Impact Assessment Directorate, WC Department of Health to author (6 November 2017). Department of Health of the Republic of South Africa, 'National Guideline to Manage Complaints, Compliments and Suggestions in the Health Sector' (2017) <www.idealhealthfacility.org.za/docs/guidelines/ Complaint-Management/National%20Guideline%20to%20Manage%20Complaints%20 Compliments%20and%20Suggestions%20March%202017.pdf.> accessed 20 December 2018.

67 For a detailed analysis of similar problems in other hospital settings, see Karl von Holdt and Bethuel Maserumule, 'After Apartheid: Decay or Reconstruction in a Public Hospital?' in Edward Webster and Karl von Holdt (eds), *Beyond the Apartheid Workplace: Studies in Transition* (University of KwaZulu-Natal Press 2005) 1; Karl von Holdt and Mike Murphy, 'Public Hospitals in South Africa: Stressed Institutions, Disempowered Management' in Sakhela Buhlungu and others (eds), *State of the Nation: South Africa* (HSRC Press and Michigan State University Press 2007) 312.

DR NALEDI: 'Yes, that meeting you attended? That was *the first* meeting that Mr Mosima *ever had* about MOU things'.

INTERVIEWER: 'Do you mean the meeting that we had with the task team?'

DR NALEDI: 'Yes, in his office. That was the *first ever* about MOU related things.'[68]

In this excerpt, the meeting referred to is a provincial-led attempt at developing a code of conduct to intervene in the poor quality of maternal care.[69] Family physicians based in primary care hospitals have a significant level of clinical and therefore at times administrative sway with higher authorities. It is important to note that for a family physician to say the above to a researcher demonstrates their frustration from the lack of accountable oversight. In this case the lack of engagement with reported incidents at hospital and district levels prompted her to speak out in this way. The incidents reported included one case of the physical assault of a patient and a series of stillbirths, which the doctor suspected resulted from neglectful service. I was unable to engage District Directors who are empowered to respond to reports of medical negligence on these and other cases. I received approvals to interview them but their doors remained closed to me as a researcher. I continued to follow-up with the hospital and the physician for a year but there had been no response from these authorities. It seems to be commonly held by staff that authorities do not respond to reports of gross negligence unless the cases are reported in the press. Thus, health system accountability is of a poor quality.

My empirical research also found that 'collective mind-sets of passivity' combined with the lack of power held outside of the top levels of management fuel challenges to the dignity and self-worth of those responsible for the bulk of direct service delivery. As one female CEO of a primary care hospital rhetorically asked in an interview:

> Why won't they [District and Chief Directors] listen to people who are here? ... So it means that even if I am here it has to take someone else to make things happen ... I have to say the system has failed me. ... Maybe people are not aware that you [Facility Manager] also have eyes to see, that you have mind. I can simply put it like that.[70]

This excerpt reveals the outright frustration felt by some primary care level CEOs. It illustrates how this derives from challenges to their self-worth by constraints on their power by the strict hierarchy of the health system.

Thus, I argue that the structure of the health system undermines primary care level staff and managers. It does so by challenging their capacity and authority

---

68 Interview with Dr Naledi, Family Physician, Primary Care Hospital (Cape Town, South Africa, 23 September 2013).

69 Honikman, Fawcus, and Meintjes (n 17).

70 Interview with Xolie Radebe, Facility Manager, Primary Hospital (Cape Town, South Africa, 9 September 2013).

through 'a system inertia'[71] that enforces complacency and tolerance of direct and structural obstetric violence. It is important to note that the majority of these civil servants are working class women, carry out the bulk of service delivery and are the least empowered healthcare professionals in the health system. This is unremarkable because the predominant social norm of gender discrimination predicts their disempowerment.

Case law and settlements for obstetric-related medical negligence

This section builds on the previous one by providing an analysis of the influence of legal mechanisms on health system accountability. Negligence case law[72] and obstetric malpractice settlements in South Africa are reviewed. I consider legal mechanisms to develop a more complete understanding of the context of binding health system accountability on obstetric violence.[73] In addition, this data demonstrates the relationship between neonatal disability and obstetric violence, justifying further why I link these in the introduction. Finally, I analyse an overview of national data on settlements for negligence claims, as well as a report of trends in increasing obstetric-related negligence in the Western Cape Province.[74] Both the national and provincial documents concern settlements for indefensible medical negligence.

---

71 Interview with Dr Thomas Gordon, Family Physician, Secondary Hospital (Cape Town, South Africa, 10 August 2013.
72 This analysis builds on an initial legal analysis provided by Camilla Pickles (email from Camilla Pickles to author (2 June 2017)); and it consists of 23 cases: *Bunge v MEC For Health, KZN* 2009 JDR 1035 (KZP); *Hoffmann v MEC for the Department of Health, Eastern Cape* 2011 JDR 1081 (ECP); *Khanyi v Premier of Gauteng* 2011 JDR 0433 (GSJ); *Khoza v MEC for Health and Social Development, Gauteng* 2015 (3) SA 266 (GJ); *Madida* (n 1); *Magqeya v MEC for Health, Eastern Cape* 2017 JDR 0598 (ECM); *Makgomarela v Premier of Gauteng* [2012] ZAGPJHC 217; *Molefe v MEC for Health* 2015 JDR 0449 (GP); *Mucavele v MEC for Health* 2015 JDR 1942 (GP); *Neveling v MEC for Health and Social Development, Gauteng Province* 2016 JDR 1219 (GJ); *Nkayiya v MEC for Health, Eastern Cape* 2015 JDR 2421 (ECM); *Ntsele v MEC For Health, Gauteng Provincial Government* 2012 JDR 2044 (GSJ); *Ntungele v MEC, Department of Health, Eastern Cape* 2015 JDR 0104 (ECM); *Nzimande v MEC for Health, Gauteng* 2015 (6) SA 192 (GP); *Sibaya v Life Healthcare Group (Pty) Ltd* 2017 JDR 0523 (KZD); *Sifumba v MEC for Health, Eastern Cape* 2015 JDR 1597 (ECM); *Tsita v MEC for Health and Social Development, Gauteng* 2015 JDR 1539 (GP); *Smith v MEC for Health, Gauteng* 2015 JDR 1819 (GP); *Sifumba v MEC for Health, Western Cape* 2015 JDR 1597; *AD v MEC for Health and Social Development, Western Cape* 2016 (7A4) QOD 32 (WCC); *Matlakala v MEC for Health, Gauteng* 2015 (7A4) QOD 22 (GJ); *Xolile v MEC for Health and Social Development, Gauteng* 2015 (3) SA 616 (GJ); *Paia v MEC for Health and Social Development* 2017 JDR 0735 (GJ); *NS v MEC for the Department of Health, Eastern Cape* 2017 JDR 0568 (ECM).
73 See Figure 6.1 for an overview of binding mechanisms.
74 David Bass, 'Western Cape Health Department: Report on Activities and Priorities' (2015); M J Mantsho, 'Steps Taken by the Department of Health to Address Issues of Medical Litigation in South Africa' (National Treasury Meeting 2015).

Analysis of case law

The 23 cases demonstrate that medical negligence litigation has been reported in four of the nine provinces in South Africa. Gauteng has the greatest number with 14 cases,[75] six in the Eastern Cape, three in KwaZulu-Natal, and one in the Western Cape. Comparison between the 23 reported cases (total 23) and the national data on negligence (4,063 obstetric-related claims in the first six months of 2017) demonstrates that the overwhelming majority of claims are settled out of court both in private and in public healthcare. A senior medical malpractice lawyer confirmed that the government 'trend is to settle through a mediator.'[76] Alice Marais explains the Western Cape Department of Health strategy is to settle clearly indefensible cases that are claiming less than ZAR one million without arbitration.[77] All of the reported cases, except one,[78] concern litigation against the state.[79] This suggests that the private sector more successfully settles and avoids a pubic scene, or that the cases have not yet been finalised. In cases against the state either the national or provincial ministers are held liable as they bear legal responsibility for negligent conduct within the health system. In this way, public servants who deliver care are not held legally responsible for their actions. As Figure 6.1 shows, patients must approach medical professional associations (or other oversight agencies) to hold a clinical professional accountable who works in the public health system.[80] Thus, case law predominantly reflects women and their families' efforts to gain material compensation.

Importantly, most of the cases concern claims for harms caused to children during birth or soon after birth, rather than harms caused to women.[81] This stands even where harm to women is very clearly present.[82] Cerebral palsy claims resulting from poor quality of care feature extensively, and the courts recognise cerebral palsy to be a serious harm. Available case law does not include the amount awarded because all of the cases, except one,[83] separated the determination of liability from the determination of 'quantum'.[84] The state (as the

---

75 Four were heard in Pretoria and 10 in Johannesburg.
76 Interview with Lynn McClure, Senior Medical Malpractice Lawyer (Johannesburg, South Africa, 22 May 2017).
77 Email from Alice Marais to author, Advisor, Medico-Legal Department, WC Department of Health to author (7 November 2017).
78 *Sibaya* (n 72).
79 Pickles (n 72).
80 Although associations are mandated to publicly report information on arbitration the SA Nursing Council, for example has not done so recently. Further, after countless attempts to gain statistics they refused.
81 Pickles (n 72).
82 Ibid. For instance, see *Mucavele* (n 72); *Hoffmann* (n 72). At times, the case law states that women claim in their personal and representative capacity. However, these claims are not separated and broken down, so it is impossible to determine what is being claimed in relation to the claimants themselves and what is being claimed on behalf of the children.
83 *Hoffmann* (n 72).
84 Also, most of the judgments are recent, and the portion of the cases concerning quantum may still be ongoing.

defendant) tends to be liable for the plaintiff's litigation costs where she is successful in establishing negligence and this adds to the state's burden in relation to the overall cost of medical negligence cases.[85]

Failure to comply with guidelines, lack of adequate monitoring and poor record keeping feature prominently in the case law.[86] The role of midwives is central to the process of legal recompense, in that the case law shows they often failed to detect foetal distress and do not seem to act with appropriate urgency.[87] Interestingly, lack of available resources, stillbirth and adverse treatment in the form of direct violence do not feature as extensively as one might expect. In *Mucavele*, procedures were performed on the mother without her informed consent (including sterilisation), but these issues were not brought before the court because her claim centred on harm to the child.[88] *Madida* exposes harm to the woman, but again this issue was not considered because claim centred exclusively on harm to the child.[89] In this instance, a midwife applied pressure to the fundus (the women's abdomen) during active labour and the child developed cerebral palsy. An expert witness to the case noted that the midwives action was dangerous for *both* the mother and foetus.[90] The court found in favour of the mother, highlighting the service rendered caused injury to the foetus and newborn.[91] Both of these cases, though not litigated for maternal traumas, show egregious forms of obstetric violence, which clearly are linked to adverse medical outcomes, including (in the former case) a permanent limitation to fertility. Judges can only consider the grievances presented to them. Thus, because the mother's involuntary sterilisation was not raised as an issue in *Mucavele*, the judge was not empowered to deliberate on this damage. This evidence demonstrates that while litigation for the recovery of damages supports compensation for injuries caused during childbirth, at present it has little bearing on staff and facility accountability, or more importantly systematic improvement of the quality of care. This sentiment is echoed by Pillay J in *Madida*: 'As unreasonable as the conduct of the defendant's employees was, any cost order drains the health budget at the expense of health services for all. It does not punish the wrong doers'.[92]

This analysis has shown that while legal protections are in place to deter medical negligence, and compensate and remedy violations of women's SRHR, they do little to hold accountable even those perpetrating direct acts of violence against women. Rather, the direct acts are invisibilised by the way they feature as evidence in the litigation.[93] Thus, like the functioning of health system

85 Pickles (n 72).
86 Ibid.
87 Ibid.
88 *Mucavele* (n 72) [7], [51], [65].
89 *Madida* (n 1) [57]–[58].
90 Ibid [57].
91 Ibid [70].
92 *Madida* (n 1) [71].
93 Pickles (n 72).

accountability the approach adopted in negligence cases also encourages tolerance of direct and structural obstetric violence.

Minister of Health: sexual and reproductive health rights

The following analysis of settled negligence claims is based on data for the first
six months of 2017 from the National Department of Health.[94] The total claims
for obstetric-related medical negligence in this period were 7,889, of which
4,063 were obstetric-related cases, and the total number of cerebral palsy cases
was 3,089. This shows that obstetric-related cases make up a high proportion of
settled cases and are probably the majority of medico-legal claims throughout
the country.[95] Not only that, obstetric claims are a higher proportion of the total
amount paid out through settlements for negligence claims.[96] That settlements
tend to be larger for obstetric-related claims makes sense. Especially considering
reported case law, which shows the majority of claims concerning disabled children result from indefensible adverse healthcare practices. The overwhelming
majority of cases are settled out of court, an action I presume results from the
Department's medico-legal teams determining claims to be indefensible.

Unfortunately, the arguments and solution put forward by the state to this
widespread problem do not acknowledge the context of poor quality and abusive health services that contribute to the scale of – indefensible – negligence
claims. The Minister of Health has consistently argued (and now the Minister
of Justice) that the increasing claims in medical negligence correlate to a preda-
tory legal fraternity, rather than the well-documented increasing crisis in public
healthcare.[97] Following this trajectory on 30 May 2018 the Minister of Justice,
after consultations with the Minister of Health, introduced the 'State Liability
Amendment Bill'.[98] This amendment bill proposed changes in the ways payments would be dispersed to women and their families who received payments
for medical negligence. In essence, it caps the lump sum amounts of compensation women could gain for damages incurred from health services. The Parliamentary Committee considering the amendment received widespread objections
to the bill, including on the basis that it will create barriers to indigent women
and their family's access to justice.[99] Meanwhile, the DoH has not proposed

---

93 Mantsho (n 74).

95 Ibid 31.

96 Ibid.

97 Chantall Presence, 'Motsoaledi: NHI Is Coming, Whether You Like It or Not' (*Independent Online*, 16 May 2017) <www.iol.co.za/news/politics/motsoaledi-nhi-is-coming-whether-you-like-it-or-not-9171470> accessed 20 December 2018; Aaron Motsoaledi, 'Health Dept Budget Vote 2016/17' (*South African Government*, 10 May 2016) <www.gov.za/speeches/debate-health-budget-vote-national-assembly-10-may-2016-dr-aaron-motsoaledi-minister-health> accessed 20 December 2018.

98 State Liability Amendment Bill, B16-2018. South African Law Reform Commission, 'Project 141: Medico-Legal Claims, Issue paper 33' (20 May 2017) <www.justice.gov.za/salrc/ipapers/ip33_prj141_Medico-legal.pdf> accessed 20 December 2018.

99 See Parliamentary Monitoring Group, 'Overview of the Session' (31 October 2018) <https://pmg.org.za/committee-meeting/27412/> accessed 28 December 2018.

any national intervention into the poor quality of reproductive healthcare or corruption draining its budget.[100] The state's approach is fundamentally flawed. Instead of showing leadership by taking responsibility the proposed legislative approach will further disempower and burden poor women and their families.[101] In the end, Parliament did not hear the matter further, allowing it to 'lapse' as per National Assembly procedure.[102] Perhaps it failed because of the strong objections to the Minister's legislative approach.

An important finding from the analysis of legal approaches to obstetric-related medical negligence is that these mechanisms do little to hold accountable health facilities and professionals perpetrating direct acts of violence to women and their kin. Thus, this avenue too tolerates direct and structural obstetric violence. While the available data on settlements are not detailed enough to show if acts of violence against women have occurred it does reveal the volume of claims, and that they are deemed indefensible. And therefore, the Department's medico-legal teams consistently determine health system or provider care to be negligent. Interestingly, this corroborates the conclusions of the scholars and state oversight bodies who assert that provider and health system 'avoidable factors' contribute to maternal and neonatal deaths.[103] Finally, the state's refusal to acknowledge its culpability reinforces impunity regarding this crisis in quality care as well as this particular form of violence against women.

Conclusion

In this chapter I defined obstetric violence and obstetric structural violence. I investigated *health system accountability mechanisms* including: the distribution and functioning of governance oversight authority and legal approaches to medical negligence. This analysis identified several ways in which these mechanisms of accountability sustain this particular form of violence against women. The main conclusion of this chapter is that the functioning of health system accountability mechanisms, legal claims and Ministerial leadership encourages the tolerance of direct and structural obstetric violence in several overlapping and reinforcing ways.

My analysis of empirical data on the governance of public hospitals in the Cape Town Metro, South Africa, found that power remains concentrated within a hierarchy. A lack of information and transparency about the reporting of negligence further concentrates power. This combined with the poor functioning of oversight and reporting processes disempowers low-level managers and staff. Unsurprisingly, these disempowered staff are predominantly black women, who are duly marginalised because of their gender and race within society. Complicating these challenges further is the fact that while community oversight of

---

100 Laetitia C Rispel, Pieter de Jager, and Sharon Fonn, 'Exploring Corruption in the South African Health Sector' (2016) 31 Health Policy Plan 239.

101 Presence (n 97).

102 See Parliamentary Monitoring Group, 'State Liability Amendment Bill' National Assembly 7 May 2019. <https://pmg.org.za/bill/797/> accessed 8 July 2019.

103 Chopra and others (n 19).

health system governance is mandated by law, this has not been largely implemented. These features of health system accountability confirm a 'system inertia' enforcing *complacency* and *tolerance* toward disempowerment and violence against women and girls. In these ways, key structural drivers, health systems and the implementation of its policies were found to sustain direct acts of violence against women.

Finally, I considered the influence of legal approaches to obstetric negligence on health system governance. This was done through an analysis of obtainable data on national case law and settlements. In addition, I examined the state's legislative solution to this crisis in obstetric healthcare. My analysis of cases and settlements reveals that these legal approaches do not hold perpetrators of direct violence accountable. The outcome of litigation on public institutions is rather their being made responsible for material compensation, with no other consequences. Furthermore, violence against women is taken as evidence in litigation and then invisibilised in judgments. I argue this acts as a tolerance of direct and structural obstetric violence. Moreover, the vast majority of negligence claims were found to be settled out of court, and resulting from being deemed 'indefensible' by the DoH's medico-legal departments. This issue points further to a crisis in the quality of reproductive healthcare. A major finding is that case law showed links between obstetric violence and indefensible claims for obstetric negligence, suggesting that there is a link between abuse and poor maternal and neonatal outcomes. Therefore, it is likely that a portion of medical negligence cases result from obstetric violence. Finally, the state's approach to 'better' manage the distribution of compensation for obstetric damages through legislation reinforces impunity for poor quality care and this particular form of violence against women. I argue that this is unacceptable. Rather the state must invest in improving the quality of care and answerability for obstetric-related medical negligence, including that which occurs as a result of the violation of women's reproductive rights.

Table of cases

AD v MEC for Health and Social Development, Western Cape 2016 (7A4) QOD 32 (WCC)
Bunge v MEC for Health, KZN 2009 JDR 1035 (KZP)
Hoffmann v MEC for the Department of Health, Eastern Cape 2011 JDR 1081 (ECP)
Khanyi v Premier of Gauteng 2011 JDR 0433 (GSJ)
Khoza v MEC for Health and Social Development, Gauteng 2015 (3) SA 266 (GJ)
Madida v MEC for Health for the Province of KwaZulu-Natal 2016 JDR 0477 (KZP)
Magqeya v MEC for Health, Eastern Cape 2017 JDR 0598 (ECM)
Makgomarela v Premier of Gauteng [2012] ZAGPJHC 217
Matlakala v MEC for Health, Gauteng 2015 (7A4) QOD 22 (GJ)
Molefe v MEC for Health 2015 JDR 0449 (GP)
Mucavele v MEC for Health 2015 JDR 1942 (GP)
Neveling v MEC for Health and Social Development, Gauteng Province 2016 JDR 1219 (GJ)
Nkayiya v MEC for Health, Eastern Cape 2015 JDR 2421 (ECM)
NS v MEC for the Department of Health, Eastern Cape 2017 JDR 0568 (ECM)

Ntsele v MEC for Health, Gauteng Provincial Government 2012 JDR 2044 (GSJ)
Ntungele v MEC, Department of Health, Eastern Cape 2015 JDR 0104 (ECM)
Nzimande v MEC for Health, Gauteng 2015 (6) SA 192 (GP)
Paia v MEC for Health and Social Development 2017 JDR 0735 (GJ)
Sibaya v Life Healthcare Group (Pty) Ltd 2017 JDR 0523 (KZD)
Sifumba v MEC for Health, Eastern Cape 2015 JDR 1597 (ECM)
Sifumba v MEC for Health, Western Cape 2015 JDR 1597
Smith v MEC for Health, Gauteng 2015 JDR 1819 (GP)
Tsita v MEC for Health and Social Development, Gauteng 2015 JDR 1539 (GP)
Xolile v MEC for Health and Social Development, Gauteng 2015 (3) SA 616 (GJ)

Bibliography

Bass D, 'Western Cape Health Department: Report on Activities and Priorities' (2015)

Bowser D and Hill K, *Exploring Evidence for Disrespect and Abuse in Facility-Based Childbirth* (Harvard School of Public Health University Research Co 2010)

Chadwick R, 'Obstetric Violence in South Africa' (2016) 106 SAMJ 5

Chadwick R J, Cooper D, and Harries J, 'Narratives of Distress about Birth in South Africa Public Maternal Settings: A Qualitative Study' (2014) 30 Midwifery 862

Chopra M and others, 'Saving the Lives of South Africa's Mothers, Babies, and Children: Can the Health System Deliver?' (2009) 374 The Lancet 835

Cooper D and others, 'Ten Years of Democracy in South Africa: Documenting Transformation in Reproductive Health Policy and Status' (2004) 12(24) Reprod Health Matters 70

Cooper D, Harries J, and Momberg M, *Assessing the Cycle of Accountability for Maternal and Child Health and Human Rights South Africa Report* (UN High Commissioner on Human Rights 2015)

Davis A, 'Racism, Birth Control and Reproductive Rights' in Angela Y Davis, *Women, Race and Class* (Random House/Women's Press 1982) 202

Department of Health of the Republic of South Africa, 'National Guideline to Manage Complaints, Compliments and Suggestions in the Health Sector' (2017)

Elloker Soraya and others, 'Crises, Routines and Innovations: The Complexities and Possibilities of Sub-District Management' in Padarath A and English E (eds), *South African Health Review 2012/13*' (Health Systems Trust 2013)

Essack Z and Strode A, '"I Feel Like Half a Woman all the Time": The Impacts of Coerced and Forced Sterilisations on HIV-Positive Women in South Africa' (2012) 26 Agenda 24

Farrell E and Pattison R C, 'Out of the Mouths of Babes – Innocent Reporting of Harmful Labour Ward Practices' (2004) 94 SAMJ 896

Geest S and Finkler K, 'Hospital Ethnography: Introduction' (2004) 59 Soc Sci Med 1995

General Comment 14 of the Committee on Economic, Social and Cultural Rights, 'Transforming our World: The 2030 Agenda for Sustainable Development' (A/RES/70/1, United Nations 2015)

Gilson L, 'Trust and the Development of Health Care as a Social Institution' (2003) 56 Soc Sci Med 1453

Gilson L and others, 'Advancing the Application of Systems Thinking in Health: South African Examples of a Leadership of Sense-Making for Primary Health Care' (2014) 12 Health Res Pol Syst 1

Haricharan H S, 'Extending Participation: Challenges of Health Committees as Meaningful Structures for Community Participation: A Study of Health Committees in the Cape Town Metropole' (University of Cape Town and the Learning Network on Health and Human Rights 2011)

Hastings-Tolsma M, Nolte A G W, and Temane A, 'Birth Stories from South Africa: Voices Unheard' (2018) 31(1) Women Birth e42

Holdt K and Maserumule B, 'After Apartheid: Decay or Reconstruction in a Public Hospital?' in Webster E and Holdt K (eds), *Beyond the Apartheid Workplace: Studies in Transition* (University of KwaZulu-Natal Press 2005)

Holdt K and Murphy M, 'Public Hospitals in South Africa: Stressed Institutions, Disempowered Management' in Buhlungu S and others (eds), *State of the Nation: South Africa* (HSRC Press and Michigan State University Press 2007)

Honikman S, Fawcus S, and Meintjes I, 'Abuse in South African Maternity Settings Is a Disgrace: Potential Solutions to the Problem' (2015) 105 SAMJ 284

Jewkes R and others, 'Why Do Nurses Abuse Patients? Reflections from South African Obstetric Services' (1998) 47 Soc Sci Med 1781

Jewkes R K and others, 'Why Are Women Still Aborting Outside Designated Facilities in Metropolitan South Africa?' (2005) 112 BJOG 1236

Kruger L and Schoombee C, 'The Other Side of Caring: Abuse in a South African Maternity Ward' (2010) 28 J Reprod Infant Psychol 84

Mantsho, M J, *Steps Taken by the Department of Health to Address Issues of Medical Litigation in South Africa* (National Treasury Meeting 2015)

McGee R and Gaventa J, 'Shifting Power? Assessing the Impact of Transparency and Accountability Initiatives' (2011) 383 IDS Working Papers 1

Mets D J, 'Out of the Mouths of Babes – Innocent Reporting of Harmful Labour Ward Practices' (2005) 95 SAMJ 284

Miller S and others, 'Beyond Too Little, Too Late and Too Much, Too Soon: A Pathway Towards Evidence-Based, Respectful Maternity Care Worldwide' (2016) 388 The Lancet 2176

Naledi T, Barron P, and Schneider H, 'Primary Health Care in South Africa since 1994 and Implications of the New Vision for PHC Re-Engineering' in Padarath A and English R (eds), *South African Health Review 2011* (Health Systems Trust 2011)

National Committee for the Confidential Enquiries into Maternal Deaths, *Saving Mothers 2008–2010: Fifth Report on Confidential Enquiries into Maternal Deaths in South Africa* (Health Department Republic of South Africa 2011)

National Committee for the Confidential Enquiries into Maternal Deaths, *Saving Mothers 2014–2016: Seventh Triennial Report on Confidential Enquiries into Maternal Deaths in South Africa (Short Report)* (Health Department Republic of South Africa 2018)

Parliamentary Monitoring Group, 'Overview of the Session' (31 October 2018)

Qadeer I, 'Unpacking the Myths: Inequities and Maternal Mortality in South Asia' (2005) 48 Development 120

Rao M, *From Population Control to Reproductive Health: Malthusian Arithmetic* (Sage Publications 2004)

Rashida Manjoo, 'Report of the Special Rapporteur on Violence against Women Its Causes and Consequences' (A/HRC/26/38, UN General Assembly 2014)

Rispel L C, Jager P, and Fonn S, 'Exploring Corruption in the South African Health Sector' (2016) 31 Health Policy Plan 239

Roberts D, *Killing the Black Body: Race, Reproduction, and the Meaning of Liberty* (Pantheon Books 1997)

Ross L J and Solinger R, *Reproductive Justice: An Introduction* (University of California Press 2017)

Rucell J, *Obstetric Violence and Colonial Conditioning in South Africa's Reproductive Health System* (DPhil thesis, University of Leeds 2017)

Sadler M and others, 'Moving beyond Disrespect and Abuse: Addressing the Structural Dimensions of Obstetric Violence' (2016) 24(47) Reprod Health Matters 47

Scott V and others, 'Exploring the Nature of Governance at the Level of Implementation for Health System Strengthening: The DIALHS Experience' (2014) 29(s2) Health Policy Plan ii59

Scott V, Mathews V, and Gilson L, 'Constraints to Implementing an Equity-Promoting Staff Allocation Policy: Understanding Mid-Level Managers' and Nurses' Perspectives Affecting Implementation in South Africa' (2011) 27 Health Policy Plan 138

Sedgh G and others, 'Induced Abortion Incidence and Trends Worldwide from 1995 to 2008' (2012) 379 The Lancet 625.

Silliman J, Bhattacharjee A, and Davis A, *Policing the National Body: Sex, Race, and Criminalization* (South End Press 2002)

South African Law Reform Commission, 'Project 141: Medico-Legal Claims, Issue paper 33' (20 May 2017)

South African National AIDS Council, 'The People Living with HIV Stigma Index, South Africa: Summary Report' (May 2015)

Strode A, Mthembu S, and Essack Z, '"She Made up a Choice for Me": 22 HIV-Positive Women's Experiences of Involuntary Sterilisation in Two South African Provinces' (2012) 20(s39) Reprod Health Matters 61

United Nations High Commissioner for Human Rights, 'Technical Guidance on the Application of a Human Rights-Based Approach to the Implementation of Policies and Programmes to Reduce Preventable Maternal Morbidity and Mortality' (A/HRC/21/22, UN Human Rights Council 2012)

United Nations High Commissioner for Human Rights, 'Follow-up Report on the Application of the Technical Guidance on the Application of a Human Rights-Based Approach to the Implementation of Policies and Programmes to Reduce Preventable Maternal Mortality and Morbidity' (A/HRC/33/24, UN Human Rights Council 2016)

World Health Organization, 'The Prevention and Elimination of Disrespect and Abuse During Facility-based Childbirth' (2014)

World Health Organization, 'Recommendations for Prevention and Treatment of Maternal Peripartum Infections' (2015)

7 Human rights law and challenging dehumanisation in childbirth

A practitioner's perspective

Elizabeth Prochaska

Introduction

We begin with an experience common to women giving birth in hospitals in countries with advanced medical care. A woman is pregnant with her first child. She labours at home before travelling to the hospital where she plans to give birth. When she arrives, a midwife insists that she perform a vaginal examination, which will be repeated every four hours. When the woman questions the necessity of the examinations and writhes in pain under the midwife's hand, she is told that they are hospital protocol. The doctor arrives as the baby crowns. Without introducing herself, she insists the woman turn to lie on her back and when the women does not move, she and the midwife turn her over themselves and place her feet in stirrups. The midwife shouts 'push'; the doctor, impatient and impersonal, tells her 'any longer and we'll need to cut'. Frightened and out of control, the woman pushes the baby into the doctor's hands. They are discharged from the hospital the next day. The birth is recorded as a spontaneous vaginal delivery, a positive outcome for the hospital. The doctor's discourtesy and rough-handling, the midwife's insistence on putting her fingers into the woman's vagina are not recorded in the hospital's notes, but the experience is etched into the mother's memory. She will recall it in flashbacks when the baby wakes in the middle of the night and in her subsequent pregnancy as she dreads giving birth again. She will remember it in her old age.

What is the appropriate legal response to this story? The law of clinical negligence struggles to offer a complete answer because it is designed to compensate women and babies for physical harm retrospectively after a clinician has failed to follow established standards or the practice of her peers. Psychological damage alone is rarely enough to substantiate a claim and negligence law cannot be used proactively by women to challenge the nature of health services or medical practice. While negligence law has evolved into incorporate concepts of individual autonomy, most recently in the Supreme Court case of *Montgomery v Lanarkshire Health Board*,[1] we must turn to human rights to give us a fuller response to disrespectful care. Human rights are a set of values that presuppose

---

1 [2015] 1 AC 1430.

a woman's humanity and dignity, enabling her to claim a remedy for violation of her physical and psychological identity and to challenge the culture and systems that perpetuate dehumanisation in childbirth.

Human rights values

Human rights are founded on a system of universal moral values that recognise the uniqueness and worth of every individual human being from birth until death. They are drawn from a fundamental belief in human dignity, which is a reflection of humans' unique status as morally conscious beings. Dignity is based on the idea, shared by many religions, that you should treat others in the way you would wish to be treated. It is most powerfully articulated in Immanuel Kant's categorical imperative: a person must be treated as an end in herself and not as means to an end.[2] Two related values emerge from the principle of human dignity: respect and autonomy. If we accept that a person is valuable and an end in herself, we must treat her as worthy of respect and relatedly capable of making decisions for herself.

The power of these values in pregnancy and childbirth is immediately apparent: pregnant women risk being viewed as a means for the creation of life rather than as an end in themselves. Their interests are often considered subordinate to those of the foetus and the sacrifice of their physical and mental health is deemed an unfortunate, or even a necessary, consequence of a woman's role as a mother. The twin values of respect and autonomy chime with the issues that research has shown to most strongly predict positive birth experiences: a respectful relationship with caregivers and a sense of control over decisions in childbirth.[3]

Human rights translate the fundamental human need for respect and control into universal values which protect individuals from threats to their autonomy by the collective power of the state and its institutions. Pregnant women are subject to the coercive control of the state: they are expected to accept antenatal care, to access hospital services in childbirth and to conform to the postnatal regime for their child. When they receive these services, they do not sacrifice their dignity and can legitimately expect to be treated according to human rights values enshrined in human rights law.

Human rights law

Human rights values were transformed into enforceable legal rights in the wake of the Second World War, when gross violations of human dignity led to the demand

---

2 Mary Gregor and Jens Timmermann (eds), *Kant: Groundwork of the Metaphysics of Morals* (CUP 2012).

3 Ellen D Hodnett, 'Pain and Women's Satisfaction with the Experience of Childbirth: A Systematic Review' (2002) 186 Am J Obstet Gynecol S160; U Waldenstrom and E Schytt, 'A Longitudinal Study of Women's Memory of Labour Pain-from 2 Months to 5 Years After the Birth' (2009) 116 BJOG 577.

for enforceable minimum standards of respect in international and national law. Human rights are now protected in international treaties, national constitutions and legislation.[4] The Council of Europe, the international organisation formed post-war and consisting of 47 member states, adopted the European Convention on Human Rights (ECHR) in 1953. The ECHR protects the fundamental right to life and requires the state to take positive action to ensure that critical health-care services, including maternity care, are available to everyone.[5] It is interpreted and enforced by the European Court of Human Rights. Rights contained in the ECHR and under international treaties, including the Convention on the Elimination of Discrimination against Women and the Convention on Human Rights and Biomedicine, extend to protecting the way in which individuals are treated by their caregivers. These include the right not to be subjected to in-human and degrading treatment, the right to informed consent and the right to non-discrimination.[6] In the United Kingdom, the Human Rights Act 1998 imposes a legal obligation on professional caregivers employed by the National Health Service to respect rights contained in the ECHR.[7]

The European Court of Human Rights has considered multiple cases brought by women challenging their treatment in childbirth. In its first judgment on childbirth rights, *Ternovszky v Hungary*,[8] the European Court of Human Rights considered a claim by a woman who challenged the refusal by the Hungarian government to regulate home birth. Anna Ternovszky argued that the failure to regulate midwives to enable them to attend home births without fear of discipli-nary or criminal sanction breached her right to respect for private life under art 8 of the European Convention.

The Court found that 'the circumstances of giving birth incontestably form part of one's private life'. This was an important recognition of the scope of art 8, which has traditionally been understood as a privacy right, but has evolved to protect physical and psychological integrity. The Court's broad definition of the protection afforded by art 8, covering all 'the circumstances of giving birth', gives women expansive protection from state incursions into their decision-making in childbirth. The Court held that that the Hungarian government's

---

4 Several South American countries have codified the concept of 'obstetric violence' in an attempt to improve conditions in maternity hospitals. See eg Venezuela's Organic Law for the Sanction, Prevention, and Eradication of Violence against Women, art 51, discussed in Rogelio Pérez D'Gregorio, 'Obstetric Violence: A New Legal Term Introduced in Venezuela' (2010) 111 Int J Gynaecol Obstet 201.

5 *Tysiac v Poland* App no 5410/03 (ECtHR, 24 September 2007). See European Court of Hu-man Rights, 'Thematic Report: Health-related Issues in the Case Law of the European Court of Human Rights' (2015) <www.echr.coe.int/Documents/Research_report_health.pdf> accessed 11 February 2019.

6 Art 3 protects the right not to be subjected to inhuman and degrading treatment; art 8 protects the right to informed consent; art 14 protect the right to non-discrimination in the enjoyment of other ECHR rights.

7 S 6 Human Rights Act 1998.

8 App no 67545/09 (ECtHR, 14 December 2010).

failure to make regulations enabling midwives to attend women giving birth at home violated art 8 and that the state was obliged to provide 'a legal and institutional environment' which respected women's choice.

The *Ternovszky* judgment was heralded as creating a positive right to home birth services throughout Europe. However, in the subsequent case of *Dubska and Krejzova v Czech Republic*,[9] the Court came under pressure from the Czech government to limit its obligation to provide specific health services where it believed there to be a risk of harm. The case was referred to the Grand Chamber of the European Court, which retreated from the position in *Ternovszky* and found that the state was not positively obliged to permit midwives to attend women at home. Mrs Dubska was free to give birth at home by herself, but the state did not have to permit a midwife to attend her. The Court considered evidence on the safety of home birth presented by the Czech government, as well as the varying home birth practices in European states, and concluded that the evidence showed an increased risk for babies born at home which entitled the state not to support women's choice of home birth. Sadly, the Court did not fully consider the conditions in Czech hospitals, which led Ms Dubska to decline hospital care and had been criticised by the UN Committee on the Convention of the Elimination of Discrimination against Women, or the risk to mother and baby of giving birth alone.

The *Dubska* case illustrates the capacity of human rights analysis to take account of broad societal considerations which may justify restriction on women's rights if they are proportionate and properly evidenced. However, the evidence presented to the Court in *Dubska* can be fairly criticised as one-sided and the Court is due to consider other childbirth claims from women in other European countries who are challenging restrictions on home birth, which may yet lead to a shift in the Court's position.[10]

The Court in *Dubska* did not resile from the broad definition of art 8 in *Ternovsky* and the principles that the Court has espoused to protect women from threats to their autonomy in a very wide range of circumstances. In *Konovalova v Russia*,[11] for example, the Court held that the failure to obtain a woman's consent to the presence of medical students during her labour constituted a violation of art 8 and stated that all medical interventions, however minor, required consent. The case has obvious ramifications for all hospitals in Europe, which should ensure that women are aware of and consent to the present of student midwives and doctors during childbirth. In *Hanzelkovi v the Czech Republic*[12] the Court found that the Czech state had violated art 8 by removing a baby from its mother's care because she had chosen to leave hospital on the day of the baby's birth rather than follow the hospital protocol and remain for two days.

---

9 App no 28859/11 and 28473/12 (ECtHR, 15 November 2016).
10 See eg *Kosaitė-Čypienė and Others v Lithuania* App no 69489/12 (ECtHR, pending).
11 App no 37873/04 (ECtHR, 9 October 2014).
12 App no 43643/10 (ECtHR, 11 December 2014).

In the United Kingdom, there have so far been few legal cases on women's reproductive rights relying on the Human Rights Act 1998,[13] but human rights principles suffused the transformative judgment on informed decision-making in the Supreme Court's case of *Montgomery v Lanarkshire Health Board*. The Court held that Mrs Montgomery, a diabetic whose baby suffered cerebral palsy after experiencing shoulder dystocia in labour, had not been properly informed about the risks of vaginal birth in her circumstances. Overturning the traditional understanding of negligence law as based on the standards of a reasonable clinician, the Court found that a doctor's actions should be judged from the patient's perspective and by whether the patient themselves would have attached significance to the risk. In its explicit recognition of patients' right to autonomy and informed choice, *Montgomery* is a human rights case which shifts the legal and clinical environment towards a principle of supported autonomy, in which the role of the clinician is to facilitate autonomous decision-making. It expands the principle of informed consent, which can be invoked pre-emptively by relying on the Human Rights Act 1998 and art 8 of ECHR, not only in cases where harm occurs, but in order to insist on personalised care.

Underpinned by the powerful and unassailable values of dignity, respect and autonomy, human rights law provides a framework in which women can make choices and ensure that those choices are respected. While human rights law, like clinical negligence law, can be invoked by women to obtain compensation for harm caused by breach of their rights in childbirth, greater force may lie in relying on human rights to proactively ensure appropriate and respectful maternity services.

Challenging dehumanisation in childbirth

By insisting on respect for women's dignity and informed choice, human rights set standards for maternity care at both a systemic and an individual level, thus enhancing women's experience of maternity care and preventing dangerous and disrespectful practice. The power of human rights law lies in its ability to compel steps to be taken to respect rights and preempt harm, as well to declare treatment unlawful and order compensation.

Under the Human Rights Act 1998, women can challenge hospital policies and practice pre-emptively, or seek compensation and a declaration of breach of their rights if they have suffered harm as a consequence of the policy. The strength of human rights values lies not only in their universalism but also in their recognition by the law, giving women recourse to external authority, in the form of regulators, ombudsmen and the legal system.

While there has been little litigation on human rights in maternity care so far in the United Kingdom, there is clear potential for claims to be brought challenging maternity policies at a local and national level, as well as women's

---

13 Human rights have been considered in cases concerning women who lack mental capacity where the Court of Protection has drawn on the principles of physical and psychological integrity in art 8 ECHR. See eg *Re CA (Natural Delivery or Caesarean Section)* [2016] EWCOP 51.

individual treatment. The following three examples of potential legal claims that could be brought under the Human Rights Act 1998 illustrate these points:

a   Many National Health Service (NHS) hospitals operate policies that restrict access to birth centres to women with a Body Mass Index (BMI) below a certain level. Women with a high BMI are told that they must give birth in obstetric units. These policies discriminate against women based on their BMI and limit their decisions about how and where they give birth. As the European Court has found, all decisions about childbirth engage the right to respect for private life protected by art 8 of ECHR. Where a policy discriminates between women, it will also engage the right to non-discrimination in art 14. While a hospital can lawfully limit access to its services to particular groups, it must justify its policy by proving that it is a proportionate response to the purported risk. This requires a clear evidence-base and proof that the hospital has considered less restrictive alternatives. In the context of restrictions based on BMI, the hospital would need to show, for example, why it permits first time mothers with a normal BMI to access the birth centre when the risk of complications is equivalent to the risk for a second time mother with a high BMI. If the justification is based on concerns about a woman with a high BMI using a birth pool, the hospital would need to show it had considered enabling a woman to use other means of pain relief in the birth centre such as the shower. The hospital's policy, or a refusal to make an exception to it, could be challenged in court under the Human Rights Act 1998. While the courts often show deference to medical decisions, and a woman would need strong evidence to counter arguments on risk, the courts will apply greater scrutiny when the decision has a discriminatory effect.

b   Hospital policies mandating repeated vaginal examinations at four hourly intervals could also be challenged on human rights grounds. Vaginal examinations during labour can be painful and traumatic, and constitute a very serious incursion on a woman's physical integrity and dignity. They require explicit and informed consent: the woman must be told the nature of the process and the reason for undertaking an examination, as well as any alternative that would be appropriate. A non-consented vaginal examination will breach a woman's right to private life and may also constitute inhuman and degrading treatment under art 3 of ECHR. If a hospital policy or clinical practice on the labour ward leads to a real risk that women are compelled to accept vaginal examinations, the hospital will be acting unlawfully and could face a claim under the Human Rights Act 1998. Any woman who is subjected to an examination without her consent can bring a claim for a declaration that her rights were breached and compensation under the Human Rights Act. It can often be difficult for a woman to prove that she did not give her consent.

c   Many NHS hospitals decline to respect women's choice of caesarean section (c-section) if they do not have an accepted medical reason for requesting one. Current NICE guidelines advise hospitals to offer c-sections to women in these circumstances and any hospital that decides not to follow the guidelines will need to provide a good reason for doing so. From a human rights perspective, declining to provide a c-section is a serious limitation on women's art 8 right to make decisions about how they give birth. The court would balance the effect on the woman, who might have compelling personal reasons for choosing a c-section, such as previous birth trauma or a history of sexual abuse, and the hospital's justification for declining to provide the operation. While additional risk and cost could provide a justification, these would need to be clearly evidenced, and the NICE guidelines would be relevant to these issues. Given that a high proportion of women will have an emergency c-section in any event, hospitals may struggle to explain why they will not offer an elective operation to women who seek one.

Human rights law offers women the potential to challenge hospitals' decisions in court and litigation can provide a very powerful incentive for change. However, the majority of women will not want or be able to seek legal redress, and human rights can be most powerfully deployed at a cultural level in maternity services to instil human rights values in caregivers and change everyday practice. Recognition that positive birth outcomes are not defined simply by clinical metrics, but by whether a woman's human dignity has been respected, can shift expectations and standards of care and put the woman at the heart of the maternity system.[14] Perhaps most importantly, human rights equip women and caregivers with the power to advocate for women and embolden people to speak out about harmful systems and behaviour in hospitals.

Conclusion

Institutionalised maternity care poses a threat to women's basic human dignity and ability to exercise their autonomy. The policies and protocols deployed by hospitals to systematise care can improve safety, but also risk dehumanisation and cause harm to women and their babies. Human rights pose a fundamental challenge to institutionalisation by putting the values of the human rather than the hospital at the heart of care. The values of dignity, respect and autonomy may be deployed to support arguments for personalised care and continuity of carer, choice of place and mode of birth – whether in the community or hospital – and to challenge any policy or practice that threatens women's inherent humanity. Human rights need not create antagonism between women and caregivers: a human rights approach offers the chance to enrich those relationships by focusing on individual, not institutional, care to the benefit of both women and the

---

14 Recent maternity policy initiatives have emphasised women's human rights. See, eg NHS England, 'A-Equip: A Model of Clinical Midwifery Supervision' (2017) <www.england.nhs.uk/wp-content/uploads/2017/04/a-equip-midwifery-supervision-model.pdf> accessed 11 February 2019.

people who seek to provide high-quality, respectful care. As the law begins to recognise the full value of human rights in healthcare, the opportunity to instil human rights values, shift maternity culture and protect women from disrespect and dehumanisation has never been greater.

Table of cases

Dubska and Krejzova v Czech Republic App no 28859/11 and 28473/12 (ECtHR, 15 November 2016)
Hanzelkovi v the Czech Republic App no 43643/10 (ECtHR, 11 December 2014)
Konovalova v Russia App no 37873/04 (ECtHR, 9 October 2014)
Kosaitė-Čypienė and Others v Lithuania App no 69489/12 (ECtHR, pending)
Montgomery v Lanarkshire Health Board [2015] 1 AC 1430
Re CA (Natural Delivery or Caesarean Section) [2016] EWCOP 51
Ternovszky v Hungary App no 67545/09 (ECtHR, 14 December 2010)
Tysiac v Poland App no 5410/03 (ECtHR, 24 September 2007)

Bibliography

D'Gregorio R P, 'Obstetric Violence: A New Legal Term Introduced in Venezuela' (2010) 111 Int J Gynaecol Obstet 201
European Court of Human Rights, 'Thematic Report: Health-related Issues in the Case Law of the European Court of Human Rights' (2015)
Gregor M and Timmermann J (ed), *Kant: Groundwork of the Metaphysics of Morals* (CUP 2012)
Hodnett E D, 'Pain and Women's Satisfaction with the Experience of Childbirth: A Systematic Review' (2002) 186 Am J Obstet Gynecol S160
NHS England, 'A-Equip: A Model of Clinical Midwifery Supervision' (2017)
Waldenstrom U and Schytt E, 'A Longitudinal Study of Women's Memory of Labour Pain – from 2 Months to 5 Years After the Birth' (2009) 116 BJOG 577

8 Leaving women behind

The application of evidence-based guidelines, law, and obstetric violence by omission

Camilla Pickles

Introduction

The World Health Organization's (WHO) statement on disrespect and abuse during childbirth helped to bring much needed global attention to the fact that healthcare professionals are subjecting pregnant and birthing women to various forms of disrespect and abuse.[1] Disrespectful and abusive treatment includes physical and verbal abuse, profound humiliation, coercive or unconsented medical procedures, lack of confidentiality, failure to get fully informed consent, refusal to give pain medication, gross violations of privacy, refusal of admission to health facilities, and neglecting women during childbirth.[2] The WHO, together with other leading maternal health organisations,[3] and obstetric violence activists and researchers actively support and encourage the provision of evidence-based care to tackle abuse and obstetric violence.[4]

Evidence-based guidelines use 'the best available research on the safety and effectiveness of specific practices to help guide maternity care decisions and facilitate optimal outcomes for mothers and their newborns'.[5] These provide the necessary framework to prevent the extreme situations of doing 'too little, too late' or 'too much, too soon' which both lead to harmful outcomes for women.[6]

1 World Health Organization, 'The Prevention and Elimination of Disrespect and Abuse during Facility-Based Childbirth' (2014) <http://apps.who.int/iris/bitstream/handle/10665/134588/WHO_RHR_14.23_eng.pdf?sequence=1> accessed 6 June 2018.

2 Ibid.

3 These organisations are listed on the World Health Organization's website, <www.who.int/reproductivehealth/topics/maternal_perinatal/endorsers.pdf> accessed 6 June 2018.

4 Simone Grilo Diniz and others, 'Abuse and Disrespect in Childbirth Care as a Public Health Issue in Brazil: Origins, Definitions, Impacts on Maternal Health, and Proposals for Its Prevention' (2015) 25 J Hum Growth Dev 377; Michelle Sadler and others, 'Moving Beyond Disrespect and Abuse: Addressing the Structural Dimensions of Obstetric Violence' (2016) 24(47) Reprod Health Matters 47.

5 Carol Sakala and Maureen P Corry, 'Evidence-Based Maternity Care: What it Is and What It Can Achieve' (2008) <www.nationalpartnership.org/research-library/maternal-health/evidence-based-maternity-care.pdf> accessed 6 June 2018.

6 Suellen Miller and others, 'Beyond Too Little, Too Late and Too Much, Too Soon: A Pathway Towards Evidence-Based, Respectful Maternity Care Worldwide' (2016) 388.10056 The Lancet 2176.

In essence, evidence-based guidelines help determine when a procedure is clinically indicated and clinical indication helps to distinguish between those procedures which should be promoted or avoided.[7] Evidence-based care offers several benefits, including improved quality of care, improved clinical decision-making, and improved support for patients' informed decision-making processes.[8] Guidelines ensure consistency of care, improve efficiency of healthcare services, facilitate standardisation of good practice, and help to contain costs.[9]

Activists rely on evidence-based guidelines to counter established practices that render childbirth a pathological event. Guidelines issued by the WHO and the International Federation of Gynecology and Obstetrics played a leading role in shaping some of the obstetric violence laws found in Latin America.[10] According to Bellón Sánchez the WHO's guidelines 'are a source of authoritative knowledge in the field of childbirth assistance that activists groups in different parts of the world use as a tool to claim more respectful healthcare assistance for women'.[11] Thus, they help to dismantle abusive maternity care in jurisdictions where there are no obstetric violence laws proscribing violence against women during childbirth.

While I accept that evidence-based guidelines help to improve maternity care services, I question whether their application will always support the fight against abuse during pregnancy and childbirth. I take the position that pregnancy and childbirth should never be the reason for any woman to experience humiliation, degradation, or any form of human rights violation. This premise demands from us that responses to abuse during childbirth should be such that no woman is left behind or sidelined during the implementation of interventions that are aimed at improving maternity care services. Further, interventions should be such that women can use them to advance their interests. We are therefore required to review critically whether interventions are adequately inclusive and accessible, bearing in mind that women are diverse, their needs are diverse, and their voices in relation to pregnancy and birth are many.

I draw from women's lived experiences of obstetric-related care to show how scientifically sound[12] evidence-based guidelines are applied in a way that silences and excludes some women from care. This process can be harmful to their psychological integrity but guidelines invisiblise these violations because there is an assumption that evidence-based care does not harm. Thereafter, I will expose

7 Ibid.
8 Steven H Woolf and others, 'Potential Benefits, Limitations, and Harms of Clinical Guidelines' (1999) 318(7182) BMJ 527.
9 Ibid.
10 Silvia Bellón Sánchez, 'Obstetric Violence: Medicalization, Authority Abuse and Sexism within Spanish Obstetric Assistance: A New Name for Old Issues' (Masters Dissertation, Utrecht University 2014) 49; Carlos Alejandro Herrera Vacaflor, 'Obstetric Violence in Argentina: A Study on the Legal Effects of Medical Guidelines and Statutory Obligations for Improving the Quality of Maternal Health' (Master's Dissertation, University of Toronto 2015) 32.
11 Sánchez (n 10) 49.
12 I assume that the guidelines are methodologically sound, and the purpose of this chapter is not to argue that the guidelines referred to herein are incorrect.

the anomaly that while evidence-based guidelines are said to be developed for women's benefit, a woman cannot use the law to compel a healthcare provider to comply with guidelines when she wants access to those benefits, or to compel a healthcare provider to disregard guidelines when she does not want access to those benefits. Finally, I demonstrate that, in these instances, evidence-based guidelines facilitate obstetric violence by omission. This underscores an overlooked concern that even the most well-developed evidence-based guidelines may leave some women behind. I argue that an obstetric violence perspective helps to clarify this harm, it declares this harm an unacceptable consequence of evidence-based care, and it supports demands for more respectful application of guidelines.

Evidence-based guidelines silence and exclude some women

On 24 May 2017, Birthrights launched its 'Maternal Request Caesarean Campaign'.[13] The Campaign recognises that there is a small group of women who feel that having a planned caesarean section is the right option for them given their circumstances but that they are experiencing barriers regarding access to care. It identified Oxford University Hospitals NHS Foundation Trust as one of the Trusts enforcing a policy of not providing caesarean sections on request.[14] I draw from existing guidelines and recommendations, and communications between Birthrights and the Trust to illustrate how healthcare professionals use highly regarded guidelines to silence some women and justify their exclusion from care. This discussion will not consider women's decision-making process in relation to elective caesarean sections and the complexity of autonomy and 'true choice' in the context of broader social and cultural experiences.[15] Instead, I focus on how healthcare professionals apply guidelines to women's requests for access to care that is not clinically indicated.

Childbirth by way of caesarean section is the subject of evidence-based guidelines or recommendations at international and national levels. At an international level, the most influential caesarean-section recommendation originates from the WHO. In 2015, the WHO confirmed its position that the ideal rate for caesarean sections is between 10 per cent and 15 per cent.[16] Drawing from

---

13 Maria Booker, 'Do I Have a Right to a C-Section? Update on Oxford University Hospitals' (21 July 2017) <www.birthrights.org.uk/2017/07/do-i-have-a-right-to-a-c-section-update-on-oxford-university-hospitals/> accessed 6 June 2018.

14 More Trusts are implicated, see Birthrights, 'Maternal Request Caesarean' (2018) <www.birthrights.org.uk/wordpress/wp-content/uploads/2018/08/Final-Birthrights-MRCS-Report-2108.pdf> accessed 30 April 2019.

15 For a discussion of the complexity of 'choosing' caesarean sections, see Katherine Beckett, 'Choosing Cesarean: Feminism and the Politics of Childbirth in the United States' (2005) 6 Fem T 251.

16 World Health Organization, 'Statement on Caesarean Section Rates' (2015) <www.who.int/reproductivehealth/publications/maternal_perinatal_health/cs-statement/en/> accessed 6 June 2018.

the latest available evidence-based data it reiterated that caesarean sections are effective in saving lives but only when 'they are required for medically indicated reasons' or when 'medically necessary'. This seems to establish a presumption in favour of vaginal childbirth that requires of women to make a positive case for access to caesarean sections. While the WHO emphasises the need for caesarean section decision-making to revolve around what is medically indicated, national guidelines take a more nuanced approach.

The National Institute for Health and Care Excellence (NICE) has issued guidelines for the provision of caesarean sections that also draws from available evidence to guide when caesarean sections are clinically indicated, but it supports a women-centred approach.[17] A women-centred approach concerns care that is directed by a woman's needs and preferences, and it requires healthcare providers to offer evidence-based information and support to enable informed decision-making. The guideline requires healthcare providers to engage meaningfully with women who elect to give birth by way of a caesarean section. They are required to discuss reasons for the election, and the risks and benefits of the procedure. The healthcare provider should offer perinatal mental health support if a woman requests a caesarean section on the grounds of anxiety. The guideline directs healthcare providers to offer a planned caesarean section if a vaginal birth is still not an option after discussion and additional support. However, it recognises that a woman cannot compel an obstetrician to provide an elective caesarean where clinical indication is absent. The attending obstetrician is required to refer the woman to another obstetrician who will carry out the caesarean section.

The Oxford University Hospitals NHS Foundation Trust's patient information leaflet on access to elective caesarean sections explains that the Trust does not make provision for maternal requests for caesarean sections because it only provides caesarean sections in cases where there are clinical indications supporting their use.[18] Healthcare professionals will refer women to another hospital in cases where they choose to go ahead with a caesarean section after being offered or receiving support regarding mode of birth.[19] The leaflet offers a rather inflexible approach and it is not clear if all women requesting caesarean sections will always be referred to another hospital. According to Birthrights[20] this approach to maternal requests for caesarean sections is not in line with the NICE guidelines and blanket policies of this nature are 'a violation of a Trust's legal duty to give

---

17 NICE, 'Caesarean Section: Clinical Guideline' (2011) <www.nice.org.uk/guidance/cg132> accessed 6 June 2018.

18 Oxford University Hospitals NHS Trust, 'I am Anxious about Giving Birth and Want to Know More about Caesarean Section' (2014) <www.ouh.nhs.uk/patient-guide/leaflets/files/10405Pcaesarean.pdf> accessed 6 June 2018.

19 Ibid.

20 Birthrights, 'Campaigns: Our Maternal Request Campaign' (2017) <www.birthrights.org.uk/campaigns/> accessed 6 June 2018.

personalised care' as confirmed in *Montgomery v Lanarkshire Health Board*.[21] According to Lady Hale:

> [A] patient is entitled to take into account her own values, her own assessment of the comparative merits of giving birth the 'natural' way and of giving birth by caesarean section, whatever medical opinion may say, alongside the medical evaluation of the risks to herself and her baby.[22]

Putting aside the issue that the Trust may be applying a blanket approach in relation to women's requests,[23] the Trust's approach is aligned with the WHO's recommendations and with the NICE guidelines in so far as access to caesarean sections is being denied because there is no clinical indication justifying this mode of childbirth. This scenario exposes some concerning consequences of the application of evidence-based guidelines: the Campaign reveals that women's voices are directly and indirectly silenced because of the application of guidelines and guidelines being applied in this way legitimise women's exclusion from care. This process can cause serious harm to women's psychological integrity, but these are rendered invisible and ignored because the harms occur while providing evidence-based care.

According to Mainz, clinical indicators are based on standards of care that are evidence-based as derived from scientific evidence or are derived from academic literature and expert panels of healthcare providers when scientific evidence is lacking.[24] Thus, 'clinical indicators' are narrowly defined and do not include factors that some women may consider to be important for their well-being during pregnancy and birth. Evidence-based guidelines can work to silence women when they are applied in contexts where there is a history of devaluing women in maternity care[25] because their adoption may merely support a shift in deference from one type of expert knowledge to another.[26] This process excludes and devalues women's knowledge rooted in their lived experiences and can overlook them as important sources of knowledge. The Trust's inflexible reverence

---

21 [2016] CSOH 133.
22 Ibid [115].
23 This is disputed. Birthrights have reports from women that they are denied access to caesarean sections without meaningful engagement while the Trust alleges that it does offer the support required by the NICE guidelines.
24 Jan Mainz, 'Defining and Classifying Clinical Indicators for Quality Improvement' (2003) 15 IJQHC 523, 524.
25 Sheila Kitzinger, *Birth and Sex: The Power and The Passion* (Pinter and Martin 2012) 84–100; Henci Goer, 'Cruelty in Maternity Wards: Fifty Years Later' (2010) 19 J Perinat Educ 33; Beverley Chalmers, 'Changing Childbirth in Eastern Europe: Which Systems of Authoritative Knowledge Should Prevail?' in Robbie E Davis-Floyd and Carolyn F Sargent (eds), *Childbirth and Authoritative Knowledge: Cross-Cultural Perspectives* (University of California Press 1997) 226–73; Norman Morris, 'Human Relations in Obstetric Practice' (1960) 275 The Lancet 913.
26 Elizabeth Kukura, 'Contested Care: The Limitations of Evidence-Based Maternity Care Reform' (2016) 31 Berkeley J Gend Law Just 241, 286.

for professional and scientific knowledge undermines women as autonomous decision-makers.[27]

Some evidence-based guidelines may indirectly silence women because they tend to speak to general populations and are not primarily concerned with individuality. This is the WHO's approach to caesarean sections and the Trust seems to support this. A generalised view has the effect of framing all women as one type of woman. This leaves little room for the consideration of other aspects relevant to care such as a woman's individual life experiences, preferences, fears, expectations, and personal perceptions of control and life circumstances.[28] Women exist beyond realms of 'clinical indication' and they are diverse. Beckett reminds us that 'women can and do find obstetric technology to be an empowering experience'[29] but some women view technological interventions as something to actively avoid too. Thus, the NICE guidelines and the WHO recommendations speak to, and facilitate, only one of many ways a woman may need to birth, and their application needs to be individualised by the Trust.

The unimportant role of women's voices in relation to determining what care is necessary for their self-determined needs creates the situation where healthcare professionals use evidence-based guidelines to justifiably exclude women from care. The Oxford University Hospitals NHS Foundation Trust adopts this approach. It presents elective caesarean sections as placing patients at risk that violates patient trust and frustrates the Trust's ability to fulfil their duties as doctors.[30] In its correspondence with Birthrights,[31] the Trust explained that its approach is not driven by the need to meet targets, but that caesarean sections are being denied on the basis that there is no clinical indication for their use and that the Trust's decision is related to good practice and to reducing short- and long-term harms to women. It recognised that some women express a fear of birth or have had a poor birth experience but that these factors do not mean that a caesarean section is 'the best option'.[32] The Trust asserted that it complies with all the relevant guidelines because it offers support to those women who

---

27 Kukura (n 26) 289. Stereotyping of this nature is ever-present in reproductive care. See Rebecca J Cook and Simone Cusack, *Gender Stereotyping: Transnational Legal Perspectives* (University of Pennsylvania Press 2010); Rebecca J Cook, Simone Cusack, and Bernard M Dickens, 'Unethical Female Stereotyping in Reproductive Health' (2010) 109 Int J Gynaecol Obstet 255; C Pickles, 'Sounding the Alarm: *Government of the Republic of Namibia v LM* and Women's Rights during Childbirth in South Africa' (2018) 21 PER 1.

28 For instance, see Ellen Lazarus, 'What Do Women Want? Issues of Choice, Control, and Class in American Pregnancy and Childbirth' in Robbie E Davis-Floyd and Carolyn F Sargent (eds), *Childbirth and Authoritative Knowledge: Cross Cultural Perspectives* (University of California Press 1997) 132; Soo Downe and others, 'What Matters to Women during Childbirth: A Systematic Qualitative Review' (2018) 13(4) PLoS ONE e0194906.

29 Beckett (n 15) 259.

30 Oxford University Hospitals NHS Trust (n 18) 4.

31 Oxford University Hospitals Trust replying letter to Birthrights, <www.birthrights.org.uk/wordpress/wp-content/uploads/2017/07/Letter-to-R-Schiller-Birthrights-from-OUH.pdf> accessed 6 June 2018.

32 Ibid.

request caesarean section procedures but that 'if no clinical indication is found despite a thorough assessment, then the woman is referred to an Obstetrician in a neighbouring Trust who may support her request'.[33] It is noteworthy that the Trust did not include rationing of maternity care service as part of its decision to deny access to caesarean sections on request. While the Trust has not specifically referenced the WHO recommendations, it quite clearly reflects the WHO's position because it justifies its position on the grounds that caesarean sections come with risks and obstetricians should not subject women and their babies to any unnecessary risk.[34]

Exclusion from care leaves women with very little options and it introduces unique concerns for women because pregnancy is time sensitive. According to Birthrights, women's referrals to other Trusts are being refused because of caseload implications and other Trusts are not offering maternal request caesareans 'in order not to become targets for women refused this choice by Oxford'.[35] Further, securing care elsewhere may require women to travel long distances, bear burdensome cost implications for accommodation for relatives, or may result in a very isolated birth when accommodation for others cannot be secured. At times women are left with very little time to make necessary arrangements because some Trusts reject requests for caesarean sections late in gestation.[36] Rejection is also very disrespectful. One woman recounts how she felt as though healthcare providers treated her like a 'child being told off for doing something wrong' and how her attending healthcare provider refused to listen to her concerns and reasons for the request.[37] Another woman expressed frustration about the fact that healthcare providers are not prepared to 'credit women with the capacity to make informed decisions regarding risks which are acceptable to her'.[38]

One can argue that the Oxford University Hospitals NHS Foundation Trust is compelling or forcing women to experience the physiological process of vaginal birth because the Trust is actively denying women access to an alternative mode of childbirth that is available at the facility. Women who were denied access to caesarean sections reported experiencing nightmares and sleeplessness, and feeling lonely, frightened, anxious, stressed, and being filled with dread while trying to secure access to a caesarean section during their pregnancies.[39] Furthermore, evidence reveals that women experience traumatic births in cases where they feel that they lacked autonomy and control, where they were denied access to a particular intervention, and when healthcare providers did not provide the necessary

---

33 Ibid.
34 Oxford University Hospitals NHS Trust (n 18) 4.
35 Birthrights replying letter to Oxford University Hospitals Trust, <www.birthrights.org.uk/wordpress/wp-content/uploads/2017/07/Second-letter-to-OUH-with-case-studies.docx> accessed 6 June 2018.
36 Ibid.
37 Ibid.
38 Ibid.
39 Ibid.

support.[40] These harms point to the fact that Trusts are compromising women's psychological integrity in rather fundamental ways. Their harms are invisiblised because evidence-based care is presented by the Trust as being the mechanism to prevent harms during childbirth. The process of invisiblising these harms allows the Trust to authoritatively assert that it is well-positioned to determine 'the best option' and the privileging of medical authority allows the Trust to assert that it is best placed to reduce short- and long-term harms.

Limited value of guidelines in law

The discussion to follow will show that a woman cannot compel a provider to comply with evidence-based guidelines to gain access to its benefits and a woman cannot compel a healthcare provider to disregard the guidelines when she does not want the benefits it has on offer. This is the situation taking place in relation to the Oxford University Hospitals NHS Foundation Trust. For women to gain access to caesarean sections they need to be able to compel an obstetrician to comply with a portion of the NICE guidelines and to compel the obstetrician to ignore the WHO recommendations.

Courts have accepted the authoritative nature of clinical guidelines as far as they are 'evidence of good medical practice'.[41] Various healthcare providers have been found negligent for failing to comply with clinical guidelines,[42] but this is not a given. In *KR v Lanarkshire Health Board*,[43] Lord Brailsford explains that guidelines

> are the result of deliberation by panels of experts who will have regard in formulating them to available scientific information and their own collective experience. The result of that process are documents which are intended to provide clinical guidance, not set down mandatory rules.[44]

Courts accept that slavish adherence to guidelines should be avoided[45] and their application should be determined by a healthcare provider's appreciation of her or his own level of knowledge and experience.[46] This means that a more experienced provider may deviate from guidelines when her or his extensive clinical

---

40 Cheryl Tatano Beck, 'Birth Trauma: In the Eye of the Beholder' (2004) 53 Nurs Res 28; Rachel Harris and Susan Ayers, 'What Makes Labour and Birth Traumatic? A Survey of Intrapartum "Hotspots"' (2012) 27 Psychol Health 1166; M H Hollander and others, 'Preventing Traumatic Childbirth Experiences: 2192 Women's Perceptions and Views' (2017) 20 Arch Womens Ment Health 515.

41 *Smith v National Health Service Litigation* [2001] Lloyd's Rep Med 90.

42 For instance see, *CP v Lanarkshire Acute Hospitals NHS Trust* [2015] SCOH 142; *DF v Healthcare NHS Trust* [2005] EWHC 1327.

43 [2016] CSOH 133 [129].

44 Ibid.

45 *Montgomery* (n 21) [203].

46 *KR* (n 43) [129].

experience and knowledge indicate this may be necessary.[47] A less experienced healthcare provider, who lacks the necessary knowledge and experience, is required to follow the guidelines since these represent distilled experience of other healthcare providers that this healthcare provider lacks.[48] This does not mean that they are compelled to comply with the guidelines; it means that the inexperienced healthcare providers should consult their more experience colleagues in cases where the application of guidelines is deemed inappropriate.[49]

Patients cannot enforce guidelines. Instead, courts adopt a flexible approach that tends to draw from and favour medical knowledge and experience as the guide to determine the justifiability of their application or deviation therefrom. Essentially, in this narrow context, the courts maintain the privileged position of medical knowledge. Medical knowledge and experience establish guidelines, and medical knowledge and experience are leading points of reference when courts seek to establish when deviation or compliance is justified. It is not overtly clear how much room is available to accommodate considerations deemed important to women that are not orientated around medical considerations, strictly construed. The current approach will do little to support women who seek to enforce one set of guidelines over another, particularly when one set of guidelines promote the consideration of what women may deem necessary (NICE guidelines) over what the medical profession deems necessary (WHO recommendations). The patient-centred approach supported in *Montgomery* may help to dismantle the privileged position of medical knowledge in the context of care during pregnancy and childbirth.

The Supreme Court recognised that a number of fundamental developments have taken place in society, medical practice, and the law, and these developments demand a change in the way that patients are cared for.[50] These developments include the fact that the patient/doctor relationship has evolved into one where patients are recognised as rights bearers; that access to information debunks the flawed assumptions that patients are medically uninformed and incapable of understanding medical-related matters; and that professional guidance encourages patient's informed involvement when making decisions about treatment.[51] Developments in law include the recognition of important common law values and rights such as self-determination and respect for private life.[52] These important values and rights support the recognition of a duty to involve patients in decision-making relating to their care and treatment.[53]

---

47 Ibid.
48 Ibid.
49 Ibid.
50 *Montgomery* (n 21) [75].
51 Ibid [75]–[79].
52 Ibid [80].
53 Ibid. See also Jonathan Herring and others, 'Elbow Room for Best Practice? Montgomery, Patients' Values, and Balanced Decision Making in Person-Centred Clinical Care' (2017) 25 Med Law Rev 582.

Collectively, these developments counter the legitimacy of medical paternalism and support a patient/doctor relationship where patients are treated as 'adults who are capable of understanding that medical treatment is uncertain of success and may involve risk, accepting responsibility for the taking of risks affecting their own lives, and living with the consequences of their choices'.[54] This translates into two important consequences. First, a healthcare provider is under a duty to ensure that a patient is aware of material risks inherent in treatment.[55] Second, a patient is entitled to decide whether not to incur that risk and the court recognises that the decision to incur risk may be informed by non-medical considerations.[56] The Supreme Court supports an understanding of risk that is patient-sensitive and the materiality of risk is not merely determined with reference to percentages. A patient-sensitive approach requires the healthcare provider to consider how the risk will affect the life of that individual patient if it were to materialise and 'the importance to the patient of the benefits to be achieved by the treatment'.[57]

Montgomery certainly helps to challenge medical paternalism.[58] Lady Hale proclaims, '[g]one are the days when it was thought that, on becoming pregnant, a woman lost, not only her capacity, but also her right to act as a genuinely autonomous human being'.[59] It establishes that clinical considerations are not the only factors relevant to decision-making about care options. It effectively gives legal weight to patient's personal perceptions of risk and the types of risk they would be willing to carry. From this perspective, women may be able to challenge the Trust's position that its approach is driven by the need to avoid long- and short-term harms, since risk of harms is seemingly being determined without the consideration of individual women's needs and what they perceive as risks worth taking in relation to their childbirth. It also helps to dispel the Oxford University Hospitals NHS Foundation Trust's notion that there is only one 'best option' and that this option should be followed because the Trust declares it the best one available. *Montgomery* allows us to recognise that the 'best option' approach may come with risks that some women are not prepared to face, and they are entitled to avoid that risk.

It is noteworthy that *Montgomery* secures the right to information to make informed decisions that are patient specific, and it establishes a duty on healthcare providers to facilitate that process. However, it does not obligate healthcare providers to ensure the realisation of those decisions. Lady Hale recognises this limitation; she states a woman cannot 'force her doctor to offer treatment which he or she considers futile or inappropriate. But she is at least entitled to

---

54 *Montgomery* (n 21) [81].

55 Ibid [82].

56 Ibid.

57 Ibid [89].

58 cf, Jonathan Montgomery and Elsa Montgomery, 'Montgomery on Informed Consent: An Expert Decision' (2016) 42 J Med Ethics 89.

59 *Montgomery* (n 21) [116].

the information which will enable her to take a proper part in that decision'.[60] *Aintree* confirms that a patient cannot demand treatment from a healthcare provider if that treatment is not clinically indicated.[61] Clinical indication reappears, and it works to limit severely women's ability to secure an experience of childbirth shaped by the autonomous and informed decisions that *Montgomery* secures. What good is it to be part of the decision-making process when the decision reached is one that does not need to be respected?

This discussion reveals that evidence-based guidelines, which are developed for the benefit of women, do not necessarily benefit all women in practice. Some women experience harms because of their application, and this needs deeper interrogation and analysis. I argue that this scenario is not merely an issue of compliance with guidelines; it is a form of violence against women.

Obstetric violence by omission

Jewkes and Penn-Kekana argue that abuse during childbirth is in fact a *subset* of violence against women.[62] They explain:

> The essential feature of violence against women is that it stems from structural gender inequality, ie, women's subordinate position in society as compared to men. This systematically devalues the lives of women and girls and thus enables the inappropriately low allocation of resources to maternity care that is found in many countries. It also disempowers women and enables the use of violence against them.[63]

According to Jewkes and Penn-Kekana, there are many lessons that can be learned from research on violence against women, especially when developing and evaluating policies and interventions.[64] They are on point. Obstetric violence activists established the importance of a violence perspective many years before Jewkes and Penn-Kekana published their comment, and I will draw from their contributions here.

I adopt a violence perceptive to argue that healthcare providers or Trusts commit acts of obstetric violence by omission when they employ evidence-based guidelines to deny women access to non-clinically indicated care, knowing that this denial of care will cause an infringement of women's psychological integrity. I support this argument by considering how obstetric violence is currently conceptualised in law and broader activism, and I build on this concept by drawing from Bufacchi's definition of violence.[65]

---

60   Ibid [115].
61   *Aintree University Hospitals NHS Foundation Trust v James* [2013] UKSC 67 [18].
62   Rachel Jewkes and Loveday Penn-Kekana, 'Mistreatment of Women in Childbirth: Time for Action on the Important Dimension of Violence against Women' (2015) 12(6) PLOS Med e1001849.
63   Ibid (footnote omitted).
64   Ibid.
65   Vittorio Bufacchi, *Violence and Social Justice* (Palgrave Macmillan 2007) 13.

'Obstetric violence' originates from Latin America.[66] The concept has grown in popularity among many activists and researchers who demand reform of the overly medicalised and violent nature of some maternity care services. It is a term employed to name the 'malaise that many women feel after childbirth, even though society tells them that everything is alright and all that is important is that the baby is alive'.[67] 'Obstetric violence' calls out unnecessary and improper use of medicine against women and their bodies, and it locates these practices within a broader framework of historical and ongoing social inequality related to gender, race, and class: 'How women are treated in labour and birth, mirrors how they are treated in society in general'.[68] An obstetric violence perspective demonstrates that disrespect and abuse during childbirth are indicators of embedded harmful attitudes towards women and their bodies.[69] These attitudes privilege medical knowledge and allow healthcare providers to enforce women's silence and compliance, and they support the imposition of routine interventions on women without consultation, informed consent, and clinical need.[70]

It is notable that 'obstetric violence' is not defined with reference to existing definitions of violence more generally. Those researchers or activists who position themselves in relation to a definition tend to draw from art 15 of the Venezuelan Organic Law on the Right of Women to a Life Free of Violence (2007).[71] It defines obstetric violence as the appropriation of women's bodies and reproductive processes by healthcare personnel which brings with it a loss of autonomy and the ability to decide freely about their bodies and sexuality, and which has a negative impact on the quality of women's lives.[72] It recognises that obstetric violence is expressed as 'dehumanised treatment', 'abuse of

---

66 Sánchez (n 10) 39, 50–51; Hanna Laako, 'Understanding Contested Women's Rights in Development: The Latin American Campaign for the Humanisation of Birth and the Challenge of Midwifery in Mexico' (2017) 38 Third World Q 379, 387.

67 Sánchez (n 10) 95.

68 Lydia Zacher Dixon, 'Obstetrics in a Time of Violence: Mexican Midwives Critique Routine Hospital Practices' (2015) 29 MAQ 437, 447.

69 Ibid 441, 444.

70 Rachel Jewkes, Naeemah Abrahams, and Zodumo Mvo, 'Why Do Nurses Abuse Patients? Reflections from South African Obstetric Services' (1998) 47 Soc Sci Med 1781; Roberto Castro and Joaquina Erviti, 'Violations of Reproductive Rights during Hospital Births in Mexico' (2003) 7 Health Hum Rights 90; Meghan A Bohren and others, '"By Slapping Their Laps, the Patient Will Know That You Truly Care for Her": A Qualitative Study on Social Norms and Acceptability of the Mistreatment of Women during Childbirth in Abuja, Nigeria' (2016) 2 SSM Popul Health 640.

71 Argentina and some states in Mexico have also introduced obstetric violence laws but the relevant provisions are not readily available to English speaking researchers, academics, and activists. For more on those jurisdictions see Caitlin R Williams and others, 'Obstetric Violence: A Latin American Legal Response to Mistreatment during Childbirth' (2018) 125 BJOG 1208. The Venezuelan obstetric violence provision was translated by Rogelio D'Gregorio in 2010 and his translation was made widely available through a prominent journal, see Rogelio Pérez D'Gregorio, 'Obstetric Violence: A New Legal Term Introduced in Venezuela' (2010) 111 BJOG 201.

72 D'Gregorio (n 71) 201.

medication', and it includes within its scope the process of converting the physiological process of childbirth into a pathological event.[73]

The Organic Law appears to promote a wide conceptualisation of obstetric
violence. Arguably, any obstetric-related conduct that takes place in relation to
a woman and her body during childbirth without her informed consent *could*
constitute obstetric violence provided that it amounts to an appropriation of
her body or that it denies her the ability to make decisions during this time.
However, art 51 narrows this broad definition because it primarily focuses on
preventing acts that pathologise childbirth. Article 51 of the Organic Law recognises that the following closed list of conduct constitutes obstetric violence:
a failure to give effective attention to obstetric emergencies; forcing women to
give birth in the supine position when the necessary means to give birth in a vertical position are available; preventing mother/child bonding and breastfeeding;
altering the natural childbirth process by using acceleration techniques without
voluntary and informed consent; performing a caesarean section without informed consent and when vaginal childbirth is possible.

D'Gregorio, an obstetrician from Venezuela, confirms that 'obstetric violence' is a narrowly construed concept in Venezuelan Law. He explains that the
Organic Law emphasises that 'medication should only be used when it is indicated, the natural processes should be respected, and instrumental or surgical
procedures should be performed only when the indication follows evidence-based
medicine'.[74] Thus, while the need for informed consent features (promoting
women's autonomy), the focal point of the obstetric violence articles relates to
preventing the use of medical interventions that are not clinically indicated and
to ensure a more humanised approach to childbirth that supports childbirth
as a physiological process. Similarly, Sánchez, who studied obstetric violence
activism in Spain, interprets obstetric violence laws as promoting the notion
that 'pregnancy does not have to be considered a pathology, but a "natural"
process'.[75] She recognises that obstetric violence laws demand that healthcare
providers recognise that women are not ill and are capable of making informed
decisions regarding their care during labour and childbirth but it seems that
these considerations are relevant in contexts where woman are looking to avoid
medicalised childbirths.

'Obstetric violence' is a helpful concept despite its narrow construction in
law. It contextualises violence against women within the obstetric care environment, it demystifies how and why this violence occurs, it helps women articulate
the harm they experience during labour and childbirth, and it works to challenge medical privilege by obligating healthcare providers to justify normalised
and routinised conduct. However, the above-mentioned application of the concept of obstetric violence creates the perception that this form of violence only
concerns healthcare provider conduct that is disrespectful of the physiological

73 Ibid.
74 Ibid.
75 Sánchez (n 10) 60.

process of childbirth or conduct (in the form of medical interventions) which is not clinically indicated and evidence-based. I argue that this conceptualisation of obstetric violence is far too narrow, and it overlooks many acts of violence that can occur in the obstetric care context.[76] Further, it does not reveal how healthcare professional subject women to violence while undergoing necessitated medicalised childbirths. This approach has the consequence of narrowing the potential for critical review and response.

Support for such a narrow construction of obstetric violence may lie in the fact that the concept of violence is not fully understood, or it may simply be a consequence of the fact that there is no accepted definition of violence, and that it is an ambiguous concept that tends to be moulded by different people who adopt different perspectives.[77] Bufacchi tackles this issue. He argues that the definition of violence should be fix and not fluid and he offers a definition that may help to develop a universally applicable conceptualisation of violence.[78]

In the main, violence is defined either very narrowly or too comprehensively.[79] A narrow definition of violence defines it as an intentional act of excessive physical force used to cause suffering or injury.[80] This approach fails to recognise the fact that violence can cause emotional and psychological suffering,[81] that it can take place indirectly through institution structures and agencies,[82] and that it is not aligned with definitions of violence found in international and regional laws.[83] This demonstrates that there is a need for a more inclusive construction of violence and there is broader support for this approach. A comprehensive definition of violence frames violence as a 'violation of rights'.[84] While this offers a more inclusive approach, it is criticised as being too comprehensive

---

76 Researchers and activists recognise a wide range of conduct as constituting violence against women during childbirth. For example, see Diniz and others (n 4) and Elizabeth Kukura, 'Obstetric Violence' (2018) 106 Georget Law J 721, 726–54.

77 Willem de Haan, 'Violence as an Essentially Contested Concept' in Sophie Body-Gendrot and Pieter Spierenburg (eds), *Violence in Europe: Historical and Contemporary Perspectives* (Springer 2007) 27; Elizabeth A Stanko (ed), *The Meanings of Violence* (Routledge 2003) 2.

78 For his arguments on how to develop an objective dimension to the definition of violence, see Bufacchi (n 65) 30–40. He frames violence as involving the perpetrator, the victim and the spectator. The spectator helps to establish the necessary objectivity.

79 Vittorio Bufacchi, 'Two Concepts of Violence' (2005) 3 Polit Stud Rev 193, 197.

80 Ibid.

81 Haan (n 77) 31.

82 Johan Galtung, 'Violence, Peace, and Peace Research' (1969) 6 *J Peace Res* 167; Bufacchi (n 79) 198.

83 See art 1 of the Inter-American Convention on the Prevention, Punishment and Eradication of Violence against Women (1995); paragraph 6 of General Recommendation 19 of the United Nations Committee on the Elimination of Discrimination against Women; art 3(a) of the Council of Europe Convention on Preventing and Combating Violence against Women and Domestic Violence (2014); art 1(j) of the Protocol to the African Charter on Human and Peoples' Rights on the Rights of Women in Africa (2005). All of these definitions adopt a much broader approach to violence against women.

84 Bufacchi (n 79) 196.

because 'almost any act can be said to violate someone's rights, making violence ubiquitous and therefore meaningless'.[85]

Bufacchi attempts to overcome these issues. According to Bufacchi:

> [A]n act of violence occurs when the integrity or unity of a subject (person or animal) or object (property) is being intentionally or unintentionally violated, as a result of an action or an omission. The violation may occur at the physical or psychological level, through physical or psychological means. A violation of integrity will usually result in the subject being harmed or injured, or the object being destroyed or damaged.[86]

Bufacchi's definition locates violence in the violation of integrity and not *all* human rights. Violence concerns the process of being reduced to a lesser being in physical and/or psychological terms.[87] He focuses on the consequence of conduct (violation of integrity) and looks at an incident from the perspective of the victim. This approach supports the argument that both acts and omissions can constitute violence since both hold the potential to cause a violation of integrity as a consequence thereof. However, Bufacchi explains that an omission can only legitimately amount to violence if two elements are present: foreseeability and alternativity.[88] These elements require that the person must be able to predict the harmful consequence and it must be possible to act in a different way, and this different act must be viable.[89] 'Viability' means that the different options must be comparable in terms of the facility of access.[90]

On the subject of intentional and unintentional causing of a violation of integrity, Bufacchi recognises that intention to cause harm is what many accept as the moral line which differentiates benevolent actions from malevolent actions, and which helps to clearly distinguish between an act of violence and a mere accident.[91] However, he recognises that there are 'hard cases' where a person's integrity is violated as a result of conduct which is not merely accidental but the harmful consequence was not intended either.[92] This will be the case when harm is a foreseeable and/or avoidable. Given that the person still experiences a violation, these hard cases make it necessary to relax the intention requirement of violence and replace it with the requirement of foreseeability of inevitable consequences of one's actions.[93] Bufacchi explains that 'an act of violence occurs when injury or suffering is inflicted upon a person or persons by an agent, and the suffering is either foreseeable and/or avoidable'.[94] Following this ap-

---

85 Ibid 197.
86 Bufacchi (n 65) 43–44.
87 Ibid 41.
88 Ibid 55.
89 Ibid 45–56.
90 Ibid 56.
91 Ibid 67, 69.
92 Ibid 73.
93 Ibid 66.
94 Ibid 85.

proach helps to broaden the definition of violence to capture unintentional but foreseeable harm, it renders visible those harms that remain invisible under the narrow definition of violence, and visibility supports demands for justification and claims for accountability.[95]

Drawing from Bufacchi's general definition of violence it is clear that the 'violence' in 'obstetric violence' concerns the violation of integrity of women within the obstetric care context. A woman's physical and psychological integrity can be violated in many ways during obstetric 'care' and this means that the appropriation of women's bodies and reproductive process is essentially only one act of many that constitute obstetric violence. Thus, medicalisation of childbirth without justification and consent is a type of obstetric violence rather than its definition. This approach exposes the fact that the current legal definition of obstetric violence, which seems to be widely supported by activists and researchers, is too narrow and this has caused certain acts of violence to be overlooked or remain undetected.

I argue that one of the acts of obstetric violence being overlooked concerns the use of evidence-based guidelines or recommendations to deny women access to non-clinically indicated care and this denial causes them foreseeable harms. This is best illustrated by referring back to the Maternal Request Caesarean Campaign.[96]

In maternal request cases, women are requesting access to caesarean sections for reasons considered important to them. Access is being denied because evidence-based guidelines and recommendations reveal that there are no clinical indications supporting this mode of childbirth. The denial of access to caesarean sections runs the serious risk of long-term psychological harms related to the trauma experienced as a result of being compelled into a particular mode of childbirth. I characterise this as a form of obstetric violence because this scenario causes a violation of women's psychological integrity. The violation occurs because of an omission on the part of attending healthcare providers. It constitutes violence because healthcare providers can predict this harmful consequence given that they consult with women antenatally and during this time women make their position in relation to vaginal birth clear. Healthcare professionals or Trusts can avoid violating women's psychological integrity because the reason for the denial of care is grounded in clinical indication and not limited resources. This scenario falls within the 'hard case' category: the violation of integrity is not an intended consequence of compliance with guidelines, but it is not an accident either. Healthcare providers do not intend the consequence of childbirth-related psychological trauma, but this consequence is foreseeable and avoidable. Therefore, it constitutes an act of obstetric violence by omission.

Embedding obstetric violence within broader debates about violence more generally reveals that pathologisation of childbirth without women's consent and the Trust's application of evidence-based guidelines to deny clinically

95 Ibid 82.
96 Booker (n 13).

non-indicated care are two sides of the same coin. In both instances women are infantilised, humiliated, and subjected to the power of others.

Leaving no woman behind: making evidence-based guidelines more effective

This chapter shows that scientifically sound evidence-based guidelines and the law can work together in particularly harmful ways for some pregnant or birthing women. For evidence-based guidelines be an effective tool to tackle abuse, as presented by the WHO and others, they need to address or challenge the underlying causes of abuse. Obstetric violence research and activism explains that the privileged position of medical knowledge and the unequal and undervalued position of women in society are the underlying causes of abuse during obstetric care. However, evidence-based guidelines do not address these causes on their own because they work with the privileged position of medical knowledge rather than challenge it. Thus, the effectiveness of guidelines is determined by those who apply the guidelines and their perceptions of women. The law allows this to occur and it will continue to occur until mechanisms of empowerment are developed for women to use when confronted with harmful application of evidence-based guidelines.

Status quo needs to be challenged because some women are being left behind and their rights are being violated. An obstetric violence perspective is particularly helpful in this context because it disrupts medical privilege. It adopts a woman's perspective by bringing into focus their experiences and this facilitates the inclusion of women's voices into spaces where they were silenced. It exposes harms that were once invisible or accepted as normal. Framing women's experiences as a form of violence against women ignites international human rights law obligations on states to 'take appropriate and effective measures to overcome all forms of gender-based violence'.[97]

The United Nations Committee on the Elimination of Discrimination against Women explains that appropriate and effective measures include legal measures such as penal sanctions, civil remedies, and compensatory provisions to protect women against all kinds of violence.[98] These should be employed *together with* other measures adopted to protect and prevent violence, such as public information and education programmes to change harmful attitudes, and to offer counselling and other support services to women who have experienced violence.[99] Importantly, the Committee confirms that a state may be responsible for private acts of violence if it fails to act with due diligence to prevent and investigate violence against women.[100] The Council of Europe Convention

---

97 General Recommendation 19 of the United Nations Committee on the Elimination of Discrimination against Women para 24(a).
98 Ibid para 24(t)(i).
99 Ibid para 24(t)(ii)–(iii).
100 Ibid para 9.

on Preventing and Combating Violence against Women and Domestic Violence supports this position; it adopts a similar approach to state obligations in the context of violence against women.[101]

It is demonstrated earlier that if evidence-based guidelines are to secure their spot as effective tools in the fight against abuse during pregnancy and childbirth, they will have to be subject to women's individual needs as self-determined. The privileged position of medical knowledge should be used *for* women rather than *against* them. Further, international human rights law emphasises that violence against women needs to be tackled from multiple perspectives. This means two things: a health systems approach to abuse is not enough and women should have effective recourse in law. Consequently, when evidence-based guidelines leave some women behind and their integrity is violated as a result thereof, there must be a remedy in law available to them. The current position that courts have adopted towards evidence-based guidelines cannot be legitimately sustained.

Conclusion

Evidence-based guidelines play an important role in maternity care. They are promoted as being developed and implemented for the benefit of women, to overcome disrespect and abuse during pregnancy and childbirth. However, this chapter tells the story of women who are silenced, excluded from care, and experience violations to their psychological integrity because of the application of evidence-based guidelines and recommendations. Further, it showed that the law has little to offer by way of leverage over those making medical decisions that have such a negative impact on them. I argue that women's experiences are not mere accidents or unfortunate but acceptable outcomes of 'good medical practice' or evidenced-based care. This is obstetric violence and this form of violence is facilitated by evidence-based guidelines because the guidelines allow the application of medical knowledge in harmful ways and they are used to justify violence against women. I suspect the reason why some of the flaws of evidence-based guidelines cannot be fully appreciated is because those promoting them do not consider abuse as a form of violence or they have a restrictively narrow understanding of the concept.[102] The recognition of these circumstances as a form of violence against women ignites important state obligations. A state must consider all possible avenues to prevent and protect women from violence. Violence can be prevented by supporting the use of evidence-based guidelines to facilitate meaningful informed decision-making rather than allowing healthcare

---

101 See arts 5 and 7.
102 For instance, the World Health Organization's researchers argue that 'violence' should be avoided because it is too narrow. They argue that 'violence' does not include unintentional harms or omissions. See Meghan A Bohren and others, 'The Mistreatment of Women during Childbirth in Health Facilities Globally: A Mixed-Methods Systematic Review' (2015) 12(6) PLOS Med e10011847; J P Vogel and others, 'Promoting Respect and Preventing Mistreatment during Childbirth' (2016) 123 BJOG 671, 672.

providers to use them make decisions for women. Further, the state should think creatively of legal ways to accommodate women's diverse needs for care, particularly when healthcare providers attempt to override and silence them because evidence-based guidelines justify this approach.

Table of cases

Aintree University Hospitals NHS Foundation Trust v James [2013] UKSC 67
CP v Lanarkshire Acute Hospitals NHS Trust [2015] SCOH 142
DF v Healthcare NHS Trust [2005] EWHC 1327
KR v Lanarkshire Health Board [2016] CSOH 133 [129]
Montgomery v Lanarkshire Health Board [2016] CSOH 133
Smith v National Health Service Litigation [2001] Lloyd's Rep Med 90

Bibliography

Beck C T, 'Birth Trauma: In the Eye of the Beholder' (2004) 53 Nurs Res 28

Beckett K, 'Choosing Cesarean: Feminism and the Politics of Childbirth in the United States' (2005) 6(3) Fem T 251

Bellón Sánchez S, 'Obstetric Violence: Medicalization, Authority Abuse and Sexism within Spanish Obstetric Assistance: A New Name for Old Issues' (Masters Dissertation, Utrecht University 2014)

Birthrights, 'Campaigns: Our Maternal Request Campaign' (2017)

Birthrights, 'Maternal Request Caesarean' (2018)

Birthrights replying letter to Oxford University Hospitals Trust

Bohren M A and others, 'The Mistreatment of Women during Childbirth in Health Facilities Globally: A Mixed-Methods Systematic Review' (2015) 12(6) PLOS Med e10011847

Bohren M A and others, '"By Slapping Their Laps, the Patient Will Know That You Truly Care for Her": A Qualitative Study on Social Norms and Acceptability of the Mistreatment of Women during Childbirth in Abuja, Nigeria' (2016) 2 SSM Popul Health 640

Bufacchi V, 'Two Concepts of Violence' (2005) 3 Polit Stud Rev 193

Bufacchi V, *Violence and Social Justice* (Palgrave Macmillan 2007)

Castro R and Erviti J, 'Violations of Reproductive Rights during Hospital Births in Mexico' (2003) 7 Health Hum Rights 90

Chalmers B, 'Changing Childbirth in Eastern Europe: Which Systems of Authoritative Knowledge Should Prevail?' in Robbie E Davis-Floyd and Carolyn F Sargent (eds), *Childbirth and Authoritative Knowledge: Cross-Cultural Perspectives* (University of California Press 1997)

Cook R J and Cusack S, *Gender Stereotyping: Transnational Legal Perspectives* (University of Pennsylvania Press 2010)

Cook R J, Cusack S and Dickens B M, 'Unethical Female Stereotyping in Reproductive Health' (2010) 109 Int J Gynaecol Obstet 255

Council of Europe Convention on Preventing and Combating Violence against Women and Domestic Violence (2014)

D'Gregorio R P, 'Obstetric Violence: A New Legal Term Introduced in Venezuela' (2010) 111 BJOG 201

De Haan W, 'Violence as an Essentially Contested Concept' in Body-Gendrot S and Spierenburg P (eds), *Violence in Europe: Historical and Contemporary Perspectives* (Springer 2007)

Diniz S G and others, 'Abuse and Disrespect in Childbirth Care as a Public Health Issue in Brazil: Origins, Definitions, Impacts on Maternal Health, and Proposals for Its Prevention' (2015) 25 J Hum Growth Dev 377

Dixon L Z, 'Obstetrics in a Time of Violence: Mexican Midwives Critique Routine Hospital Practices' (2015) 29 MAQ 437

Downe S and others, 'What Matters to Women during Childbirth: A Systematic Qualitative Review' (2018) 13(4) PLoS ONE e0194906

Galtung J, 'Violence, Peace, and Peace Research' (1969) 6 J Peace Res 167

General Recommendation 19 of the United Nations Committee on the Elimination of Discrimination against Women

Goer H, 'Cruelty in Maternity Wards: Fifty Years Later' (2010) 19 J Perinat Educ 33

Harris R and Ayers S, 'What Makes Labour and Birth Traumatic? A Survey of Intrapartum "Hotspots"' (2012) 27 Psychol Health 1166

Herrera Vacaflor C A, 'Obstetric Violence in Argentina: A Study on the Legal Effects of Medical Guidelines and Statutory Obligations for Improving the Quality of Maternal Health' (Masters Dissertation, University of Toronto 2015)

Herring J and others, 'Elbow Room for Best Practice? Montgomery, Patients' Values, and Balanced Decision Making in Person-Centred Clinical Care' (2017) 25 Med Law Rev 582

Hollander M H and others, 'Preventing Traumatic Childbirth Experiences: 2192 Women's Perceptions and Views' (2017) 20 Arch Womens Ment Health 515

Inter-American Convention on the Prevention, Punishment and Eradication of Violence against Women (1995)

Jewkes R and Penn-Kekana L, 'Mistreatment of Women in Childbirth: Time for Action on the Important Dimension of Violence against Women' (2015) 12(6) PLOS Med e1001849

Jewkes R, Abrahams N, and Mvo Z, 'Why Do Nurses Abuse Patients? Reflections from South African Obstetric Services' (1998) 47 Soc Sci Med 1781

Kitzinger S, *Birth and Sex: The Power and the Passion* (Pinter and Martin 2012)

Kukura E, 'Contested Care: The Limitations of Evidence-Based Maternity Care Reform' (2016) 31 Berkeley J Gend Law & Just 241

Kukura E, 'Obstetric Violence' (2018) 106 Georget Law J 721

Laako H, 'Understanding Contested Women's Rights in Development: The Latin American Campaign for the Humanisation of Birth and the Challenge of Midwifery in Mexico' (2017) 38 Third World Q 379

Lazarus E, 'What do Women Want? Issues of Choice, Control, and Class in American Pregnancy and Childbirth' in Davis-Floyd R E and Sargent C F (eds), *Childbirth and Authoritative Knowledge: Cross Cultural Perspectives* (University of California Press 1997)

Mainz J, 'Defining and Classifying Clinical Indicators for Quality Improvement' (2003) 15 IJQHC 523

Maria Booker, 'Do I Have a Right to a C-Section? Update on Oxford University Hospitals' (21 July 2017)

Miller S and others, 'Beyond Too Little, Too Late and Too Much, Too Soon: A Pathway Towards Evidence-Based, Respectful Maternity Care Worldwide' (2016) 388.10056 The Lancet 2176

Montgomery J and Montgomery E, 'Montgomery on Informed Consent: An Expert Decision' (2016) 42 J Med Ethics 89

Morris N, 'Human Relations in Obstetric Practice' (1960) 275 The Lancet 913

NICE, 'Caesarean Section: Clinical Guideline' (2011)

Oxford University Hospitals NHS Trust, 'I am Anxious about Giving Birth and Want to Know More About Caesarean Section' (2014)

Oxford University Hospitals Trust replying letter to Birthrights

Pickles C, 'Sounding the Alarm: Government of the Republic of Namibia v LM and Women's Rights during Childbirth in South Africa' (2018) 21 PER 1

Protocol to the African Charter on Human and Peoples' Rights on the Rights of Women in Africa (2005)

Sadler M and others, 'Moving Beyond Disrespect and Abuse: Addressing the Structural Dimensions of Obstetric Violence' (2016) 24(47) Reprod Health Matters 47

Sakala C and Corry M P, 'Evidence-Based Maternity Care: What It Is and What It Can Achieve' (2008)

Stanko E A (ed), *The Meanings of Violence* (Routledge 2003)

Vogel J P and others, 'Promoting Respect and Preventing Mistreatment during Childbirth' (2016) 123 BJOG 671

Williams C R and others, 'Obstetric Violence: A Latin American Legal Response to Mistreatment during Childbirth' (2018) 125 BJOG 1208

World Health Organization, 'The Prevention and Elimination of Disrespect and Abuse during Facility-Based Childbirth' (2014)

World Health Organization, 'Statement on Caesarean Section Rates' (2015)

9 Childbirth, consent, and information about options and risks

Lisa Forsberg

Introduction[1]

This chapter focuses on autonomy violations consisting in patients being deprived of information about different treatment options and their risks by their physicians. It argues that in order for what we value in respect of patients' personal autonomy to be protected, their interests in receiving information about options and risks ought to be robustly protected. The aim is to challenge the assumption that *respect for women's autonomy* in childbirth requires only that healthcare professionals 'not interfere with an unassisted delivery',[2] and to introduce some arguments that may serve as a starting point for thinking about what information women should receive in the context of childbirth.

Section one outlines how English law on consent regulates the provision by physicians of information about different treatment options and risks to patients in medical consent transactions.[3] Section two sketches how inadequate information about options and risks in medical consent transactions interferes with or undermines patient autonomy. Section three considers some difficulties relating to proving causation of non-remote legally recognised injury in non-disclosure cases and argues that it is unsurprising that patients should face such difficulties, given that the harm to patients in non-disclosure cases is distinct from the outcome's disvalue and its causal history. It argues that for what we value in respect of autonomy to be protected, the law should directly recognise the harm to patients arising in failures of information about treatment options and risks. Section four considers an objection to the proposal of direct recognition of autonomy violations by insufficient information from the fundamental principles of medical law, and gestures at a possible way in which more robust protection for patients' interests in receiving information about options and

---

1 I am extremely grateful to Anthony Skelton and Isra Black for their very helpful comments on earlier drafts of this chapter.
2 See eg Jessica Flanigan, 'Obstetric Autonomy and Informed Consent' (2016) 19 Ethical Theory and Moral Pract 225, 234.
3 Treatment options include non-treatment.

risks could avoid this objection and be made consistent with the fundamental principles of medical law, at least in the context of childbirth.

The chapter focuses on the civil law on consent in England and Wales. I focus on medical consent transactions involving one patient (P), and one physician (D). I stipulate that in all cases considered, P possesses decision-making capacity,[4] and her consent has not been unduly influenced.[5] Moreover, All consent transactions considered are such that a duty exists between D and P. Finally, for the sake of argument, I accept that the patient interests we are concerned with broadly relate to patient autonomy, and that a failure to respect patients' interests in consenting to or refusing medical interventions and receiving sufficient information about options and risks to enable them to do so in a way that is consistent with their values can be understood broadly as autonomy violations of some kind. There might be better ways to describe them, but I take autonomy violations to be an intuitively plausible shorthand for the *kind* of interests of concern here. In any case, the overall argument does not depend on these interests being best understood as (all) relating to patients' personal autonomy.[6]

English civil law on consent and information about options and risks

English law regulating medical consent by patients with decision-making capacity and information disclosure relevant to it has two pillars. First, battery protects individuals from physical interferences subject to the qualification that some interferences may be warranted, and therefore the law has, *inter alia*, established that individuals may waive the inviolability of their bodies. In order to benefit from such a waiver in the medical context, D needs valid consent from P who, in the usual course of things, determines which interferences with her bodily integrity to permit. Second, there is a requirement on D to provide such information that is sufficient to avoid a successful claim in negligence (for failure to warn).

The standard that information provision has to meet in order to avoid liability in battery is as follows: P's consent to φ is valid when P has been informed

---

4 In England and Wales, this is governed by the Mental Capacity Act 2005, ss 1–3.
5 *Re T (Adult: Refusal of Treatment)* [1993] Fam 95 (CA).
6 These could instead be construed as interests in not being wronged in certain ways, for example by being deceived, coerced, manipulated, and so on. We can take consent to be (very) morally important without grounding its moral importance in autonomy or respect for autonomy, see, eg, Onora O'Neill, 'Autonomy: The Emperor's New Clothes' (2003) 77 Proc Aristot Soc Suppl Vol. Neil C Manson and Onora O'Neill, *Rethinking Informed Consent in Bioethics* (CUP 2007). O'Neill understands consent to protect against P being wronged in some way, eg by being deceived, coerced, manipulated, and so on rather than these things being violations of P's autonomy.

'in broad terms of the nature of the procedure'.[7] As long as *P* has been informed in broad terms of the nature of φ, then 'the cause of the action on which to base a claim for failure to go into risks and implications [of φ] is negligence, not trespass' (battery).[8]

The standard that information provision has to meet in order to avoid, all else being equal,[9] liability in negligence is as follows: *P*'s consent to φ is sufficiently informed when *D* has taken reasonable care to ensure that *P* 'is aware of any material risks involved in any recommended treatment, and of any reasonable alternative or variant treatments'.[10] A risk is material if 'in the circumstances of the particular case a reasonable person in the patient's position would be likely to attach significance to the risk, or the doctor is or should reasonably be aware that the particular patient would be likely to attach significance to it'.[11]

The requirement to provide *P* with (sufficient) information about options and risks, then, is decoupled from the requirement to gain *P*'s valid consent. Moreover, the protection in respect of patient autonomy or consent offered by the torts of battery and negligence is limited in various ways. In battery, failures to obtain *P*'s valid consent are actionable only if they involve interference with bodily integrity via touching.[12] In negligence, failures to provide sufficient information are not actionable *per se*, but only when other conditions are met: that negligent disclosure has a non-remote historical connection to a legally recognised form of injury.

Autonomy, the value of options, and information about risks

The moral significance of withholding information about options and their inherent risks is generally taken to derive from respect for patients' personal autonomy, or something like it. Autonomy is a contested concept, but on all standard accounts it has at its core something like self-governance or being able to ive one's life in accordance with one's values, considered preferences, and so

---

7 *Chatterton v Gerson* [1981] QB 432, 433.

8 Ibid.

9 That is, there has to be a historical connection that is non-remote too, in order for there to be liability.

10 *Montgomery v Lanarkshire Health Board* [2015] UKSC 11 [87]. 'Reasonable care' implies that *D* need only make *P* 'aware' of material risks, etc., not ensure that *P understands* what's entailed. *D* need not disclose information that is covered by the 'therapeutic exception' established in *Montgomery*, whereby *D* is not 'required to make disclosures to her patient if, in the reasonable exercise of medical judgment, she considers that it would be detrimental to the health of her patient to do so'; ibid [85]. I stipulate that none of the consent transactions we are concerned with her are covered by therapeutic privilege.

11 Ibid [87].

12 Broadly construed, touching can be via instruments, etc.

on.[13] This is so whatever view of the *value* of autonomy one might take, that is, whether it is taken to be intrinsically or instrumentally valuable.

Information about treatment options and their risks in medical consent transactions matters to autonomy because P's preference for any given option is comparative in nature, and the value P assigns to any given option is not fully determined by considerations related to P's health and the consequences of each available option for it. The value of each of the options in P's option set (and thus which of these it is instrumentally rational for P to choose) is influenced by the other options within the option set. The choice-worthiness of a particular option, Z, then, is determined in part by how it compares to the other options, Å, Ä, and Ö. Making options available allows possibly for a 'better' (depending on decision rule) option to be chosen. That the value P assigns to any given option will not be fully determined by health-related considerations matters because of the way in which the knowledge is distributed across P and D in medical consent transactions. In the typical case, D possesses knowledge of the in principle available options and their inherent risks that P typically lacks, whereas P possesses knowledge of her values, preferences, plans, circumstances, etc., which in addition to the medical considerations bear on which of the available options will be better for her (information that D typically lacks).

In medical consent transactions in which more than one option is available to P – by available I mean available in principle, that is, that D or some other D *could* offer these interventions to P, not that all options are such that D *would in fact* offer the interventions to P – which of these options is better for P will depend on the risk-benefit profile of each option, how these risks and benefits are assessed from P's point of view, and how each option compares to the risk-benefit profiles of alternative options.

In some cases, the risk-benefit profiles of the options are such that one of the options will almost certainly be the better option for P. Take a situation in which P has a broken leg. The risk-benefit profile of the options available to P in this scenario {having broken leg mended; not having broken leg mended} is such that the option {having broken leg mended} will almost certainly be better for P. Such cases seem to be swamping cases, that is, cases in which the value of one option dominates the others.[14]

Not all medical consent transactions are like this, however. In many consent scenarios, there will be a variety of options available (in principle), each with a

---

13 This is a very rough sketch. Of course, not *any* preferences will do. Most accounts will have some further specification regarding which preferences count: rational preferences, preferences consistent with one's second-order preferences, etc. For our purposes, it is not necessary to choose one account; our account should be compatible with as many (reasonable) accounts of the nature and value of autonomy as possible.

14 This is not to say that other values are not at play in such cases, but merely that the value given to each option will in the typical case be such that the dominant option is most choice-worthy for P (from her point of view).

different risk-benefit profile. Which of the options will be prudentially better for *P* in such cases is less obvious. Judgements about betterness or choice-worthiness here will depend on the disvalue of the risks, and the value of the potential benefits, *from P's point of view*. Consider:

> *Analgesia. P* is having a tumour removed from her diaphragm. Following the operation, *P* needs analgesia to enable her to breathe and cough comfortably, thereby preventing lung collapse and pneumonia. Option A is a thoracic epidural that more effectively serves this purpose but carries a small risk of spinal-cord injury, which might cause paraplegia. Option B is an intravenous narcotic infusion. The risk of pneumonia and lung collapse is considerably greater, and might have serious consequences.[15]

Based on the facts about A's and B's respective effects on *P*'s health, it might *seem* better for *P* to have A. However, more knowledge about *P* and her particular circumstances and values might tell us otherwise. *P* may be an avid sportswoman for whom being able to play sports with her friends is an important part of what, in her view, gives her life meaning. The risk of spinal-cord injury, even if small, may therefore be significant to her, and something she would be prepared to pay a high price in terms of, for example, enduring pain, in order to avoid. With this additional information in mind, it may no longer seem so obvious that it would be better, all things considered, for *P* to have A. Whether it will be better for *P* to have A or B, then, will depend in part on the medical facts and risks, but also in part on other relevant facts about *P*, what she values or cares about, and so on, and the implications for the significance of the risks and potential benefits of each of the options open to her.[16]

Some argue that while the particular expertise *D* possesses makes her well-placed to appraise the *medical* risks and benefits of each of the options and recommend some option over others, *D* possesses no particular expertise in respect of determining what is good for patients in general or for a particular patient *all things considered*. *P* herself seems *prima facie* best placed to make all things considered judgements about what is good for her.[17] Of course, *D* might have knowledge that makes her well-placed to say what will be good for *P* in some cases. She might for example know a lot about what patients in general in *P*'s situation find better for them. But whether or not *P* herself (as opposed to, say, *D*) is in fact best placed to make such decisions, we need to acknowledge that such decisions cannot be made *in the absence of* value judgements, not all of which relate to *P*'s health.

---

15 Adapted after Julian Savulescu, 'Rational Non-Interventional Paternalism: Why Doctors Ought to Make Judgments of What Is Best for Their Patients' (1995) 21 J Med Ethics 327.

16 Ibid.

17 For example, Ian Kennedy, *The Unmasking of Medicine* (Granada 1983); Harry Lesser, 'The Patient Right to Information' in *Protecting the Vulnerable: Autonomy and Consent in Health Care* (Routledge 1991).

We might consider a childbirth scenario which is, like *Analgesia,* a two-option case – a simplified version of the scenario in *Montgomery v Lanarkshire*:

> *Childbirth.* P is about to give birth. There are two options available to her: vaginal birth (VB) and caesarean section (CS). VB (for P) carries a 9–10 per cent risk of shoulder dystocia (risk SD). CS does not carry the particular risk SD, although it carries other risks (which we can assume for the sake of argument are of a similar magnitude, but different in kind).

P in *Childbirth* might, like P in *Analgesia,* have particular circumstances, preferences, and values such that she would be prepared to pay a high price to avoid risk SD. It might be that risk SD threatens much of what, in her view, gives her life meaning and value. Here, like in *Analgesia,* it seems intuitively plausible that it should be up to P to decide to which risks she is willing to expose herself.[18]

Imagine now that D neglects to inform P that CS is an option; she mentions option VB only. D also neglects to inform P that VB (for P) carries risk SD. Since D does not mention option CS, she does not inform P that CS does not carry the particular risk SD (although it does carry other risks). Here, it seems that depriving P of the information necessary for her to be able to make a decision about whether to expose herself to risk SD violates her autonomy in some way.

Insufficiently informed consent, autonomy, and redress

What are P's opportunities for legal redress in scenarios such as *Childbirth* above, in which she has been insufficiently informed about options and risks? Battery seems an unpromising route in non-disclosure cases of this kind. In order to succeed, P would need to demonstrate that her consent was so flawed so as to render it invalid for the purposes of battery, that is, making it so that it was as if

---

18 It may be objected that comparing *Analgesia* and *Childbirth* is misleading. It might be argued that the former is a one-person case whereas in *Childbirth,* we must consider not just any harms to P but also harms to the foetus/baby. Perhaps this means that we have to put the childbirth scenarios in a different category. It could then either be that P is assumed to assign so much value to the health of her future baby that that whatever option promotes its health is taken always to be dominant. Or it might be that P and her future baby are taken to be two patients whose interests should be considered separately and then the option that promotes both of their health is taken as dominant. The former does not seem plausible. Negative consequences for the woman vary considerably and some are very serious indeed. It seems that not all of these would be outweighed by some benefit to the foetus/baby, especially not if they could have been avoided (which the variation suggests they sometimes can be). If the latter is the case – that is, the woman and foetus/baby are taken to be two different patients each of which D owes a duty of care, and some benefit to the foetus/baby is taken to justify D's decision in favour of, say, VB over CS, then there seems to be a compelling argument in favour of making this explicit rather than couching the decision in terms of what is allegedly better for P herself.

she had not validly consented, and that any interference with her bodily integrity would thus be unlawful.[19] Given that *D* needs only to describe φ in broad terms for *P*'s consent to φ to be valid, and given judicial hostility to the use of battery in non-disclosure cases and against medical professionals,[20] a claim in battery seems unlikely to succeed.

Negligence, then, seems to be *P*'s most promising route to redress. But also here *P* faces obstacles. To succeed in negligence, recall, *P* needs to establish breach, causation, and non-remote legally recognised injury.[21] In the actual *Montgomery* case, *P* could demonstrate loss because the materialisation of risk SD caused *P*'s baby brachial plexus injury and cerebral palsy.[22] *P* could further demonstrate that she would not have consented to VB had she been informed of risk SD, because *D* herself admitted that one of the reasons that she had ne-glected to inform *P* of risk SD was that most women in *P*'s situation would opt for CS over VB if informed of the relevant risks, including SD.[23] *D*'s admission made the counterfactual claim plausible, such that on the balance of probabilities it did not look like abuse of hindsight on *P*'s part.

But we can easily imagine other cases in which *P*'s consent is insufficiently informed but where it might be considerably harder for her to demonstrate causation of non-remote legally recognised injury. One reason for this is that there is an assumption that birth-related injuries are, at least to some extent, unavoidable, or should have been expected by *P*, or are a natural part of life and of childbirth and childbirth-related interventions. This makes it hard for *P* to prove that *D*'s insufficient information disclosure caused her to suffer non-re-mote legally recognised injury. First, when *some* injury is expected, it might be hard to distinguish injuries that result from *D*'s behaviour from injuries that are a 'normal part of childbirth', making it hard for *P* to prove causation. Even if the court were to agree that *D*'s failure to perform φ was negligent, *P* will still need to establish that it was *D*'s negligence, rather than, say, some underlying condition or circumstance to do with *P*'s physical characteristics or the foetus' positioning that caused the injury. Second, it might be hard for *P* to demonstrate that the risk of the *particular injuries* that she sustained was such that it would have caused her to refuse the treatment option that she in fact had, had she been

19 Note that invalid consent is generally taken to permit treatment in *P*'s best interests, for example when *P*'s consent is invalid due to incapacity or undue influence. This is different from what we are concerned with here. When, as in our case, the problem is with the information supplied, it is as if *P* did not give valid consent. Therefore any treatment will be unlawful, and cannot be made lawful.

20 For example, *Chatterton* (n 7) and *The Creutzfeldt-Jakob Disease Litigation* (1995) 54 BMLR 1 (QBD) 6 (May J): 'A person may succeed in a claim for failure to inform or warn only if the failure alleged amounts to negligence. To frame such a claim in battery is not only deplorable but insupportable in law'.

21 We do not need to consider duty since all the consent transactions we are concerned with take place in the context of the doctor-patient relationship which is an established duty situation.

22 *Montgomery* (n 10) [22].

23 Ibid [13], [19].

informed of it, especially when there might be no 'no-injury options' realistically available to *P*.

It may be objected, of course, that it is not clear that the *level* or *extent* of injury that seems to be expected or accepted in fact ought to be so. Birth-related injuries vary considerably across countries and regions within countries, and many such variations cannot be explained by socio-economic or pre-existing health differences. Differences might depend on differences in guidelines, or in practices adopted in particular hospitals, or might vary according to views of individual healthcare professionals regarding the most appropriate practices to adopt.[24] The existence of such significant variations seems to make it less plausible that *P* should expect or accept whatever injuries *in fact* occur (within some limits). We might think, then, that the expectation or acceptance of injury poses more of an obstacle to *P*'s success in negligence claims than it ought to.

There is a larger point here. As we have seen, *P* faces various obstacles to a successful claim in negligence because she will often struggle to prove that the outcome that in fact ensued constituted a non-remote legally recognised injury to her and that it was caused by *D*'s conduct. But if information about options and risks is necessary for the kind of consent that tracks or enables what is valuable in respect of patient autonomy, it seems that *P*'s autonomy has been undermined or violated in some way in medical consent transactions in which *D* fails to inform her of options and risks. It seems intuitively compelling both that (a) *P* has been harmed or treated unjustly in some way by *D* and ought therefore to have access to a legal remedy against *D* of some kind, and (b) that *D* has wronged or unjustly treated *P* in some way and therefore ought to expect some kind of legal action to be taken against her.[25] It seems, then, that *P*'s options for legal redress do

---

24 There are, for example, huge variations in episiotomy use across countries. Just within Europe, according to the 2010 European Perinatal Health Report:

> Episiotomy rates ranged from 5 per cent to 70 per cent of vaginal deliveries. They were around 70 per cent in Cyprus, Poland, Portugal, and Romania, 43–58 per cent in Wallonia and Flanders in Belgium and in Spain, 16–36 per cent in Wales, Scotland, Finland, Norway, Estonia, France, Switzerland, Germany, Malta, Slovenia, Luxembourg, the Brussels region in Belgium, Latvia, and England, and five to seven per cent in Denmark, Sweden, and Iceland. Episiotomy rates have fallen or stayed the same in many countries with data from 2004, with the exception of England, Scotland, and the Netherlands, where they rose.
>
> European Perinatal Health Report: Health and Care of Pregnant
> Women and Babies in Europe in 2010, 19

> Patients who undergo episiotomies are significantly more likely to suffer faecal incontinence, and patients in settings that used them as a matter of routine are significantly more likely to suffer perineal trauma, pain, and complications. Other research has found the prevalence of obstetric interventions to vary with the time of day or day of the week: David A Webb and Jennifer Cullhane, 'Hospital Variation in Episiotomy Use and the Risk of Perineal Trauma during Childbirth' (2002) 29 Birth 132.

25 These issues are discussed in Roger Crisp, 'Medical Negligence, Assault, Informed Consent, and Autonomy' (1990) 17 J Law Soc 81.

not correspond very well to our intuitions about what is going on, normatively, in such cases.

This is perhaps unsurprising. The structure of negligence is such that it is not very well equipped to protect patient autonomy, at least not in any robust or comprehensive way. It seems that, *from the point of view of autonomy*, the harm in cases in which *P* is not informed about options and risks does not just lie in a risk materialising or in some negative consequences ensuing for *P* or in *P* being made worse off. It seems that, from the point of view of autonomy, what matters is whether *P* was able to choose whether to undergo A and expose herself to risk R, or whether to opt for B instead. This explains why we do not think that *P* has suffered any kind of autonomy violation in a case in which she was informed that A carried risk R and about options available to her other than A and she decided to undergo A and R materialised. We do not think of this as an autonomy violation even if *P* is very badly off following A. And conversely it also seems that *P* may have suffered an autonomy violation when she has not properly consented to some intervention even if the intervention leaves *P* better off. We might think, then, that whether or not risk SD materialises, *P* has been harmed in some way by *D* when she is not informed of it in *Childbirth*.

One way in which to understand this is to argue that in cases such as these, *P* suffers a type of loss that is not (directly) recognised in law and for which legal redress is unlikely, a form of loss that consists in an influence that somehow undermines *P*'s autonomy or prevents her from exercising it, or 'when a person acts in such a way that control over a single and, usually, important decision in the life of another person is removed from the sphere of that other person's practical reason'.[26] Roger Crisp illustrates this idea by asking us to consider the following case:

> *Charity*. I know that you have been considering whether to give away all your possessions with a view to entering a religious order, or to remain a rich stockbroker. You have left the form surrendering your possessions on your desk. While you are at work, mulling over your future, I take the form to Oxfam, who immediately transfer your assets into their account. If, during the day, you decided that you were going to tear up the form, my action would be a patent global exercise violation. But let us assume that you had in fact yourself decided to take the form to Oxfam the very next day. Surely, it is still the case that I have violated your autonomy. I have wrested control from you over one of the most important decisions of your life.[27]

Whether or not Stockbroker is worse off in the end, it seems that his autonomy has been interfered with in some way or that he has been prevented from exercising it. It further seems that this is some kind of harm to Stockbroker and

---

26 Ibid 84.
27 Ibid. The assumption here is that Stockbroker has a considered preference to possess control over this decision.

that it is distinct from the worseness of the outcome (if it is worse). The *Charity* case, Crisp argues, is analogous to cases in which *D* interferes with *P*'s autonomy by withholding information about options and risks *P* needs to exercise her autonomy.[28] It seems plausible that the wrong consists in something like depriving *P* of reasonable options or of opportunities or of discretion to decide on the risks to which to expose herself in accordance with her values. We might think that *P* is not just harmed when she is not informed of her preferred option, A, but also when she is not informed of her non-preferred option, B, unless her non-preferred option is *clearly* worse, such that no reasonable person in *P*'s position could prefer it over A. Moreover, autonomy violations of this kind seem to be a wrong both on views on which autonomy has intrinsic value, and on views on which autonomy has only instrumental value, for example, because it allows *P* to promote her prudential good.[29]

The harm to *P*, then, seems to be located somewhere other than in the negative consequences ensuing from the flawed consent transaction. Further, it seems that if we wanted to offer opportunities for legal redress for *this* wrong, the requirements that *P* would need to meet should focus on the consent transaction itself rather than on demonstrating negative consequences ensuing from it. The autonomy violation, it seems, could be present whether or not the risk materialises. The autonomy violation itself is not necessarily any less serious in a case in which the physical or psychological injury fails to ground a successful claim in negligence than in a case in which *P* has sustained injury such that her claim would succeed (even though cases in the latter category might be more serious all things considered). And it seems that in cases in which *P* has suffered an actionable (under current negligence rules) injury, the harm she has suffered is not limited to the actionable injury, and the actionable injury cannot fully account for the ways in which she has been harmed in the flawed consent transaction.[30]

If these kinds of autonomy violations indeed constitute harms to *P*, we might think that they should be more directly recognised or actionable in law, at least if the harms to *P* are serious. And we might have reason to think that the harms to patients whose medical consents are insufficiently informed about treatment options and risks *are* serious, at least in some cases.

One option, if this is right, is to attempt to compensate autonomy violations under the existing negligence framework and, if necessary, tweak the negligence rules in cases when we think that the harm to *P* is sufficiently serious but are unclear on whether the loss and causation requirements could be met, as has

---

28 Ibid.

29 Even on views that allow paternalism it is unclear that *D*'s failure to inform would be justified: It would be so only if *D* knew (better than *P*) how to promote *P*'s welfare.

30 This seems analogous to how autonomy violations are treated in battery. If, for example, *P* cannot reasonably be taken to lack capacity, but is treated as if she lacks capacity – a violation of her autonomy – the law provides redress notwithstanding that the intervention was in *P*'s best interests, or would have been something she would have chosen for herself. The wrong here is treated as independent of the good outcome.

been done in some cases.[31] But we might think that a route to redress that either recognised autonomy violations as a separate wrong in law or accepted that autonomy violations could be actionable damage for the purposes of negligence would be preferable. A legal remedy that compensated for the autonomy violation itself would seem to more accurately reflect the normative nature of the harm to *P* in non-disclosure cases and its location. This would also reflect the fact that in cases in which non-remote legally recognised injury to *P* has been caused by *D*, it seems that this is an additional harm to *P*, for which she ought, all else being equal, to be compensated (and will be under the existing negligence framework that compensates physical or psychological injury), but that the autonomy violation *P* suffers when *D* fails to inform her of options and risks is distinct from this injury.

An objection from the fundamental principles of medical law

At this point it may be objected that any proposal that imposed more onerous duties on *D* to inform *P* about alternatives to the treatment *D* recommends, and legal sanctions where such information was lacking, would risk inconsistency with the fundamental principles of medical law. Informing *P* that CS is an alternative to VB, one may argue, would essentially amount to making CS available as an option, or letting *P* choose between VB and CS. This would be inconsistent with the medical law principle according to which *P* does not have a right to have her requests for particular interventions granted.[32] The lawfulness of the provision of φ depends, among other things, on φ being, in *D*'s professional judgement, good for *P*. Professional judgement is a constraint on patient autonomy, except in the case of refusals.

This objection is hard to avoid, especially in cases like *Childbirth*. As Emily Jackson observes, while there is a strong emphasis within the National Health Service (NHS) on women's active participation in the management of pregnancy and childbirth – something that suggests a commitment to *P*'s autonomy – this 'does not generally extend to giving women the "right" to choose an elective caesarean section' (although *P*'s preferences will be taken into account in decisions about whether it is provided).[33] It would, Jackson notes, often not be negligent of *D* not to offer CS.[34]

---

31 Eg as in *Chester v Afshar* [2004] UKHL 41. For criticisms of the decision in *Chester v Afshar*, see eg Tamsyn Clark and Donal Nolan, 'A Critique of *Chester v Afshar*' (2014) 34 Oxf J Leg Stud 659.

32 *R (on the application of Burke) v General Medical Council* [2005] EWCA Civ 1003.

33 Emily Jackson, *Regulating Reproduction: Law, Technology and Autonomy* (Hart 2001) 117.

34 Ibid. It might be in some cases. If *D*'s refusal to offer CS as an alternative leads *P* to refuse option (medically assisted) VB, then plausibly *D* would be under an obligation to offer CS, because it would be negligent to send *P* home in light of the likely consequences of going it alone in a situation when medical assistance was needed. But such cases seem likely to be rare.

The principle that *P* does not have a right to have her requests for particular interventions granted by *D* is justified directly on grounds that medical professionals should not be compelled to act against their professional judgement, but is widely taken to (also) be indirectly justified on grounds of resource allocation considerations. We might think that the case of different treatment options in childbirth illustrates very well why this policy is defensible and perhaps necessary: caesarean deliveries are more expensive than vaginal ones (in general) and this is often used to maintain that 'given the inevitability of rationing scarce resources in the NHS, it would be difficult to argue that women have a right to a comparatively expensive procedure requested against medical advice'.[35]

But even if *P* does not have a right to CS due to medical law principles and perhaps reasonable constraints on how healthcare resources are used, it does not follow that *D* is justified in withholding information about CS from *P*. This is because CS, it seems, is a reasonable alternative, or at least not a clearly unreasonable one. Given that CS is not an unreasonable alternative, *P* should be informed about CS and other reasonable alternatives, and the risks attached to each. Respect for *P*'s autonomy would seem to require that professional judgement is exercised in a way that accommodates a plurality of conceptions of the good life.

Unless such a duty was imposed on D, professional judgement might be used to restrict women's decision-making in ways that are inconsistent with respect for patient autonomy. We see an example of this in *Montgomery v Lanarkshire*. Here, *D* accepted that the nine to ten per cent risk of shoulder dystocia was a high risk, but explained that she had a policy of not discussing this particular risk with her patients, because 'in her estimation, the risk of a grave problem *for the baby* resulting from shoulder dystocia was very small'.[36] Moreover, she said, if the risk was mentioned, 'most women will actually say, "I'd rather have a caesarean section"'. *D* stated that 'if you were to mention shoulder dystocia to every [diabetic] patient ... then everyone would ask for a caesarean section, and *it's not in the maternal interests for women to have caesarean sections*'.[37] We might call this the *maternal interests claim*. Note that, in *D*'s view, having CS would *not* be good for *P*, notwithstanding both the relatively low general medical risks associated with planned caesareans (suggested by professional and NICE guidance) and the special medical risks associated with VB for this particular patient.

---

35 Ibid. Some uses of this relative costs argument are controversial. Planned caesareans are considerably cheaper than emergency caesareans, and it is not clear that the most appropriate comparator is always used when the relative costs of the procedures are appealed to. If we are concerned with the costs for the healthcare service of each alternative – VB or CS – it seems that some of the most serious costs associated with VB, that is, costs for repairs of birth injuries such as severe tears leading to faecal and urinary incontinence, pelvic floor damage, etc., many of which occur or are reported only much later or go unreported, should be included in any calculation of relative costs of the different modes of delivery. That said I grant that the average CS is more expensive than the average VB.

36 *Montgomery* (n 10) [13], emphasis added.

37 Ibid, emphasis added.

D's *maternal interests claim*, then, indicates that there were, in *D*'s view, some reasons *other than* medical risk to *P* that counted against CS in general, including for *P*.[38] Moreover, the reasons in favour of VB were in *D*'s view such that they made it all things considered better for *P* to have VB over CS even given the medical reasons in favour of CS in *P*'s case.

Lady Hale seems to have taken *D*'s judgement to be based on what *D* saw as non-medical reasons against CS, saying that:

> Whatever [*D*] may have had in mind [when she made the *maternal interests claim*], this does not look like a purely medical judgment. It looks like a judgment that vaginal delivery is in some way morally preferable to a caesarean section: so much so that it justifies depriving the pregnant woman of the information needed for her to make a free choice in the matter.[39]

Lady Hale then hints at some possible such (non-medical) reasons:

> Giving birth vaginally is indeed a unique and wonderful experience, but it has not been suggested that it inevitably leads to a closer and better relationship between mother and child than does a caesarean section.[40]

Even if we grant the benefits alluded to here – empirically dubious as they may seem – we might think that *D* in making her judgement about VB being better for *P* (and acting on it) relied on a conception of the good life that is too narrow to be compatible with respect for patient autonomy. *D*, it seems (if we accept Lady Hale's reconstruction of her reasoning), essentially imposed on *P* a value judgment which *P* might reasonably reject.[41] She decided that not only was VB good for some moral (or at least non-medical) reason, but also that the value of its purported benefit was such that it outweighed any reasons against VB in *P*'s case, including the medical reasons against. This is attaching

---

38 Something like this seems to be the Supreme Court's interpretation of *D*'s reasoning in this case, which I will for the sake of argument accept here. For another interpretation of *D*'s reasoning, see Jonathan Montgomery and Elsa Montgomery, 'Montgomery on Informed Consent: An In-expert Decision?' (2016) 42 J Med Ethics 89.

39 *Montgomery* (n 10) [114], emphasis added.

40 Ibid.

41 This is especially apt here, since women make birth decisions on the basis of a wide range of value judgements, many of which may be considered controversial by others. We see this in the approach to pain and pain management in childbirth, compared to in respect of other health conditions and medical interventions: We would never consider extracting a tooth or undergoing surgery without adequate pain management; yet in childbirth there is a movement that advocates just that. For a philosophical examination of 'possible justifications for the seemingly common idea that natural childbirth, understood as birth without the assistance of pain medication, is in some sense superior to pain-managed birth', see Jennifer Baker, 'Natural Childbirth Is for the Birds: An Analysis of the Normativity of Natural' in Sheila Lintott (ed), *Motherhood: Philosophy for Everyone* (Wiley-Blackwell 2010). See also Rebecca Kukla, 'Measuring Mothering' (2008) 1 Int J Fem Approaches Bioeth 67.

considerable weight to a particular value among a set of values. Doing so seems to be something that we – insofar as we are committed to personal autonomy – might let *P* do (eg by refusing treatment that is in her best interests, medically speaking). But it is not clear that it would be legitimate for *D* to engage in a weighing exercise of this kind on *P*'s behalf, without her permission. We must take care, then, to avoid letting professional judgement restrict patients' information about options and risks in ways that are inconsistent with respect for patient autonomy.

Of course, *D* in *Montgomery* was held to have acted negligently when she did not disclose the risks of VB and how they compared to those of CS in this particular case. It was held that patients ought to be given the choice of whether to forego any benefits of VB, because patient autonomy is important and patients have a right, it was said, to make decisions about whether to undergo particular medical interventions in light of that which they valued, or in accordance with their conception of the good life. But redress in this case was made possible because *P*'s baby suffered severe injuries as a result of *D*'s failure to inform *P* of the relevant risks. It seems, however, that if we accept the arguments in the preceding sections, *P* would have been harmed in some way by *D*'s failure to disclose these risks even if such injuries had not been sustained.

The new standard introduced in *Montgomery* seems to provide more robust protection for patients' interests in receiving information about options and risks, and to capture some of what matters to the protection of patient autonomy. It requires *D* to take reasonable care to ensure that *P* is informed of any material risks involved in the intervention that *D* recommends to *P* in the present situation, and also of 'any reasonable alternative or variant treatments',[42] and holds that risks are material if in the circumstances of the particular case a reasonable person in *P*'s position would be likely to attach significance to it, or if *D* is or should reasonably be aware that *P* in particular would be likely to attach significance to it.[43]

But it is not clear that the *Montgomery* standard captures all of what matters. *D* might not know all of what *P* is likely to attach significance to and facts about this may not fall into the category of what it is reasonable for *D* to know or be aware of in the situation. For example, discussions with *P* about her values and so on might reveal that some risks, while risks of φ generally, are not relevant risks of φ *for P*. Some standard (medical) risks of CS, such as risks of infection and haemorrhage, will be relevant to all patients. But other risks considered by *D* in the standard case may not be relevant in the individual case. Suppose, for example, that *P* is certain that she does not, following this pregnancy, want to have any additional children. This information about *P*'s values and preferences as it applies to future pregnancies renders some standard risks irrelevant risks *for P*. Risks of placental abruption, miscarriage, stillbirth, or a further CS are all standard risks of CS, but given her preference for not going through

42 Ibid [87].
43 Ibid.

any future pregnancies, *P* will take these to be irrelevant when considering the benefits and costs of each of the available options.[44] This makes the risk profile in the choice between VB and CS substantially different in *P*'s case, compared to the standard risk profile on the basis of which *D* makes her decision about which course of action would be best to adopt. *D* may not know beforehand which of the options would be best for *P*, since particular risks might by *D* mistakenly be thought to be relevant risks for *P*. Since *D* may not know beforehand whether particular risks are relevant risks *for P*, *D* ought to disclose them to *P*.

In childbirth, there are many different risks associated with different options, for which women may have a varying degree of tolerance depending on their lifestyles and what they value. Even when a risk is a relevant risk for *P*, it might be a risk that she is more or less willing to accept. The risk of unplanned hysterectomy in CS is, for example, often cited as a reason in favour of VB, but as one woman notes:

> Ask a woman to weigh a 0.07% risk of unplanned hysterectomy to a significantly higher risk of spending the rest of her life peeing a little when she laughs, coughs, sneezes, runs, lifts, and other general life activities, and her answer might not be so obvious.[45]

Risks primarily associated with VB, such as urinary and faecal incontinence and pelvic organ prolapse, can have devastating debilitating consequences for women's quality of life, sometimes for the rest of their lives.[46] Given the nature of judgements about the tolerability of different risks, it may seem that the presumption should be one in favour of letting *P* determine to which risks she is willing to expose herself. The things that are not (in the typical case) known by *D* (relating to *P*'s values, life plans, and so on) are highly relevant to decisions regarding the tolerability of various risks and, therefore, whether VB or CS will be better for *P*.[47] For these considerations – highly relevant to autonomy – to be given their proper place, the idea of 'reasonable options' needs to be construed broadly. That seems to require information about reasonable alternatives, including those that may not in practice be available to *P*, eg because of resource

---

44 It might be objected that *P* cannot be certain that she will never want to go through another pregnancy and that she ought therefore to give some weight to the risk of a future CS. But this applies in all cases in which *P* can change her mind about her values. It does not seem that the fact that she might in the future change her mind about her life plans and what she values is a reason for her to now give weight to a risk that is at the moment irrelevant. This is not how we typically make decisions about other medical procedures.

45 Kavin Senapathy, 'Giving Birth Made Me Question the Informed Consent Process during Childbirth' (Self, 14 May 2018) <www.self.com/story/informed-consent-in-childbirth> accessed 12 September 2018.

46 See eg Oonagh E Keag and others, 'Long-Term Risks and Benefits Associated with Cesarean Delivery for Mother, Baby, and Subsequent Pregnancies: Systematic Review and Meta-Analysis' (2018) 15(1) PLoS Med e1002494.

47 Except perhaps in cases where *P* and *D* have a long-standing relationship.

constraints, and ones that this particular physician would not prefer or recommend for P.[48]

In the case of VB and CS, it seems that neither should be excluded on the basis of the magnitude of a risk it carries, or the magnitude of its combined risks (ie combination of all risks) associated with it. Notably, D is generally taken to be under an obligation to disclose non-treatment options, even when those carry very great risks (eg in the case refusal of life-prolonging treatment).

The risks each of VB and CS carries are very different in kind, but arguably this makes the case for disclosure stronger, since it makes it more likely that P has strong preferences for one kind of risk over others, based on how tolerable the risks are to her given her circumstances, lifestyle, values, and so on. We recognise and accept in other contexts that patients make decisions based on the value they place on different considerations, including those that do not relate to their physical health, and also the value they place on certain health values over other health values (eg lucidity vis-à-vis pain in the context of pain management).

If this is the case, it would seem that D should be taken to be under an obligation to disclose various birth options and the risks they carry, including CS, also when P has no medical indication that favours CS. An argument can be made to the effect that even if P does not have an enforceable right to be provided with a particular intervention such as CS by D, we have good reasons to construe D's obligations to provide P with information about options and risks as more onerous than has often been assumed.

Conclusion

In this chapter, I focused on autonomy violations that consist in patients being deprived of information about different treatment options and their risks by their physicians. I outlined how English law on consent regulates the provision by physicians of information about different treatment options and risks to patients in medical consent transactions. I then briefly outlined how inadequate information about options and risks in medical consent transactions interferes with or undermines patient autonomy. I considered some difficulties faced by patients seeking legal redress in non-disclosure cases, relating to proving causation of non-remote legally recognised injury. I argued that it is unsurprising that patients should face such difficulties, because the harm to patients in non-disclosure cases is distinct from the outcome's disvalue and its causal history. I argued that for what we value in respect of autonomy to be protected, the law would need to directly recognise the harm to patients arising in failures of information about treatment options and risks. I then considered an objection to the proposal of directly recognising autonomy violations by insufficient information from the fundamental principles of medical law, and gestured at a possible way in which more robust protection for patients' interests in receiving information

---

48 Having this information would enable P to seek a second opinion, for example.

about options and risks could avoid this objection and be made consistent with the fundamental principles of medical law, at least in the context of childbirth, by construing the idea of reasonable alternatives (of the kind that the physician is under an obligation to disclose) in such a way that it allows for a plurality of conceptions of the good life. The hope is that these arguments could serve as a starting point for thinking about what information women should receive in the context of childbirth.

Table of cases

Chatterton v Gerson [1981] QB 432
Montgomery v Lanarkshire Health Board [2015] UKSC 11
R (on the application of Burke) v General Medical Council [2005] EWCA Civ 1003
Re T (Adult: Refusal of Treatment) [1993] Fam 95 (CA)

Bibliography

Baker J, 'Natural Childbirth Is for the Birds: An Analysis of the Normativity of Natural' in Lintott S (ed), *Motherhood: Philosophy for Everyone* (Wiley-Blackwell 2010)

Clark T and Nolan D, 'A Critique of *Chester v Afshar*' (2014) 34 Oxf J Leg Stud 659

Crisp R, 'Medical Negligence, Assault, Informed Consent, and Autonomy' (1990) 17 J Law Soc 81

Flanigan J, 'Obstetric Autonomy and Informed Consent' (2016) 19 Ethical Theory and Moral Pract 225

Jackson E, *Regulating Reproduction: Law, Technology and Autonomy* (Hart 2001)

Keag O E and others, 'Long-Term Risks and Benefits Associated with Cesarean Delivery for Mother, Baby, and Subsequent Pregnancies: Systematic Review and Meta-Analysis' (2018) 15(1) PLoS Med e1002494

Kennedy I, *The Unmasking of Medicine* (Granada 1983)

Kukla R, 'Measuring Mothering' (2008) 1 Int J Fem Approaches Bioeth 67

Lesser H, 'The Patient Right to Information' in *Protecting the Vulnerable: Autonomy and Consent in Health Care* (Routledge 1991)

Manson N C and O'Neill O, *Rethinking Informed Consent in Bioethics* (CUP 2007)

Montgomery J and Montgomery E, 'Montgomery on Informed Consent: An Inexpert Decision?' (2016) 42 J Med Ethics 89

O'Neill O, 'Autonomy: The Emperor's New Clothes' (2003) 77 Proc Aristot Soc Suppl 1–21

Savulescu J, 'Rational Non-Interventional Paternalism: Why Doctors Ought to Make Judgments of What Is Best for Their Patients' (1995) 21 J Med Ethics 327

Webb D A and Cullhane J, 'Hospital Variation in Episiotomy Use and the Risk of Perineal Trauma during Childbirth' (2002) 29 Birth 132

10 Court-authorised obstetric intervention

Insight and capacity, a tale of loss

Samantha Halliday

Introduction: childbirth and the rhetoric of choice[1]

The battleground of abortion is alive to shouts of a woman's right to choose, but choice does not relate solely to the decision whether to continue or terminate a pregnancy; a woman's right to make choices continues throughout her pregnancy and becomes particularly important in the context of childbirth and delivery choices.[2] Choice is a central tenet of maternity care and its importance is emphasised in policy documents;[3] however, the lived experience is often rather different. In the twenty-first century, birth is framed as a medical procedure,

With thanks to Professor Roger Brownsword for his extremely valuable comments on an earlier draft of this chapter. Thanks also to the delegates of the 2018 workshop 'Childbirth: Vulnerability, Violence, and Control' for their very useful feedback.

1 In this chapter I build upon my previous work that focused upon the tension between a pregnant woman's autonomy and actions taken to protect the foetus, considering the case law in England and the United States and the ambit of the duty to protect foetal life in Germany, see Samantha Halliday, *Autonomy and Pregnancy: A Comparative Analysis of Compelled Obstetric Intervention* (Routledge 2016). This chapter builds upon that work by focusing upon the relationship between insight and capacity in more recent cases where courts have authorised obstetric intervention in the face of the woman's refusal.

2 Choice is a recurrent theme throughout pregnancy; another important context in which it arises is in relation to non-invasive prenatal testing (NIPT) where a choice must be made to have NIPT, when to have it, how to respond to a positive result (termination, continuing the pregnancy with the opportunity to prepare for the future). Throughout pregnancy these choices are not exercised in a neutral context, rather the technological imperative dominates; there is an expectation that women will take advantage of technology, that NIPT will be regarded as part of the routine procedures performed during pregnancy. I am indebted to Roger Brownsword for pointing out this further example of 'choice' and the way it is circumscribed by technology and expectations. On NIPT see Roger Brownsword and Jeff Wale, 'Testing Times Ahead: Non-Invasive Prenatal Testing and the Kind of Community We Want to Be' (2018) 81 MLR 646.

3 See for example National Maternity Review, 'Better Births: Improving Outcomes of Maternity Services in England. A Five Year Forward View for Maternity Care' (2016) <www.england.nhs.uk/wp-content/uploads/2016/02/national-maternity-review-report.pdf> accessed 10 March 2019. UK Department of Health and Social Care, 'National Service Framework: Children, Young People and Maternity Services' (4 October 2004) <www.gov.uk/government/publications/national-service-framework-children-young-people-and-maternity-services> accessed 10 March 2019.

rather than a natural process. It is protocol-led and available choices are dictated by clinical guidelines and local policies, regardless of whether one gives birth in an obstetrician led unit, or a midwife-led birthing centre. The medical discourse is powerful and has successfully constructed pregnancy and birth as risky, as a procedure to be managed by experts using technology to ensure that nothing goes wrong.[4] The consequence of this is reduced choice for women who are cautioned to act responsibly, but where women fail to acquiesce and comply with medical advice, the question arises as to whether they can be forced to make the 'right' choice.

This chapter focuses upon how choices are managed where the woman's choice diverges from the advice of clinicians. As Hedley recognised in *PC v City of York Council*[5] the Court of Protection's powers 'can be both invasive and draconian'. This is no more apparent than in the case of women with a serious mental illness (SMI) compelled to accept obstetric intervention in the furtherance of their best interests; deprived of the right to make the decision for themselves, the decision will be made in line with their best interests, as assessed by somebody else. The very fact that the woman has refused to accept medical advice opens up the question of capacity; thereafter, her disagreement with medical advice raises questions about her insight, rendering her yet more vulnerable to a finding of incapacity. Ruck Keene has described the impact of a finding of incapacity as a 'cliff edge off which one falls into the clinging embrace of paternalism'.[6] A finding of incapacity will deprive a woman of the right to determine how she gives birth, the right to refuse a caesarean, or instrumental birth. As Lady Hale recognised in *Montgomery v Lanarkshire Health Board*, this is an intensely personal decision,[7] but if the woman is judged to lack the necessary capacity to make this decision, it will be transferred to a third party who has only to consider the woman's wishes and feelings, rather than to give effect to them as part of the best interests assessment.

This chapter builds upon my previous work in the area of court-authorised obstetric intervention by focusing upon the role of insight in determining capacity and the degree of respect afforded to the woman's delivery choices within the assessment of her best interests. It interrogates the relationship between insight

---

4 On medicalisation and risk see for example Judith McAra-Couper, Marion Jones, and Liz Smythe, 'Caesarean-section, My Body, My Choice: The Construction of "Informed Choice" in Relation to Intervention in Childbirth' (2012) 22 Fem Psychol 81; Alphia Possamai-Inesedy, 'Confining Risk: Choice and Responsibility in Childbirth in a Risk Society' (2006) 15 Health Sociology Review 406; Julie Jomeen, 'Choice in Childbirth: A Realistic Expectation?'(2007) 15 Br J Midwifery 485; Maria Zadoroznyj, 'Social Class, Social Selves and Social Control in Childbirth' (1999) 21 Sociol Health Illn 267.

5 [2013] EWCA Civ 478 [13].

6 Alex Ruck Keene, 'Capacity Is Not an Off Switch – Case Commentary' (*Mental Capacity Law and Policy Newsletter,* 1 October 2015) <www.mentalcapacitylawandpolicy.org.uk/capacity-is-not-an-off-switch/> accessed 10 March 2019.

7 [2015] UKSC 11 [115].

and capacity through the lens of two recent cases,[8] recognising that in both cases the perceived lack of insight was fatal to the women's capacity, forcing them over the figurative cliff edge and suggesting that in the context of women with an SMI or a learning difficulty the notion of patient-centred, choice-led maternity care is illusionary.

Setting the scene

Individuals with capacity have an almost absolute right to refuse treatment; in the words of Butler-Sloss LJ they can do so 'for rational or irrational reasons or for no reason at all'.[9] Moreover, as Lord Donaldson MR observed, 'This right of choice is not limited to decisions which others might regard as sensible',[10] a sentiment that is incorporated in s 1(4) Mental Capacity Act (MCA) 2005 recognising that 'A person is not to be treated as unable to make a decision merely because he makes an unwise decision'. During the 1990s, in a series of cases,[11] the courts in England and Wales demonstrated a willingness to police pregnancy,[12] declaring that it would be lawful for caesareans deemed necessary to be performed, notwithstanding the pregnant woman's refusal of consent.[13] Whilst the majority of the US courts have engaged with this issue by considering foetal interests, often in the guise of the state's interest in potential life,[14] the English courts have refused to consider foetal interests, at least explicitly, except in the very first case where a caesarean was authorised to save the life of both the pregnant woman and the foetus.[15] Instead, the English courts approach the matter as a question of capacity – if the woman has capacity she may refuse all treatment, including that required to safeguard a foetus. The twentieth-century cases culminated in two Court of Appeal decisions that emphasised that a woman's autonomy was not impacted by pregnancy, that a woman with capacity could:

---

8 *The NHS Acute Trust & The NHS Mental Health Trust v C* [2016] EWCOP 17 and *A University Hospital NHS Trust v CA* [2016] EWCOP 51.

9 *Re MB* [1997] 2 FLR 426 [436]–[437].

10 *T (Consent to Medical Treatment) (Adult Patient), Re* [1993] Fam 95 [653].

11 *Re S* [1993] Fam 123; *Tameside and Glossop Acute Services Trust v CH* [1996] 1 FLR 762; *Norfolk and Norwich Healthcare (NHS) Trust v W* [1996] 2 FLR 613; *Rochdale Healthcare NHS Trust v C* [1997] 1 FCR 274; *Re MB (Medical Treatment)* [1997] 2 FLR 426; *St George's Healthcare NHS Trust v S (NO 2), R v Collins and others*, ex parte S (NO 2) [1998] EWCA Civ 1349 [1999] Fam. 26.

12 Sara Fovargue and Josè Miola, 'Policing Pregnancy: Implications of the Attorney General's Reference (No. 3 of 1994)' (1998) 6 Med Law Rev 265.

13 For a detailed critical analysis of the English case law, see Halliday (n 1) 40–89.

14 See for example *Jefferson v Griffin Spalding County Hospital Authority* 74 SE 2d 457 (1981); *Re AC* 573 A.2d 1235 (1990); *Re Madyun* (1986) 573 A 2d 1259 (DC 1990); *Pemberton v Tallahassee Memorial Regional Medical Center* 66 F.Supp.2d 1247 (N D Fla 1999); *Samantha Burton v Florida* 39 So 3d 263 (Fla Dist Ct App 2010); but cf. *In re Baby Boy Doe, a Fetus v Mother Doe* 632 NE 2d 326 (1994).

15 *Re S* (n 11).

for religious reasons, other reasons, for rational or irrational reasons or for no reason at all, choose not to have medical intervention, even though ... the consequence may be the death or serious handicap of the child she bears, or her own death.[16]

Two years later the Court of Appeal confirmed the central holding of *Re MB*, concluding that:

> While pregnancy increases the personal responsibilities of a woman it does not diminish her entitlement to decide whether or not to undergo medical treatment. ... [An unborn child's] need for medical assistance does not prevail over her rights. She is entitled not to be forced to submit to an invasion of her body against her will, whether her own life or that of her unborn child depends on it. Her right is not reduced or diminished merely because her decision to exercise it may appear morally repugnant. The infringement of the mother's autonomy could not, therefore, be justified by the perceived needs of the foetus.[17]

Whilst the Court of Appeal appears to have given a ringing endorsement to a woman's autonomy in these cases, it is significant that thus far no court has considered the question of capacity in such a case, where the issue was still live, rather than on appeal, and found the woman to have the necessary capacity to refuse treatment. It seems a rather hollow victory to say that a woman with capacity may refuse treatment given the unlikelihood of a woman refusing treatment necessary to save the foetal life being adjudged competent.

The issue of court-authorised obstetric intervention resurfaced with *Re AA*,[18] a case involving an Italian national that gave rise to sensational media reports suggesting that AA had been subjected to a caesarean against her will in order to enable social workers to take the child into care.[19] AA was detained under the Mental Health Act 1983 and had previously had two caesarean sections; there was said to be a one per cent risk of uterine rupture if she were to give birth vaginally. In an *ex tempore* judgment, having summarily dismissed AA's capacity to decide for herself, Mostyn J granted a declaration that it would be in AA's best interests for her baby to be delivered by caesarean section, with the use of reasonable restraint if necessary and appropriate.[20]

---

16 *Re MB* (n 11) [436]–[437] (Butler-Sloss LJ).
17 *St George's Healthcare NHS Trust v S (NO 2); R v Collins and others, ex parte S* (NO 2) (n 11) [50] (Judge LJ).
18 *Re AA (Mental Capacity: Enforced Caesarean)* [2012] EWHC 4378 (COP).
19 The first report was made by Christopher Booker, 'Operate on This Mother so that We Can Take Her Baby' (*The Telegraph*, 30 November 2013).
20 There are a number of concerning features about this case, not least that it was not reported until media reporting highlighting the lack of transparency in Court of Protection cases made the continued failure to publish the judgment untenable. For a detailed analysis of the case, see Halliday (n 1) 64–71.

During the last five years, at least ten women have been required to submit to a caesarean following a finding of incapacity. The true number of cases is probably much higher because even those cases considered by the court are rarely reported and in the majority of cases the women will be treated under the general authority, s 5 MCA. Unlike the previous tranche of cases, the new cases almost all involve women with an SMI, primarily schizophrenia or bipolar disorder;[21] the remaining three cases involved women with a learning difficulty.[22] Moreover, all of the recent cases have been pre-emptive applications, and none involved an immediate risk to either the woman or the foetus; rather orders were sought permitting doctors to perform a caesarean against the wishes of the pregnant women in order to avoid risks associated with a 'natural' delivery.

Serious mental illness

Howard's research demonstrates that most women with a psychotic disorder will have children,[23] but as Taylor points out, 'SMI … is associated with a range of adverse consequences in pregnancy and the postpartum period'.[24] Even where a woman's illness is well managed, there is a risk of psychiatric decompensation during pregnancy, a risk that is increased by the discontinuation or reduction in dosage of psychotropic medication due to the teratogenic effect it can have. In an ideal world consideration of the woman's reproductive health would form part of the care of all women of childbearing age with an SMI so that the impact of drugs upon a pregnancy could be taken into account and a detailed treatment plan be developed pre-conception to facilitate the optimum management of her mental health during pregnancy. However, whilst best practice, all too often that is not the case. Pregnancy does represent a challenge for women with an SMI as a balance has to be struck between continuing the drugs that allow her to maintain her mental health and well-being and safeguarding the foetus from the teratogenic and neurodevelopmental risks posed to the foetus by psychotropic medication. For example, sodium valproate is used to treat bipolar disorder, but can lead to malformations in the foetus and should not be used by women or girls of childbearing age unless a pregnancy prevention plan is in place. In each

---

21 Including *Re AA (Mental Capacity: Enforced Caesarean)* [2012] EWHC 4378 (COP); *Re P* [2013] EWHC 4581 (COP); *Great Western Hospitals NHS Foundation Trust v AA, BB, CC & DD* [2014] EWHC 132 (Fam); *Royal Free NHS Foundation Trust v AB* (2014), unreported; *North Somerset Council v LW and others* [2014] EWCOP 3; *NHS Trust and others v FG* [2014] EWCOP 30; *The NHS Acute Trust & The NHS Mental Health Trust v C* [2016] EWCOP 17.

22 *The Mental Health Trust, The Acute Trust & The Council v DD & BC* [2014] EWCOP 11 (COP); *V* (2016), unreported, but referred to in subsequent proceedings: *A Hospital Trust v V and Ors* [2017] EWCOP 20; *A University Hospital NHS Trust v CA* [2016] EWCOP 61.

23 Louise M Howard, R Kumar, and Graham Thornicroft, 'The Psychosocial Characteristics of Mothers with Psychotic Disorders' (2001) 178 Br J Psychiatry 427.

24 Clare L Taylor and others, 'The Characteristics and Health Needs of Pregnant Women with Schizophrenia Compared with Bipolar Disorder and Affective Psychoses' (2015) 15 BMC Psychiatry 88.

pregnancy a risk-benefit assessment will have to be undertaken weighing the risks of untreated mental health problems against the risks to the foetus posed by the drugs.[25]

Whether patients can ever truly be described as 'consumers of health services' is debatable, but the notion of choice in childbirth has been described as an illusion.[26] That is particularly the case where the woman has an SMI, a condition that automatically marks her out as different and as requiring special treatment. Online support groups and the Internet more generally provide access to a significant amount of information, both lived experiential and theoretical, allowing women to become informed and knowledgeable consumers of healthcare,[27] both in relation to the treatment and management of their SMI, but also the management of their pregnancy and labour. This 'new medical pluralism'[28] can equip women 'to better evaluate their choices and challenge expert knowledge';[29] however, it must be recognised that there is very little choice for women with an SMI. The limited number of mother and baby units and speciality perinatal mental health services reduces choice throughout pregnancy, but for the delivery women with an SMI will inevitably be allocated to obstetrician-led care, rather than midwife-led care, so that they will be required to give birth in hospital. Birth in hospital brings with it the prospect of cascading interventions,[30] for example, an epidural, or the use of electronic foetal monitoring increases the likelihood of obstetric intervention being required. A direct correlation can be observed as the use of technology increases and patient choice reduces in line with increasing predictability for medical professionals.

Whilst policy documents speak of patient choice, not all childbirth options are available to all women, nor will all options be considered valid, or even responsible options. This is particularly the case when a woman has an SMI. Her choices are easily dismissed, attributed to her SMI, or a more general lack of insight, extending beyond her SMI into her pregnant state. As the recent cases demonstrate, unless the woman is able to comply with instructions and willing to submit to all of the interventions deemed necessary to manage and monitor

25 National Institute for Health and Care Excellence, 'Antenatal and Postnatal Mental Health: Clinical Management and Service Guidance' (*National Collaborating Centre for Mental Health*, 2018) <www.nice.org.uk/guidance/cg192/evidence/full-guideline-pdf-4840896925> accessed 10 March 2019.

26 Judith A Lothian, 'Choice, Autonomy, and Childbirth Education' [2008] J Perinat Educ 35; Michele L Crossley, 'Childbirth, Complications and the Illusion of "Choice": A Case Study' (2007) 17 Fem Psychol 543.

27 Felicia Wu Song and others, 'Women, Pregnancy, and Health Information Online: The Making of Informed Patients and Ideal Mothers' (2012) 26 Gend Soc 773, 777.

28 Kristin K Barker, 'Electronic Support Groups, Patient-Consumers, Medicalization: The Case of Contested Illness' (2008) 49 J Health Soc Behav 20.

29 Song (n 27) 775.

30 Kirstie Coxon, Jane Sandall, and Naomi J Fulop, 'To What Extent Are Women Free to Choose Where to Give Birth? How Discourses of Risk, Blame and Responsibility Influence Birth Place Decisions' (2014) 16 Health Risk Soc 51, 52.

the progress of labour, her desire for a vaginal delivery is likely to be dismissed on the basis of safety. The cases demonstrate that risk is constructed in two very different ways. On the one hand vaginal delivery is constructed as risky, as requiring oversight by professionals, as McAra-Couper observed: '[T]he belief that birth is risky – along with a dependence on hospitalisation, intervention and technology to ensure safety – actually constrains and regulates choice'.[31] This framing of risk is not particular to women with an SMI; all vaginal birth that takes place without obstetric oversight is categorised as risky. However, in the case of a woman with an SMI a second source of risk is apparent, the woman herself is constructed as risky, rather than at risk, as dangerous, rather than in danger. She is described as posing a risk to the foetus and to healthcare professionals, as needing to be managed, to avoid agitation, rather than needing to be supported through the delivery. The medical model that is adopted in these cases problematises the person – she is regarded as a person with an SMI, the SMI becomes the focus, rather than the person and thus objectified, she becomes an object for clinical intervention. As the cases demonstrate, clinicians see a risky person wanting to have a risky procedure and they double down on the management of risk, requiring the woman to submit to the safest, most controlled, delivery available, a caesarean under general anaesthetic. Nevertheless, it is important to recognise that the calculation of risk is very one-sided; it does not take account of the additional degree of risk posed to the pregnant woman by a caesarean birth in comparison with that associated with vaginal delivery, nor does it take account of the additional risk incurred through the use of a general rather than local anaesthesia.

Insight and capacity

Insight is a clinical construct, a clinical term of art that originated in the psychiatric literature, particularly in relation to schizophrenia. As Diesfeld and Sjöström have pointed out, 'Most of the vernacular meanings [of insight] relate to understanding something about the exterior world'.[32] When we say that someone has made insightful comments we praise their astute contribution to the discussion and recognise the high level of their perception; however, in the context of mental illness the term insight is used in relation to that which is going on inside the individual – it is internal, rather than external facing. As Fulford suggests, like the concept of time, insight is easier to use than define.[33] There is no single accepted definition of insight, but the common elements relate to awareness of one's own condition and behaviour. In 1934 Lewis defined

---

31 McAra-Couper and others (n 4) 84.

32 Kate Diesfeld and Stefan Sjöström, 'Interpretive Flexibility: Why Doesn't Insight Incite Controversy in Mental Health Law?' (2007) 25 Behav Sci Law 85, 89.

33 Bill (K W M) Fulford, 'Insight and Delusion: From Jaspers to Kraepelin and Back Again via Austin' in Xavier Amador and Anthony David (eds), *Insight and Psychosis: Awareness of Illness in Schizophrenia and Related Disorders* (OUP 2004) 73.

insight as 'a correct attitude to morbid change in oneself'.[34] The fact that insight requires a correct attitude suggests that anyone who disagrees with the clinician will have an 'incorrect' attitude and thus insight would appear to mandate compliance. David has argued that insight is not a binary concept, and suggested that it comprises three dimensions: '(a) awareness of illness, (b) the capacity to relabel psychotic experiences as abnormal, and (c) treatment compliance.'[35] It is suggested that this third dimension is of critical importance in the obstetric context. As I have suggested elsewhere,[36] the trigger for a capacity assessment is often refusal to follow medical advice; none of the reported cases concern women willing to do as their doctor suggested. That being so it is difficult to disagree with Høyer that 'those agreeing with their treating psychiatrist have insight, those who disagree have not'.[37]

Perkins and Moodley describe the concept of insight as arrogant, criticising its promotion of 'a single, rather narrow, perspective – that of "scientific psychiatry"'.[38] Insight may refer to many issues – to the presence, or nature of mental illness, to the proposed treatment measures, or even, as in these cases be unrelated to the SMI. The court-authorised obstetric case law demonstrates that the concept is being used much more broadly, that it is being applied outside the psychiatric context to other areas of medicine, used as a device to question the woman's ability to make decisions about birth rather than her SMI. Holstein has argued, 'patient testimony that contradicts expert opinion is not treated as a countervailing report, but instead is seen as a symptom itself'.[39] Clinicians who give evidence do so with the status of expert, whilst the patient is rarely involved in these cases and is stigmatised by her status as mentally ill.[40] In the reported cases there is no attempt to demonstrate why the individual lacks insight; rather a blanket assertion is made that she does. The patient's voice is not heard, she certainly is not represented by the Official Solicitor, and the scene is set to discount her wishes and feelings and give effect to the clinician's advice as serving her best interests. As demonstrated in the two cases discussed below, the clinical construct of insight has been adopted by obstetricians in order to further demonstrate the deviance of women who refuse to comply with medical advice, pathologising their refusal. The woman's non-compliance is utilised as evidence in itself of her lack of insight qua capacity.

Diesfeld and Sjöström have suggested that insight acts as a bridge between legal and clinical discourses,[41] but it is important to recognise that insight is not

---

34 Aubrey Lewis, 'The Psychopathology of Insight' [1934] J Psychol Psychother 332, 333.
35 Anthony S David, 'Insight and Psychosis' (1990) 156 Br J Psychiatry 798, 805.
36 Halliday (n 1).
37 Georg Høyer, 'On the Justification for Civil Commitment' (2000) Acta Psychiatr Scand 65, 67.
38 Rachel Perkins and Parimala Moodley, 'The Arrogance of Insight?' (1993) 17 BJPsych Bull 233, 234.
39 James A Holstein, *Court-ordered Insanity: Interpretive Practice and Involuntary Commitment* (Aldine Transaction 1993) 102.
40 Ibid.
41 Diesfeld and Sjöström (n 32) 85.

part of the capacity test incorporated into the MCA; it is not mentioned in the Mental Health Act or in the Codes of Practice. Nevertheless, the label 'lack of insight' is powerful, but it is not a neutral observation; rather as Richardson has argued, 'At its core lies a judgement about the patient's ability to accept certain experiences, or behaviour as pathological, thus giving it an inherently subjective character'.[42] Case's research demonstrates that during the eight year study period, one third of cases involving capacity referred to P (the person who is subject to Court of Protection proceedings is known) as lacking insight. Within those cases, a number invoked a lack of insight in relation to the diagnostic threshold, but others raised insight as part of the assessment of whether P satisfied the functional capacity criteria.[43] As Case suggests, reference to insight is unproblematic in relation to the first test, but its application to the functional criteria is a cause for concern and it is this application that is found in the obstetric intervention cases. The functional criteria already provide significant latitude in assessing whether or not P satisfies the criteria to be able to make a decision herself. The danger is that by applying seemingly scientific language weight is added to the 'expert' opinion, rendering the already vulnerable woman more vulnerable, more likely to be deemed to lack the ability to make decisions about birth herself and thereafter paving the way to dismissing her views when they fall to be considered in assessing her best interests. In this way, it is suggested that the use of insight may subvert the patient-centred ethos of the best interests tests; it may fundamentally undermine the ideology of the MCA to empower and facilitate the taking of decisions by individuals wherever possible.[44]

Patient choice and capacity in the context of the MCA 2005

At the heart of the MCA is a commitment to patient-centred care, care that should reflect the patient's values regardless of whether she has capacity at the time or not. This ethos finds voice in the presumption of capacity (s 1(2) MCA). The Act adopts a two-stage capacity test, s 2(1) MCA. The diagnostic criterion calls for the assessment of whether or not the individual has 'an impairment of, or disturbance in the functioning of the mind or brain'. Thereafter the functional threshold requires the determination of whether the impairment or disturbance renders the individual incapable of making the decision in question, s 3(1) MCA, providing that the person will be unable to make the decision for herself if she cannot understand, retain and use or weigh the information relevant to the decision, or communicate her decision. The diagnostic threshold

---

42 Genevra Richardson, 'Rights Based Legalism: Some Thoughts from the Research' in Bernadette McSherry and Penny Weller (eds), *Rethinking Rights-Based Mental Health Laws* 181, 190.
43 Paula Case, 'Dangerous Liaisons? Psychiatry and Law in the Court of Protection – Expert Discourses of "Insight" (and "Compliance")' (2016) 24 Med Law Rev 360, 360, 368.
44 See for example Lord Falconer's statement in the foreword to the Code of Practice: 'It will empower people to make decisions for themselves wherever possible' in *Mental Capacity Act Code of Practice, Foreword* (TSO 2007).

will be easily satisfied, perhaps too easily satisfied, as Okai's systematic review of psychiatric inpatients suggests that the majority of such patients retain capacity to make their own treatment decisions with rates of incapacity generally in line with that found in general hospital inpatients.[45]

Significantly, although the first element of the test for incapacity relates to diagnosis and therefore is correctly left to clinicians, the second element, the functional test that applies after the diagnostic threshold has been satisfied, is not merely a medical matter, but it should also be subject to stringent assessment in court. This is emphasised by a number of judicial pronouncements such as Baker J in observing that although the professionals agreed that *KK* lacked capacity,

> These opinions are of course important evidence, but ... it is the court alone that is in the position to weigh up all the evidence as to the functional test and thus it is the court that must make the ultimate decision.[46]

Nevertheless, as Case demonstrates, experts do give evidence on both arms of the test,[47] with psychiatric evidence 'routinely sought on whether P is "unable to make a decision"' as well as on the question of impairment.[48] Clough's observation that 'the judges often accept professional's view that the person lacks capacity without necessarily scrutinising the particular requirements outlined in the Act'[49] is amply demonstrated in the case law relating to court-authorised obstetric intervention.

Together with the functional test of capacity the Act emphasises that it is the decision-making process rather than the content of the decision that is assessed, though it can be questioned to what extent that principle has translated in practice. The right to make an unwise decision has long been recognised in case law[50] and is preserved by s 1(4) MCA 2005. However, it is well recognised that treatment refusals act as a trigger for capacity assessments[51] and the danger is particularly clear in the obstetric intervention cases where treatment refusals or non-compliance are pathologised, seen as evidence of the woman's inability to make the decision. As the House of Lords' Select Committee concluded: 'The concept of unwise decision-making faces institutional obstruction due to

---

45 David Okai and others, 'Mental Capacity in Psychiatric Patients: Systematic Review' (2007) 191 Br J Psychiatry 291, 295.

46 *CC v KK & STCC* [2012] EWCOP 2136 [62]; in a similar vein see *London Borough of Islington v QR* [2014] EWCOP 26 (Batten J), 'The decision on capacity is one for the judge to make' [84].

47 Case (n 43) 364.

48 Ibid 361.

49 Beverley Clough, 'People Like That: Realising the Social Model in Mental Capacity Jurisprudence' (2014) 22 Med Law Rev 53, 56.

50 Cf *Re T* (n 10) [113] (Lord Donaldson MR); *Re MB* (n 9) [436]–[437] (Butler-Sloss LJ).

51 See for example Paula Case, 'Negotiating the Domain of Mental Capacity: Clinical Judgement or Judicial Diagnosis?' (2016) 130 Med Law Int 174, 188, citing an interesting study by Isobel Sleeman and Kate Saunders, 'An Audit of Mental Capacity Assessment on General Medical Wards' (2013) 8 Clin Ethics 47, noting that all patients whose capacity had been assessed had disagreed with the medical team about their treatment.

prevailing cultures of risk-aversion and paternalism'.[52] The danger is that pathologising non-compliance undermines the statutory framework designed to empower and facilitate people making their own decisions. There can be no right to make an unwise decision if an unwise decision is deemed to be evidence of a lack of insight, thereby demonstrating an inability to make the decision itself.

Following a finding of incapacity, the woman must be treated in accordance with her best interests. As Jackson argues, the meaning of 'best interests' has changed significantly since the principle was established in *Re F (Mental Patient: Sterilisation)* (1989) where whilst recognising the importance of consulting relatives about an individual's best interests, Lord Goff did not appear to even consider that the individual herself should be consulted.[53] Although the individual's past and present wishes and feelings must be considered (s 4(6)(a) MCA), they are not prioritised above other factors to be considered in assessing her best interests, s 4 MCA.[54] This provides significant leeway to decision-makers in balancing the competing factors, an exercise that Peter Jackson J deems intuitive rather than mechanical.[55] In cases where there is a threat to the woman's life her best interests will almost always require that she be treated.[56] In *Aintree*, the Supreme Court accepted that this was the starting point, but stressed that notwithstanding the fact that 'a profound respect for the sanctity of human life is embedded in our law and our moral philosophy',[57] there is a strong, not an absolute, presumption that it is in a person's best interests to stay alive.[58] Post *Aintree* there are indications that the courts are now less inclined to start from the position that the preservation of life will trump all other considerations in the assessment of best interests, adopting instead a more patient-focused approach that looks to prioritise the decision that P would have made herself.[59]

In *Aintree* the Supreme Court held that a patient-centred approach should be adopted, holding that:

> The purpose of the best interests test is to consider matters from the patient's point of view. That is not to say that his wishes must prevail, any more than those of a fully capable patient must prevail. We cannot always

---

52 House of Lords – Select Committee on the Mental Capacity Act 2005, *Mental Capacity Act 2005: Post-Legislative Scrutiny* (The Stationery Office, London, 13th March 2014) [104].

53 Emily Jackson, 'From "Doctor Knows Best" to Dignity: Placing Adults Who Lack Capacity at the Centre of Decisions about Their Medical Treatment' (2018) 81 MLR 247, 252.

54 Explanatory Notes to the Mental Capacity Act 2005, para 28.

55 *Re E (Medical treatment: Anorexia) (Rev 1)* [2012] EWCOP 1639 [129].

56 See for example *Re M (Adult Patient) (Minimally Conscious State: Withdrawal of Treatment)* [2011] EWHC 2443 [249] (Baker J) emphasising that '[T]he importance of preserving life is the decisive factor in this case'; *A Local Authority v E* [10§1] EWHC 1639.

57 *Airedale NHS Trust v Bland* [1993] AC 789 [808] (Sir Thomas Bingham MR).

58 *Aintree University Hospitals NHS Foundation Trust v James* [2013] UKSC 67 [35].

59 See for example *Briggs v Briggs* [2016] EWCOP 53 [62]. For a detailed discussion of this shift see Jackson (n 53) 253–255.

have what we want. ... But insofar as it is possible to ascertain the patient's wishes and feelings, his beliefs and values or the things which were important to him, it is those which should be taken into account because they are a component in making the choice which is right for him as an individual human being.[60]

As Series points out, a shift has occurred in the thinking about the relevance and weight to be given to an individual's wishes and feelings since the introduction of the MCA 2005. Although simply one factor to be considered under the statutory checklist set out in s 4, the Supreme Court Decision in *Aintree* and the adoption of the United Nations Convention on the Rights of Persons with Disabilities, including art 12, have shifted the focus away from the paternalistic justification for treatment provided by the MCA (that a third party should decide how to treat an individual in accordance with her best interests) to the question of to what extent can best interest decisions accommodate that individual's wishes and feelings.[61]

However, the approach in the case of women with SMI has been very different. P is not the centre of the decision, and she is not the subject of the decision; rather she is treated as an object, a recipient of care, a risk to be managed. In many of the recent cases, the risk has been one of potential harm to the foetus, to the woman, or to the healthcare professionals treating her and it is a risk based upon the woman losing control during labour, becoming agitated, not complying with directions ... that is, it is the woman herself who poses the threat. In assessing the woman's best interests the woman's wishes have been considered, but pathologised, regarded as evidence of her lack of insight and in putting themselves in the place of the patient, the courts have considered what a prudent patient who fulfils the maternal ideological role would do, concluding that she would be willing to accept any intervention necessary to ensure the safe delivery of the foetus.[62] Intuitively the ability to ensure a controlled and safe delivery is prioritised over giving effect to the woman's expressed wishes for a vaginal delivery. This means that in the context of pregnant women with an SMI often they cannot have the birth experience that they desire; rather to an even greater extent than occurs with other women, their birth will be managed. The cases discussed below demonstrate that the management is determined by factors such as staff availability and risk assessments, rather than her wishes and feelings. As the House of Lords' Select Committee concluded in its post-legislative scrutiny of the MCA: 'Best interests decision-making is often not undertaken in

---

60 *Aintree University Hospitals NHS Foundation Trust* (n 58) [45] (Hale LJ).
61 Lucy Series, 'The Place of Wishes and Feelings in Best Interests Decisions: *Wye Valley NHS Trust v Mr B*' (2016) 79 MLR 1101, 1101.
62 *Re MB* (n 9) [439] (Butler-Sloss LJ), 'It must be in the best interests of a woman carrying a full-term child whom she wants to be born alive and healthy that such a result should if possible be achieved'.

the way set out in the Act: the wishes, thoughts and feelings of P are not routinely prioritised. Instead, clinical judgments or resource-led decision-making predominate'.[63]

Insight in the Court of Protection: two examples from the case law

In *The NHS Acute Trust & The NHS Mental Health Trust v C*[64] the applicants sought a declaration that C lacked the capacity to make decision about her obstetric care and treatment and that it would be in her best interests for her to receive treatment in accordance with a care plan that included a caesarean. C had a long history of bipolar affective disorder, but her condition had been generally well controlled by psychotropic medicine. She was referred to a midwife at 15 weeks at which point there were no concerns about her own health, or the pregnancy.[65] However, in late pregnancy she was detained under s 2 Mental Health Act 1983, suffering a manic episode with psychotic symptoms.[66] During her time in the hospital she had not always taken her medication and was frequently agitated. Whilst C maintained her preference for a vaginal delivery, the consultant obstetrician considered that a caesarean performed under general anaesthetic would be necessary due to C's inability to remain still and her unpredictable behaviour.

In her evidence the consultant obstetrician set out two options for the delivery of C's foetus, either a pre-planned caesarean performed under general anaesthetic, or to induce C and proceed to an emergency caesarean if necessary, dismissing C's preference for a natural birth:

> C would not be able to tolerate labour and comply with the necessary directions required to keep her and her baby safe throughout that period. ... She will not tolerate the examinations and treatments that may be necessary throughout the birth process. ... Without appropriate clinical interventions the risk to mother and baby during a natural vaginal delivery are high and this is exacerbated by C's current presentations and lack of engagement.[67]

The case demonstrates that in the medical model of obstetric care, management of labour and childbirth is a proactive process; women's choices may not be accepted or respected. It is based on the view that order is created through medical

---

63 House of Lords – Select Committee on the Mental Capacity Act 2005 (n 52) [104].
64 [2016] EWCOP 17.
65 Ibid [15]–[16].
66 The relapse was attributed to pregnancy; although no details are provided about how her mental health had been managed during pregnancy there is an increased rate of relapse in the case of bipolar disorder during pregnancy, Adele C Viguera and others, 'Risk of Recurrence in Women with Bipolar Disorder during Pregnancy: Prospective Study of Mood Stabilizer Discontinuation' (2007) 164 Am J Psychiatry 1817.
67 *The NHS Acute Trust & The NHS Mental Health Trust* (n 64) [26]–[27].

management and reaffirms the view of birth as a disordered process in need of control. As Davis-Floyd has argued, normal hospital routines incorporate technology as part of the childbirth process, normalising the use of such technology and creating an expectation of compliance from women.[68] The obstetrician expressed clear concern for the safety of both the woman and the foetus, but at no stage is the risk to either specified in terms of degree or the form it might take. Rather C is portrayed as risky, as dangerous due to her inability to keep still and the consultant obstetrician's concern that she might refuse to follow directions during labour. Monitoring of labour is very much a part of modern-day obstetrics; blood pressure, temperature, vaginal examinations, and abdominal palpation take place regularly throughout labour and foetal heart monitoring may be undertaken. Each of these practices enables healthcare professionals to assess progress in labour, but although they are routine in obstetric-led care, many women opt not to have such interventions and there is a well-recognised causal link between increased intervention and instrumental birth.[69] Nevertheless, C's expected 'inability' to allow such monitoring is framed as deviant, as risky, and is portrayed as resulting in a high level of risk to both herself and the foetus.

The consultant obstetrician's view that a caesarean will be necessary is based upon C's lack of engagement with her and a clear lack of compliance on C's behalf. During the first trimester C was well, she was looking after herself, in a steady relationship with A, and was positive about the pregnancy. She was supported in her choice of a natural delivery by her mother and A.[70] The judgment states that she was referred to a midwife at 15 weeks, although that is rather later than usual, but she did engage and attended most of the scheduled antenatal appointments, cooperating with most of the examinations deemed necessary. Whilst detained under the MHA C's interactions with consultant obstetrician had become confrontational and angry. She was unable to tolerate ten minutes of continuous foetal heart rate tracing; however, she was described as suffering a manic episode at the time and that would make remaining still for lengthy periods of time extremely difficult. C did undergo an ultrasound and is described as tolerating a discussion with the obstetrician and consultant psychiatrist about the risks of vaginal delivery and the possibility of a caesarean. The court heard that she had interrupted their explanations and refused to repeat back what had been said, becoming 'bitter, angry and confrontational with staff'.[71] C was clearly very unwell, but given that she had developed her own birth plan and that she still wanted to have a natural birth it is perhaps unsurprising that she

---

68 Robbie E Davis-Floyd, *Birth as an American Rite of Passage* (2nd edn, University of California Press 2004).

69 See for example Kirstie Coxon, Jane Sandall, and Naomi J Fulop, 'To What Extent Are Women Free to Choose Where to Give Birth? How Discourses of Risk, Blame and Responsibility Influence Birth Place Decisions' (2014) 16 Health Risk Soc 51, 52. Pam Lowe, *Reproductive Health and Maternal Sacrifice* (Palgrave Macmillan 2016) 147.

70 *The NHS Acute Trust & the NHS Mental Health Trust* (n 64) [15]–[16].

71 Ibid [19].

was agitated when faced with professionals telling her that she would have to have a caesarean and moreover one performed under general anaesthetic.[72] Although C had had more contact, over a longer period, with her midwife, little is reported of those interactions, other than to confirm the consultant obstetrician and consultant psychiatrist's evidence regarding C's lack of insight, inability to concentrate, and unpredictable behaviour.

The way in which C is described is designed to emphasise the impact of her mental illness upon her, it defines her, who she is and how she is likely to behave. Although heavily pregnant C was not due to give birth imminently, and the remaining weeks of pregnancy could, it is suggested, have made a key difference in stabilising her mental health and enabling her to participate in the decision about how to give birth. Whilst it is clear that the diagnostic threshold would be met, it is less clear that the functional elements were not met and as Holman J stressed in *Re SB* a finding that P does suffer 'an impairment of, or a disturbance in the functioning of, the mind or brain ... is the beginning not the end of the enquiry'.[73] The consultant psychiatrist confirmed that C was still very unwell, saying that she has no insight into her mental state and concluded that she lacked capacity to decide on her obstetric care because her inability to concentrate for long periods prevented her from understanding the whole context and that she lacked the ability to retain information. However, this emphasises one of the dangers of importing the clinical term 'insight' to the functional aspects of capacity. Although insight might be understood to signify a deeper understanding of the issue, that is not what is required by the law. It is not necessary for P to understand every detail; rather she must understand and weigh the salient details relevant to the decision at hand.[74] As Case observes, requiring a deeper understanding would '[conflict] with judicial insistence that the threshold for capacity should not be set too high'.[75] It would undermine the principle that the individual should be enabled to decide for herself wherever possible.

It is regrettable that Theis J did not avail herself of the opportunity to speak to C herself, as Peter Jackson J recognised in *Wye Valley NHS Trust v B*, although there were 'two excellent recent reports of discussions with [P], ... there is no substitute for a face-to-face meeting'.[76] Case law demonstrates how very important such a step can be,[77] for example, in *Re SB (termination of pregnancy)* Holman J recognised that even where the SMI might impact upon P's decision-making, it did not, without more, render her unable to make a decision, saying that 'my assessment of this case has been enormously illuminated by her attendance and by the considerable oral evidence which she has given'.[78]

---

72 The anaesthetist considered a spinal epidural would not be suitable due to the risk that C would not keep still, increasing the risk of nerve damage. The rationale for using a general anaesthetic was that it would limit the amount of time that she would be subject to physical restraint.

73 *Re SB* [2013] EWCOP 1417 [37].

74 *LBL v RYJ* [2010] EWHC 2664 (Fam) [58] (Macur J).

75 Case (n 43) 375.

76 *Wye Valley NHS Trust v B* [2015] EWCOP 60 [18].

77 See for example *Re TZ* [2013] EWCOP 2333.

78 *Re SB* (n 73) [29].

From the information provided in the judgment it seems unlikely that C would have been found to have the requisite capacity to refuse a caesarean, but following the finding that she lacked capacity an assessment of her best interests was required. 'Best interests' incorporate consideration of the patient's previously expressed wishes and feelings; unlike many of the cases concerning obstetric intervention C had drafted a birth plan approximately three months earlier, at a time when her mental health was unimpaired. Theis J did consider C's wishes and feelings, recognising that C still wanted to have a natural delivery. She noted that earlier in the pregnancy, before decompensation, C had wanted a water birth, but that this was no longer an option. Although the judge did not speak to C herself, she was advised by the solicitor acting on behalf of the official solicitor who had visited C. At that meeting C confirmed that she wanted to have a natural birth in line with her birth plan. She wanted as little intervention as possible, but would consent to a caesarean if it was an emergency. If a caesarean did become necessary, C said that she wanted to be awake for it (that is she did not want a general anaesthetic); she wanted the baby to be given to her immediately for as much skin to skin contact as possible and to be accompanied by her birth partner.[79] Reading these requests, it is hard to conclude that C did not understand the context in which she was making her decision.

Both consultants advised that C was unlikely to be able to tolerate a vaginal delivery, that she was likely to find labour traumatic, and that she might react in an extreme manner, including physical resistance that would pose a risk to herself, the foetus, and staff. From the perspective of best interests, the only relevant risk is that to C herself; staffing concerns should play no part in the assessment of a patient's best interests. Although the clinicians recognised that a caesarean would be difficult for C, they felt it would be less distressing for her and argued that she should have a planned caesarean under general anaesthetic, that is precisely what C did not want. They concluded that C had 'no insight' into her current condition, or need for treatment. In this respect it is important to note that her current condition related to pregnancy and the need for a caesarean, not merely her mental illness. The focus of the medical evidence therefore was upon management of risk (that is management of the woman, not just pregnancy, or mental illness) and the benefits of intervention (that is control) rather than the hazardous natural birth. Technology is assumed to be a benefit, despite the fact that the use of technology leads to cascading interventions,[80] and that many women object to the use of technology. However, C's non-compliance was regarded as demonstrating her lack of understanding, or recognition of the benefit of technology – it demonstrated a lack of insight.

On the basis of the evidence presented to her, Theis J concluded that C had 'demonstrated limited or no insight into what [a natural birth] will involve'.[81] However, looking at the comments C made to the solicitor it is difficult to conclude that C lacked insight into what was involved. Indeed, one might suggest

79 Ibid [41].
80 Lowe (n 69) 147.
81 *The NHS Acute Trust & the NHS Mental Health Trust* (n 64) [58].

that no woman facing her first labour has insight into what is involved; no amount of preparation can prepare you for the event.

Theis J granted the declarations sought on the basis of the consultant obstetrician's evidence that anything other than a planned caesarean under general anaesthesia would be more likely to harm and risk the safety of C, the foetus, and those 'conducting the delivery'. The choice of words is telling; Theis J spoke of 'those conducting the delivery', but a baby is not a parcel delivered by a courier. A baby is delivered by a woman, the product of her labour. By casting C in the passive role Theis J further objectifies her, identifying her as a passive observer in the process rather than as an actor. The consultant obstetrician's view that constant foetal heart monitoring would be necessary throughout labour was a very important factor in this case, prompting Theis J to reject the possibility of a vaginal delivery, or a caesarean under local anaesthetic that would have allowed C to remain awake for the procedure. She found that the consultant obstetrician and psychiatrist had taken account of the likely impact the different modes of delivery would have upon C and weighted the risks of performing a caesarean under general anaesthesia. The fact that the clinicians had undertaken this weighing is one thing; the assessment of best interests remains, however, one for the court and reading the judgment it is difficult to avoid the conclusion that this is one of those excessively deferential judgments that Lord Woolf suggested were a thing of the past.[82] Theis J recognised that C's mental health had improved somewhat over the last two days, and was satisfied that the clinicians would review the situation before deciding whether to go ahead with a planned caesarean, should they still believe that C lacked capacity to decide for herself. The judgment concludes with a postscript confirming that C gave birth to a child subsequently; the means of delivery is not given.

Theis J reached her decision without speaking to C, although she was made aware of C's current and previous wishes and did receive evidence from both C's mother and the 'father'. Nevertheless, it is clear that C was not enabled to participate in this decision in any meaningful way, that her wishes and feelings were dismissed as impractical, as demonstrating a lack of insight into her situation, that of a pregnant woman who is regarded as a danger to herself and others due to an SMI. It is suggested that the contrast between the way pregnant women and others are treated is extremely clear when this case is compared to the case of *Wye Valley NHS Trust v B* (2015).[83] In this case Peter Jackson J held that it would not be in B's best interests to amputate his foot in order to save his life in the face of his firmly held objections to the operation. Like C, B lacked the capacity to understand the information and weigh it to reach a decision, but Jackson J emphasised that 'a conclusion that a person lacks decision-making capacity is not an "off-switch" for his rights and freedoms'.[84] In that case he concluded by

82 Lord Woolf, 'Are the Courts Excessively Deferential to the Medical Profession?' (2001) 9 Med Law Rev 1.
83 *Wye Valley NHS Trust* (n 76).
84 Ibid [11].

saying that 'There is a difference between fighting on someone's behalf and just fighting them. Enforcing treatment in this case would surely be the latter'.[85] It is suggested that the same is true in the case of C.

In *A University Hospital NHS Trust v CA*[86] Baker J granted a declaration that it would be lawful to perform a caesarean on a woman with a diagnosis of autism and learning disability. CA was born in Nigeria, but had lived in the United Kingdom for almost ten years. It was reported that as a child she had been subjected to abdominal 'tribal cutting' to release bad blood, during which she had been physically restrained, and that she had been subjected to female genital mutilation (FGM).[87] The judge recognised that in these circumstances a caesarean could be traumatic.[88] CA would not agree to blood being taken and objected to physical examinations; it had not been possible to perform a gynaecological examination. However, she had undergone an ultrasound and permitted the midwife to perform minimal examinations such as taking her blood pressure. Her midwife reported that she had little understanding of labour, but that she had watched a DVD about it, commenting that she would not have an epidural. CA was reluctant to discuss the delivery, adamant that she wanted a home delivery and was reported to have said 'no one can touch you at home, I trust no one'.[89] The midwife reported that she had formed a good relationship with CA, but that she continued to be challenging and difficult. Shortly before the application was made medical staff sought to admit her to hospital due to concern about her condition, but CA refused.[90]

A consultant psychiatrist examined CA and concluded that she has a learning difficulty and is autistic, although he was unable to carry out a full assessment and was unable to access her medical records. He reported that she was selective about which information she retained and that which she dismissed; and that she was unable to weigh information to make an informed choice.[91] The midwife confirmed that CA was unable to repeat back information she had been given about pain relief, although she had rejected the need for pain relief and told the psychiatrist that she did not believe labour would be painful, based on her friend's experience.[92] The midwife concluded that CA lacked capacity or insight into what was going to happen. The Official Solicitor clearly had some qualms about whether CA lacked capacity to make her own decision about treatment, but was persuaded that the functional test was satisfied.[93] Baker J concluded that CA lacked the capacity to understand, retain, weigh, and use information

---

85 Ibid [45].
86 [2016] EWCOP 61.
87 Ibid [11]–[13].
88 Ibid [14].
89 Ibid [17].
90 Ibid [16]–[18].
91 Ibid [20]–[26].
92 Ibid [17], [26].
93 Ibid [27].

and thus was unable to make decisions about medical treatment, particularly the delivery. He described her as lacking 'any real understanding of the realities of childbirth. ... [S]he was extremely selective as to the information she retained and [could] relate back'.[94] He stressed that medical staff had taken all practicable steps to assist CA to make the decision, but found that she lacked 'the capacity to weigh up and use the information about childbirth – blood tests, internal examinations, pain relief, methods of delivery, how to describe what she feels, whether and when to push, and generally what to do'.[95]

Recognising the importance of CA's wishes and feelings Baker J went into considerable detail about what she had told the Official Solicitor's representative. She had started the conversation by saying that she wanted the case closed and did not want to talk about it. She explained that she wanted to have a home birth, that hospitals were associated with too many bad memories for her. She said that blood tests and medical examinations were out of the question, could think of no risk to the baby of a home delivery, and said she was sure nothing could go wrong as her whole family would be there for her and the baby. She could not explain why she did not want a caesarean and responded to the representative's statement that a judge would have to decide the case by saying that 'the judge was not having the baby but she was.'[96] Baker J noted CA's strong independence and ardent wish to have a home birth, but said it was clear from the evidence that she had little understanding of what labour and childbirth entail.[97] In *Wye Valley NHS Trust v B*, B was described as fiercely independent,[98] but his views were not dismissed on the basis of his limited understanding of what the amputation of his foot would entail. For B there was a clearly identifiable consequence of him not undergoing the recommended treatment, death through septicaemia; by comparison the risks to CA involved in not undergoing a caesarean were at best imprecise. A comparison of the way in which pregnant women and other individuals found to lack capacity suggests that the level of understanding required of a pregnant woman is significantly higher than the more rudimentary understanding required in other contexts. As Quinn has argued:

> [T]here is a profound contradiction between tolerating extremely poor choices and decision-making in non-disabled people on the one hand and then raising the bar exceedingly high for persons with disabilities – so high that most non-disabled people would have difficulty surmounting it![99]

94 Ibid [29].
95 Ibid [29] and [30].
96 Ibid [34].
97 Ibid [35].
98 *Wye Valley NHS Trust* (n 76) [21].
99 See for example Gerard Quinn, 'Personhood & Legal Capacity: Perspectives on the Paradigm Shift of Article 12 CRPD' (*Harvard Law School*, 20 February 2010) <https://www.inclusionireland. ie/sites/default/files/attach/basic-page/846/harvardlegalcapacitygqdraft2.doc> accessed 10 March 2019.

The consultant obstetrician concluded that an elective caesarean would be best, particularly because her history of non-compliance meant that she was likely to decline examinations and foetal monitoring, leading to the risk of a poor foetal outcome which would, in turn, impact upon CA. Other key benefits of a caesarean included avoiding the risk of tearing due to FGM, allowing CA sufficient time to process information about the caesarean; hospital-based caregivers could plan for any complications and other caregivers could plan for CA and the baby.[100] Of course on the negative side of the balance sheet CA would suffer post-delivery pain; she would have another abdominal scar and physical recovery would take longer than that associated with vaginal delivery. The consultant psychiatrist concluded that a vaginal delivery was not an option, arguing that her reluctance to comply with instructions would lead to an uncoordinated labour process. He suggested that the most damaging outcome would be if CA were to require an emergency caesarean, that the safest option would be a planned caesarean where CA would be supported by an assembled team of familiar faces, which would reduce the risk of chaos.[101] Baker J accepted these views and concluded that it would be in CA's best interests to conduct a caesarean, granting the necessary declaration. In a postscript to the judgment it is noted that a planned caesarean was performed the day after the hearing and that the only restraint that had been necessary was to hold her hand to administer intravenous sedation.[102]

Whilst the Official Solicitor's representative was significantly more proactive in challenging the clinical evidence in this case than is usual, it is important to recognise that the role of the official solicitor is to represent P's best interests, not to represent P. This is significant because CA did not participate in the hearing, and Baker J did not speak to her directly; therefore, she had no voice in the hearing and no representation. Her views were reported and dismissed on the basis that she lacked insight. Whereas C's non-compliance was framed as evidence of lack of insight, in the case of CA, her lack of insight was considered to lead to non-compliance. By relying upon 'insight', a technical, objective term, the clinicians and judge were able to avoid the question of whether CA's refusal of a caesarean was reasonable. From the facts reported in the judgment it is clear that CA did not have a relationship based on trust with the healthcare professionals caring for her. She did not want to be admitted to hospital, did not want to be examined, and did not want a caesarean, preferring to deliver her baby at home. Taking account of her personal history (tribal cutting and FGM) this is not surprising and seems an entirely understandable response;[103] indeed a choice for a home birth is a choice made by many women. On behalf of the Official Solicitor Ms Gollop emphasised that CA had been cut repeatedly by men against her will

---

100 *A University Hospital NHS Trust v CA* (n 86) [37], [40].
101 Ibid [42]–[43].
102 Ibid [49].
103 See also Rosemary Auchmuty, Marie Fox, and Jaime Linsey, 'Health Law, Medicine and Ethics. Debate 1 Are Women More Likely to Have Their Healthcare Decisions Overruled?' in Rosemary Auchmuty (ed), *Great Debates in Gender and Law* (Macmillan 2018) 124.

and that she would not necessarily find a caesarean less traumatic than vaginal delivery, particularly as she was adamant that she did not want a caesarean, or indeed a hospital birth at all.[104] As Hughes suggests:

> 'Lack of insight' is a label that positions people in a certain light. Once it is declared that a person 'lacks insight' he or she is regarded as having a significant mental illness, which seamlessly calls into question decision-making, judgements and abilities, while raising worries about risk-taking and safety.[105]

Thus framed the clinical authority was foregrounded, CA's non-compliant behaviour was seen as a result of her lack of insight.

Conclusion

In 2001, Lord Woolf, the then Master of the Rolls, suggested that the courts were no longer excessively deferential to the medical profession;[106] however, a reading of the most recent tranche of cases suggests that nothing has changed since the end of the twentieth century when the pregnant woman has an SMI, that the golden principle of medical law (patient autonomy) is just as compromised as it ever has been. From the cases discussed above it is clear that the decision-making process and the hearing of the application are dominated by the medical discourse. A refusal to follow medical advice is equated with a lack of insight, that insight not merely into the SMI but also into pregnancy and birth is becoming increasingly important; indeed it would appear that insight is being subsumed within the capacity test. Noticeably, the way in which clinicians describe the patient's condition (particularly her pregnant condition) is recontextualised[107] and rendered in terms that speak to the legal definition of capacity. As Diesfeld and Sjöström argue, the use of insight medicalises arguments, 'framing the person's self-perceptions and choices as evidence of pathology'.[108] It is suggested that a psychiatric term of art has no place in the legal test of capacity, a test that incorporates not merely a diagnostic threshold but also a functional test.

My critique of the reliance on 'lack of insight' draws on two separate objections. First, it is conclusory; it presents the conclusion of an assessment rather than the reason for it (generally that the woman refuses to consent to treatment deemed necessary by the healthcare professionals caring for her). Second, it blurs the boundaries between the diagnostic threshold and the functional criteria, allowing healthcare professionals to assume control of the second stage of the

---

104 *A University Hospital NHS Trust v CA* (n 86) [36].
105 Julian C Hughes, 'Insight: The Concept, the Assessment and the Label' (2019) 25 BJPsych Adv 131, 132.
106 Lord Woolf, 'Are the Courts Excessively Deferential to the Medical Profession?' (2001) 64 MLR 1.
107 See Stefan Sjöström, *Party or Patient? Discursive Practices Relating to Coercion in Psychiatric and Legal Settings* (Borea 1997). Diesfeld and Sjöström (n 32) 87.
108 Diesfeld and Sjöström (n 32) 98.

capacity assessment as well as the first. Use of insight to negate the functional criteria threatens to undermine the central aim of the MCA to engage and facilitate decision-making by P wherever possible. There can be no doubt that alongside the inherent flexibility of the definition of incapacity, insight has provided significant interpretative flexibility, facilitating intervention and opening the door to treatment aligned with clinical advice, but classified as best interests.

The themes of risk and control run throughout the cases – women are supposed to remain in control, but what is actually meant is compliant. The courts' consideration of the women's capacity and best interests foregrounds their diagnoses; the following discussion is dominated by experts and their views of the safest way forward. However, it is important to note that the risks considered are generally risks to the foetus and the healthcare professionals, not to the woman herself. The woman is the risk, the source of danger that must be neutralised by complete anaesthetic rendering her compliant. In this context caesareans are equated with safety; vaginal ('natural') birth is constructed as risky and dangerous. The notion of avoidable harm is persistent. Sheila Kitzinger was responsible for introducing birth plans to the United Kingdom in the mid-1970s, responding to what she described as a 'factory-farm system of childbearing. ... [Where] care was task rather than women-centred'.[109] Reading through the descriptions of plans for the delivery of the foetus in these cases, it is hard to avoid concluding that this approach still applies at least to women with an SMI. These women are accused of being a risk, to themselves, to the foetus; they are viewed as egocentric because they refuse to conform to the dominant ideology of maternity. This contrasts with the vision set out in *Better Births*[110] that emphasises the need for personalised care centred upon the woman, baby, and her family and the provision of better postnatal and perinatal mental healthcare.[111] The review concludes that 'Women should be informed of risks and be supported to make decisions which would keep them as safe as possible. ... Once a woman has made her decisions, she should be respected and the services should wrap around her'.[112] Thus, the vision provided centres upon the woman, rather than framing her as a passive recipient of care. However, this vision remains an illusion in the case of women with SMI who are constructed as passive subjects, and if they are not passive enough then restraint will be used to ensure their subjectivity.

The underlying philosophy of the MCA is that individuals should be empowered to take decisions for themselves wherever possible, and therefore s 1(3) MCA requires that all practical steps be taken to enable the individual to take the decision for herself without success before she is deemed to lack the capacity to decide for herself. This requirement is likely to be particularly important in relation to non-consensual caesareans, as the case law prior to the enactment of the MCA often raises the question of whether more could have been done to

---

109 Sheila Kitzinger, 'Birth Plans: How Are They Being Used?' (1999) 7 Br J Midwifery 300.
110 National Maternity Review (n 3).
111 Ibid 8–10.
112 Ibid 48.

enable the women to take decisions for themselves. Psychological intervention at an earlier point in the pregnancy, for example, might have put the women in a position to be able to take decisions for themselves; instead no action was taken to empower or facilitate the decisional capabilities of the women. With the onset of labour imminent, recourse was had to court orders to compel the performance of a caesarean on the basis that the women were unable to make the necessary decision for themselves. This is precisely the scenario that CA found herself in. Despite the fact that her GP had been aware of her pregnancy from the 30th week, the application for a declaration was not submitted until two weeks before CA's due date, earning the Trusts significant criticism from Baker J.[113] During those eight weeks significant progress could have been made using behavioural psychotherapy to develop a relationship of trust, where CA could feel safe, and addressing her fears of being touched and examined. In such a way, CA could have been assisted to participate more fully in the decision-making process, and a clearer picture of the FGM and cutting could have been developed, instead of the rather opaque information on which the court was left to rely.

Similarly, as a woman with bipolar affective disorder, it was foreseeable that C might relapse during pregnancy.[114] She had written a birth plan and discussed it with her midwife whilst well, at a time where there were no concerns about her capacity to make decisions for herself. It is regrettable that the opportunity was not taken to consider how she would want to be treated if her mental health were to deteriorate, to develop an advance decision for such an eventuality, rather than the more common, but non-binding, aspirational birth plan. It is suggested that the best way to put the woman at the centre of these undeniably difficult decisions is through greater use of advance decision-making, maximising the opportunity for the woman to participate in the decision and for her views to carry significant weight in any best interests decision that has to be made, for example due to non-applicability of the advance decision to the situation that arises at a time when the woman lacks capacity.[115]

Taken against the backdrop of the changing landscape Peter Jackson J identified in *Wye Valley*, it seems undeniable that pregnant women are treated differently to other patients, that the usual rules do not apply to them, and that the retreat from the figurative cliff edge of capacity has yet to occur in the obstetric context. Whilst the use of 'insight' may give the appearance of scientific objectivity and professional detachment, it is suggested that it acts as a mask, hiding value

---

113 Baker J criticised the Trust for failing to comply with the guidance issued by Keehan J in *NHS Trust 1 v G: Practice Note* [2014] EWCOP 30 [6], [19] which stressed the need for early identification of an individual for whom an application might need to be made and that except in an emergency, applications should be made at least four weeks before the expected due date.

114 There is an increased rate of relapse in the case of bipolar disorder during pregnancy, Adele C Viguera and others (n 66).

115 A detailed consideration of advance decision-making in this context falls outside the scope of this chapter, but can be found in Samantha Halliday, 'Conceiving Better Birth Plans: Mental Illness, Pregnancy and Court Authorised Obstetric Intervention' (2019) Medical Law International.

judgements and enabling maximum management of the process of birth, whilst minimising the potential for women deemed to lack capacity to participate in such a deeply personal decision about the manner in which they will give birth. In such a context, to talk of choice and of woman-centred care is illusionary.

Table of cases

A Hospital Trust v V and Ors [2017] EWCOP 20

A Local Authority v E [10§1] EWHC 1639

A University Hospital NHS Trust v CA [2016] EWCOP 61

Aintree University Hospitals NHS Foundation Trust v James [2013] UKSC 67

Airedale NHS Trust v Bland [1993] AC 789

Briggs v Briggs [2016] EWCOP 53

CC v KK & STCC [2012] EWCOP 2136

Great Western Hospitals NHS Foundation Trust v AA, BB, CC & DD [2014] EWHC 132 (Fam)

In re Baby Boy Doe, a Fetus v Mother Doe 632 NE 2d 326 (1994)

Jefferson v Griffin Spalding County Hospital Authority 74 SE 2d 457 (1981)

LBL v RYJ [2010] EWHC 2664 (Fam)

London Borough of Islington v QR [2014] EWCOP 26

Montgomery v Lanarkshire Health Board [2015] UKSC 11

NHS Trust 1 v G: Practice Note [2014] EWCOP 30

NHS Trust and others v FG [2014] EWCOP 30

Norfolk and Norwich Healthcare (NHS) Trust v W [1996] 2 FLR 613

North Somerset Council v LW and others [2014] EWCOP 3

PC v City of York Council [2013] EWCA Civ 478

Pemberton v Tallahassee Memorial Regional Medical Center 66 F.Supp.2d 1247 (N D Fla 1999)

Re AA (Mental Capacity: Enforced Caesarean) [2012] EWHC 4378 (COP)

Re AC 573 A.2d 1235 (1990)

Re M (Adult Patient) (Minimally Conscious State: Withdrawal of Treatment) [2011] EWHC 2443

Re Madyun (1986) 573 A 2d 1259 (DC 1990)

Re MB (Medical Treatment) [1997] 2 FLR 426

Re MB [1997] 2 FLR 426

Re P [2013] EWHC 4581 (COP)

Re S [1993] Fam 123

Re SB [2013] EWCOP 1417

Re TZ [2013] EWCOP 2333

Rochdale Healthcare NHS Trust v C [1997] 1 FCR 274

Royal Free NHS Foundation Trust v AB (2014)

Samantha Burton v Florida 39 So 3d 263 (Fla Dist Ct App 2010)

St George's Healthcare NHS Trust v S (NO 2), R v Collins and others, ex parte S (NO 2) [1998] EWCA Civ 1349 [1999] Fam 26

T (Consent to Medical Treatment) (Adult Patient), Re [1993] Fam 95

Tameside and Glossop Acute Services Trust v CH [1996] 1 FLR 762

The Mental Health Trust, The Acute Trust & The Council v DD & BC [2014] EWCOP 11 (COP)

The NHS Acute Trust & The NHS Mental Health Trust v C [2016] EWCOP 17

The NHS Acute Trust & The NHS Mental Health Trust v C [2016] EWCOP 17 and A University Hospital NHS Trust v CA [2016] EWCOP 51
Wye Valley NHS Trust v B [2015] EWCOP 60

Bibliography

Auchmuty R, Fox M, and Linsey J, 'Health Law, Medicine and Ethics. Debate 1 Are Women More Likely to Have Their Healthcare Decisions Overruled?' in Auchmuty R (ed), *Great Debates in Gender and Law* (Macmillan 2018) 124

Barker K K, 'Electronic Support Groups, Patient-Consumers, Medicalization: The Case of Contested Illness' (2008) 49 J Health Soc Behav 20

Brownsword R and Wale J, 'Testing Times Ahead: Non-Invasive Prenatal Testing and the Kind of Community We Want to Be' (2018) 81 MLR 646

Case P, 'Dangerous Liaisons? Psychiatry and Law in the Court of Protection – Expert Discourses of "Insight" (and "Compliance")' (2016) 24 Med Law Rev 360

Case P, 'Negotiating the Domain of Mental Capacity: Clinical Judgement or Judicial Diagnosis?' (2016) 130 Med Law Int 174

Clough B, 'People Like That: Realising the Social Model in Mental Capacity Jurisprudence' (2014) 22 Med Law Rev 53

Coxon K, Sandall J, and Fulop N J, 'To What Extent Are Women Free to Choose Where to Give Birth? How Discourses of Risk, Blame and Responsibility Influence Birth Place Decisions' (2014) 16 Health Risk Soc 51

Crossley M L, 'Childbirth, Complications and the Illusion of "Choice": A Case Study' (2007) 17 Fem Psychol 543

David A S, 'Insight and Psychosis' (1990) 156 Br J Psychiatry 798

Davis-Floyd R E, *Birth as an American Rite of Passage* (2nd edn, University of California Press 2004)

Diesfeld K and Sjöström S, 'Interpretive Flexibility: Why Doesn't Insight Incite Controversy in Mental Health Law?' (2007) 25 Behav Sci Law 85

Felicia Wu Song and others, 'Women, Pregnancy, and Health Information Online: The Making of Informed Patients and Ideal Mothers' (2012) 26 Gend Soc 773

Fovargue S and Miola J, 'Policing Pregnancy: Implications of the Attorney General's Reference (No. 3 of 1994)' (1998) 6 Med Law Rev 265

Fulford B K W M, 'Insight and Delusion: From Jaspers to Kraepelin and Back Again via Austin' in Amador X and David A (eds), Insight and Psychosis: Awareness of Illness in Schizophrenia and Related Disorders (OUP 2004)

Halliday S, *Autonomy and Pregnancy: A Comparative Analysis of Compelled Obstetric Intervention* (Routledge 2016)

Halliday S, 'Conceiving Better Birth Plans: Mental Illness, Pregnancy and Court Authorised Obstetric Intervention' (2019) Medical Law International (forthcoming)

Holstein J A, *Court-ordered Insanity: Interpretive Practice and Involuntary Commitment* (Aldine Transaction 1993)

Howard L M, Kumar R, and Thornicroft G, 'The Psychosocial Characteristics of Mothers with Psychotic Disorders' (2001) 178 Br J Psychiatry 427

Høyer G, 'On the Justification for Civil Commitment' (2000) Acta Psychiatr Scand 65

Hughes J C, 'Insight: The Concept, the Assessment and the Label' (2019) 25 BJPsych Adv 131

Jackson E, 'From "Doctor Knows Best" to Dignity: Placing Adults Who Lack Capacity at the Centre of Decisions about Their Medical Treatment' (2018) 81 MLR 247

Jomeen J, 'Choice in Childbirth: A Realistic Expectation?'(2007) 15 Br J Midwifery 485

Kitzinger S, 'Birth Plans: How Are They Being Used?' (1999) 7 Br J Midwifery 300

Lewis A, 'The Psychopathology of Insight' [1934] J Psychol Psychother 332

Lord Falconer, *Mental Capacity Act Code of Practice, Foreword* (TSO 2007)

Lord Woolf, 'Are the Courts Excessively Deferential to the Medical Profession?' (2001) 9 Med Law Rev 1

Lothian J A, 'Choice, Autonomy, and Childbirth Education' [2008] J Perinat Educ 35

Lowe P, *Reproductive Health and Maternal Sacrifice* (Palgrave Macmillan 2016)

McAra-Couper J, Jones M, and Smythe L, 'Caesarean-Section, My Body, My Choice: The Construction of "Informed Choice" in Relation to Intervention in Childbirth' (2012) 22 Fem Psychol 81

National Maternity Review, 'Better Births: Improving Outcomes of Maternity Services in England. A Five Year Forward View for Maternity Care' (2016)

Okai D and others, 'Mental Capacity in Psychiatric Patients: Systematic Review' (2007) 191 Br J Psychiatry 291

Perkins R and Moodley P, 'The Arrogance of Insight?' (1993) 17 BJPsych Bull 233

Possamai-Inesedy A, 'Confining Risk: Choice and Responsibility in Childbirth in a Risk Society' (2006) 15 Health Sociology Review 406

Richardson G, 'Rights Based Legalism: Some Thoughts from the Research' in McSherry B and Weller P (eds), *Rethinking Rights-Based Mental Health Laws* (Hart Publishing 2010) 181

Series L, 'The Place of Wishes and Feelings in Best Interests Decisions: Wye Valley NHS Trust v Mr B' (2016) 79 MLR 1101

Sjöström S, *Party or Patient? Discursive Practices Relating to Coercion in Psychiatric and Legal Settings* (Borea 1997)

Sleeman I and Saunders K, 'An Audit of Mental Capacity Assessment on General Medical Wards' (2013) 8 Clin Ethics 47

Taylor C L and others, 'The Characteristics and Health Needs of Pregnant Women with Schizophrenia Compared with Bipolar Disorder and Affective Psychoses' (2015) 15 BMC Psychiatry 88

UK Department of Health and Social Care, 'National Service Framework: Children, Young People and Maternity Services' (4 October 2004)

Viguera A C and others, 'Risk of Recurrence in Women with Bipolar Disorder during Pregnancy: Prospective Study of Mood Stabilizer Discontinuation' (2007) 164 Am J Psychiatry 1817

Zadoroznyj M, 'Social Class, Social Selves and Social Control in Childbirth' (1999) 21 Sociol Health Illn 267

11 Obstetric violence through a fiduciary lens

Elizabeth Kukura

Introduction

In recent years, consumer advocates in the United States have encouraged people to come forward with their stories of mistreatment by healthcare providers during childbirth. Such advocacy has shown victims they are not alone, while also situating accounts of abuse and coercion within a legal framework of informed consent, autonomy, and birthing rights. Yet despite these developments, it is still difficult for many – both within and outside the mainstream medical system – to recognise certain practices as obstetric violence and to understand how such mistreatment harms pregnant people, their babies, and their families.[1] At the heart of all stories of obstetric violence is the idea of betrayal. A pregnant patient places trust in a physician to care for the patient's health and well-being, and to help facilitate safe delivery of a baby. When that patient experiences abuse, coercion, or disrespect at the hands of a trusted healthcare provider, the betrayal of trust may have a profoundly negative impact on the patient.

Given the central role of trust and betrayal in cases of obstetric violence, the principles of fiduciary law provide a useful lens for examining obstetric violence. Fiduciary principles help reveal how certain conduct violates a patient's trust, leading to physical, emotional, and psychological harms. Fiduciary law prioritises loyalty and the protection of the vulnerable party from abuse of power by the fiduciary who has been entrusted to act in the beneficiary's best interests. Although physicians were not among the original fiduciaries, courts have subsequently recognised that fiduciary principles are at the heart of the doctor-patient relationship. Fiduciary law's concern with the transfer of power to a party with greater expertise, the risk that conflicts of interest might influence the exercise of

---

1 This chapter refers to the gender-neutral 'pregnant people' or 'patient' out of recognition that some men experience pregnancy and childbirth. Robin Marantz Henig, 'Transgender Men Who Become Pregnant Face Social, Health Challenges' (*NPR*, 7 November 2014) <www.npr.org/sections/health-shots/2014/11/07/362269036/transgender-men-who-become-pregnant-face-health-challenges> accessed 19 November 2018. However, where discussing specific research on women's experiences or individual women's accounts of mistreatment, gendered language will be used. More research is needed on the experiences of transgender individuals seeking maternity care in mainstream healthcare institutions.

that power, and the resulting vulnerability on the part of the transferring party make it a valuable framework for examining the dynamics that enable and tolerate obstetric violence. By examining mistreatment during childbirth through a fiduciary lens, it becomes clear that certain common maternity care practices depart from the values that characterise the doctor-patient relationship and therefore should constitute a breach of fiduciary duty.

This chapter begins in the 'Fiduciary basics: trust and loyalty' section by summarising the key principles that characterise fiduciary law and make it useful for analysing obstetric violence claims. The 'Evolving norms: the physician as fiduciary' section examines how the modern conception of physician as fiduciary has evolved, as reflected in case law and in formal statements by leading medical organisations. Then, in the 'Applying fiduciary principles to obstetric violence' section, the chapter applies fiduciary principles to obstetric violence, looking specifically at the role of competing loyalties and conflicts of interest, the problems with using the language of maternal-foetal conflict to describe disagreements over clinical care, and how coercing a patient's consent to treatment may constitute a form of impermissible patient abandonment. Finally, the 'The limitations of fiduciary protections in childbirth' section briefly describes the current limitations of fiduciary law in providing a remedy to patients who experience obstetric violence and the future potential of fiduciary principles to expose and disrupt harmful maternity care practices.

Fiduciary basics: trust and loyalty

Originally developed in courts of equity, a fiduciary relationship derives from the 'conferral of trust on another'.[2] A fiduciary is someone who is 'entrusted with power or property to be used for the benefit of another and legally held to the highest standard of conduct'.[3] Fiduciaries must be loyal to the entrustor and act in a manner that furthers the entrustor's best interests, embodying fairness, honesty, and good faith.[4] The fiduciary typically has specialised knowledge or expertise that the fiduciary uses on behalf of the beneficiary, enabling the fiduciary to 'serve as a substitute for the entrustor'.[5] The fundamental principle of fiduciary obligation is the duty of loyalty to the entrusting party.

When the entrustor seeks a fiduciary's services, the entrustor delegates power to the fiduciary, making the entrustor dependent on the fiduciary. The exercise of this power is solely for the entrustor's benefit, not to serve the interests of the fiduciary.[6] However, there is always a risk that the fiduciary will misuse the

2 Eileen A Scallen, 'Promises Broken vs. Promises Betrayed: Metaphor, Analogy, and the New Fiduciary Principle' (1993) U Ill LR 897, 971.
3 Marc A Rodwin, 'Strains in the Fiduciary Metaphor: Divided Physician Loyalties and Obligations in a Changing Health Care System' (1995) 21 Am J L & Med 241, 243.
4 Deborah A Demott, 'Beyond Metaphor: An Analysis of Fiduciary Obligation' (1998) 48 Duke LJ 879, 882.
5 Tamar Frankel, 'Fiduciary Law' (1983) 71 Calif LR 795, 808.
6 Ibid 809.

power delegated by the entrustor. Thus, fiduciary law has developed to protect the vulnerable entrustor from the potential abuse of power by the fiduciary.[7] In addition to concern about the entrustor's dependence on the fiduciary and the entrustor's resulting vulnerability, fiduciary principles also address the entrustor's inability to protect herself from abuse by the fiduciary. This inability to cover may arise from the loss of power that results from delegation to the fiduciary or from a deficit in knowledge on the part of the entrustor.

In interpreting and applying the fiduciary's obligations, courts are attuned to potential conflicts of interest. Concern for the entrustor's vulnerability shifts the parties' burdens, focusing judicial attention on the fiduciary's violation of duty rather than the injury suffered by the beneficiary. Indeed, a fiduciary may be liable for violating a duty of loyalty even in the absence of a measurable injury on the part of the beneficiary.[8] Rather than require the entrustor to prove actual reliance on the fiduciary, the law permits the entrustor to rely on the trustworthiness of the fiduciary and instead requires the fiduciary to prove fulfilment of his or her duty to the entrustor.[9] In instances of breach, the entrustor is entitled to restitution of the benefit the fiduciary received as a result of the breach, or recovery of any loss suffered due to the breach of duty. The courts' willingness to impose disgorgement as a remedy 'suggests that a betrayal of trust is qualitatively different from an ordinary breach of promise'.[10] Commentators have noted that judicial opinions 'applying the fiduciary constraint are distinctive, among private law cases, in that they frequently and explicitly use the language of moral obligation to justify their outcomes'.[11] The moralistic tone of cases applying fiduciary principles reflects the extent to which fiduciary law is concerned with dependence, vulnerability, the inability to cover – and ultimately betrayal of trust.

Evolving norms: the physician as fiduciary

Fiduciary principles originally applied to trustees, administrators, and bailees, but as the concept has evolved over time, the number of relationships considered to be fiduciary has grown.[12] The twentieth century saw a significant expansion of fiduciary law in response to the complexity of society, as individuals increasingly looked to experts to help them solve problems or navigate their public and private responsibilities.[13] It is in this context that courts began applying fiduciary principles to the doctor-patient relationship.[14]

---

7 Ibid 810, Demott (n 4) 902.
8 Demott (n 4) 905–06.
9 Frankel (n 5) 824.
10 Scallen (n 2) 912.
11 Demott (n 4) 891.
12 Frankel (n 5) 795–96.
13 Ibid 802–04.
14 Ibid 796.

Fiduciary law is useful for understanding the nature and scope of the doctor-patient relationship. Physicians have specialised knowledge and expertise that patients lack; in fact, patients seek doctors who have elite training and extensive clinical experience, leading to situations where the gap between patient and provider knowledge is even wider. Physicians also control patient access to information and treatment; without a doctor's recommendation to obtain a particular type of care, the patient would likely be unaware of the possibility and lack even the basic information necessary to investigate treatment options. Even with the development of more robust informed consent requirements and the greater involvement of patients in medical decision-making as a result, physicians influence how patients sort information about treatment risks, benefits, and alternatives, and can emphasise certain considerations that align with the physicians' values or preferences.

Like other fiduciary relationships, patients are generally unable to assess whether physicians are acting loyally. Some patients do independent research or seek a second opinion and may be well-positioned to interrogate a provider's recommendation, but most patients lack the resources, ability, or time to investigate independently. Ultimately, many patients rely on physicians as medical experts to make treatment decisions for them and are unable to protect themselves adequately from conflicts of interest that bias physician decision-making or other misuse of the physician's power.

Courts across the United States have recognised the physician as a fiduciary and have applied fiduciary principles when analysing doctors' obligations to their patients.[15] In a prominent 1990 case dealing with breach of fiduciary duty arising from a physician conflict of interest, a doctor failed to disclose the extent of his personal economic interest in blood and tissue removed from the patient's body for medical research.[16] When the patient sued, the *Moore* court reasoned that while the fiduciary obligation does not require the fiduciary to sacrifice its own interests entirely, the fiduciary must nevertheless refrain from putting its interests ahead of the beneficiary's interests.[17] A physician must disclose possible conflicts 'not because he has a duty to protect his patient's financial interests, but because certain personal interests may affect professional judgment'.[18]

The *Moore* court focused on the conflict created by the physician's economic interest in the clinical research, but physician conflicts may arise in a variety of

15 *Emmett v E Dispensary & Cas Hosp* 396 F2d 931, 935 (DC Cir 1967) where it is stated that 'We find in the fiducial qualities of [the physician–patient] relationship the physician's duty to reveal to the patient that which in his best interests it is important that he should know'; *Hammonds v Aetna Cas & Sur Co* 243 F Supp 793, 799 (ND Ohio 1965) holding physicians owe patients 'the duty of secrecy' and 'the duty of undivided loyalty'; *Neade v Portes* 710 NE2d 418 (Ill App Ct 1999) recognising existence of fiduciary relationship between physician and patient; *Shadrick v Coker* 963 SW2d 726, 736 (Tenn 1998) same; *Lockett v Goodill* 430 P2d 589, 591 (Wash 1967) where it is stated that 'The relationship of patient and physician is a fiduciary one of the highest degree'.

16 *Moore v Regents of the University of California* 271 Cal Rptr 146 (Cal 1990), cert denied 499 US 936 (1991).

17 Ibid 150–51.

18 Ibid 152, n 10.

other contexts, including the desire to avoid malpractice exposure, obligations to hospitals and third-party payors, and the economic interest in higher reimbursement rates for certain procedures. Such conflicts may influence how a physician counsels a patient about the risks and benefits of treatment. Given the prominence of vulnerability, dependence, and control in the doctor-patient relationship, the fiduciary concept has become the 'dominant metaphor in medical ethics and law today and is presumed by much of the legal and ethical analysis of physicians' conflicts of interest'.[19]

In addition to judicial recognition of the physician as fiduciary, the American Medical Association (AMA) has invoked fiduciary principles in guidance to members about navigating conflicts of interest. The AMA states that conflicts 'must be resolved to the patient's benefit', based on the 'physician's role as a fiduciary, ie a person who, by his undertaking, has a duty to act primarily for another's behalf'.[20] The idea that physicians should put their patients' interests first and avoid personal conflicts of interest that might compromise the physicians' loyalty is also reflected in statements from other medical professional groups, including the American College of Physicians[21] and the American College of Surgeons.[22] The notion of physicians as fiduciaries also forms the implicit basis for an extensive literature on medical ethics, including the concept of patient-centred care.

Applying fiduciary principles to obstetric violence

The moral themes of power, vulnerability, and dependence at the heart of fiduciary law make it a powerful lens through which to analyse claims of obstetric violence. First developed by Latin American women's health advocates, the term obstetric violence refers to a variety of types of conduct ranging in severity from verbal and physical abuse to coercion to subtler forms of humiliation and disrespect. There is no established definition of obstetric violence in the global health literature, but the World Health Organization has recognised that, 'Many women across the globe experience disrespectful, abusive or neglectful treatment during childbirth in facilities', which 'constitutes a violation of trust between women and their health-care providers'.[23] In previous work, I have identified three broad categories of obstetric violence – abuse, coercion, and disrespect – to theorise how different types of conduct cause harm and why

19 Rodwin (n 3) 242.
20 American Medical Association, Report of the Council on Ethical and Judicial Affairs, Report A (I-86): Conflicts of Interest (1986) 11.
21 American College of Physicians Ad Hoc Committee on Medical Ethics, 'American College of Physicians Ethics Manual, Part 1' (1984) 101 Ann Internal Med 129, 134.
22 American College of Surgeons, 'Statements on Principles' (12 April 2016) <www.facs.org/about-acs/statements/stonprin.> accessed 11 February 2019.
23 World Health Organization, 'The Prevention and Elimination of Disrespect and Abuse during Facility-BasedChildbirth'(2015)<http://apps.who.int/iris/bitstream/handle/10665/134588/WHO_RHR_14.23_eng.pdf;jsessionid=3B08D11EE3E3DE1BBB3ADFA59F862A84?sequence=1> (accessed 11 February 2019).

such acts betray patient trust.[24] While the severity of the harm depends on the individual circumstances of the patient, certain dynamics appear consistently in many accounts of obstetric violence.

Women who report obstetric violence often describe provider mistreatment as arising from disagreements at critical decision points during labour and delivery. In particular, the decision of whether to induce or augment labour artificially using medication, whether to pursue a caesarean delivery, or whether to use another medical intervention – such as vacuum delivery or episiotomy – is often the focus of the doctor-patient conflict that leads to abuse or coercion. Each of these practices bears risk of complication, and different women have different levels of risk tolerance, which may vary based on their medical histories, plans for future procreation, and personal, cultural, or religious values. In addition, some practices that are common in US-based maternity care were adopted without rigorous research on their health and safety benefits.[25] A growing body of evidence questioning the wisdom of certain practices – such as restricting access to vaginal birth after caesarean (VBAC), continuous electronic foetal monitoring, restrictions on mobility during labour, or immediate cord clamping – leads some women to question their physicians and decline particular interventions, which, in turn, may lead to heightened conflict between the patient and her care providers. Instead of welcoming these moments as opportunities for more discussion about risks and benefits, or further clarification of values around intervention and manner of delivery, some physicians perceive patient refusal as a challenge to their medical expertise and instead resort to other techniques of obtaining consent – including threatening to obtain a court order compelling treatment, reporting the woman to child welfare authorities, or using fear to pressure the patient.

In addition to conflict with physicians over treatment decisions, another consistent feature of women's accounts of obstetric violence is silence about the experience, along with feelings of shame. Women stay silent about mistreatment during childbirth for various reasons. Strong privacy norms that protect health information make some people reticent to discuss their medical care publicly. For some patients, it takes time to identify what happened during the delivery that made the experience painful or traumatic – especially when dealing with the demands of newborn care and postpartum healing. Others may fear their complaints will not be believed, will be trivialised, or will be too traumatic to share. Shame is also a powerful silencer; women may blame themselves for not being more assertive about their decisions or not resisting more forcefully once

---

24 Elizabeth Kukura, 'Obstetric Violence' (2018) 106 Geo LJ 721, 728–54. Existing research on obstetric violence suggests that certain women in the United States experience obstetric violence at disproportionately higher rates – especially women of color, poor women, young women, and religious minorities – whether due to disadvantages that make them especially vulnerable to abuse of power by a physician or due to heightened concern about complications in future pregnancies.

25 Judith Pence Rooks, *Midwifery and Childbirth in America* (1997) 25.

they experienced pressure to consent. The idea that a physician would betray a patient's trust is hard for many people to accept. Family members may encourage a woman to acquiesce 'because the doctor knows best', reflecting the dissonance they feel when observing doctor-patient conflict. When women do speak up about mistreatment, they often hear a consistent message, 'but you have a healthy baby, so just be grateful'. While this sentiment may reflect society's understandable discomfort with the possibility of mistreatment by healthcare providers, it minimises women's experiences of harm. It can be difficult to understand how a woman might have a healthy baby and also suffer deep emotional wounds as a result of being abused or coerced while giving birth. The violation of trust between a doctor and patient may be challenging to confront – and even harder to put into words.

The remainder of this section will draw on fiduciary principles to show how certain types of conduct reflect problematic breaches of physician loyalty. The first section identifies various physician conflicts of interest that should be disclosed to maternity care patients, including economic incentives that influence clinical decision-making, liability avoidance, internal hospital policies that dictate physician conduct without patient knowledge, and the perceived duty to treat the foetus as a separate patient. 'Invoking the language of maternal-foetal conflict' then considers how the framing of doctor-patient disagreements as 'maternal-fetal conflict' reflects a breach of physician loyalty to the pregnant patient. Finally, 'Coercion as patient abandonment' suggests that VBAC restrictions – along with other coercive practices that require women to relinquish their rights in order to continue receiving care – are a form of impermissible patient abandonment.

Competing loyalties and conflicts of interest

Fiduciary law concerns itself with disloyalty that results from competing commitments or interests on the part of the fiduciary. Such conflicts of interest – whether economic, legal, or moral in nature – may influence how the physician counsels the patient about treatment options. Where such conflicts of interest are obscured from the patient, she is unable to protect herself from harm by investigating whether the conflict has indeed influenced the physician's conduct.

Economic incentives

Healthcare in the United States is big business, with healthcare spending constituting nearly 18 per cent of gross domestic product in 2016[26] and maternity care representing the largest category of hospital reimbursements for most

---

26 Irene Papanicolas, Liana R Woskie, and Ashish K Jha, 'Health Care Spending in the United States and Other High-Income Countries' (*Jama*, 13 March 2018) <https://jamanetwork.com/journals/jama/fullarticle/2674671> accessed 11 February 2019.

public and private insurers.[27] It is the rare physician whose professional life is untouched by financial concerns, whether related to reimbursement rates, hospital economics, provider compensation, the cost of malpractice insurance, high drug prices, or the availability of research funds. In maternity care, there are economic incentives that influence physicians' practice of medicine, either implicitly or explicitly. For-profit hospitals are concerned with producing value for their shareholders, implementing policies designed to maximise the financial bottom line, and non-profit hospitals often pursue similar strategies in order to compete with for-profit institutions. Research demonstrates that a procedure's price tag may influence clinical decision-making by healthcare providers. For example, higher reimbursement rates for caesarean deliveries, combined with the need for longer hospitalisation and related ancillary procedures (including anaesthesia), incentivise physicians to recommend caesareans in the absence of medical necessity.[28] Hospitals report higher caesarean rates for women with private, fee-for-service insurance than for women covered by public insurance, women who lack insurance coverage, or women covered by health maintenance organisations that limit reimbursement per patient.[29] Other research has linked differences in caesarean rates with the profit orientation of the hospital or the likelihood of increased reimbursement for caesarean deliveries.[30]

Financial incentives lurk elsewhere in maternity care. The availability of increased payment for additional tests and procedures may influence a physician's assessment of their necessity or value. Many routine actions associated with delivery – including administration of intravenous (IV) fluids, bladder catheterisation, rupture of membranes to release amniotic fluid, foetal monitoring, episiotomy, shaving pubic hair, epidural anaesthesia, and forceps-assisted or vacuum-assisted delivery – may result in additional fees about which the patient is unaware. At best, such interventions are benign, causing minor disruption, annoyance, or discomfort, in addition to the added expense. But some procedures that are considered routine or mundane may have important clinical consequences. For example, artificial rupture of the membranes may be offered to expedite contractions, but it can also shorten the amount of time a woman is able to labour naturally before the doctor recommends a caesarean to prevent possible infection; a woman who does not know that the intervention her physician recommends increases the physician's reimbursement rate, while starting the countdown clock to an unnecessary or unwanted caesarean, cannot advocate

---

27 Elisabeth Rosenthal, 'American Way of Birth, Costliest in the World' (*The New York Times*, 30 June 2013) <www.nytimes.com/2013/07/01/health/american-way-of-birth-costliest-in-the-world.html> accessed 11 February 2019.

28 Kukura (n 24) 767.

29 Emmett B Keeler and Mollyann Brodie, 'Economic Incentives in the Choice between Vaginal Delivery and Cesarean Section' (1993) 71 Milbank Q 365, 374.

30 Jonathan Gruber and Maria Owings, 'Physician Financial Incentives and Cesarean Section Delivery' (1996) 27 Rand J Econ 99. Nathanael Johnson, 'For-profit Hospitals Performing More C-sections' (*California Watch*, 13 September 2010) <https://khn.org/news/californiawatch-profit-hospitals-performing-more-c-sections/> accessed 11 February 2019.

adequately on her own behalf because she lacks relevant information that her fiduciary has withheld.

Similarly, administration of IV fluids or foetal monitoring may be desirable from the provider's perspective, as they increase the amount of reimbursement the hospital can seek and enable providers to follow standard protocols for all labouring patients, but being attached to an IV pole and foetal monitor limit the pregnant person's mobility, preventing gravity from assisting the foetus' descent and precluding the patient from finding more comfortable positions in which to labour. Less mobility often means longer labours or more surgical deliveries because the physician is concerned that too much time has elapsed. The influence of economic incentives on physicians may be subconscious, but the relationship between reimbursement and clinical decision-making is sufficiently established to make it reasonable to expect physician disclosure of the difference in cost, or the existence of separately billed fees, to patients who are deciding between multiple treatments.

Maternity care providers also face pressure to keep patient care flowing at a fast pace, making beds available for additional patients. Because more patients delivering at the hospital means more revenue, physicians may be encouraged to apply stricter enforcement of guidelines on how long active labour should last or how long a woman should push before a caesarean is encouraged. Concern about efficiency may also incentivise the use of interventions to hasten labour or expedite delivery, even when not medically indicated. There has been some reporting in the popular press on the control of delivery timing for provider convenience, highlighting research that shows more babies are born on weekdays than on weekends.[31] But without physician disclosure of potential economic conflicts of interest, patients are unlikely to be aware of the role that revenue generation for hospitals and physicians may play in shaping clinical recommendations.

Avoidance of malpractice exposure

Because obstetricians face the highest malpractice insurance premiums of all physicians in the United States, fear of malpractice and the perception of high malpractice risk loom large for many maternity care providers. Seeking to minimise liability, some hospitals and individual providers adopt policies that deviate from evidence-based principles and put women and their babies at greater risk of complications. Two common examples of such policies are VBAC restrictions and mandatory electronic foetal monitoring.

---

31 Lena H Sun, 'What Time of Day Are Most Babies Born?' (*The Washington Post*, 8 May 2015) <www.washingtonpost.com/news/to-your-health/wp/2015/05/08/what-time-of-day-are-most-u-s-babies-born/?noredirect=on&utm_term=.3d2c84e75eb2> accessed 11 February 2019; Zan Armstrong, 'Why Are so Many Babies Born Around 8:00 A.M.?' (*Scientific American*, 20 June 2017) <https://blogs.scientificamerican.com/sa-visual/why-are-so-many-babies-born-around-8-00-a-m/> accessed 11 February 2019.

Restrictions on VBAC are perhaps the most common form of coercion in the US maternity care system, with hundreds of hospitals and providers preventing women with scars from previous caesareans from delivering vaginally during subsequent births. With approximately one-third of all births ending in caesarean surgery, widespread restrictions on access to VBAC mean that many women will have surgical births in later pregnancies, regardless of whether a caesarean is medically indicated.[32] But research shows that for women experiencing low-risk pregnancies, VBAC presents a lower risk of complications than elective repeat caesarean.[33] The risk of uterine rupture during VBAC – usually caused by an opening of the prior caesarean scar, necessitating surgery – is less than one per cent, even with multiple scars,[34] and the risk of infant death resulting from rupture is approximately 1 in 2,000.[35] A pregnant person's risk of emergency hysterectomy or death is statistically no different between VBAC and repeat caesarean, but a caesarean imposed due to VBAC restrictions increases the risk of complications associated with caesareans, including maternal death, blood clots and stroke, surgical injury, longer hospitalisation, rehospitalisation, infection, poor birth experience, less early contact with babies (with negative impact on breastfeeding, bonding, and regulation of infant body temperature and maternal hormones), intense and prolonged postpartum pain, poor overall mental health, and poor overall functioning.[36]

The decision to pursue VBAC requires thoughtful weighing of risks and benefits, but VBAC-restrictive policies convey the message that VBAC is undoubtedly a riskier choice. Because successful obstetrics malpractice claims overwhelmingly result from infant injury or death, rather than maternal birth injury due to caesarean, physicians perceive that they lessen their malpractice exposure by recommending caesarean delivery, even when not medically necessary. Failure to disclose the potential consequences of VBAC restrictions on patient health and well-being – suggesting, contrary to the evidence, that elective repeat caesarean is necessarily the safer choice – is a violation of the physician's fiduciary duty. Furthermore, failure to disclose the true basis for that policy – protecting

---

32 Joyce A Martin and others, 'Births: Final Data for 2015' (National Vital Statistics System, US Dept of Health and Human Services 2017) 9.

33 Elizabeth Kukura, 'Contested Care: The Limitations of Evidence-Based Maternity Care Reform' (2016) 31 Berkeley J Gender L & Just 241, 269–70; John Zweifler and others, 'Vaginal Birth after Cesarean in California: Before and after a Change in Guidelines' (2006) 4 Annals Fam Med 228, 230.

34 Mark B Landon and others, 'Risk of Uterine Rupture with a Trial of Labor in Women with Multiple and Single Prior Cesarean Delivery' (2006) 108 Obstet Gynecol 12; Mona Lydon-Rochelle and others, 'Risk of Uterine Rupture during Labor among Women with a Prior Cesarean Delivery' (2001) 345 New Eng J Med 3. The incidence of rupture is even lower when no drugs are used to induce or augment labour. Ron Gonen and others, 'Results of a Well-Defined Protocol for a Trial of Labor after Prior Cesarean Delivery' (2006) 107 Obstet Gynecol 240, 243.

35 Lydon-Rochelle (n 34) 7.

36 Carol Sakala, 'Vaginal or Cesarean Birth?: A Systematic Review to Determine What Is at Stake for Mothers and Babies' (Childbirth Connection 2006) 3–4.

the hospital and provider from liability exposure, rather than protecting the patient from safety risk – is also a violation of the physician's duty of loyalty to the patient.

Continuous electronic foetal monitoring (EFM) enables doctors and nurses to capture real-time foetal heart rate data; the labouring patient wears a band across the belly to secure the monitor, which transmits information to a computer. Hospitals adopted EFM widely in the 1970s to prevent cerebral palsy, but subsequent research indicates that regular use of EFM has not reduced its incidence.[37] Nevertheless, hospitals continue to use EFM routinely because the easy-to-read tracings lessen the burden of malpractice defense should a birth result in litigation. Continuous EFM also enables a higher patient-to-nurse ratio, as nurses can monitor multiple patients simultaneously through a central portal located at the nurses' station. This results in less personal interaction on the labour and delivery floor, along with less support for the labouring patient.

Not only does continuous EFM interfere with personal support for the patient, it also restricts pregnant patients' mobility during labour, disrupting the ability of gravity to assist with the foetus' descent into the birth canal. EFM also inhibits the use of water as a natural form of pain relief; labouring patients cannot sit in the tub to ease the intensity of contractions while holding the monitor in place. Thus, EFM can prolong the duration of labour and increase reliance on pain medication, both of which increase the likelihood of further intervention such as forceps, vacuum, or caesarean. In addition, EFM sometimes results in false positives that prompt physicians to recommend caesarean. For all of these reasons, research links use of continuous EFM to the high rate of medically unnecessary caesareans in the United States.[38] Labouring patients are led to believe that continuous EFM increases safety during childbirth and does not pose risk of harm. Women who try to decline continuous EFM in order to maintain mobility or take a shower report being told they cannot opt to remove the monitor, despite the existence of alternative evidence-based methods of monitoring foetal heart rate.[39] The failure of physicians to disclose the risks of prolonged labour, increased likelihood of intervention, and resulting need for further treatment to address the side effects of those interventions violates their fiduciary duty to patients. The use of continuous EFM for liability-minimising purposes without discussion of the potential consequences reflects an undisclosed conflict of interest that precludes the patient from making an informed decision.

The desire to minimise liability exposure may influence how physicians counsel patients about treatment options in other contexts. For example, a doctor who has previously been sued for complications related to a breech delivery may steer patients away from vaginal breech delivery without counseling the patient

---

37 Rebecca Dekker, 'The Evidence on: Fetal Monitoring' (*Evidence Based Birth*, 17 July 2012, updated 21 May 2018) <https://evidencebasedbirth.com/fetal-monitoring/> accessed 11 February 2019.

38 Ibid.

39 Ibid.

about risks of caesarean delivery or the possibility of external cephalic version to resolve the breech position. Steering a patient towards a particular treatment without information about potential risks and benefits means the physician has prioritised his or her own interest in improving the physician's malpractice record over the patient's best interests. With specialised training in obstetrics, the physician can control what information the patient has and how she weighs different risks and benefits against one another. Without disclosure of the conflict, the patient is unlikely to be aware of the physician's specific interest in avoiding malpractice liability and is unlikely to have information about the physician's prior experience with malpractice litigation. It is understandable that physicians may be more cautious than usual after a bad outcome with a patient, but where fear of litigation produces biased counseling in favour of elective repeat caesarean without disclosure of the risks to future fertility, or results in any counseling without information about potential risks and benefits, the physician is violating the duty of loyalty.

Internal hospital policies

Some hospitals have developed explicit policies in anticipation of conflict between a physician and pregnant patient who declines recommended treatment. When a physician practicing at a hospital that maintains such a policy fails to disclose its existence to pregnant patients, the physician violates his duty of loyalty. The recent case of Dray has illustrated the impact of internal policies on pregnant patients' ability to refuse treatment. In 2011, Dray sought care at Staten Island University Hospital (SIUH) because she wanted to deliver vaginally after two previous caesareans and SIUH boasted higher VBAC rates than other area hospitals.[40] As a Hasidic Jew, Dray hoped to have a large family and thus was motivated to avoid another caesarean in order to reduce the risk of complications in future pregnancies. When she went into labour, the doctor on-call at the hospital began pressuring her to consent to a caesarean, despite the lack of any complications. The doctor continued to insist on a caesarean, telling her 'that she would be committing the equivalent of child abuse and that her baby would be taken away from her' if she did not consent.[41] The doctor consulted the director of maternal-foetal medicine and the hospital attorney, who advised that no court order was necessary to compel Dray to undergo unwanted surgery; the director noted in Dray's chart that she was competent to refuse surgery but that he was overriding her refusal to consent, and the doctors performed the caesarean as she continued to beg for more time to labour.[42] Dray delivered a healthy baby by caesarean, but the doctor cut her bladder in the process, an injury requiring further surgery.[43]

40 Anemona Hartocollis, 'Mother Accuses Doctors of Forcing a C-Section and Files Suit' (*The New York Times*, 16 May 2014) <www.nytimes.com/2014/05/17/nyregion/mother-accuses-doctors-of-forcinga-c-section-and-files-suit.html> accessed 11 February 2019.

41 Ibid.

42 Ibid.

43 Ibid.

In subsequent litigation, the hospital disclosed that it maintained a policy regarding situations where a pregnant patient refuses treatment. The policy applies when several doctors agree that the treatment bears a 'reasonable possibility of significant benefit' to the foetus that 'outweigh[s] the possible risks to the woman' and the doctor has made 'reasonable efforts to persuade the pregnant woman to change her mind'.[44] If the patient continues to decline a caesarean, the policy provided that the attending physician, director of obstetrics, and the hospital's legal department may authorise treatment without the patient's consent, overriding the refusal without seeking a court order.[45] Under the policy, a physician may override the patient's wishes immediately, at his or her sole discretion, if the physician deems it to be an emergency situation.[46] This concentrates tremendous power in the physician, especially in a field of medicine where reasonable physicians often disagree among themselves about how best to balance treatment risks and benefits.

Dray's attorneys have subsequently characterised SIUH's caesarean protocol as a 'secret policy', as it was never disclosed during Dray's prenatal care or labour.[47] The fact that the hospital maintained an undisclosed policy of overriding a competent patient's caesarean refusal without judicial intervention is a breach of the physicians' fiduciary duty. In the wake of the Dray litigation, investigative reporting has identified the existence of similar policies at other New York-area hospitals.[48] That this practice extends to other regional facilities suggests that hospitals across the United States may also maintain 'secret' policies about which patients are never informed but which may dramatically impact their medical care during childbirth.

In addition to policies that explicitly override a patient's informed refusal, hospitals and individual providers may maintain other unidentified policies or practices that can lead a physician to disregard a patient's best interests in service of other goals. Some women are told they must undergo labour induction once they have reached a certain point in pregnancy, regardless of whether induction is medically indicated under the circumstances. Others are told after they have laboured for a prescribed amount of time that they must have a caesarean

---

44 Molly Redden, 'New York Hospital's Secret Policy Led to Woman Being Given C-Section against Her Will' (*The Guardian*, 5 October 2017) <www.theguardian.com/us-news/2017/oct/05/new-york-staten-island-university-hospital-c-section-ethics-medicine> accessed 11 February 2019.

45 Ibid.

46 Ibid. This policy conflicts with 2014 guidance issued by the American Academy of Pediatrics and the American College of Obstetricians and Gynecologists, which declared: 'Even the strongest evidence for fetal benefit would not be sufficient ethically to override a pregnant woman's decision to forgo fetal treatment'. The American College of Obstetricians & Gynecologists, American Academy of Pediatrics, Committee Opinion No 501, 'Maternal-Fetal Intervention and Fetal Care Centers' (*ACOG*, August 2011) <www.acog.org/Clinical-Guidance-and-Publications/Committee-Opinions/Committee-on-Ethics/Maternal-Fetal-Intervention-and-Fetal-Care-Centers> accessed 11 February 2019.

47 Redden (n 44).

48 Ibid.

without reference to specific medical necessity. Women who question the need for intervention are often informed they must comply because 'it is hospital policy'. Most patients in such situations believe they have no options other than to acquiesce, whether because they are unaware of their legal rights, are uncomfortable challenging the medical expertise of doctors, or realise they have nowhere else to obtain maternity care. In active labour, it is unlikely that a patient would be able to review underlying documentation detailing the policies invoked by the physician, if it even exists; it is also rare that patients have access to a patient advocate or hospital ethicist to help the parties navigate the situation. In short, the pregnant patient is powerless, lacking information and resources to advocate on her own behalf and no longer able to trust that the physician is prioritising her needs. Hospital policies become tools for providers to coerce consent from unwilling patients, enabled in part by the lack of disclosure of such policies during prenatal care, hospital tours, or the labouring woman's admission to the hospital. Where patient care is influenced by such policies and the physician has not disclosed the policy to the patient, the physician violates his duty of loyalty by prioritising other concerns over the patient's best interests.

Two-patient model of care

The concept of the two-patient model of maternity care developed in the mid-twentieth century alongside the emergence of the ultrasound, which enabled a physician to visualise the foetus and make foetal diagnoses that were previously beyond the physician's capabilities.[49] Doctors began to understand themselves as caring for two separate patients, despite the fact that the foetus is entirely dependent on the woman for survival and flourishing. Legal scholar Oberman has described how the two-patient model that dominates modern US-based maternity care reflects flawed legal and ethical reasoning in that the pregnant patient is the only one with capacity to consent to medical treatment.[50] In healthcare, the doctor-patient relationship is understood to begin when the patient seeks care (except in situations involving mentally incapacitated patients or emergencies where the patient is unconscious). Therefore, the physician has no basis on which to adopt the foetus as a separate patient in the absence of consent by the foetus or the foetus' guardian – which properly puts the focus back on the woman and her informed decision-making.

Concern for foetal well-being is an important component of high-quality maternity care, but when a physician pursues the interests of the foetus as a separate patient, the quality of care provided to the pregnant patient may suffer.

49 FA Manning, 'Reflections on Future Directions of Perinatal Medicine' (1989) 13 Semin Perinatol 342; J Whitridge Williams, Jack A Pritchard, and Paul C MacDonald, *Williams Obstetrics* (16th edn, Appleton-Century-Crofts 1980) where it is stated that 'Happily, we have entered an era in which the fetus can be rightfully considered and treated as our second patient'.

50 Michelle Oberman, '"Mothers and Doctors" Orders: Unmasking the Doctor's Fiduciary Role in Maternal-Fetal Conflicts' (2000) 94 Nw U L Rev 451, 472.

Such divided loyalties can impact the type of disclosure, counseling, and support a patient receives from the physician when facing a decision about medical care. Similarly, a woman who made an informed decision about what treatment to accept or decline may encounter hostility from a physician who is harbouring a separate loyalty to the foetus. For example, in 1996, when Pemberton was pregnant for the second time, she decided to deliver at her home in Florida because she could not locate a provider to support her informed decision to pursue a VBAC.[51] Wanting a large family, she sought to avoid an unnecessary caesarean and the risks it would pose in future pregnancies. After labouring for about a day without complication, she decided to seek IV fluids at the hospital to avoid dehydration. The doctors considered VBAC too risky for the foetus and refused to provide fluids unless she consented to a caesarean, even though there was no indication a caesarean was medically necessary. A sympathetic nurse alerted Pemberton that the hospital intended to pursue a court order compelling her to submit to surgery, so she left the hospital surreptitiously and returned home to continue active labour. Shortly thereafter, the sheriff and state's attorney came to her house and forced her to return to the hospital, strapping her legs together on the stretcher. Ultimately, the judge granted an order compelling the surgery, even though Pemberton could feel the foetus progressing into her birth canal, signalling that delivery was imminent. Pemberton's subsequent legal challenge for negligence, false imprisonment, and violation of her constitutional rights was dismissed.[52] In rejecting her claims, the court accepted the hospital's arguments that its action was necessary to protect the foetus.[53]

Although adherence to the two-patient model of care differs from more familiar types of physician conflicts involving financial interests, this type of divided loyalty arises regularly in maternity care. A physician who perceives risk to the foetus may not inform a woman about potential courses of treatment that she would prefer. Similarly, a physician acting on behalf of the foetus as a second patient may discourage a woman from pursuing surgery she considers worthwhile or pressure a woman to accept unwanted intervention. Failure to disclose that the physician believes himself to be serving two patients means that the pregnant patient has incomplete information about the motivations and biases of the physician on whom she relies for comprehensive and accurate medical information. If it is possible that a physician will force unwanted treatment on a pregnant patient based on the physician's perceived obligation to the foetus as a second patient, the pregnant patient deserves to have this information in order to be able to protect herself adequately from abuse of power by the physician as fiduciary – whether by discussing this scenario in advance, obtaining legal counsel, or seeking maternity care elsewhere.[54]

---

51 *Pemberton v Tallahassee* Mem'l Reg'l Med Ctr, 66 F Supp 2d 1247, 1249 (ND Fla 1999).
52 Ibid 1250.
53 Ibid (n 2) 1251–54.
54 Oberman (n 50) 497–99.

Invoking the language of maternal-foetal conflict

As the two-patient model of maternity care has taken hold, language has developed to describe situations where the woman's decision-making is perceived to conflict with foetal interests. The term 'maternal-fetal conflict' is used to describe this dynamic both in clinical settings and in the academic literature. Where maternal-foetal conflict language is invoked, the phrase usually reflects the physician's treatment preference. The physician identifies his recommendation as promoting of foetal health and safety, and a pregnant patient who disagrees is characterised as neglectful of foetal well-being. This framing ignores how concern for the foetus has factored into the patient's decision about a preferred course of treatment. For example, rather than assume a woman who declines a caesarean has determined that the potential benefits to her baby of vaginal delivery – such as increased newborn lung function and natural production of oxytocin to support breastfeeding – make vaginal delivery more desirable than a caesarean, the idea of maternal-foetal conflict predisposes the physician to scepticism, viewing her disagreement as a sign of selfishness or disregard for the foetus.

By asserting his treatment preference under the guise of foetal protection, the physician subordinates his duty to the pregnant patient to his perceived duty to the foetus.[55] In this way, the adoption of maternal-foetal conflict language violates fiduciary principles because it enables the doctor to assert his own values over the patient's values in the name of protecting the foetus. Oberman argues that it would be more appropriate to refer to these situations as 'maternal-doctor conflicts', as they involve 'doctors' seemingly well-motivated efforts to promote maternal or foetal well-being by imposing their perception of appropriate medical care on their pregnant patients.[56] In such situations, the physician 'invests the fetus with interests and rights that directly coincide with his own personal treatment preferences', making the doctor a 'seemingly neutral arbitrator' settling the 'conflict'.[57] The language of maternal-foetal conflict obscures the extent to which the physician has helped create and extend the conflict by not heeding the wishes of the competent adult patient.[58]

Maternal-foetal conflict language is powerful. It conceptually cleaves apart the mother and baby, even though they remain physically intertwined and interdependent. There are a variety of ways that a woman and the foetus she carries impact each other negatively during and after pregnancy, but this results in so-called maternal-foetal conflict in only a narrow set of circumstances. For example, a woman who develops gestational diabetes during pregnancy has an increased risk of developing type-II diabetes later in life, but society does not understand this as a moment of conflict between a woman and her foetus or attempt to find fault, even where the risk of subsequent adverse health outcome

---

55 Ibid 477.
56 Ibid 454.
57 Ibid.
58 Ibid 455, 482.

is significant. Instead, a physician will recommend appropriate monitoring and treatment to minimise the risk of harm. Although maternal and foetal interests could be deemed to 'conflict' in a variety of circumstances, it seems clear that maternal-foetal conflict is unidirectional: it refers to maternal interests that are perceived to threaten foetal interests.

Indeed, the one-sidedness of maternal-foetal conflict is reflected in the language of the SIUH 'secret' policy that was invoked to justify Dray's unconsented caesarean: 'Because of the physiologic dependence of the fetus on the pregnant woman, the burden of consequences of her actions on the fetus should be taken into account by her doctors and staff'.[59] The nature of pregnancy means that the pregnant person bears responsibility for the well-being of another, and society measures her actions against the archetype of a self-sacrificing mother – one who sacrifices her body and self to satisfy the needs of her child.[60] But although women bear this maternal responsibility, the decisions they make in service of this responsibility are not always respected by healthcare providers. A woman who asks for more information, questions a recommendation, or disagrees with a treatment decision suggested by her doctor may be accused of acting selfishly, elevating her own interests above the interests of her foetus, even when the decision rests on the woman's belief that her preferred course of treatment is in the best interests of the foetus.

The framing of clinical disagreements as maternal-foetal conflict reflects the influence of abortion jurisprudence, which explicitly balances the woman's interests in avoiding pregnancy against the state's interest in potential life. Starting with the Supreme Court's *Roe v Wade* decision in 1973, US abortion law and policy have developed within a framework that weighs maternal and foetal interests against each other.[61] Where courts have been asked to order a woman to submit to caesarean surgery, or have heard subsequent challenges to compelled treatment, they look to abortion doctrine for guidance and reason that if the state's interest in potential life is significant enough after viability to overcome a woman's interest in avoiding pregnancy, it must be significant enough to outweigh her interest in avoiding a caesarean – typically characterised as a misleadingly neutral 'manner of delivery', rather than major abdominal surgery.[62] Although abortion and childbirth are two distinct reproductive experiences, the balancing of interests in the abortion context has been uncritically imported into the childbirth context in the form of perceived maternal-foetal conflict, eroding the woman's ability to direct the course of her own medical care. In this way, the interest-weighing of abortion law and the language of maternal-foetal conflict operate together to reinforce the misconception that a baby needs protection from its mother.

59 Redden (n 44).
60 Kukura (n 24) 776.
61 *Roe v Wade* 410 US 113 (1973).
62 Pemberton (n 51) 1251–52. Elizabeth Kukura, 'Revisiting *Roe* to Advance Reproductive Justice for Childbearing Women' (2018) 94 Notre Dame L Rev Online 20, 21–22.

The language of maternal-foetal conflict thrusts the pregnant patient into conflict with her own foetus. By applying this label to the situation, the doctor enables other third parties – including hospital administrators, lawyers, and the state – to identify the pregnant patient as violating a norm and acting inappropriately as a mother. This strengthens the ability of the physician to coerce the patient into consenting to unwanted treatment, or simply emboldens the doctor to override the patient's refusal. When the doctor exposes the patient to the risk of such regulation, the doctor breaches his or her duty of loyalty to the patient. The invocation of maternal-foetal conflict language serves to diminish the pregnant patient and her autonomy – violating the physician's fiduciary duty to the patient.

Coercion as patient abandonment

Many of the coercive tactics women report experiencing during childbirth essentially amount to an ultimatum: 'Consent to this treatment or I will not provide any care at all'. By conditioning continued care on the patient's willingness to cede her right to informed consent, this type of threat constitutes a form of patient abandonment. If the patient is unwilling to sacrifice her rights, she can no longer rely on the physician to provide needed medical care. A physician who abandons a patient during treatment violates his fiduciary duty to the patient, betraying the patient's trust and violating the duty of loyalty at the core of the relationship.

The most prominent example of coercion as patient abandonment occurs in the form of VBAC restrictions. At the very least, current research supports the position that women should have a choice between VBAC and repeat caesarean, and should be encouraged to consider a trial of labour after a caesarean (TOLAC) to be a safe and reasonable option in the absence of individual risk factors.[63] Women who live in VBAC deserts – without a hospital or provider willing to support their VBAC attempt – have the choice of elective repeat caesarean, relocating to another region where VBAC is accessible, or attempting an unassisted home birth. Given that most women lack the ability to move elsewhere to give birth and fear attempting delivery without support, they form a relationship with a healthcare provider where the foundation of the relationship is a coercive ultimatum.

Other coercive practices may similarly breach a physician's fiduciary duty to the patient by making the patient choose between unwanted treatment or foregoing physician care entirely. When a care provider withholds treatment or threatens to withhold treatment, the physician engages in a form of emotional manipulation to secure the patient's consent. Women have reported that their physicians have threatened to withdraw care while in active labour if they do not agree to labour augmentation with Pitocin or have threatened to withhold epidural anaesthesia

63 See (n 34).

if they do not consent to a caesarean.[64] A woman in this situation has nowhere to go; once in active labour, it is unlikely she can comfortably get up and leave the hospital. Even if she could, she may not have access to another hospital willing to treat her, or any other hospital in the area at all, meaning that she has no alternative but to consent to the unwanted treatment. When a physician uses coercion to secure a patient's acquiescence to unwanted treatment, the physician prioritises something other than the patient's stated interests and should be considered to have breached the physician's fiduciary duty to the patient.[65]

The limitations of fiduciary protections in childbirth

Fiduciary law is well-suited to holding physicians responsible for obstetric violence because it accounts for patient dependence and vulnerability by shifting the burden of proof to the fiduciary. When a conflict arises between a fiduciary and entrustor, the fiduciary must show that it dealt fairly with the entrustor – in contrast to other areas of law where the party alleging breach bears the burden of proof.[66] Furthermore, the harm caused by a breach of fiduciary duty 'is less tangible and more dignitary in nature', making the fiduciary concept useful for identifying and explaining physician misconduct in the maternity care context.[67] But in practice, the enforcement of fiduciary law against physicians is weak, limiting its immediate application for patients harmed by obstetric violence. The doctor-patient fiduciary relationship currently lacks a framework of regulation and oversight comparable to other fiduciaries.[68]

Courts hold physicians liable for breaching their fiduciary duties to patients in a limited set of circumstances. Judges may enforce a physician's duty to keep information confidential, to disclose financial interests in medical research, and to refrain from abandoning patients, as well as the duty to obtain informed consent.[69] Beyond these specific duties, licensing boards and medical associations have not explicitly defined the duties of a physician as fiduciary or any legal consequences for the violation of such duties.[70] In effect, a physician is likely to be held liable for breach of fiduciary duty only when such a breach also constitutes medical malpractice,[71] limiting the utility of fiduciary principles to address misconduct that is currently beyond the reach of tort law.[72]

---

64 Kukura (n 24) 750–51.
65 Oberman (n 50) 477.
66 Demott (n 4) 900.
67 Oberman (n 50) 490.
68 Rodwin (n 3) 242.
69 Ibid 247–48. *Canterbury v Spence* 464 F2d 772, 780 (DC Cir), cert denied 409 US 1064 (1972); *Miller v Kennedy* 522 P2d 852, 860 (Wash Ct App 1974), aff 'd 530 P2d 334 (1975); *Cobbs v Grant* 502 P2d 1, 7–8 (Cal 1972); *Lockett v Goodill* 430 P2d 589, 591 (Wash 1967); *Hammonds v Aetna Cas & Sur Co* 243 F Supp 793, 801–02 (D Ohio 1965).
70 Rodwin (n 3) 249–51.
71 Oberman (n 50) 459.
72 Kukura (n 24) 779–90.

But enforcement of fiduciary principles in medicine does not have to be weak. Fiduciary law can and should be responsive to claims by patients that physicians have violated their fiduciary duties by coercing unwanted treatment or engaging in other forms of obstetric violence. The process of developing appropriate regulation requires courts to focus on the potential for abuse of power by the fiduciary in the specific context in which that fiduciary exercises power.[73] To make fiduciary law a meaningful source of protection and redress for patients harmed by obstetric violence, courts should enforce rules to prevent physician conflicts of interest from influencing maternity care decision-making. Such enforcement would require enhanced scrutiny of how physicians counsel patients about their options during labour and delivery, including whether and how physicians discuss potential conflicts related to economic interests (of physicians or the hospitals where they work), concerns about minimising malpractice exposure, the existence of blanket policies that may impede patients' access to care, or a perceived duty to the foetus as a second patient. Holding physicians accountable for failure to disclose competing loyalties would shed light on practices that strip pregnant people of their autonomy and dignity during childbirth but which are so common that they seem unexceptional. By recasting these practices, such as the use of coercion to obtain consent to caesarean surgery, as impermissible breaches of loyalty, the law would provide more meaningful protection to the vulnerable and dependent parties in the typical doctor-patient relationship.

Outside the medical context, a plaintiff alleging breach of fiduciary duty does not bear the burden of establishing that an injury resulted from the breach, but the equivalent rule does not exist as applied to physicians.[74] Similarly, when non-physician fiduciary conduct is challenged, courts require fiduciaries to prove they have not violated the trust of the beneficiary, but this requirement does not apply in medicine.[75] Applying this rule to physician breaches of patient loyalty would provide a potential avenue for recourse to patients who experience obstetric violence. Rather than having to prove that a physician conflict caused the physician to subordinate the patient's interests to other physician concerns, the law would put the onus on the physician to show that the conflict did not interfere with the physician's loyalty to the patient. As courts continue to articulate the fiduciary duties of physicians, they should pay attention to the value of burden-shifting in ensuring that the party with less knowledge and expertise can adequately protect herself from abuse.

Currently, doctors 'pose as fiduciaries to their pregnant patients' but are unaccountable as such to the patients they serve.[76] Courts should be troubled by the 'gap between the fiduciary ideal and practice' in medicine, especially when grappling with birth injury claims arising out of obstetric violence.[77] As fidu-

---

73 Frankel (n 5) 818.
74 Oberman (n 50) 490.
75 Rodwin (n 3) 249.
76 Oberman (n 50) 482.
77 Rodwin (n 3) 247.

ciary norms continue to evolve, advocates should press for the strengthening of fiduciary law as applied to physicians. This doctrine fills a need that remains unsatisfied by tort law and other legal frameworks; it is precisely because obstetric violence constitutes a fundamental betrayal of patient trust, involves an imbalance between physician and patient in terms of informational resources and power, and reflects a profound dignitary harm that development of robust regulation of physicians as fiduciaries is a worthwhile pursuit for advocates concerned about coercion and abuse in maternity care.

Table of cases

Canterbury v Spence 464 F2d 772 (DC Cir), cert denied 409 US 1064 (1972)
Cobbs v Grant 502 P2d 1 (Cal 1972)
Emmett v E Dispensary & Cas Hosp 396 F2d 931 (DC Cir 1967)
Hammonds v Aetna Cas & Sur Co 243 F Supp 793 (ND Ohio 1965)
Hammonds v Aetna Cas & Sur Co 243 F Supp 793 (D Ohio 1965)
Lockett v Goodill 430 P2d 589 (Wash 1967)
Miller v Kennedy 522 P2d 852 (Wash Ct App 1974), aff'd 530 P2d 334 (1975)
Moore v Regents of the University of California 271 Cal Rptr 146 (Cal 1990), cert denied 499 US 936 (1991)
Neade v Portes 710 NE2d 418 (Ill App Ct 1999)
Pemberton v Tallahassee Mem'l Reg'l Med Ctr, 66 F Supp 2d 1247 (ND Fla 1999)
Roe v Wade 410 US 113 (1973)
Shadrick v Coker 963 SW2d 726 (Tenn 1998)

Bibliography

American College of Physicians Ad Hoc Committee on Medical Ethics, 'American College of Physicians Ethics Manual, Part 1' (1984) 101 Ann Intern Med 129

American Medical Association, Report of the Council on Ethical and Judicial Affairs, Report A (I-86): Conflicts of Interest (1986)

Demott D A, 'Beyond Metaphor: An Analysis of Fiduciary Obligation' (1998) 48 Duke LJ 879

Frankel T, 'Fiduciary Law' (1983) 71 Calif LR 795

Gonen R and others, 'Results of a Well-Defined Protocol for a Trial of Labor after Prior Cesarean Delivery' (2006) 107 Obstet Gynecol 240

Gruber J and Owings M, 'Physician Financial Incentives and Cesarean Section Delivery' (1996) 27 Rand J Econ 99

Keeler E B and Brodie M, 'Economic Incentives in the Choice between Vaginal Delivery and Cesarean Section' (1993) 71 Milbank Q 365

Kukura E, 'Contested Care: The Limitations of Evidence-Based Maternity Care Reform' (2016) 31 Berkeley J Gender L & Just 241

Kukura E, 'Obstetric Violence' (2018) 106 Geo LJ 721

Kukura E, 'Revisiting Roe to Advance Reproductive Justice for Childbearing Women' (2018) 94 Notre Dame L Rev Online 20

Landon M B and others, 'Risk of Uterine Rupture with a Trial of Labor in Women with Multiple and Single Prior Cesarean Delivery' (2006) 108 Obstet Gynecol 12

Lydon-Rochelle M and others, 'Risk of Uterine Rupture during Labor among Women with a Prior Cesarean Delivery' (2001) 345 New Eng J Med 3

Manning F A, 'Reflections on Future Directions of Perinatal Medicine' (1989) 13 Semin Perinatol 342

Martin J A and others, 'Births: Final Data for 2015' (National Vital Statistics System, US Dept of Health and Human Services 2017)

Martin J A and others, *Births: Final Data for 2015,* National Vital Statistics System, US Dept of Health and Human Services (2017)

Oberman M, '"Mothers and Doctors" Orders: Unmasking the Doctor's Fiduciary Role in Maternal-Fetal Conflicts' (2000) 94 Nw U L Rev 451

Rodwin M A, 'Strains in the Fiduciary Metaphor: Divided Physician Loyalties and Obligations in a Changing Health Care System' (1995) 21 Am J L & Med 241

Sakala C, *Vaginal or Cesarean Birth?:A Systematic Review to Determine What Is at Stake for Mothers and Babies* (Childbirth Connection 2006)

Scallen E A, 'Promises Broken vs. Promises Betrayed: Metaphor, Analogy, and the New Fiduciary Principle' (1993) U Ill LR 897

Whitridge Williams J, Pritchard J A, and MacDonald P C, *Williams Obstetrics* (16th edn, Appleton-Century-Crofts 1980)

World Health Organization, 'The Prevention and Elimination of Disrespect and Abuse during Facility-Based Childbirth' (2015)

Zweifler J and others, 'Vaginal Birth after Cesarean in California: Before and after a Change in Guidelines' (2006) 4 Annals Fam Med 228

12 Reflections on criminalising obstetric violence

A feminist perspective

Karen Brennan

Introduction[1]

Obstetric violence (OV) – mistreatment, abusive, or disrespectful treatment of women in childbirth – has gained increasing attention in recent years. However, there is little research on its legal aspects,[2] including the question of whether it is or should be a target of the criminal law, though there are at least three jurisdictions in Latin America where specific statutes protecting women against OV have been enacted.[3] And, in the South African context, Pickles has argued that OV should be criminalised there.[4] This chapter provides the first exploration of the question of criminalisation of OV in England and Wales.

OV is identified in the literature as a form of gender-based violence: it is against women and stems from patriarchal gender norms.[5] Recognition that an act of violence is a form of violence against women reveals not only the harm done to the individual victim but also the role such violence plays in reinforcing gender norms and oppression of women in general. Traditionally, however, violence against women has been unacknowledged and minimised (for example domestic violence, marital rape), not only in society but also in law, and the criminal law has struggled to accommodate women's experiences of abuse and violence.[6]

---

1 I am grateful to the editors of this collection and Professors Sabine Michalowski and Donald Nicolson for their comments on early drafts of this chapter.

2 For some exceptions see Michelle Oberman, 'Mothers and Doctors' Orders: Unmasking the Doctor's Fiduciary Role in Maternal-Fetal Conflicts' (2000) 94 Northwest University Law Rev 451; Camilla Pickles, 'Eliminating Abusive "Care": A Criminal Law Response to Obstetric Violence in South Africa' (2015) 54 SACQ 5; Farah Diaz-Tello, 'Invisible Wounds: Obstetric Violence in the United States' (2016) 24(47) Reprod Health Matters 56.

3 See Lydia Z Dixon, 'Obstetrics in a Time of Violence: Mexican Midwives Critique Routine Hospital Practices' (2015) 29 Med Anthropol Q 437, 443 (referring to Venezuela and the Mexican state of Veracruz); Carlos H Vacaflor, 'Obstetric Violence: A New Framework for Identifying Challenges to Maternal Healthcare in Argentina' (2016) 24(47) Reprod Health Matters 65 (discussing the legal framework in Argentina).

4 Pickles (n 2).

5 See discussion below at nn 35–44.

6 For example, marital rape was only recognised as a crime in the 1990s: see *R v R* [1991] 4 All ER 481 (HL).

Feminist analyses show that the law is patriarchal[7] and that criminal law doctrine is based on the male, not the female, subject.[8] Historically, the male character of the criminal law is most evident in, for example, the common law defence of provocation which in its classic formulation facilitated lenient treatment for killings done in 'righteous male anger' – the murder of an unfaithful wife and/or her lover, being the quintessential example[9] – and the way the offence of rape was originally conceived of as a crime against the property interests of the victim's husband or father.[10] As Nicolson has observed, 'the criminal legal subject is male … it is [male] behaviour which informs the norms of criminal law and the response of actors of the criminal justice system'.[11]

In recent decades, there has been increasing feminist focus on criminal reform to address the law's gender bias against women. This has met with some success such as through replacing provocation with a new defence of loss of control,[12] reforming rape laws,[13] and the introduction of new offences to target gender-based violence such as domestic abuse[14] and 'revenge porn'.[15] The government has also recently announced plans to criminalise 'upskirting'.[16] Recently, feminist scholars have also highlighted the need to create specific offences to capture the gendered harms that women experience in the context of image-based sexual abuse.[17]

It is against this context – the gendered nature of OV, and the law's inherent maleness and consequent historical failing to address the concerns of women – that the issue of enacting a specific offence of OV is considered. It will be argued that the criminalisation of OV requires a specific statutory crime. It is important

7 Carol Smart, 'Legal Regulation or Male Control' in *Law, Crime and Sexuality: Essays in Feminism* (Sage Publications 1995). Janet Rifkin, 'Toward a Theory of Law and Patriarchy' [1980] Harv Women's Law J 83.

8 Generally, Nicola Lacey, 'Unspeakable Subjects, Impossible Rights: Sexuality, Integrity and Criminal Law' in Nicola Lacey, *Unspeakable Subjects: Feminist Essays in Legal and Social Theory* (Hart Publishing 1998).

9 Jill Radford, 'Marriage Licence or Licence to Kill? Womenslaughter and the Criminal Law' (1982) 11 Fem Rev 88; Susan Edwards, 'Male Violence against Women: Excusatory and Explanatory Ideologies in Law and Society' in Susan Edwards (ed), *Gender, Sex and the Law* (Croom Helm 1985).

10 Lacey (n 8) 106.

11 Donald Nicolson, 'Criminal Law and Feminism' in Donald Nicholson and Lois Bibbings (eds), *Feminist Perspectives on Criminal Law* (Cavendish Publishing 2000).

12 Coroners and Justice Act 2009, s 54–56.

13 Sexual Offences Act 2003, s 1(rape), 74–76 (consent).

14 Serious Crimes Act 2015, s 76 (Controlling or Coercive Behaviour in an Intimate of Family Relationship).

15 Criminal Justice and Courts Act 2015, s 33 (Disclosing Private Sexual Photos and Films with Intent to Cause Distress).

16 UK Ministry of Justice and Lucy Frazer QC MP, 'Government Acts to Make "Upskirting" a Specific Offence' (*GOV.UK*, 15 June 2018) <www.gov.uk/government/news/government-acts-to-make-upskirting-a-specific-offence> accessed 19 January 2019.

17 Clare McGlynn, Erica Rackley, and Ruth Houghton, 'Beyond "Revenge Porn": The Continuum of Image-Based Sexual Abuse' (2017) 25 Fem Leg Stud 25.

to highlight from the outset that my suggestion is not that all instances of mis-treatment identified in the literature be subject to the criminal law, and more will be said on that as the argument develops. However, what is important is that the law takes an approach focused on women's experiences of violence and which seeks to challenge the gender norms on which OV is based. While the discussion will focus on the legal position in England and Wales, much of what is said will be applicable to other jurisdictions, at least those with a similar social, cultural, and legal context.

The 'OV: Meaning, scope, and its gendered roots' section outlines the concept of OV and explains its conception as a form of gender-based violence. The 'Crim-inalising obstetric violence' section, focusing on non-fatal offences against the person (NFOAP) and the new wilful neglect and ill-treatment offences found in the Criminal Justice and Courts Act (CJCA) 2015, explores limitations of the current criminal law with regard to targeting abusive treatment of women in childbirth. Following on from this discussion, it is argued in 'The argument for a woman-centred offence' section that a specific offence of OV which takes a woman-centred approach would: first, identify abuse of women in childbirth as a matter that demands a specific criminal response, draw attention to this issue and properly label the wrong/harm involved; and, second, enable the law to be formulated to take account of the particular experiences of women in childbirth. The final section will conclude the chapter.

OV: meaning, scope, and its gendered roots

'OV' is a broad concept used by activists and writers to draw attention to and address mistreatment of women in childbirth.[18] Other terminology describing the phenomenon includes 'disrespect and abuse' of women in childbirth, 'dehu-manised care', 'birth rape', 'mistreatment of women', and 'childbirth abuse'.[19] There is no consensus on the terminology. Some writers use the terms inter-changeably, while others seek to distinguish 'mistreatment' from 'violence' on the ground that the former is a more inclusive term that captures the broader range of experiences described in the research.[20] In this chapter, I will mainly rely on the term OV, but I will also use other terminology such as 'abuse' and 'mistreatment'. Although I recognise that these terms could hold different meanings, and that there is a wider debate about appropriate terminology, I will use them interchangeably.

---

18 For example, see Dixon (n 3); Rachelle Chadwick, 'Obstetric Violence in South Africa' (2016) 106 S Afr Med J 423.

19 J P Vogel and others, 'Promoting Respect and Preventing Mistreatment during Childbirth' (2015) 123 BJOG 671, 672; Rachelle Chadwick, 'Ambiguous Subjects: Obstetric Violence, Assemblage and South African Birth Narratives' (2017) 27 Fem Psychol 489, 491; Meghan A Bohren and others, 'The Mistreatment of Women during Childbirth in Health Facilities Glob-ally: A Mixed-Methods Systematic Review' (2015) 12(6) PLoS Med e1001847.

20 Bohren and others (n 19).

Although there is no settled definition, Chadwick summarises the consensus: '[OV] includes both direct violence (physical, verbal and sexual abuse), subtler forms of emotional violence (dehumanisation, disrespect, and undignified care) and structural violence (stigma, discrimination, and systematic deficiencies)'.[21] It covers a wide range of conduct, perpetrated with different degrees of culpability, and includes (but is not limited to) the following examples: forced/non-consented to medical procedures (eg caesarean sections, episiotomies, inductions, forceps delivery, vaginal examinations); unnecessary, but apparently consented to, medical treatments; withholding medical treatment/pain relief; slapping, pinching, restraining of women during labour; verbal and emotional abuse (eg shouting, threats, coercion, being lied to obtain compliance/consent); neglect; and disrespectful treatment (eg putting the needs of the care provider ahead of those of the woman; ignoring the woman's embodied experience).[22] A key aspect of OV is that it undermines, indeed strips women of their autonomy and dignity.[23] Understanding these examples of abuse/mistreatment as 'violence' takes the concept beyond traditional accounts which view it as involving a physical attack. Indeed, as a concept, OV intentionally 'confront[s] problematic practices, which have often been hidden, invisible, unacknowledged, as forms of violence',[24] and 'seek[s] to name phenomena which are not easily or normatively recognised as forms of violence … as *violence*'.[25] Thus, OV serves to reveal and identify what is otherwise hidden and to challenge minimisation of women's experiences of abuse in childbirth.

The concept of OV emerged in the fight for a humanised approach to childbirth, and sought to highlight the damage perpetrated on women by medicalised childbirth.[26] As such, it embraces routine obstetric practices in a technological age within medical settings, identifying the unnecessary/improper use of routine biomedical interventions as 'violence'.[27] Consequently, OV may be perpetrated by individual care providers (eg midwives, obstetricians), and at a systematic level by health institutions and services through their policies, protocols, working environments, and resources. Indeed, as Freedman and Kruk have summarised, research shows that 'this is not the phenomenon of a few bad apples. Rather, it runs wide and deep in the maternity services of many countries'.[28]

---

21 Chadwick (n 19) 492.

22 For example, see Vogel (n 19) 672; Chadwick (n 19) 491–492; Ana Flávia Pires Lucas d'Oliveira, Simone Grilo Diniz, and Lilia Blima Schraiber, 'Violence against Women in Health-Care Institutions: An Emerging Problem' (2002) 359 The Lancet 1681, 1683; Bohren (n 19).

23 Joanna N Erdman, 'Bioethics, Human Rights, and Childbirth' (2015) 17 Health Hum Rights 43, 45; Bohren and others (n 19).

24 Chadwick (n 18) 423.

25 Chadwick (n 19) 492, emphasis in the original.

26 Ibid 491.

27 Dixon (n 3) 437–38, 441–42.

28 Lynn P Freedman and Margaret E Kruk, 'Disrespect and Abuse of Women in Childbirth: Challenging the Global Quality and Accountability Agendas' (2014) 384 The Lancet 42; Rachel Jewkes, Naeemah Abrahams, and Zodumo Mvo, 'Why Do Nurses Abuse Patients? Reflections

Mistreatment and abuse of women in childbirth is a global phenomenon. Although much of the literature has focused on Latin American and African countries,[29] there is also evidence of women's experiences of mistreatment in childbirth in high-income settings.[30] For example, Reed and others in their study of women who experienced post-birth trauma across the globe, including Australia, North America and Europe, highlighted that many women reported being lied to and threatened to get their agreement to medical interventions. These threats often focused on the welfare of the baby ('the dead baby threat'); that a caesarean would be performed without consent; or that the woman would be reported to social services, and her baby taken from her, if she did not comply with medical authority.[31] Women's experiences of trauma included violence and physical abuse, and they used language associated with sexual assault to describe these experiences.[32] An English study by Baker and others highlighted a number of examples of mistreatment of women in childbirth, including problems in relation to decision-making with regard to obstetric interventions such as episiotomies and inductions.[33] Women in this study indicated that they had little choice over decisions about such procedures in that they were given inadequate information by staff and/or that their preferences and embodied experiences were ignored. Some women reported that they were 'talked into' or 'bullied' to obtain their consent.[34]

OV is identified as a form of gender-based violence.[35] In other words, it stems from and reflects oppressive cultural attitudes to women and wider structural gender inequality.[36] As highlighted by Dixon, 'how women are treated in labour and birth ... mirrors how they are treated in society'.[37] A number of researchers have identified parallels between OV and intimate-partner violence because similar coercive tactics are employed to those used by abusive men (eg manipulation, intimidation, violence) and because it is based on gender norms.[38]

---

from South African Obstetric Services' (1998) 47 Soc Sci Med 1781, 1791–92; d'Oliveira and others (n 22) 1683.

29 See Bohren and others (n 19) for overview.

30 See Sarah R Baker and others, '"I Felt as Though I'd Been in Jail": Women's Experiences of Maternity Care during Labour, Delivery and the Immediate Postpartum' (2005) 15 Fem Psychol 315; Bohren and others (n 19) (systematic review of 65 studies across 34 countries, including high-income settings); Rachel Reed, Rachael Sharman, and Christian Inglis, 'Women's Descriptions of Childbirth Trauma Relating to Care Provider Actions and Interactions' (2017) 17 BMC Pregnancy and Childbirth 21 (worldwide study, mainly comprised of participants from Australia, Oceania, North America, and Europe); Diaz-Tello (n 2) (discussing forced caesarean sections in the United States).

31 Reed and others (n 30) 25.

32 Ibid 25–26.

33 Baker and others (n 30) 324–25.

34 Ibid 324.

35 For example, see Rachel Jewkes and Loveday Penn-Kekana, 'Mistreatment of Women in Childbirth: Time for Action on This Important Dimension of Violence against Women' (2015) 12(6) PLoS Med e1001849; Dixon (n 3).

36 Jewkes and Penn-Kekana (n 35).

37 Dixon (n 3) 447.

38 For further discussion, see Jonathan Herring in this collection. See also Dixon (n 3) 447–450; Sonya Charles, 'Obstetricians and Violence Against Women' (2011) 11(12) Am J Bioeth 51;

Although all patients are susceptible to paternalistic medical practices and infringements of their autonomy in medical decision-making, as Dodds has highlighted, women are especially vulnerable in this respect, particularly in the context of reproductive health decisions: patriarchy, the choices women have to make, and normative ideas that women are 'irrational' mean that their autonomy is undermined.[39] Specifically in relation to childbirth, it is understood that the relationship between birthing women and their midwives/obstetricians is affected by oppressive patriarchal gender norms about the value of women and how 'good' women/mothers should behave. In her South African study into why midwives abuse their patients, Chadwick found that 'class, racialised and gendered imperatives about "good mothers" and "good women" intertwine ... with medical norms surrounding the ideal of the "good patient", to create relational networks of discipline, punishment, normalising judgment and coercion'.[40] The role of patriarchal gender norms that devalue women is also found in high-resource settings and 'Western' cultures where prominent ideals of 'maternal sacrifice', which expect that women put their babies first, even where this is against their own interests, make them more susceptible to medical authority, pressure, and abuse.[41]

Related to this is the cultural value of the foetus and the impact of advances in technology on medical perceptions of the foetus as a 'second-patient'.[42] This can create a maternal-foetal conflict, in medical eyes, with, in more extreme cases, medical personnel viewing their role as being to protect the foetus/baby *against* its mother.[43] Fear of civil liability if the child is injured through negligent medical treatment during childbirth may also make medical professionals/institutions push for certain kinds of treatment or intervention against the wishes of the birthing woman. As Baker and others argue in relation to their English study:

> The pursuit of the 'birth machine' with its ever-increasing use and reliance on technologies and interventions ... enacted within a fetocentric environment in which the life of the foetus ... and fear of litigation dominate, mean that the rhetoric of informed choice ... is just that – rhetoric ... . In the context of childbirth, 'choice' is potentially coercive as it ignores the asymmetrical relations and the cultural impediments enforced through the obstetric hegemony, which operates within a patriarchal culture.[44]

Meghan A Bohren and others, '"By Slapping their Laps the Patient Will Know that you Truly Care for Her": A Qualitative Study of Social Norms and Acceptability of the Mistreatment of Women During Childbirth in Abuja, Nigeria' (2016) 2 Popul Health 640, 642.

39 Susan Dodds, 'Choice and Control in Feminist Bioethics' in Catriona Mackenzie and Natalie Stoljar (eds), *Relational Autonomy: Feminist Perspectives on Autonomy, Agency and the Social Self* (OUP 2000).

40 Chadwick (n 19) 501.

41 See generally Pam Lowe, *Reproductive Health and Maternal Sacrifice: Women, Choice and Responsibility* (Palgrave-Macmillan 2016), chs 2, 5 and 6.

42 Samantha Halliday, *Autonomy and Pregnancy: A Comparative Analysis of Compelled Obstetric Intervention* (Routledge 2016) 1–4; Sheena Meredith, *Policing Pregnancy: The Law and Ethics of Obstetric Conflict* (Ashgate 2005) 1–2, 5–6.

43 Oberman (n 2) 451–452.

44 Baker and others (n 30) 334.

Thus, ideals of maternal sacrifice and 'good' motherhood, alongside an increased focus on foetal safety and welfare, can make women in childbirth more vulnerable to abuse, and, in particular, to treatment that undermines autonomy.

The question I seek to address in this chapter is the role of the criminal law in responding to this. In the following section, I explore the limits of the criminal law in responding to OV, before examining the potential of existing offences to capture some examples of OV.

Criminalising obstetric violence

My argument proceeds on the basis that at least some of the harms perpetrated on women by abusive obstetric practices merit criminalisation, and, indeed, as explored in this section, are already potentially captured by existing offences. Taking this as my starting point, I will argue that if we seek to criminalise OV, what is needed is a specific statutory offence. As I demonstrate, while existing offences might be used to target obstetric abuse, they may not be particularly effective at capturing the gendered violence involved. A specific offence would not only label the crime correctly, it would also enable the law to take account of and respond to the role of gender norms in the perpetration of abusive obstetric practices, as well as the gender-based harms perpetrated on childbearing women, notably, but not exclusively, those involving autonomy-infringements. A specific offence may also serve to challenge oppression of women in this context, and resist minimisation of their experiences of abuse.

As explained, OV is a broad and somewhat ill-defined spectrum ranging from relatively minor (eg being rude or disrespectful in attitude) to very serious harms/ wrongs (eg forced medical procedures). From a legal perspective, the issue is what role the criminal law can play in relation to some, but not all, instances of OV. There are complex issues that arise when considering questions of whether conduct could or should be criminalised, including practical considerations such as what we might seek to achieve by criminalisation; and whether this would be best realised through the criminal law, or whether other forms of legal regulation would provide a more effective response.[45] We must also be cognisant of the limits of the criminal law. Indeed, whilst criminalisation may be appealing, it should never be taken lightly because, unlike with other forms of legal regulation, it involves the coercive power of the state, allowing for state punishment and condemnation of wrongdoing.[46] The criminal law, therefore, should be used

---

45 Other legal responses to OV could include tort and human rights litigation, and regulatory frameworks. See Karen Yeung and Jeremy Horder, 'How Can the Criminal Law Support the Provision of Quality in Healthcare?' (2014) 23 BMJ Qual Saf 519.

46 Andrew Ashworth, 'Conceptions of Overcriminalization' (2008) 5 Ohio St J Cr L 407, 408, 410; Douglas Husak, 'The Criminal Law as Last Resort' (2004) 24 Oxf J Leg Stud 207; A P Simester and others, *Simester and Sullivan's Criminal Law: Theory and Doctrine* (6th edn, Hart Publishing 2016) 659–660.

with restraint. For example, Mill's 'harm principle',[47] which is often considered central to the question of the limits of the criminal law, argues that the only rationale for criminalisation is the prevention of harm to others, which means that criminalisation is justified if it will prevent harm.[48] This approach does not mandate criminalisation in such circumstances, however; it merely permits it, and there will be other factors to take into account.[49]

One of the restrictions generally accepted by theorists on the scope of the criminal law is that, due to the significant consequences of criminalisation for individuals, we should only criminalise *serious* blameworthy harms.[50] This would suggest that only serious incidents of OV would lend themselves to criminalisation. However, although I do not wish to suggest that mistreatment of women in childbirth always warrants criminalisation, we should, following what was said in the previous section,[51] guard against trivialisation of birthing women's experiences of violence. In particular, in determining what merits a criminal response it is necessary to challenge the criminal law's traditional male approach to violence and harm. The question of what conduct would cross the threshold to become the concern of the criminal law should be informed by women's experiences and cognisant of and responsive to the gendered roots of the harm involved. What might appear to be 'trivial' on an objective assessment may take on a different level of gravity when considered from the perspective of women in labour and when account is taken of the gendered nature of the violence involved.

First, as noted earlier, in the OV literature, the term 'violence' is used to describe phenomena not normally viewed as violent[52] and it would be important that the law took a broad approach to conceptualising violence. Indeed, the Supreme Court in *Yemshaw* recognised that for the purposes of the Housing Act 1996, domestic violence included emotional, psychological, and financial abuse.[53] Traditionally the criminal law's offences of violence (NFOAP, discussed below) have focused on requirements of physical touching and/or injury of a particular nature (either physical or psychiatric) and degree.[54] As Herring argues, referring to this issue in the context of domestic violence, the law ignores the impact of the context of the relationship in which the violence occurred as well as the broader social context when considering the severity of the attack; this can mean that women's experiences of violence are trivialised within the traditional criminal law framework.[55]

---

47 John S Mill, *On Liberty* (Dover Publications 2002), ch 1.

48 For example, see generally Jonathan Herring, *Great Debates in Criminal Law* (3rd edn, Palgrave 2015), ch 1; Simester and others (n 46) 660–67.

49 Ibid.

50 For example, see Ashworth (n 46).

51 See discussion above at nn 24–25.

52 Ibid.

53 Jonathan Herring, 'The Meaning of Domestic Violence: *Yemshaw v London Borough of Hounslow* [2001] UKSC 3' (2011) 33 J Soc Wel & Fam L 297.

54 In the offences of battery/assault; Actual Bodily Harm; Wounding or Grievous Bodily Harm, discussed below at nn 64–116.

55 Herring (n 53) 300–301.

Second, recognising that OV is a form of gender-based violence also increases its seriousness because not only is the injury to the individual victim identified, but so too is the wider public harm in terms of the role this violence plays in oppression of women in general.

Notwithstanding this, it seems there will be examples of OV that would not be serious enough to warrant criminal sanction. An example might be where a midwife/obstetrician spoke to a woman in a harsh or demeaning way (though there may be situations where verbal abuse would cross the threshold). Further, even if serious harm was caused, there would be no criminalisation in the absence of fault (eg if it was caused accidentally). However, there are other instances of abuse/mistreatment that should attract the attention of the criminal law, such as, for example: deliberately withholding pain relief, where this was not warranted on medical grounds; and blameworthy autonomy-infringements, such as that which occurs where medical procedures are performed without consent, or where women submit to medical procedures/examinations due to improper pressure, lies, lack of information, or threats. Indeed, as is explored in the following section, some of these examples are already captured by the criminal law.

Obstetric violence under current offences

Historically the criminal law has had little to do with medical practice, and, except in cases where death was caused through gross negligence, medical professionals had not faced criminalisation for harms perpetrated on their patients.[56] The Francis Report into serious mistreatment and neglect of patients at Mid-Staffordshire National Health Services (NHS) Foundation Trust highlighted the inadequacies of the existing criminal law framework, namely that, unless it could be shown that death had resulted, it was impossible to criminalise medical professionals who mistreated, neglected, or abused patients in their care.[57] Consequently, two new offences were created, which are largely concerned with criminalising poor, abusive or unsafe (medical) care. Sections 20 and 21 of the CJCA 2015 specifically target 'care workers' (including medical professionals) and 'care providers' (for example NHS Trusts). The section 20 offence criminalises individuals who ill-treat or wilfully neglect those in their care.[58] The section 21 crime criminalises 'care providers', and would enable criminalisation of, for example, an NHS Trust, where a medical professional ill-treated/wilfully

56 Hannah Quirk, 'Sentencing White Coat Crime: The Need for Guidance in Medical Manslaughter Cases' (2013) 11 Crim LR 871; Amel Alghrani and others, 'Healthcare Scandals in the NHS: Crime and Punishment' (2011) 37 J Med Ethics 230.
57 Robert Francis, 'Report of the Mid Staffordshire NHS Foundation Trust Public Inquiry' (The Stationery Office 2013). For discussion, see Alghrani and others (n 56); Yeung and Horder (n 45).
58 For a brief outline, see Zia Akthar, 'Vulnerable Patients, Wilful Neglect and Proof of Sufficient Certainty: Part 1' (2017) 181 JNP 385.

neglected a patient; the Trust's activities were organised or managed in a way which amounted to a gross breach of a relevant duty of care to the patient; and in the absence of such breach, the ill-treatment/neglect would not have occurred or would have been less likely to occur.

Crucial to these offences is the fact that the conduct in question did not meet accepted standards of care and that the professional had knowledge, recklessness, or a 'couldn't-care-less' attitude in this regard.[59] The wilful neglect offence, for example, is committed where the professional deliberately refrained from acting or refrained from acting because of not caring whether action was required or not.[60] The ill-treatment offence requires deliberate conduct which could properly be described as ill-treatment, where the perpetrator either appreciated that he was inexcusably ill-treating the patient, or was reckless in this regard.[61] Proof of harm, such as physical or psychological injury or suffering, or actual or threatened damage to health, is not required.[62]

Clearly these offences which capture substandard medical practice could be used in cases involving abuse/mistreatment/neglect of women in labour. For example, if a woman was denied pain relief where this denial breached accepted medical standards of care, and where the midwife or obstetrician had the requisite degree of fault (ie knowledge, recklessness, or couldn't care less attitude with regard to their failure to provide pain relief), the wilful neglect offence would arguably be committed. It is unclear the extent to which these offences will be effective at capturing autonomy-infringements. Arguably, however, carrying out a medical procedure that was either unnecessary or not consented to could constitute ill-treatment.

A question may arise as to whether it will be more difficult to prove the legal requirements for these crimes in situations where the patient is under the care of medical professionals for a relatively short period of time, as may be the case for a woman in labour, and where the incident in question involved a one-off failure in care that had no long term or serious consequences for the patient? Arguably not: these offences do not require persistent neglect or ill-treatment, and, as noted, proof of harm is not required. However, the decision on whether to prosecute may be influenced by whether the woman experienced physical, mental, or emotional suffering or harm. Indeed, consideration of sufficiency of evidence of the offence requirements is only one aspect of the decision, with prosecutors

---

59 See guidance from following cases: *R v Newington* (1990) 91 Cr App R 247; *R v Sheppard* [1981] AC 394; *R v Turbill and Broadway* [2014] 1 Cr App R 7; *R v Patel* [2013] EWCA Crim 965. Crown Prosecution Service, *Ill-Treatment or Wilful Neglect – Sections 20 to 25 of the Criminal Justice and Courts Act 2015* (17 October 2017) <www.cps.gov.uk/legal-guidance/ill-treatment-or-wilful-neglect-sections-20–25-criminal-justice-and-courts-act-2015> accessed 19 November 2018.

60 *R v Turbill and Broadway* [2014] 1 Cr App R 7.

61 *R v Newington* (1990) 91 Cr App R 247.

62 Ibid; *R v Patel* [2013] EWCA Crim 965.

also having to consider the likelihood of conviction, based on that evidence, and whether prosecution is in the public interest.[63]

In this regard, it is plausible that prosecutions will be reserved for particularly egregious instances of neglect and ill-treatment such as those involving vulnerable patients with pressing medical needs where the failure in care caused or risked serious suffering or harm. In OV cases, will prosecutions be taken against medical staff where ultimately no harm was caused/risked to the woman or her baby, notwithstanding the significant distress and indignity she may have suffered due to neglect/ill-treatment during labour, and the longer-term impact this may have on her? Given what has been said about the impact of gender norms and the importance of foetal welfare, will women who report instances of ill-treatment/neglect encounter disbelief or dismissive attitudes from the police and prosecutors and ultimately be less protected than other patients?

It may also be possible to criminalise some instances of OV, particularly non-consented to medical interventions, through non-fatal offences against the person (NFOAP). These crimes cover non-consented to touching (battery), and also situations where harm (physical or psychological) was unlawfully caused, either through a battery or other means, through the actual bodily harm (s 47), grievous bodily harm and wounding offences (s 20/18) found in the Offences Against the Person Act 1861. A key rationale of these crimes is the protection of bodily integrity and autonomy: 'The fundamental principle, plain and incontestable, is that every person's body is inviolate. It has long been established that any touching of another person, however slight, may amount to a battery'.[64] Although these crimes are not specifically targeted at medical professionals, they have, in theory, the potential to capture non-consented to medical treatment.

Consent plays a vital role in delineating what conduct the criminal law will criminalise in the context of NFOAP. In summary, any unconsented to touching outside of what is acceptable as part of everyday life constitutes a battery.[65] This includes non-consensual medical treatment. If surgery was involved, it could constitute the more serious unlawful wounding offence (s 18/20),[66] or, if an unconsented to intervention resulted in some other legally recognised harm to the patient (including diagnosed psychiatric harms, such as depression and post-traumatic stress disorder, but not emotional harms such as fear, anxiety, and

---

63 Crown Prosecution Service, 'The Code for Crown Prosecutors' (October 2018) <www.cps.gov.uk/sites/default/files/documents/publications/Code-for-Crown-Prosecutors-October-2018.pdf> accessed 23 February 2019.

64 *Collins v Wilcock* [1984] 3 ALL ER 374 QBD [1177] (Lord Goff).

65 Ibid.

66 A 'wound' requires that both layers of the skin were cut (*Moriarty v Brookes* (1834) 6 C & P 684, 172 ER 1419; *M'Loughlin* (1838) 8 C & P 635, 173 ER 651), as would be the case with surgical interventions.

distress),[67] it could amount to actual bodily harm[68] or grievous bodily harm.[69] Mentally competent patients can, therefore, refuse medical treatment, even if this refusal would result in serious harm to them or another person, including death: no matter how foolish or irrational their decision may appear to be, the choices of a mentally competent patient must be respected; non-consensual medical treatment is a criminal offence.[70]

In legal doctrine, birthing women are not treated differently to other patients. Providing she has mental capacity,[71] a woman can refuse medical interventions, such as vaginal examinations, inductions, episiotomies, and caesarean sections, even if this puts not only her own life/health at risk but also that of the foetus/baby.[72] In particular, normative expectations about 'good motherhood' and medical imperatives to preserve the life/health of mother/foetus/child have no bearing on legal doctrine. As emphasised by the Court of Appeal in *S v St George's NHS Trust*, the foetus' 'need for medical assistance does not prevail over [the pregnant woman's] right. She is entitled not to be forced to submit to an invasion of her body against her will, whether her own life or that of her unborn child depends on it'.[73]

However, in medical and legal practice it is not so straightforward. As Farrell and Devaney argue, the right to not be compelled to undergo medical treatment does not necessarily mean that patients are empowered to make choices about their care: medical hegemony creates a 'power asymmetry' which makes patients vulnerable to paternalistic medical practices.[74] As noted, women in labour may be particularly vulnerable to having their choices with regard to treatment challenged due to gender norms surrounding 'good motherhood', the position of the foetus as second-patient, and fears of litigation if harm results.[75] Because a woman's decisions carry implications not only for her own health but that of the foetus/baby, medical professionals may struggle to act in accordance with her wishes if they believe her choices endanger the foetus. As Baker and others state:

> [T]he power and influence of obstetric hegemony, with its philosophy of pathology and a paternalistic model of care enacted within a fetocentric

---

67 *Chan-Fook* [1994] 2 All ER 552; *Burstow* [1998] AC 147.
68 Actual bodily harm is 'any hurt or injury calculated to interfere with the health of comfort' of the victim, but it must be more than 'slight and trifling': *Donovan* [1934] KB 498; *Miller* [1954] 2 QB 282.
69 Grievous bodily harm means 'really serious harm': *DPP v Smith* [1961] AC 290.
70 For example, see *Airedale NHS Trust v Bland* [1993] AC 789, Re T [1992] EWCA Civ 18; *Re MB (An Adult: Medical Treatment)* [1997] 2 FLR 426; *St George's NHS Trust v S, Regina v Collins & Ors, Ex Parte S* [1999] Fam 26.
71 The issue of capacity is discussed further below at nn 99–113.
72 *St George's NHS Trust* n (70).
73 Ibid [50].
74 Anne-Maree Farrell and Sarah Devaney, 'When Things Go Wrong: Patient Harm, Responsibility and (Dis)empowerment' in Catherine Stanton and others (eds), *Pioneering Healthcare Law: Essays in Honour of Margaret Brazier* (Routledge 2016).
75 See the text above at nn 35–44.

environment, acts to control, discipline and disempower women and their bodies during childbirth.[76]

Normative expectations of 'good motherhood' may also affect how women make decisions; for example, they may submit to medical treatment they do not want due to pressure in the delivery room and/or because they have internalised social norms about their obligations as 'mothers'.[77]

The literature on OV shows that consent may be undermined in a variety of subtle and hidden ways in the privacy of the delivery room such as through threats, pressure, exploitation, manipulation, deception, inadequate information, or lack of consultation. Although from an ethical perspective we may consider that consent obtained in such circumstances is not a true consent, the law is more circumspect in its approach. Indeed, although the courts have become more willing to find no consent due to deceptions/pressure in the context of sexual offences,[78] there is little evidence of a similar approach being taken for NFOAP, particularly in medical settings. One problem is that there is limited guidance on the meaning of consent in the context of NFOAP;[79] another is that, even if we did have a coherent doctrine of consent, it may not, in its generic form, cater well for the particular issues that arise in obstetric situations.

Consent does not require an express oral or written agreement; agreement may be implied from the circumstances (eg if a patient moved position to allow an examination to be conducted). Further, failure to communicate a lack of consent, for example through resistance or protest, does not mean that the patient has consented.[80] There is the potential for misunderstanding, but where this occurs – ie where a medical professional mistakenly believes a patient was consenting when in fact they were not – they cannot be liable for a criminal offence, something which reflects the requirement for blameworthiness in the criminal law.[81]

In criminal law, the basic consent principles are: consent must be expressly or impliedly given; the patient must have mental capacity; and, consent will be vitiated by frauds as to the nature or quality of the act or the identity of the perpetrator, and by certain threats.[82] There are difficulties, however, in determining

---

76　Baker and others (n 30) 319.

77　Catriona MacKenzie and Natalie Stoljar, 'Introduction: Autonomy Reconfigured' in Catriona MacKenzie and Natalie Stoljar (eds), *Relational Autonomy: Feminist Perspectives on Autonomy, Agency and the Social Self* (OUP 2000).

78　This is based on an interpretation of the meaning of consent for the purposes of sexual offences only, found in section 74 of the Sexual Offences Act 2003. For examples of cases taking broader approaches, see *Assange v Swedish Judicial Authority* [2011] EWHC 2849 (Admin); *McNally* [2013] EWCA Crim 1051; *R(F)* [2013] EWHC 945 (Admin), where deceptions as to wearing a condom, gender, and withdrawal prior to ejaculation were held to vitiate consent on the ground that there was no freedom to choose.

79　Simester and others (n 46) 786.

80　*Malone* [1998] 2 Cr App R 447.

81　*Morgan* [1976] AC 182; *Jones* (1986) 83 Cr App R 375.

82　See generally David Ormerod, *Smith and Hogan Criminal Law* (12th edn, OUP 2008) 591–596.

the precise meaning and scope of these common law rules. There is limited case law, particularly regarding medical contexts, and none which address unwanted medical interventions on birthing women.

The general position on frauds is that a deception (which can include a failure to disclose information) as to the nature or quality of the conduct[83] or the identity of the perpetrator negates consent.[84] However, there is little guidance on the meaning of 'nature' and 'quality'. The only case law from the criminal courts in medical contexts does not offer much insight, dealing with situations involving deceptions as to medical qualifications[85] or professional registration,[86] or where the medical procedure was carried out for a wholly non-medical (and sexual) purpose.[87]

One issue that arises is whether failure to disclose the risks of a procedure would invalidate consent. The criminal courts have interpreted 'nature' to mean the central features of the conduct in question, but to not extend to collateral matters.[88] It was held, in the context of criminalising HIV transmission through consensual sexual intercourse under NFOAP (as section 20/18 offences), that the 'nature' of an act includes the risk of harm attached,[89] which would suggest that failure to disclose to a patient the risks involved in a procedure would vitiate consent to that procedure, leaving open the possibility of conviction for NFOAP. However, the approach taken by the courts to consent in the context of civil battery (which is defined in the same way as a criminal battery) suggests that a narrower approach would be taken in medical contexts. Although failure to inform a patient about a risk involved in a procedure may give rise to a negligence claim, providing inadequate disclosure caused harm to the patient,[90] the civil courts have refused to find a battery in such situations, in one case holding that it would be 'deplorable' and 'insupportable' to do so, and this is due to the implication that a crime had also been committed.[91] In civil law battery cases providing the patient was 'informed in broad terms about the nature of the procedure' there is a true consent.[92]

83 See *Tabassum* [2000] Cr App R 328.
84 Ormerod (n 82) 592–596.
85 *Tabassum* [2000] Cr App R 328, where women were deceived as to the defendant being medically qualified to carry out breast examinations for research purposes, it was held that there was no consent because the women had been deceived as to the quality of the act (ie that it was for a medical purpose).
86 *Richardson* [1998] Cr App R 200, where it was held there was a valid consent from dental patients notwithstanding that the defendant, who was a qualified dentist, was suspended from practice.
87 *Green* [2002] EWCA Crim 1501.
88 Ormerod (n 82) 594–595.
89 *Dica* [2004] EWCA Crim 1103; *Konzani* [2005] EWCA Crim 706.
90 Informed consent in the context of negligence requires disclosure of material risks: *Montgomery v Lanarkshire Health Board* [2015] AC 1430.
91 *The Creutzfeldt-Jacob Disease Litigation* (1996) 54 BMLR 79 (QB) 80.
92 *Chatterton v Gerson* [1981] QB 432.

To take another example, if a woman is deceived not about the risks of the treatment but about the risks to her/baby of not undergoing that procedure, would this constitute a fraud which vitiates consent? Possibly, the deception could be construed as relating to the purpose of the act – for example, where the risk to the baby is over-stated and it is said that the procedure is necessary to save the baby's life; arguably this involves a deception as to purpose. However, it is unclear whether deceptions as to purpose fall within the scope of legally recognised negations of consent.[93] One factor that might be relevant in such cases is the professional's reason for the treatment. For example, if they acted out of genuine, albeit misguided, concern for the woman and her baby, would the courts be less likely to find vitiated consent (ie that there was a relevant deception), than in a case where the doctor acted for an objectively 'bad' motive such as, for example, to meet targets or for financial gain?[94] Although the conventional view is that motive is irrelevant on the question of whether particular criminal offences have been committed (unless it is a specific offence requirement), there is jurisprudence indicating that motive is not always ignored in criminal cases. Interestingly, two such cases have involved medical contexts where the doctor's motive appears to have been influential in persuading the court that they had not committed an offence.[95]

It might be possible to argue that such a deception constituted a threat (eg 'if you don't comply, your baby will die'), but, again, we have limited clarity on when threats suffice to negate consent for the purposes of NFOAP.[96] To take another example, if a woman agreed to treatment she did not want because she was threatened with having her child taken into care or with court-authorised medical treatment (eg she was told that if she did not consent her mental capacity would be challenged and that a court would likely order that the procedure be carried out against her will in her best interests), would this vitiate consent? Most likely such examples would be dealt with on a case-by-case basis, it being for the jury to decide whether the nature of the threat/pressure and its impact on the victim meant that her will was overborne so that she submitted, rather than consented, to the act in question.[97] Medical contexts will present particular difficulties. First, it seems likely that 'threats' are likely to take the more subtle form of pressure, manipulation, persuasion, or exploitation.[98] Second, some level of persuasion and indeed pressure ought to be acceptable, and medical professionals should not be deterred by fear of legal action, and in particular

---

93 Unless as in *Tabassum* (n 83) this was then construed as being a lie as to the quality of the act.

94 For example, in one case of civil battery where the courts did find that consent was vitiated, despite the fact that the patients were aware of the nature of the procedure performed, the professional, a dentist, had carried out extensive but unnecessary dental work on patients for financial gain: *Appleton v Garrett* 34 BMLR 23.

95 *Bodkin Adams* [1957] Crim LR 365; *Gillick v West Norfolk and Wisbech AHA* [1985] 3 All ER 402 (HL).

96 Ormerod (n 82) 596; Simester and others (n 46) 788–790.

97 Simester and others (n 46) 789–790.

98 Emily Jackson, *Medical Law: Text, Cases and Materials* (4th edn, OUP 2016) 314–315.

criminalisation, from persuading their patients to accept a particular treatment, especially in situations where the treatment is necessary, or highly desirable, to prevent harm to the patient (including harm to her baby).

Finally, there is the issue of mental capacity. On this matter the law is well developed and clear, but its application indicates that in practice birthing women's autonomy is not well protected.[99] Although there can be no legally valid consent where mental capacity is lacking, this does not mean that medical procedures cannot be performed in such cases. Indeed, the law facilitates non-consented to medical treatment where a patient lacks capacity, providing this is in the patient's best interests.[100] What this means is that if a woman refuses consent to, for example, a caesarean section, challenging her mental capacity provides a route to facilitating that procedure without risking criminal liability.

First, section 5 of the Mental Capacity Act 2005 allows for clinical judgments about a patient's capacity and best interests to enable lawful medical treatment without the patient's consent. Provided reasonable steps were taken to ascertain mental capacity, and there was a reasonable belief that the patient lacked capacity and that the treatment was in her best interests, no offence is committed. In essence, this provision enables clinicians to make their own determinations about mental capacity, and thus exercise their medical authority to determine the patient's best interests.[101] Jackson, however, highlights that medical professionals do not always understand this test or how to apply it.[102]

Medical teams may also avoid criminal liability by seeking a declaration of incapacity and court-authorised treatment.[103] Indeed, in obstetric cases this is the recommended course of action where women who refuse to agree to a proposed procedure (usually a caesarean section) are suspected to lack capacity, rather than relying solely on clinical judgments about capacity/best interests.[104] Whether this happens in practice is another matter. Further, it seems the courts only pay lip service to autonomy rights in this context: there have been numerous cases of court-authorised caesareans based on incapacity/best interests.[105] This is despite the fact that in *St George's Healthcare NHS Trust v S* a competent pregnant woman's right to refuse medical treatment was upheld, even where this put her own and/or the foetus' life at risk, and the Court of Appeal clearly recognised the importance of a woman's autonomy rights, which were not diminished by her state of pregnancy.[106]

---

99 Halliday (n 42), ch 2; Sabine Michalowski, 'Court-Authorised Caesarean Sections – The End of a Trend?' (1999) 62 MLR 115.
100 Mental Capacity Act 2005, s 2–5.
101 See generally Emily Jackson, 'From "Doctor Knows Best" to Dignity: Placing Adults Who Lack Capacity at the Centre of Decisions about Their Medical Treatment' (2018) 81 MLR 247.
102 Ibid 249.
103 Mental Capacity Act, 2005, s 2–4, 15.
104 *NHS Trust and Ors v FG* [2014] EWCOP 30; see Jackson (n 101) 258.
105 See Halliday (n 42) ch 2, for an overview.
106 (n 70) [43–50].

However, despite legal principles that clearly uphold a competent pregnant woman's right to refuse treatment, in practice there has yet to be a case where the issue of whether a caesarean could be performed was still live and the courts upheld the woman's capacity and allowed her refusal of treatment to stand.[107] Although the Court of Appeal in *St George's* did find in the woman's favour, the procedure had already been carried out. In other words, the life/health of the baby was no longer at stake. As Halliday argues, the decision might have been different had it been an emergency situation where the life of the mother/foetus was at risk.[108]

The court-authorised caesarean case law highlights that the practice of the law may not necessarily reflect the legal principles. Although gender norms play no role in the legal rules, as Halliday's analysis of the case law both before and after the *St George's* decision indicates, there remains significant scope for paternalistic and gendered attitudes to infuse the law's application.[109] Indeed, Halliday argues that where medical professionals are of the view that a woman's refusal to consent to a caesarean endangers the foetus, the law on incapacity is used as a 'device' to order that the procedure be carried out in her best interests.[110] Further, as Michalowski highlights, although the same legal principles apply, in practice it seems women in childbirth are treated differently to other patients in that there are few cases involving other patients where the courts have been so willing to authorise medical intervention on the grounds of incapacity/best interest.[111] Where a woman's decision to refuse treatment threatens foetal safety, the courts seem willing to protect the foetus, despite the fact that the law does not support such an approach.[112] In fact, Halliday suggests, rather than protecting women, the law on capacity ensures they meet the 'socially constructed view of motherhood which requires women to act altruistically, doing whatever is necessary for the foetus'.[113]

The approach taken in these cases suggests that women who claim that a criminal offence was committed against them are likely to meet many obstacles, not least the challenge of overcoming normative expectations and how these may affect the interpretation and application of the law. In other words, the idea that everyone's body is inviolate, and that everyone has the right to refuse medical treatment, may not provide much protection for women in obstetric cases. This is not only due to potential shortcomings in current legal doctrine but also to how gender norms affect the application of legal rules, something that is very apparent in how the law has been applied in capacity cases. Indeed, as experiences with other gender-based crimes, such as sexual offences, have shown,

---

107 Halliday (n 42) ch 2, 40, 85.
108 Ibid 58.
109 Ibid, ch 2, for an overview.
110 Ibid 86–87, 91.
111 Michalowski (n 99) 126.
112 Ibid 126–27; Halliday (n 42) 85.
113 Halliday (n 42) 89.

where crime is embedded in gender norms those same norms also affect how criminal justice actors involved in processing the case, from the police through to jurors, interpret and implement the law.[114]

Linked to this is the fact that women in such situations may not realise they have been the victim of a crime. Ultimately, the violence of the act is invisible to both victims and the criminal justice system. As Bibbings has observed in relation to NFOAP in the context of domestic violence, victims internalise gender norms and may not interpret what has happened to them as 'violence'[115]:

> [T]he gender of the perpetrator and victims, combined with the context in which the violence occurs, has an effect upon whether incidents which potentially constitute offences will actually be perceived as such and, if so, reported, charged, prosecuted and found to attract criminal liability.[116]

Following the analysis in this section, it is evident that overall the current criminal law provides an inadequate response to OV. Of course, the argument could be made that many patients may experience similar harms and, given that specific crimes to target abuse in the medical context were created in 2015, surely OV should be dealt with under these offences; if there are any gaps, these could be closed by the creation of additional offences (or amendment to existing offences) to ensure that all patients are equally protected. In other words, why should birthing women be treated differently to other patients?

My suggestion for a specific OV offence is not based on the notion that women in childbirth need additional protection compared to other patients. Rather, the argument is that because their experiences are different, women in childbirth require different protection which can take account of and respond to the particular circumstances involved, notably the following features: unlike with other patients whose vulnerability to abuse/mistreatment/violence stems from their physical and/or mental weakness and disempowerment due to illness, women in childbirth are not 'sick'; the additional moral and social pressure on women to make decisions not only for themselves but also for their unborn children, and in particular that normative expectations of 'good motherhood' make them vulnerable to unwanted medical interference and abusive care; finally, the perception of the foetus as 'second-patient', the ethical dilemma faced by medical staff where the woman's decision could lead to death or injury to the foetus, and the perceived maternal-foetal conflict that therefore arises may make medical professionals more willing to cross the line into seriously unprofessional standards of

---

114 See generally Nicolson (n 11); Nicola Lacey, 'General Principles of Criminal Law? A Feminist View' in Donald Nicholson and Lois Bibbings (eds), *Feminist Perspectives on Criminal Law* (Cavendish Publishing 2000).

115 Lois Bibbings, 'Boys Will Be Boys: Masculinity and Offences against the Person' in Donald Nicholson and Lois Bibbings (eds), *Feminist Perspectives on Criminal Law* (Cavendish Publishing 2000).

116 Ibid 231.

care that are properly the concern of the criminal law. The earlier analysis argues that existing legal doctrine would likely struggle to incorporate these experiences of violence and normative understandings would likely affect the interpretation and implementation of the law. There is therefore a need for a separate offence that is tailored to address the particular factors involved and which can counteract rather than reinforce gender norms in how the law is applied.

The argument for a woman-centred offence

Following the analysis in the previous section, there are two arguments in favour of establishing a specific offence to target violent obstetric practices: first, to identify and properly label the wrong/harm done and in so doing to draw attention to this issue and express the community's intolerance of abuse of women in childbirth; second, to allow for a woman-centred approach to the definition and scope of the offence, which acknowledges women's experiences of violence and appreciates the gendered nature of the harm/wrong involved.

First, even if some aspects of OV are captured by existing criminal offences, it may be important to explicitly recognise this as a separate crime which properly identifies and labels the harms involved. The concept of OV acknowledges as violence incidents that traditionally do not attract that label and, in so doing, challenges the minimisation of women's experience of maternity abuse. However, if violence against women in childbirth is subsumed within standard criminal law offences, it is hidden, and the public, women themselves, and criminal justice officials may not perceive that a crime has been committed; the harm in question is not identified and indeed is rendered invisible. The expressive potential of the criminal law is also diminished. As McGlynn and others argue with regard to 'image-based sexual abuse', 'shoe-horning practices into conventional privacy-related offences risks obscuring the nature of the abuse and reducing any potential expressive effect of the criminal law'.[117] Further, drawing on Vera-Gray's work on street-harassment, they also highlight the problem of normalisation of women's experiences of abuse – on the street and online – and the importance of the criminal law, and proper labelling of crimes, to 'name' the conduct in question as abuse, thus 'reflect[ing] women's experiences and ... resist[ing] minimisation of these forms of harm'.[118] A statutory crime of 'OV', or some other suitably labelled offence, would not only draw attention to this issue but would also allow for identification of the specific harms done to women who are victims of serious and blameworthy abusive maternity care and resist minimisation of their experiences.

Related to this, it is suggested that the state should recognise OV as a *crime*. As Duff argues, certain wrongs[119] *should be* criminalised 'to mark them out as

117 McGlynn (n 17) 31.
118 Ibid 40.
119 Taking a legally moralist approach, he views crimes as 'wrongs' rather than 'harms'.

public wrongs, which must be condemned as such, and for which their perpetrators must be called to answer'.[120] He sees crimes as wrongs that 'properly
concern ... the public'[121] because they involve an attack on our core community
values, and therefore warrant a collective community response.[122] In this regard,
unlike with other forms of regulation, the criminal law can demonstrate societal
intolerance of violence against birthing women and perform an important expressive function. As Yeung and Horder observe in relation to the creation of the
2015 offences, the criminal law is the 'most powerful and important social institution through which we hold to account, and express public censure of, those
who have mistreated others in a wholly unacceptable and highly culpable way'.[123]

Second, the law, as it stands, fails to recognise and address the specifically
gendered aspects of OV. I have focused on the law's approach to consent,
which links in with infringements of autonomy and bodily integrity, in the
previous section. Arguably there are also other facets of the existing law that
would fail to accommodate women's experiences of abuse in childbirth, such
as for example the law's limited understanding of violence and harm. The laws
discussed in the previous section, particularly NFOAP, are 'male' laws that
were not created to capture the sort of harms perpetrated on women by OV.
As Bibbings has argued, despite being ostensibly gender neutral, these offences
are ultimately masculinist in nature.[124] Feminist scholarship has revealed that
the meaning and scope of the criminal law are affected by sex and gender.[125]
Thus, for the criminal law to play any role in responding to these situations it
needs to take a more woman-centred approach to issues such as consent (and
autonomy), violence, and harm. In particular, it should be recognised that the
harm involved is one involving autonomy and dignity infringements that have
gendered roots.

Further, the concepts of autonomy and choice, so central to the issue of
consent for the purposes of NFOAP, are *male*. The traditional conception of
autonomy as individualist and rationalistic is 'inextricably bound up with mas-
culine character ideals'.[126] This fails to capture the position of birthing women.
Indeed, it could be said that the whole idea of 'choice' in the context of use
of medical interventions in childbirth is suspect.[127] As discussed earlier, she
is, or least is perceived to be, in a relational rather than an individualistic position by virtue of her role in bringing forward human life. This may affect
not only her own self-perception with regard to the choices she makes but also

---

120 R A Duff, *Answering for Crime: Responsibility and Liability in the Criminal Law* (Hart
 Publishing 2009) 89.
121 Ibid 141.
122 Ibid 140–46.
123 (n 45) 5.
124 Bibbings (n 115).
125 Lacey (n 114) 88, 96–98.
126 Mackenzie and Stoljar (n 77) 3, 5–12.
127 Katherine Beckett, 'Choosing Cesarean: Feminism and the Politics of Childbirth in the United
 States' (2005) 6 Fem Theory 251, 262–269.

how others, particularly medical professionals and those close to her, view her choices and the extent to which she should be free to choose when her decision is thought to endanger the foetus. These are issues that need to be considered in the criminal law's understanding of consent. In this regard, feminist theories of relational autonomy allow us to take account of the impact of socialisation and social relationships on autonomy.[128] For instance, in this context it would facilitate a better understanding of the impact of oppressive gender norms on the woman's decision-making. These feminist critiques of traditional masculinist autonomy and their understandings of relational autonomy could help to inform criminal law in any law reform agenda.

Conclusion

In approaching the creation of a specific OV offence, we must be cognisant of what criminalisation entails – coercive state censure and punishment – and understand that the decision to criminalise is not something that should be taken lightly. The fact that the criminal law already targets non-consensual medical treatment, albeit not particularly effectively, as well as abusive/negligent treatment of patients by doctors/nurses suggests that criminalisation of this specific aspect of medical care would not necessarily be inappropriate. However, it will not always be desirable to criminalise medical professionals who mistreat women in childbirth. There is a need to ensure that medical professionals are not inhibited from doing their jobs effectively through fear of criminalisation, and that there is a clear line between legal and illegal conduct, not forgetting that improper or unethical medical treatment does not always merit criminalisation: we are only concerned with serious and blameworthy incidents.

What is crucial to ensure is that the construction of an OV offence is based on the understanding that this is a form of gender-based violence. It is beyond the scope of this chapter to suggest a possible framework as a number of issues would need to be explored in detail. For now, I suggest that in considering an offence of OV, the approach to harm, consent, seriousness, fault, and defences (and other matters) must be informed by the experiences of women and must understand the gendered context and the imbalance in power in the relationship in which OV occurs. The vulnerable position the woman is in due to the role of patriarchal norms and her relationship with the foetus should be taken account of so that the law protects women against normative expectations, rather than drawing on these norms to undermine the protection offered by the law.

---

128 Mackenzie and Stoljar (n 77) 4, 13, 20. Carolyn McLeod and Susan Sherwin, 'Relational Autonomy, Self-Trust, and Healthcare for Patients Who Are Oppressed' in Catriona Mackenzie and Natalie Stoljar (eds), *Relational Autonomy: Feminist Perspectives on Autonomy, Agency and the Social Self* (OUP 2000).

Finally, questions may arise about whether criminalisation would be the best outcome for women. Women as victims of gendered crimes, such as rape and domestic violence, are often revictimised by the criminal justice system; they are disempowered when the state takes over their grievance; and let down when conviction and punishment do not follow. Indeed, as Lacey has argued, focusing solely on criminal law doctrine is an inadequate response because this does nothing to change cultural attitudes that affect how the criminal law is then interpreted and utilised by the police, prosecutors, judges, and juries. As the experience with rape has shown, irrespective of changes to legal definitions, problematic gender norms – rape myths – still play a crucial role in the outcome of these cases.[129] This does not mean we should not strive to improve the law, but to remind us that legal reform is only part of the answer.

Table of cases

Airedale NHS Trust v Bland [1993] AC 789, Re T [1992] EWCA Civ 18

Assange v Swedish Judicial Authority [2011] EWHC 2849 (Admin)

Bodkin Adams [1957] Crim LR 365

Burstow [1998] AC 147

Chan-Fook [1994] 2 All ER 552

Chatterton v Gerson [1981] QB 432

Collins v Wilcock [1984] 3 ALL ER 374 QBD

Dica [2004] EWCA Crim 1103

Donovan [1934] KB 498

Gillick v West Norfolk and Wisbech AHA [1985] 3 All ER 402 (HL)

Green [2002] EWCA Crim 1501

Jones (1986) 83 Cr App R 375

Konzani [2005] EWCA Crim 706

M'Loughlin (1838) 8 C & P 635, 173 ER 651

Malone [1998] 2 Cr App R 447

McNally [2013] EWCA Crim 1051; *R(F)* [2013] EWHC 945 (Admin)

Miller [1954] 2 QB 282

Morgan [1976] AC 182

Moriarty v Brookes (1834) 6 C & P 684, 172 ER 1419

NHS Trust and Ors v FG [2014] EWCOP 30

R v Newington (1990) 91 Cr App R 247

R v Newington (1990) 91 Cr App R 247; *R v Patel* [2013] EWCA Crim 965

R v Patel [2013] EWCA Crim 965

R v R [1991] 4 All ER 481 (HL)

R v Sheppard [1981] AC 394

R v Turbill and Broadway [2014] 1 Cr App R 7

Re MB (An Adult: Medical Treatment) [1997] 2 FLR 426

St Georges NHS Trust v S, Regina v Collins & Ors, Ex Parte S [1999] Fam 26

Tabassum [2000] Cr App R 328

The Creutzfeldt-Jacob Disease Litigation (1996) 54 BMLR 79 (QB) 80

---

129 Lacey (n 114) 99.

Bibliography

Akthar Z, 'Vulnerable Patients, Wilful Neglect and Proof of Sufficient Certainty: Part 1' (2017) 181 JNP 385

Alghrani A and others, 'Healthcare Scandals in the NHS: Crime and Punishment' (2011) 37 J Med Ethics 230

Ashworth A, 'Conceptions of Overcriminalization' (2008) 5 Ohio St J Cr L 407

Baker S R and others, '"I Felt as Though I'd Been in Jail": Women's Experiences of Maternity Care during Labour, Delivery and the Immediate Postpartum' (2005) 15 Fem Psychol 315

Beckett K, 'Choosing Cesarean: Feminism and the Politics of Childbirth in the United States' (2005) 6 Fem Theory 251

Bibbings L, 'Boys Will Be Boys: Masculinity and Offences against the Person' in Donald Nicholson and Lois Bibbings (eds), *Feminist Perspectives on Criminal Law* (Cavendish Publishing 2000)

Bohren M A and others, '"By Slapping Their Laps the Patient Will Know that You Truly Care for Her": A Qualitative Study of Social Norms and Acceptability of the Mistreatment of Women during Childbirth in Abuja, Nigeria' (2016) 2 Popul Health 640

Bohren M A and others, 'The Mistreatment of Women during Childbirth in Health Facilities Globally: A Mixed-Methods Systematic Review' (2015) 12(6) PLoS Med e1001847

Chadwick R, 'Obstetric Violence in South Africa' (2016) 106 S Afr Med J 423

Chadwick R, 'Ambiguous Subjects: Obstetric Violence, Assemblage and South African Birth Narratives' (2017) 27 Fem Psychol 489

Charles S, 'Obstetricians and Violence against Women' (2011) 11(12) Am J Bioeth 51

Crown Prosecution Service, 'The Code for Crown Prosecutors' (October 2018)

d'Oliveira A F P L, Grilo Diniz S, and Schraiber L B, 'Violence against Women in Health-Care Institutions: An Emerging Problem' (2002) 359 The Lancet 1681

Diaz-Tello F, 'Invisible Wounds: Obstetric Violence in the United States' (2016) 24(47) Reprod Health Matters 56

Dixon L Z, 'Obstetrics in a Time of Violence: Mexican Midwives Critique Routine Hospital Practices' (2015) 29 Med Anthropol Q 437

Dodds S, 'Choice and Control in Feminist Bioethics' in Catriona Mackenzie and Natalie Stoljar (eds), *Relational Autonomy: Feminist Perspectives on Autonomy, Agency and the Social Self* (OUP 2000)

Duff R A, *Answering for Crime: Responsibility and Liability in the Criminal Law* (Hart Publishing 2009)

Edwards S, 'Male Violence against Women: Excusatory and Explanatory Ideologies in Law and Society' in Susan Edwards (ed), *Gender, Sex and the Law* (Croom Helm 1985)

Erdman J N, 'Bioethics, Human Rights, and Childbirth' (2015) 17 Health Hum Rights 43

Farrell A and Devaney S, 'When Things Go Wrong: Patient Harm, Responsibility and (Dis)empowerment' in Catherine Stanton and others (eds), *Pioneering Healthcare Law: Essays in Honour of Margaret Brazier* (Routledge 2016)

Francis R, 'Report of the Mid Staffordshire NHS Foundation Trust Public Inquiry' (The Stationery Office 2013)

Halliday S, *Autonomy and Pregnancy: A Comparative Analysis of Compelled Obstetric Intervention* (Routledge 2016)

Herring J, 'The Meaning of Domestic Violence: *Yemshaw v London Borough of Hounslow* [2001] UKSC 3' (2011) 33 J Soc Wel & Fam L 297

Herring J, *Great Debates in Criminal Law* (3rd edn, Palgrave 2015)

Husak D, 'The Criminal Law as Last Resort' (2004) 24 Oxf J Leg Stud 207

Jackson E, 'From "Doctor knows Best" to Dignity: Placing Adults Who Lack Capacity at the Centre of Decisions about Their Medical Treatment' (2018) 81 MLR 247

Jackson E, *Medical Law: Text, Cases and Materials* (4th edn, OUP 2016)

Jewkes R and Penn-Kekana L, 'Mistreatment of Women in Childbirth: Time for Action on This Important Dimension of Violence against Women' (2015) 12(6) PLoS Med e1001849

Jewkes R, Abrahams N, and Mvo Z, 'Why Do Nurses Abuse Patients? Reflections from South African Obstetric Services' (1998) 47 Soc Sci Med 1781

Lacey N, 'Unspeakable Subjects, Impossible Rights: Sexuality, Integrity and Criminal Law' in Lacey N, *Unspeakable Subjects: Feminist Essays in Legal and Social Theory* (Hart Publishing 1998)

Lacey N, 'General Principles of Criminal Law? A Feminist View' in Donald Nicholson and Lois Bibbings (eds), *Feminist Perspectives on Criminal Law* (Cavendish Publishing 2000)

Lowe P, *Reproductive Health and Maternal Sacrifice: Women, Choice and Responsibility* (Palgrave-Macmillan 2016)

Lynn P Freedman and Kruk M E, 'Disrespect and Abuse of Women in Childbirth: Challenging the Global Quality and Accountability Agendas' (2014) 384 The Lancet 42

MacKenzie C and Stoljar N, 'Introduction: Autonomy Reconfigured' in Catriona MacKenzie and Natalie Stoljar (eds), *Relational Autonomy: Feminist Perspectives on Autonomy, Agency and the Social Self* (OUP 2000)

McGlynn C, Rackley E, and Houghton R, 'Beyond "Revenge Porn": The Continuum of Image-Based Sexual Abuse' (2017) 25 Fem Leg Stud 25

McLeod C and Sherwin S, 'Relational Autonomy, Self-Trust, and Healthcare for Patients Who Are Oppressed' in Catriona Mackenzie and Natalie Stoljar (eds), *Relational Autonomy: Feminist Perspectives on Autonomy, Agency and the Social Self* (OUP 2000)

Meredith S, *Policing Pregnancy: The Law and Ethics of Obstetric Conflict* (Ashgate 2005)

Michalowski S, 'Court-Authorised Caesarean Sections – The End of a Trend?' (1999) 62 MLR 115

Mill J S, *On Liberty* (Dover Publications 2002)

Nicolson D, 'Criminal Law and Feminism' in Donald Nicholson and Lois Bibbings (eds), *Feminist Perspectives on Criminal Law* (Cavendish Publishing 2000)

Oberman M, 'Mothers' and Doctors' Orders: Unmasking the Doctor's Fiduciary Role in Maternal-Fetal Conflicts' (2000) 94 Northwest University Law Rev 451

Ormerod D, *Smith and Hogan Criminal Law* (12th edn, OUP 2008)

Pickles C, 'Eliminating Abusive "Care": A Criminal Law Response to Obstetric Violence in South Africa' (2015) 54 SACQ 5

Quirk H, 'Sentencing White Coat Crime: The Need for Guidance in Medical Manslaughter Cases' (2013) 11 Crim LR 871

Radford J, 'Marriage Licence or Licence to Kill? Womenslaughter and the Criminal Law' (1982) 11 Fem Rev 88

Reed R, Sharman R, and Inglis C, 'Women's Descriptions of Childbirth Trauma Relating to Care Provider Actions and Interactions' (2017) 17 BMC Pregnancy and Childbirth 21

Rifkin J, 'Toward a Theory of Law and Patriarchy' [1980] Harv Women's Law J 83

Simester A P and others, *Simester and Sullivan's Criminal Law: Theory and Doctrine* (6th edn, Hart Publishing 2016)

Smart C, 'Legal Regulation or Male Control' in *Law, Crime and Sexuality: Essays in Feminism* (Sage Publications 1995)

Vacaflor C H, 'Obstetric Violence: A New Framework for Identifying Challenges to Maternal Healthcare in Argentina' (2016) 24(47) Reprod Health Matters 65

Vogel J P and others, 'Promoting Respect and Preventing Mistreatment during Child-birth' (2015) 123 BJOG 671

Yeung K and Horder J, 'How Can the Criminal Law Support the Provision of Quality in Healthcare?' (2014) 23 BMJ Qual Saf 519

Afterword

Emily Jackson

Several interlinked and overlapping themes run through the chapters in this edited collection. First, childbirth has become increasingly medicalised. Even though falling perinatal and maternal mortality rates may owe more to general improvements in women's standard of living than to increased technological intervention in pregnancy and childbirth, it is widely assumed that there is a simple causal relationship between the routine clinical management of childbirth and better health outcomes. Second, while the primary focus of obstetric care is to protect the life and health of the pregnant woman, mortality in high-income countries as a result of pregnancy and childbirth is now sufficiently low that maternal mortality rates are of very little value as an indicator of obstetric success or failure. Instead, the key indicator for contemporary obstetric practice has become the health and well-being of the foetus/baby.

Third, in addition to the routine clinical management of childbirth, directed towards avoiding even very small risks to the foetus/baby, there is a widely shared assumption that maternal self-sacrifice should come very easily to women, and that there is something worryingly abnormal about a woman who is reluctant to undergo any interventions which a doctor judges necessary. When the tendency towards medicalisation is accompanied by the presumption that a woman will agree to whatever a doctor recommends in order to avoid any risk of harm to the foetus, it is perhaps unsurprising that the harms women experience through medical interventions during labour become completely invisible.

The preceding chapters have all been concerned in different ways with what the conventional understanding of childbirth leaves out or obscures. The relatively new concept of 'obstetric violence' is a way of trying to capture the idea that childbirth can sometimes involve doing things to women's bodies against their wishes and without their consent, and that the invisibility of this may mirror other previously hidden forms of violence against women, such as domestic abuse. In this volume, Herring draws a very direct link between domestic abuse and obstetric violence. Although there is seldom the same malicious intent during traumatic births, and birth involves a team of healthcare professionals, rather than a one-to-one intimate relationship, both develop from initially caring relationships, both involve undermining the victim's self-confidence and both happen in intimate, private spaces which instead become unsafe and frightening.

Obstetric violence does not just refer to extreme examples, like pinning a resisting woman down in order to forcibly cut open her abdomen, but has extended to include many more practices that have conventionally been regarded as normal practice in the delivery room. Episiotomy, in which a cut is made from the woman's vagina to her anus, is certainly not necessary in all births (in the United Kingdom, it happens in one in seven births). In some countries, however, episiotomy rates are as high as 92 per cent, meaning that almost all women are expected to submit to often unnecessary actual bodily harm with distressing long-term consequences.[1] Yet because women's suffering from sexual dysfunction and incontinence tends to be private and hidden, the long-term damage routine episiotomy causes to women's bodies is out of sight and overlooked.

When teaching classes on surrogacy, it is striking how students who are generally in favour of liberal access to surrogacy are often horrified by the prospect of a woman hiring a surrogate because she does not want to go through childbirth. If asked to articulate what would be wrong with this, a common response is that a woman who wants to avoid childbirth is unlikely to be a good mother, because she has failed to grasp something important about what motherhood 'is'. Shirking the opportunity to demonstrate, through significant physical trauma, her capacity to put her child's interests above her own must be an indication that she might likely be a selfish, and hence unfit, mother. The question of whether it would therefore be sensible to subject fathers to a physical endurance test in order to establish their capacity for paternal self-sacrifice tends to be brushed off as patently absurd.

This, it could be argued, is an instance of unconscious bias, through which we make judgements about people and situations without realising that we are doing it. What the concept of 'obstetric violence' is intended to achieve, therefore, through the startling linkage of childbirth and violence, is the exposure of harm that has been so thoroughly hidden and obscured that it has become non-existent as harm.

There are very good reasons to challenge what is often assumed to be ordinary obstetric practice, and to highlight the invisibility of harms to women. The reporting in 2011 of a large-scale 'birthplace' survey is a case in point.[2] This study demonstrated that giving birth at home is always safer for women, and that giving birth in hospital may be safer for firstborn children, but that it is no safer for subsequent births. But the study was not reported as having made any findings at all about the safest place for women to give birth. Instead the headlines, not only in the tabloid press but also in scholarly and specialist articles, were simply that home birth is risky, especially for first pregnancies. Harms to women from

---

1 Shalini Singh and others, 'Provider Perspective on Use of Episiotomy in Obstetric Practice' (2016) 2 JRHM 101–103; F Althabe, J M Belizán and E Bergel, 'Episiotomy Rates in Primiparous Women in Latin America: Hospital Based Descriptive Study' (2002) 324 BMJ 945–946.
2 Birthplace in England Collaborative Group, 'Perinatal and Maternal Outcomes by Planned Place of Birth for Healthy Women with Low Risk Pregnancies: The Birthplace in England National Prospective Cohort Study' (2011) 343 BMJ.

giving birth in hospital were not just treated as less important than any risk to the foetus; they were not reported as harms.

Consider also the suggestion that a pregnant woman might be under a duty to undergo a caesarean section as part of a general duty of 'easy rescue' towards her foetus.[3] It is surely extraordinary to describe non-consensual surgery as 'easy', or as a trivial or insignificant harm. This claim is possible only because the harms to women from common interventions in childbirth are simply invisible, and because assumptions about maternal self-sacrifice are so deeply ingrained that being cut open becomes no sacrifice at all. Similarly, to say that giving birth at home is like 'driving without a seatbelt'[4] does not just misrepresent the evidence, although it undoubtedly does that: there is a very small increased risk to first babies from home birth, whereas seat belts reduce the risk of death by 45 per cent, and cut the risk of serious injury by 50 per cent, while causing no physical damage at all to the person wearing the belt.[5] Comparing the harms to women from episiotomy, caesarean section and forceps delivery with 'putting on a seat-belt' simply proves the point that harm to women during childbirth has become completely invisible as harm.

For some women childbirth is so traumatic that it triggers post-traumatic stress disorder. But to most people it is imperceptible as a trauma-inducing stressor, in part because we assume that, however painful it might be, the birth of a healthy child is an unqualified source of joy. It is 'common knowledge' that the pain of childbirth is quickly eclipsed by the joy of meeting one's baby for the first time, and the profound feelings of love and responsibility that follow. The birth of a healthy baby is often described as a 'blessing'. And it is difficult to complain about being blessed, especially when some women who give birth endure the almost unimaginable horror of stillbirth. A woman who is lucky enough to have a healthy baby is often made to feel as though complaining about how she was treated during labour would be to display distinctly unmaternal levels of ingratitude or selfishness.

Of course, some women find it difficult to adjust to motherhood; postnatal depression is also not uncommon; however, this fact does not dent the conventional understanding of childbirth as painful, but worth it. Tort law can exacerbate this because it is impossible to obtain damages for negligently inflicted psychological damage when the trauma of birth can be described as 'normal'. Traumatic childbirth is generally medicalised childbirth, and most people find it hard to believe that healthcare professionals and babies could be the cause of post-traumatic stress disorder. While pain is the worst part of childbirth for some women, for others it is obstetric intervention, being ignored, or inadequate communication and support.

---

3 Julian Savulescu, 'Future People, Involuntary Medical Treatment in Pregnancy and the Duty of Easy Rescue' (2007) 19 Utilitas 1–20.
4 Lachlan de Crespigny and Julian Savulescu, 'Homebirth and the Future Child' (2014) 40 J Med Ethics 807–812.
5 Birthplace in England Collaborative Group (n 2).

If a woman did not consent to an invasive intervention, like cutting, which results in actual bodily harm, a criminal offence has been committed. Prosecutions from non-consensual obstetric interventions are vanishingly rare, however. Women are unlikely to go to the police, and even if they do, it may be difficult to establish that they did not consent to the intervention. In another parallel with violence between intimates, there may be an honest doctor who is convinced that the woman did consent, and a woman who is clear that she did not.

Are there any potential downsides to an expansive definition of obstetric violence? Might there be any disadvantages to categorising being ignored or treated disrespectfully as violence against women? Conduct can be wrong without being criminal, and it may be that there are more effective ways than criminalisation to improve the way in which women are treated during childbirth. We know from other contexts that criminalisation often has unintended consequences. Criminalising HIV transmission, for example, can operate as a disincentive to testing, thus paradoxically increasing the risk of transmission. Would the threat of criminal prosecution for obstetric violence be likely to promote better communication with patients, and expand options for women, or might it instead make hospital managers more risk averse and prescriptive? Criminalisation also has the potential to individualise what may in fact be structural and systemic reasons for poor care during childbirth. Of course, there are times when individual healthcare professionals are culpable in the mistreatment of women during childbirth, but there may be other times when inadequate resources and poor training are to blame.

It is important to ensure that the disrespectful and dehumanising treatment of women during childbirth is considered as a wrong in itself. If it can be challenged only when it can plausibly be described as a species of gender-based violence, there might be a danger that, in practice, it will tend to capture only deliberately non-consensual treatment, while the regular and indeed routine ways in which women are expected to submit to medical authority during childbirth remain unchallenged.

Labouring women are not the only people who may encounter condescending attitudes from healthcare professionals, or whose dignity may be insufficiently safeguarded. Elderly patients, or those suffering from mental health disorders, sometimes find themselves ignored, or their compliance is taken for granted. Person-centred care is important for everyone, and what is needed is a way to ensure that disrespectful and degrading treatment is seen as a breach of the most fundamental duty of a healthcare professional, which should not only be to make the clinical care of one's patients one's first concern but also to ensure the protection of their dignity.

While the problem of patronising and demeaning care may extend beyond childbirth, it could be argued that describing what many women put up with during childbirth as violence is a way of shocking healthcare professionals, and others, into recognising the harm that is done when women routinely face bullying, silencing and the loss of autonomy during childbirth. If the multiple indignities women experience during 'routine' childbirth have become completely invisible as harm, it may be necessary to spell it out using language which is hard to ignore. What is needed most of all is a culture change in which women are not the invisible subjects of childbirth, whose needs and interests are not only not taken sufficiently seriously, but not even registered as interests in the first place.

Bibliography

Althabe F, Belizán J M and Bergel E, 'Episiotomy Rates in Primiparous Women in Latin America: Hospital Based Descriptive Study' (2002) 324 BMJ 945–946.

Birthplace in England Collaborative Group, 'Perinatal and Maternal Outcomes by Planned Place of Birth for Healthy Women with Low Risk Pregnancies: The Birthplace in England National Prospective Cohort Study' (2011) 343 BMJ.

De Crespigny L and Savulescu J, 'Homebirth and the Future Child' (2014) 40 J Med Ethics 807–812.

Savulescu J, 'Future People, Involuntary Medical Treatment in Pregnancy and the Duty of Easy Rescue' (2007) 19 Utilitas 1–20.

Singh S and others, 'Provider Perspective on Use of Episiotomy in Obstetric Practice' (2016) 2 JRHM 101–103.

Index

abandonment 2, 43, 68, 84, 205, 210,
221–22; *see also* neglect
abortion 36, 117–18, 178, 220
abuse: abuse during childbirth 1–8, 30–1,
34, 41–2, 46, 68–9, 79, 99, 111, 141,
157, 210, 229, 244 (*see also* obstetric
violence); abuse of power 204–6, 218,
223; child abuse 215; childhood abuse
51; disrespect during childbirth 46,
68–9, 89–92, 99, 105, 108, 111, 132,
139; domestic abuse 35, 67, 70–2,
74–7, 84, 227, 247, 251; emotional
abuse 14, 18, 24–5, 30, 46, 69, 204,
221, 229, 233; facility-based abuse
3, 30, 126, 231–2 (*see also* violence);
image-based sexual abuse 227, 244;
intimate-partner violence 35, 230;
maternity abuse 35, 90–1, 128, 141,
224, 244; medical abuse 31, 70, 91–2,
105–6, 234; online abuse 5, 244;
physical 5, 14, 30–5, 50, 68–9, 111,
120–2, 140, 153–4, 208, 229–30, 245;
sexual 21, 30, 50–1, 68–9, 81–2 138
229–30 (*see also* rape); verbal 30–31,
68–69, 73, 234
accountability 4, 6, 9, 26, 111, 113–28
accountability mechanisms 114, 116, 118,
120–1, 127
activism 150, 152, 156
AD v MEC for Health and Social
Development, Western Cape 123
Aintree University Hospitals NHS
Foundation Trust v James 150, 188–9
Airedale NHS Trust v Bland 188, 237
American Medical Association (AMA) 208
analgesia 165–6
Assange v Swedish Judicial Authority 238
authority 7, 9, 14, 241, 254; *see also*
epistemic authority

autonomy: autonomy violation 161–2,
169–71, 176; loss of autonomy 5, 16,
31, 45, 70, 151 254; liberal autonomy 8

battery 71, 163, 166–7, 236, 239
black women, maternal mortality 17, 33
birth: birth injury claims 223; birth plan
16, 73, 75, 191, 193, 199–200; birth
process management 8, 176, 251; birth
trauma *see* trauma; caesarean sections
(c-section) 24, 38, 54, 58, 70, 78, 80–2,
104, 114, 137–8, 142–7, 152, 155,
166, 171–4, 181, 229, 237, 241, 253;
facility-based childbirth 2, 111; fear
of childbirth 54, 56, 58–9, 200, 221;
home birth 106, 134–5, 196–7, 221,
252–3; hospital birth 25, 183–4, 190,
197–8; subjective birth experience 39,
52, 54, 69; vaginal birth 80, 103, 136,
143, 146, 155, 166, 184, 209
Bodkin Adams 240
Birthrights 142–6
Briggs v Briggs 188
Bunge v MEC for Health, KZN 123
Burstow 237

C v Slovakia 69
Canterbury v Spence 222
capacity 7, 21, 79, 100, 146–9, 178–90,
198–201, 237–8, 240–2
care 6, 77, 148–9; institutionalised
maternity care *see* obstetric care;
interpersonal care 99, 103; patient
care 98, 212, 217; respectful care
102–3, 132; transformative care 90;
unsafe medical care 117, 234, 251;
withdrawing care 42, 221; *see also*
obstetric care
CC v KK & STCC 187

Chan-Fook 237
Chatterton v Gerson 239
Cobbs v Grant 222
coercion 10, 31–5, 42, 45–6, 79, 111,
    114, 140, 204–5, 208–10, 213, 217,
    221–4, 229–32
coercive control 5, 9, 67–72, 74–5,
    85, 133
Collins v Wilcock 236
Committee on Equal Opportunities for
    Women and Men 76
consent: capacity to consent 82; informed
    consent 10, 70, 125, 134, 136–7,
    140, 151–2, 162–3, 166, 204, 207,
    221; valid consent 82–3, 167; vitiated
    consent 240–2; *see also* medical consent
    transactions
contraception 114
control 8–9, 51, 54–6, 118, 132–3,
    145–6, 189–91, 207–8, 227; *see also*
    coercive control
Convention on the Elimination of All
    Forms of Discrimination against
    Women 77
court-authorised medical treatment 178–9,
    181, 185, 187, 240–2
CP v Lanarkshire NHS Trust 147
Creutzfeldt-Jacob Disease Litigation
    167, 239
criminalisation 226–7, 232–4, 241,
    246, 254

dehumanisation 22, 132–3, 138–9, 228–9
delivery *see* birth
denying treatment 9, 69, 76, 146,
    150, 155
depression 53–4, 56, 236, 253
deprivation of information 10, 161, 166,
    173, 176
Dica 239
dignity 70–2, 112, 133, 254
distress 41, 55–6, 193, 236–7, 252
Donovan 237
Dubska and Krejzova v Czech Republic
    135, 139

ectopic pregnancy 116, 174
Electronic foetal monitoring (EFM) 101,
    183, 209, 212, 214
Emmett v E Dispensary & Cas
    Hospital 207
epistemic: epistemic agency 33–4, 43–7;
    epistemic authority 14–5, 33, 39, 43;
    epistemic injustice 14, 18, 20, 33,

44, 47; epistemic violence 7, 30–5,
    37–8, 45–6
evidence-based care 4, 140–4, 147
evidence-based guidelines 10, 140–7, 150–7

facility-based care 2, 114; *see also* health
    care facilities; toxic facility cultures
fathers 252
Female Genital Mutilation (FGM) 195,
    197, 200
feminism 26, 31–2, 46, 83, 90, 111–2,
    226–7, 245–6
feminist phenomenology 14
feminist scholarship 245
femininity 9, 79, 83
foetal interest (interest of the child /baby)
    73, 78, 84, 180–1, 185–6, 188, 217,
    219–20, 252
foetus 72–5, 78, 84, 96, 125, 133, 189–
    91, 210, 216–23, 231, 241–3, 251
force *also see* coercion; forced medical
    procedure 10, 81–2, 229, 232, 237;
    forced treatment 136, 140, 149–51,
    181, 195, 218, 221, 229, 240–2
fraud 238–40
fundamental principles medical law 162,
    171, 176

gaslighting 6, 14, 18–27
gender bias 227
gender norms 226, 228–32, 236–7, 242–7
gender violence 14, 22, 30, 77
gender-based crimes 242
gender-based violence 156, 226–30, 234,
    246, 254
gender-violence *see* gender-based violence
gendered harms 227
Gillick v West Norfolk and Wisbech
    AHA 240
Great Western Hospital NHS Foundation
    Trust v AA, BB, CC & DD 182
Green 239
gynaecology 15, 27, 114, 141, 195

Hammonds v Aetna Cas & Sur Co 207, 222
Hanzelkovi v Czech Republic 135
harm 5–7, 69–75, 124, 142–56, 168–71,
    236–9, 244–6
harm-principle 233
health system reform 9, 120, 151
healthcare
healthcare facilities 9, 30, 43, 115, 118,
    127, 140, 208; *see also* toxic facility
    cultures

healthcare providers 6, 24, 38, 41, 43–4, 89, 91–2, 143–52, 155, 208–13, 220, 234
healthcare professionals *see* medical professionals
Hoffmann v MEC for the Department of Health, Eastern Cape 123–4
hospital: facility policies 2, 99, 106, 112–3, 136–8, 210, 215–7; hospital protocol 132, 135, 216; internal hospital policies 210, 215
A Hospital Trust v V and Others 182
human dignity 133, 138

In re Baby Boy Doe, a Fetus v Mother Doe 180
infantilisation 14, 16, 23, 27, 156
informed decision 136, 141, 143, 146–50, 157, 214, 217–18
injuries 51, 95, 125, 167–8, 174
institutional obstruction 187
institutionalised standards 94
insurance 211–2
integrity 134–7, 141–4, 147, 150, 154–5, 157, 161, 236, 245
International Confederation of Midwives 92
interpersonal relations 49, 99, 103
intersectionality 84
intuition dismissal 15, 103, 169
inviolability of the body 163, 236, 242
invisible harm 34, 253–55

Jefferson v Griffin Spalding County Hospital Authority 180
Jones 83

Khanyi v Premier of Gauteng 123
Khoza v MEC for Health and Social Development, Gauteng 123
Konovalova v Russia 135
Konzani 239
Kr v Lanarkshire Health Board 147, 239
Kosaitė-Čypienė and Others v Lithuania 135

labelling 186, 198, 221, 228, 232, 244
labour *see* birth
lack of consent *see* consent
lack of insight 7, 178–80, 183–97
law: civil law 10, 162–3, 239; criminal law 243–7; fiduciary law 204–8, 222–4; human rights 3, 9–11, 30, 69–70, 116, 132–9, 141, 154–7; medical law 162, 171–2, 176, 198

LBL v RYJ 192
A Local Authority v E 188
Lockett v Goodill 207, 222, 224
London Borough of Islington v QR 187, 233

M'Loughlin 236
Madida v MEC for Health for the Province of KwaZulu-Natal 111, 123, 125
Magqeya v MEC for Health, Eastern Cape 123
Makgomarela v Premier of Gauteng 123
male power 6, 90, 92
malicious intent 251
Malone 238
malpractice exposure 10, 208, 212–3, 223
manipulation 18–9, 71, 83, 221, 230, 238–40
marginalisation 35–6, 47, 96
marital rape 226; *see also* rape
maternal request cases 142–3, 146, 155
maternal-foetal conflict 205, 210, 215, 219–21, 231, 243
maternal mortality 89, 115–7; *see also* black women maternal mortality
Matlakala v MEC for Health, Gauteng 123
McNally 238
medical consent transactions 161–8, 176
medical intervention 135, 152–3, 162, 174, 181, 209, 230, 236–9, 242, 251
medical negligence 11, 113, 120, 122–8
medical professionals: doctors 16, 25, 74, 84, 89–91, 101, 135, 182, 207, 215–20; doctor-patient relationship 10, 204–8, 217, 223, 246; midwives 6, 8, 26, 88–108, 125, 135, 231; nurses 16, 25, 38–44, 77, 91–101, 121, 214
medical risks 7, 165, 172
medical technologies 88, 95, 145, 179, 183–4, 191–3, 231
mental capacity 180, 237–41
mental health 53–62, 181–6, 190–4, 200, 213, 254
The Mental Health Trust, The Acute Trust & The Council v DD & BC 182
Miller v Kennedy 222
miscarriage 15, 27, 50, 116, 174
misconduct 222
misogyny 27, 76, 91
mistreatment 68–9, 204–5, 209–10, 226–35
Molefe v MEC for Health 123

Montgomery v Lanarkshire Health Board
    82, 132, 136, 144, 148–50, 163,
    166–7, 172–4 179, 239
Moore v Regents of the University of
    California 207
Morgan 238
Moriarty v Brook 236
motherhood 3579, 83, 105, 232, 237–8,
    242–3, 252
Mucavele v MEC for Health 123–5

Neade v Portes 207
neglect 69, 106, 115, 120–2, 208, 219,
    228–9, 234–6
negligence 10–2, 114, 119–28, 132, 136,
    163, 167–71, 234, 239
neonatal death 52, 116, 127
Neveling v MEC for Health and Social
    Development, Gauteng Province 123
The NHS Acute Trust & The NHS
    Mental Health Trust v C 180
The NHS Acute Trust & The NHS
    Mental Health Trust v C [2016]
    EWCOP 17 and A University Hospital
    NHS Trust v CA 180
NHS Trust 1 v G: Practice Note 200
NHS Trust and others v FG 182
NICE guidelines 138, 143–8
Nkayiya v MEC for Health, Eastern
    Cape 123
non-consented medical interventions 68,
    89, 137, 229, 236, 241
non-treatment 162, 175
Norfolk and Norwich Healthcare 180
North Somerset Council v LW and
    others 182
NS v MEC for the Department of Health,
    Eastern Cape 123
Ntsele v MEC for Health, Gauteng
    Provincial Government 123
Ntungele v MEC, Department of Health,
    Eastern Cape 123
Nzimande v MEC for Health,
    Gauteng 123

ob-gyn *see* gynaecology
objectifying 1–2, 27, 79, 194
obstetric care: antenatal care 37, 59, 104,
    133, 155, 191; intra-partum care 104;
    maternity care 8, 89–91, 136, 146,
    151, 180, 205, 209–11, 217–24, 244;
    perinatal care 59; post-natal care 199;
    prenatal care 73, 216–17
obstetric violence 5–6, 14, 32, 89–91,
    140–2, 151–3, 155

oppression 14, 18, 31–3, 45–7, 103
    230–232, 246
overriding patient refusal 215–6, 221

Paia v MEC for Health and Social
    Development 123
paternalistic medical practices 7, 189,
    231, 237
pathology 31, 39, 52, 70, 95, 141, 152,
    185–9
patient: patient abandonment 205, 210,
    221; patient inferiority 77
patient-doctor relationship *see* doctor-
    patient relationship; patients
    decision-making 134, 136, 141–2,
    148–50, 162–3, 192–4, 199–200, 217,
    219, 246
patriarchy 9, 26–7, 76–85, 90–2, 226–7,
    231, 246
PC v City of York Council 179
Pemberton v Tallahassee Memorial
    Regional Medical Center 180
Post-Traumatic Stress Disorder (PTSD)
    49–61, 236, 253
practitioner *see* medical professionals
pregnancy 33–6, 72–3, 116–7, 133,
    149–52, 180–3, 223, 241–2
privacy 140, 209
professional practice 93, 101–4
protocol 212, 216, 229
psychological damage 235, 253

R v Newington 235
R v Patel 235
R v R 226
R v Sheppard 235
R v Turbill and Broadway 235
race 32, 84, 112, 121, 151
rape 21, 81–2, 227–8, 247
rationality 26, 93, 180–1
Re AA (Mental Capacity: Enforced
    Caesarean) 181–2
Re AC 180
Re M (Adult Patient) (Minimally
    Conscious State: Withdrawal of
    Treatment) 188
Re Madyun 180
Re MB (Medical Treatment) 180
Re MB 180–1, 187, 189
Re P 182
Re S 180
Re SB 192
Re TZ 192
recovery 57, 197
refusal of treatment 162, 242

relationship: in a couple 50, 55–6 with a doctor *see* doctor-patient relationship; with a partner 54, 61, 74, 193; mother-child relationship 56–7, 172
Remy v MacDonald 73
reproductive rights 117, 128; *see also* sexual and reproductive health and rights
respectful treatment of women 88–9, 91, 102–3, 106, 136, 141–2, 208, 229
right to information 149
Rochdale Healthcare NHS Trust v C 180
Roe v Wade 220
Royal Free NHS Foundation Trust v AB 182

Samantha Burton v Florida 39 So 3d 263
self-governance *see* autonomy
self-worth 71, 122
serious blameworthy harms 233
sexual offences 227, 238, 242; *see also* rape
Sexual and Reproductive Health and Rights (SRHR) 70, 111–2, 115, 126
sexuality 80, 115, 151
Shadrick v Coker 207
shame 21, 24, 36–7, 209
Sibaya v Life Healthcare Group (Pty) Ltd 123–4
Sifumba v MEC for Health, Eastern Cape 123
Sifumba v MEC for Health, Western Cape 123
silencing 15, 21, 30–7, 42–6
simulation based medical training 97–8
serious mental illness (SMI) 179–85, 190–2, 198–9; *see also* mental health
Smith v MEC for Health, Gauteng 123
Smith v National Health Service Litigation 147
social inequalities 33, 46, 151
St George's Healthcare NHS Trust v S 241
St George's Healthcare NHS Trust v S (NO 2), R v Collins and others, ex parte S (NO 2) 180–1
stillbirths 96, 122

T (Consent to Medical Treatment) (Adult Patient), Re 180
Tabassum 239–40
Tameside and Glossop Acute Services Trust v CH 180
technocracy 97
technology 15, 40, 179, 183–4, 193

teenage pregnancy 35–7; *see also* pregnancy
Term Breech Trial 101
Ternovszky v Hungary 134–5
threats 42, 78, 133, 221, 230
transparency 113, 120–1
trauma: trauma-focused psychological therapies (TFPTs) 60–2; traumatic childbirth 23–5, 102–3, 137, 146, 193, 196, 209
treatment guidelines 94, 96, 140–6, 179; *see also* evidence-based guidelines
trust 14–9, 67, 73–5, 79, 94, 99, 102–3, 204–10, 220–4
Tsita v MEC for Health and Social Development, Gauteng 123
Tysiac v Poland 134

United Nations Committee on the Convention on the Elimination of all forms of Discrimination against Women 153, 156
United Nations Convention on the Rights of Persons with Disabilities 189
United Nations High Commissioner for Human Rights 2, 115–6
universal vulnerability 7–8
A University Hospital NHS Trust v CA 180, 182, 195
unwanted touching 67, 71

vaginal birth after caesarean (VBAC) 209–10, 212–21
vaginal examination 69, 114, 132, 137, 191, 229, 237
violation of rights 153
violence against women *see* gender-based violence
violence during childbirth *see* abuse during childbirth
vulnerability 7–8, 54, 111, 205–6, 222

White Ribbon Alliance 92, 106
woman-centred care 95
woman-centred approach 228, 244
women's knowledge 15–18, 26–7, 31–3, 39–44, 101, 144–5, 183, 210
World Health Organisation (WHO) 1, 69, 111, 208
Wrong 67–74, 170–1, 228, 232, 244–5
Wye Valley NHS Trust v B 189, 192, 194, 196, 200

Xolile v MEC for Health and Social Development, Gauteng 123